History & Women, Culture & Faith

Volume 2

History and Women, Culture and Faith:
Selected Writings of Elizabeth Fox-Genovese
David Moltke-Hansen, General Editor

History & Women

Culture & Faith

Selected Writings of
Elizabeth Fox-Genovese

David Moltke-Hansen, General Editor

Volume 2

*Ghosts and Memories: White and Black
Southern Women's Lives and Writings*

Edited by Kibibi Mack-Shelton and Christina Bieber Lake
Foreword by Mark Bauerlein

The University of South Carolina Press

© 2011 University of South Carolina

Published by the University of South Carolina Press
Columbia, South Carolina 29208

www.sc.edu/uscpress

Manufactured in the United States of America

20 19 18 17 16 15 14 13 12 11   10 9 8 7 6 5 4 3 2 1

Library of Congress Cataloging-in-Publication Data
Fox-Genovese, Elizabeth, 1941–2007.
  History and women, culture and faith : selected writings of Elizabeth Fox-
Genovese / David Moltke-Hansen, general editor.
      p. cm.
  Includes bibliographical references and index.
  ISBN 978-1-57003-990-4 (cloth : alk. paper) — **ISBN 978-1-57003-991-1 (cloth :
alk. paper)** — ISBN 978-1-57003-992-8 (cloth : alk. paper) — ISBN 978-1-57003-993-5
(cloth : alk. paper) — ISBN 978-1-57003-994-2 (cloth : alk. paper) 1. Women—History.
2. Culture. 3. Feminism. 4. Fox-Genovese, Elizabeth, 1941–2007. I. Moltke-Hansen,
David. II. Title.
  HQ1121.F64 2011
  305.409—dc22

                                    2010048764

Publication of *History & Women, Culture & Faith* is made possible in part by
the generous support of the Watson-Brown Foundation.

This book was printed on Glatfelter Natures, a recycled paper with 30 percent
postconsumer waste content.

Contents

General Editorial Note

This is one of five volumes of the selected essays and reflections of Elizabeth Fox-Genovese. First conceived a week after Fox-Genovese's funeral service, the project received generous support from the Watson-Brown Foundation, on whose Hickory Hill Forum advisory board Fox-Genovese served. Also making this edition possible was the collaboration of a dozen of her former colleagues and students, as well as her sister. Helping this diverse group keep on schedule, the Institute for Southern Studies of the University of South Carolina provided administrative support and the superb assistance of history graduate student Ehren K. Foley, compiler of the selected bibliographies for the first four of the five volumes of the edition.

Because the essays and chapters included were published in some seventy-five different venues, spelling and punctuation vary. No effort was made to standardize either these things or the forms of citation. English spellings are not as common as American but do occur. The editors did correct an occasional, obvious error silently or did insert in brackets missing words or elements of citations. In addition they put all original notes at the ends of pieces. The few editors' notes are placed as footnotes.

Each volume stands on its own, covering an area of Fox-Genovese's long-term scholarly and intellectual involvements. The fifth volume, the reader, is drawn largely from the others to give a broad sampling of the range of her work. It does, nevertheless, also include a couple of items by Fox-Genovese not found in the first four volumes, together with a number of remembrances of her.

The decisions about the contents of individual volumes were the responsibility of the editor or editors of each volume. The editors of the first four volumes nominated items for inclusion in the reader. They were guided in the selections for their own volumes by principles to which they all subscribed at the outset or, in a couple of cases, when joining the project a bit later on. Selections from the books Fox-Genovese wrote, co-wrote, and saw through publication are excluded. These titles are widely known and available. The editors also generally tried to choose more substantial over more popular pieces and limited each volume to a little over one hundred thousand words of her writings and some thirty thousand words of apparatus, including notes and bibliography. These decisions necessitated exclusion of at least a third of her fugitive writings. As a result the present edition includes no more than roughly 20 percent of her total published work.

For background to these materials and for related correspondence, readers are directed to the Southern Historical Collection of the University of North Carolina at Chapel Hill, repository of Elizabeth Fox-Genovese's papers. An aid to finding the papers is currently available at http://www.lib.unc.edu/mss/inv/f/Fox-Genovese,Elizabeth.html.

Foreword

A Literary Theorist of the Positive Kind

Mark Bauerlein

People more or less familiar with Elizabeth Fox-Genovese's historical work and cultural commentaries might be surprised at how much the pieces in this volume mark her as a perceptive literary critic, and sometimes as a literary theorist. Historians are assumed to read literature for its representation of historical realities, not for its "literariness," "self-referentiality," "textuality," and other prominent counterrepresentational touchstones in the field. Literary theory purports to be radical, too, a trait that runs contrary to the varieties of moral, political, and educational conservation Betsey expressed in the productive last two decades of her life.

That identity suggests why one notable rendition of Betsey in the world of literary studies presents her as a sober, nontheoretical moderate in defense of a literary canon. It appears in the summer 1991 issue of *Critical Inquiry*, the high-cachet quarterly of literary theory in which Paul de Man, Stanley Fish, and other distinguished figures published some of their most important essays, where leading feminist literary critics Sandra M. Gilbert and Susan Gubar stage a whimsical closet drama titled "Masterpiece Theatre: An Academic Melodrama."[1] The characters in the drama come right out of the late-1980s academic culture wars and literary theory, and they include William Bennett, Lynne Cheney, Allan Bloom, J. Hillis Miller, Harold Bloom, Gerald Graff, Helen Vendler, Henry Louis Gates, and many others. At the center of their exchanges sits a text: What does it mean? What does it signify? Who (or what) is the author?

The episodes pass in brief conversational vignettes. In one of them, Betsey arrives on the scene in a taxi and observes the radicals and the traditionalists argue back and forth before stepping in to mediate. After feminist scholar Lillian Robinson demands that professors hearken only to works marginalized or forsaken by canonical thinking, Betsey speaks up (Gilbert and Gubar insert actual words she had written elsewhere into her statement— they appear in quotation marks):

I can't agree with you there. "The 'radical' critics of the purportedly irrelevant canon have sacrificed the ideal of collective identity that constituted its most laudable feature. To settle for education as personal autobiography or identity is tacitly to accept the worst forms of political domination." (711)

Bennett listens and accuses her of spouting "ideology," then pledges, "I'll get *you*, too!" (711; the versions of Bennett and Cheney are altogether ridiculous). Betsey ignores him and offers a middle course between completely dispensing with the traditional literary canon and totally adhering to it.

I'm just trying to point out that "unless we agree that there is a place for some canon, the apparent issue of whether or not to introduce gender, race, and class is no issue at all. . . . Let me offer you a paradox: It may well be that those who reject the narrowness of the established canon, but who remain committed to the validity of some canon . . . are the true custodians of liberal education or of the humanities." (711–12)

Professor Robert Scholes, noted semiotician and future-president of the Modern Language Association, replies with the standard leftist point that any "book list" is arbitrary and autocratic. Worse, he adds, it turns education into "political conformity to some kind of conservative definition of national identity" (712).

Betsey's reply:

Your spirit is "touching," Bob, but your "politics are misguided. Mr. Bennett is, in this respect, correct. The status of the canon is of large political significance. . . . The unpleasant implications of Mr. Bennett's proposals lie not in his attempt to shore up the canon, but in his related—and thinly veiled—determination to reverse [the] expansion [of] and restrict access to higher education."

The position is broad minded and judicious, a Burkean gradualism of curricular reform. We admit modifications to the canon here and there because of salient shifts in thinking about gender, race, and class, but we also conserve a canonical ambition and the hierarchy that goes with it. Furthermore, at the same time, we do not let the identity politics of canon-busting obscure the real politics of higher education ("custodianship" and "access").

Betsey's approach, of course, pleases none of the adversaries, and we can extend the response to academia at large. In academic debates over identity and curriculum, where debates often acquire a simmering psychopolitical undercurrent, the middle ground is the least popular. In fact Betsey's moderation, not her putative controversial identity, explains why so many colleagues at Emory and elsewhere found her a troubling figure. In a habitat of cliques and sects, as the humanities had become in the late 1980s, the colleague who partly agrees with you and partly disagrees with you is more trying than the colleague who disagrees with you all the way.

Gilbert and Gubar were right to assign her this disconcerting forensic stance, for in classrooms, in academic gatherings, and in private conversations, she displayed it again and again. In discussing just about anything involving intellectual or political judgment, as soon as one began to settle into a firm understanding and expected her to concur, Betsey would insert a thoughtful qualification or gentle warning. The easy targets of academia—political correctness, various tribalisms, and the like—encouraged expressions of moral assurance and lineups of good guys vs. bad guys, and she battled them repeatedly on principle. But she also understood well the complacency and extremism they could foster in parties on both sides of the question. Extremism was an intellectual vice. In one essay included here, "My Statue, My Self: Autobiographical Writings of Afro-American Women," Betsey says so explicitly.[2] In explaining literary tradition, she writes, "The coherence of such a tradition consists as much in unfolding strategies of representation as in experience itself. Some would even argue that the coherence of a tradition is only to be sought in the strategies of representation; the self is a function of discourse—a textual construct—not of experience at all. Others, including many black feminist critics, would emphasize black women's writing as personal testimony to oppression, thus emphasizing experience at the expense of text. Neither extreme will do" (44). The implication is that we should appreciate the significance of textuality in any literary understanding but curb it with an appreciation of experience—and vice versa. It is a dialectical position, and it asks scholars to assume a difficult and unstable mental posture once again, the middle ground that rejects the comforts of either polarity.

In the *Critical Inquiry* piece, we see that dialectic collapse. A novice reader in the scene, a young woman who frankly enjoys novels, thanks Betsey for supplying the confidence to proceed in spite of the epistemological skepticism of the theorists. "I'm not going to let these others interrogate you either right now," she tells the text. "I'm just going to *read* you" (712). It must be said, however, that Betsey would have mistrusted such a pure and simple engagement just as much as she did the hyperabstract ruminations of high-textuality theory.

The scene proceeds as the theorists protest, Frank Lentricchia telling the novice contemptuously, "Don't be naïve. No act of reading is innocent" (712). That is a glib way of stating a complex truth, and Betsey does not bother with it. But if readers of "Masterpiece Theatre" come away believing

that Betsey was antitheory and hermeneutically naive, essays in this volume
will disabuse them. The pages to follow amply demonstrate not only an erudite grasp of literary tradition, especially the lineage of African American
women's writing, but also a productive theoretical practice. The substantive
examination "My Statue, My Self" is a strong example.

The essay opens with an explicit call to theory. The autobiographies of
black women, she declared, "command an attention to theory and method
that respects their distinctiveness as a discourse" (44). The theorizing that
proceeds operates in stark contrast to the theory we have become accustomed to since the 1970s, to be sure, but it is no less theoretical because of
it. Literary theory has adopted a deconstructive, problematizing mode in
one way or another for more than three decades, but here the argument
aims to clarify and chart a constructive approach to the text. In a word Betsey laid out the right principles for reading black women's autobiography.
That means identifying the distinguishing features and tensions of the genre
in order to improve our understanding of the text. All of the representa-
tional cruxes of contemporary theory are present, for instance, when Betsey
recognized that we cannot "take any of the history offered in the texts at
face value" but that we must "accept the text as bearing some (possibly distorted) relation to reality" (47).

They are recognized, however, in order to advance a determination of
the text, not block it. Instead of sinking into the mire of theoretical difficulties, aporias, and uncertainties, she set out to assemble the right interpretative framework for comprehending *Autobiography of a Slave Girl, Our Nig,
Incidents in the Life of a Slave Girl,* and the rest. She began with "careful
consideration of extratextual conditions" (46), actual circumstances such as
the pressure on black women authors to authenticate their composition. For
slave and ex-slave authors, Betsey argued, their authorship had to override
not only their status as chattel, but also their unstable gender, that is, the
absence of forms of gender identification for black women in antebellum
America (captured by Sojourner Truth's query "Ar'n't I a Woman?"). If
autobiography tells the story of a human being in the process of becoming
a self, a black woman's autobiography adds to it the uphill task of en-
visioning a self that one might become. While northern and southern societies at the time handed white women a gender identity that they might
don, they provided black women no such thing. A careful reading of black
women's autobiography, then, incorporates that absence into the interpretation.

A careful interpretation also discerns the division of anticipated audiences into black and white, men and women. As Betscy said, "There is little

evidence that black women autobiographers assumed that any significant number of other black women would read their work" (50). That so few readers would share the racial makeup of the author raises yet another interpretative variable, namely, a troubled relation of author to reader. "The tension at the heart of black women's autobiography derives in large part," she maintained, "from the chasm between an autobiographer's intuitive sense of herself and her attitude toward her probable readers" (52–53). While other authors might affirm an intimate relation with readers, black women authors face a "possible adversarial relation" (55).

For Betsey these are not accidents extraneous to a theoretical understanding of black women's literature. They are constituents of the theory. If the first premise of literary theory is that representation is a complicated matter, Betsey acknowledged it—and then sought to manage it, not reduce it, with sound principles of reading appropriate to the genre.

Other essays in this volume display the same forward progress of interpretation, as well as a penetrating eye for literary detail. Her analysis of Kate Chopin's *The Awakening* is the best treatment of the novel that I have seen, and it displays minute stylistic details and broad historical contexts with equal dexterity. Moreover it orients those points toward an ambition most satisfying to a reader's curiosity and a student's frustration, that is, to lay bare the text, to get at its truth.

For me, coming through graduate school in English in the 1980s when deconstruction and its derivatives (Lacanian interpretation, postcolonialism, trauma theory) acquired the status of professional protocol, Betsey's approach to literary study was a welcome antidote. In those heady high-theory days, we were taught to suspect empirical claims, to conduct inquiry not by amassing evidence but by problematizing it, and to regard assertions about what the text means as a quaint throwback to precritical times. We almost looked forward to the first-year graduate student in a seminar who presented the day's text as an expression answerable to what-does-this-mean questions. One naive remark and we started to pounce. Even more amusing was the hotshot visiting theorist who might deliver a sparkling lecture to the department on the latest cutting-edge indeterminacy only to have a near-retirement Old Boy rise to cite a few archival snippets that might resolve the indeterminacy of this text or that one. The visitor would smile an indulgent smile, then rehearse a few catchphrases about the need to interpret the snippets before we use them to interpret the text; the need to acknowledge the textuality of the evidence; or the need to unveil various unconscious, ideological, metaphysical, identity-grounded underpinnings of the whole meaning-ascribing endeavor.

Such performances imparted well the style, the manner, the mores of critical acumen. We soaked it up as the professional attitude. Perhaps when pressed we would have admitted that the plodding collection of evidence took more time and energy than mastering the skeptical premises of literary theory. But the gestures of theory had something else to back them up, namely, the aura of smartness. To speak them well and to eschew the nuts and bolts of empirical work and basic decision making ("Yes, this means this and not that") was to certify one's training and to flash credentials.

Like all institutional rituals, it grew old quickly. After twenty conference panel discussions in which one person after another stepped forth to proclaim, "Who's to say which works should be in the canon?" and "Let's not reinscribe the myth of objectivity by trying to settle the final meaning of the text," theory in the textuality grain lost its allure. It got repetitive, predictable, and invariably negative—save for the politically correct pieties of the moment, which one posited with ostentatious fervor. By the early 1990s, one could already sense the onset of ennui and exhaustion that so afflict literary studies today. In effect it amounted to a paralyzing game, and the irony was that playing it well—dismantling, subverting, undermining, and unmasking positive interpretations—signified higher intelligence and greater professionalism.

The habit was hard to break. It had planted itself too deeply in one's formation, and it had all the might of disciplinary etiquette. To take the podium and announce "This means this" was just plain bad taste, no matter how much erudition and documentation backed it up. That is why it took a learned mind with an independent personality to resist the skeptical theoretical disposition. Never intimidated by popular dogmas, Betsey disdained the conformity mind-set that allowed negative theory to dominate the field for so many years. She also possessed astonishing learning that saved her from practitioners who thought that they might cast her as an antitheory reactionary who did not possess the brainpower necessary to divine the theory breakthrough. On the contrary she entered literary studies not as an antitheorist but as a positive theorist. She understood theory not as a method of undoing but a method of doing better. Her question to negative theorists could only be taken generously: "How does your theory help us understand the material? I see how it helps us avoid the traps of uncritical assertions and simplistic readings, but how does it generate positive knowledge or positive decisions about the text?" Her example remains a model of critical responsibility.

Notes

1. Sandra M. Gilbert and Susan Gubar, "Masterpiece Theatre: An Academic Melodrama," *Critical Inquiry* 17 (Summer 1991): 693–717. Further citations are made parenthetically in text.

2. Elizabeth Fox-Genovese, "My Statue, My Self: Autobiographical Writings of Afro-American Women," in *The Private Self: Theory and Practice of Women's Autobiographical Writings,* ed. Shari Benstock (Chapel Hill: University of North Carolina Press, 1988), 63–89: reprinted in this volume, pp. 42–66. In-text citations are to the version in this volume.

Introduction

Vision and Voice—Women Who Wrote the South

Kibibi Mack-Shelton and Christina Bieber Lake

After the publication of *Within the Plantation Household,* there could be no doubt that Elizabeth Fox-Genovese was a gifted historian who was interested in the lives of extraordinary—and ordinary—women. She read diaries, interviews, and narratives of southern African American women and white women with great textual sensitivity, bringing into balance the historian's eye for larger themes and context and the archivist's attention to detail. *Within the Plantation Household* established Fox-Genovese as a premier historian, and it set the standard for scholarship about the lives of southern women.

But even more remarkably, *Within the Plantation Household* revealed Fox-Genovese as a premier literary scholar. Hardly a brief afterthought, its epilogue presents a compelling and unparalleled reading of Harriet Jacobs's autobiographical narrative *Incidents in the Life of a Slave Girl.* Historians of lesser skill might be tempted to do what Alan Jacobs describes some of his philosopher friends as doing when they come to him wanting "juicy literary 'examples'" to illustrate their philosophical points but "never imagine that these poems and stories and plays could actually shape philosophical reflection, could be themselves philosophically significant. . . . For them, philosophical work as they know it is the fruit; literature provides, at most, leafy ornamentation."[1]

Fox-Genovese never succumbed to "using" literature to illustrate her historical or theoretical arguments. She believed that attention to narrative as narrative, with all its tensions and ambiguities, is crucial to historical discovery. In recognition of Fox-Genovese's versatility as a historian and a literary critic, we have divided this volume into two parts. The first part, "Women—Making History," is focused on her historical writings, and the second part, "Women—Redefining Southern Culture," is focused on her literary analysis.

Women—Making History

Fox-Genovese's quest to understand the distinctive intricacies of southern culture and its women fueled her continuing examination of southern women's history through their own words. Her insights were thus productive of new historical models. In "Strategies and Forms of Resistance: Focus on Slave Women in the United States" (1986), Fox-Genovese joined the few scholars who were attempting to explicate women's gender-specific roles in resisting slavery. She supported the findings of Herbert Aptheker's pioneering study, *American Negro Slave Revolts* (1943), that women also participated in active resistance, arguing cogently that an understanding of the "how and why" of these women's roles in resistance required further examination of the impact of their African culture. In addition she pointed out the danger of "insisting upon the specific experience of women as women" and overlooking the "individual soul or consciousness" of black women who saw themselves as slaves and women whose oppression from both statuses were inextricably linked.[2]

Fox-Genovese understood that the only way for a responsible historian to consider the "data" of individual souls and consciousness is to examine the writers' personal voices found in autobiographies, journals, diaries, memoirs, and oral history accounts. Writings such as Jarena Lee's *The Religious Experience and Journal of Mrs. Jarena Lee, Giving an Account of Her Call to Preach the Gospel* (1849), Julia Foote's *A Brand Plucked from the Fire: An Autobiographical Sketch* (1886), and Amanda Smith's *An Autobiography* (1893) present autobiographies as being "testimonials to the power of their God" in which the narratives show how struggling lives were transformed into missionary ones that served their people. Similarly Fox-Genovese showed that Mrs. A. E. Johnson's *Clarence and Corinne; or, God's Way* (1890) and *The Hazeley Family* (1894), along with Emma Dunham Kelley's *Four Girls at Cottage City* (1898), also used "religious and domestic models" to explore "situations that test moral fortitude in the small encounters of everyday life."[3]

In "To Write the Wrongs of Slavery," Fox-Genovese applauded the discovery of fresh voices in an extensive review of the thirty-volume *Schomburg Library of Nineteenth-Century Black Women Writers* (1986). These rediscovered texts, she argued, are indispensable to place experiences of African American women in the larger picture of antebellum southern life. Although they strategically de-emphasized race, they wisely used religious tones to reflect on their dreams of freedom, their femaleness, or the evils of slavery. Phillis Wheatley, for example, wrote poetry in "a language alien to most blacks," yet her strong "invocation of Christianity" held whites "up to the implications of their belief." She also asserted that "freedom [was] a universal natural right."[4]

Fox-Genovese critically exposed attempts "to integrate" these black women writers "into the [white] cultural mainstream" rather than recognize that these women had their own "spirited independence and force of character that prompted [them] to write for publication." She examined the "attestations, introductions, and testimonials" that accompanied the original publications, as in the case of Reverend Bishop Mallalieu's introductions to *The Narrative of Bethany Veney: A Slave Woman* (1889) and *The House of Bondage or Charlotte Brooks and Other Slaves* (1890). Though these women narrated the horrors of slavery, Fox-Genovese showed how Mallalieu found it necessary to "accentuate the positive and downplay the negative" by emphasizing the authors' "sense of 'the joy of deliverance'" and asserting about Octavia V. Rogers Albert that, "loving her race, she 'would gladly have died for their enlightenment and salvation.'" Elizabeth Keckley's memoir, *Behind the Scenes, or Thirty Years a Slave, and Four Years in the White House* (1868), lacked the usual introduction or attestation, but she herself stated that, although she might have "portrayed the dark side of slavery," she also had "painted the bright side."[5]

In her examination of black female autobiographies in "My Statue, My Self" (1988), Fox-Genovese disagreed with those who suggested that they should be evaluated solely on their "merits" and that they reflected the "romanticism and humanism" of personal experience, thus lacking "intellectual excellence," which, according to the "white male cultural elite," "requires depersonalization and abstraction." She defended these firsthand accounts, likening them to "bear[ing] witness to a collective experience" similar to a personal "report from the war zone." She offered Zora Neale Hurston's troubling autobiography, *Dust Tracks on a Road,* as a good example. Fox-Genovese explained how "self-representation" can be presented as a statue, or fixed image of the ego ideal at the same time as it draws on and conveys aspects of the actual "self of everyday life—the contingent self."[6]

Fox-Genovese acknowledged these writings as "necessarily personal and unique . . . commentary" that documents "the collective experience of black women in the United States." She recognized that black women's common experience of being black and female "in a specific society at a specific moment and over succeeding generations" strongly established these autobiographies as a "subgenre" with its own "integrity." "My Statue, My Self" thus redefined the position of black female autobiography in historiography.[7]

Fox-Genovese's attention to the special problems of self-representation for all women enabled her to make unique contributions to the historical debate over a woman's identity in relation to her community and larger regional culture. In "Between Individualism and Community: Autobiographies of Southern Women" (1990), she turned to autobiographies, such as Ellen Glasgow's *The Woman Within* (1954), Katharine Du Pre Lumpkin's *The Making of a Southerner* (1946), and Maya Angelou's *I Know Why the Caged Bird Sings* (1969), to make a case for a much more conflicted story than is typically described. For example Fox-Genovese outlined the internal struggles, described in book 3 of *The Making of a Southerner,* that shaped Lumpkin as she faced the "sharp contrast between the impermanency of her family's residencies, the uncertainty of their material situation, and the permanency and certainty of their beliefs," notably, white supremacy and black inferiority.[8] These uncertainties and certainties worked together to form Lumpkin's conflicted identity.

In "Family and Female Identity in the Antebellum South: Sarah Gayle and Her Family" (1991), Fox-Genovese examined the journal of elite southern housewife Sarah Gayle to illustrate how her identity as a woman resulted from her evolving roles as wife and mother in a slaveholding household. Antebellum southern women's writings are invaluable to the historian precisely because they were not solely about "self" but described day-to-day happenings, including accounts of unmanageable slaves, household production, motherhood and parenting, female behavior, and the ravages of war. Similarly in her introduction to *A Blockaded Family: Life in Southern Alabama during the Civil War* (1991), Fox-Genovese looked beyond Parthenia Hague's romantic apologia to the struggles of Alabama women to survive and to maintain their dual patriotism to both the South and the Union. Through this narrative Fox-Genovese revealed the elite woman's willingness to suffer rather than take handouts from her foe, the Union army. She waded through Hague's nostalgia for her beloved South in order to deepen historical understanding of the impact of the social and economic deprivations southerners experienced from the wartime blockade.[9] Finally Fox-Genovese's foreword to Kibibi Mack's *Parlor Ladies and Ebony Drudges* (1999) illustrates how actively she recognized emerging scholarship that invited scholars "to follow new paths of inquiry" for writing southern African American women's history. Like historians Stephanie Shaw and Darlene Clark Hine's scholarship on southern African American women, *Parlor Ladies and Ebony Drudges* further "broadened . . . our understanding of the intricate tapestry of black women's work."[10]

Women—Redefining Southern Culture

If the first half of this volume illustrates Elizabeth Fox-Genovese's sensitivity to rhetorical concerns as a historian, the second half illustrates her maturation as literary critic. This section outlines questions that Fox-Genovese believed only a skilled literary critic could answer fully: How do individual southern women make sense of their lives, particularly when marred by slavery? What stories are southern women writers able to tell—and not able to tell—and why? And how do the stories both shape and reflect the larger communities in which they lived and worked?

Her repeated visit to this last question in particular illustrates how Fox-Genovese kept pace with, or even anticipated, the work of some of the most influential literary critics of the late twentieth century. The pieces reprinted here cover ground very similar to that covered by Elaine Showalter in *A Literature of Their Own: British Women Novelists from Brontë to Lessing* (1977); Sandra M. Gilbert and Susan Gubar in *The Madwoman in the Attic: The Woman Writer and the Nineteenth-Century Literary Imagination* (1979); and Jane Tompkins in *Sensational Designs: The Cultural Work of American Fiction, 1790–1860* (1985). Much of Fox-Genovese's work was concurrent with these studies, illustrating her early sensitivity to the concerns that would reshape the discipline of English literature for years to come.

Many scholars, for example, credit Tompkins's *Sensational Designs* with opening the domestic sentimental novel to critical scrutiny. Literary critics had largely ignored domestic fiction because it had been written by Hawthorne's famous "damned mob of scribbling women"—women who wrote unabashedly for the public and not for the cultural elite. Insisting on the validity of reader-response criticism, Tompkins claimed that she wanted to redefine literary study, to see literary texts "not as works of art embodying enduring themes in complex forms, but as attempts to redefine the social order."[11] These texts are interesting, Tompkins insisted, because they provide examples of how the culture thinks about itself and its problems. But these texts do more than passively reflect culture. As their authors had "designs upon their audiences," these texts must be studied precisely because of their popularity, especially with women readers. Women, after all, have always been the primary readers of novels.[12]

Fox-Genovese had long been reading popular domestic fiction through a similar, culturally sensitive lens. Her essay "Scarlett O'Hara: The Southern Lady as New Woman" (1981) takes as its subject a novel that many adolescent women read but that no one ever studied in school, *Gone with the Wind*. Fox-Genovese's piece illustrates that this novel was a product of Margaret Mitchell's personal and historical imagination, which needed to make sense of the new woman (the "flapper") and to justify the southern way of life to the rest of the country. Fox-Genovese wrote that "for Mitchell, the New South, of which she was trying to make sense as a setting for female life, needed to be understood in the mainstream of American life. The middle-class values which were being challenged by the ferment of the 1920s had

to be anchored in a national culture, not limited to sectional idiosyncra-
sies."[13] Mitchell had designs on her readers, in other words, and quite ambitious ones at that. Fox-Genovese continued, "Mitchell reread Southern
history through a prism of conservative progressivism. . . . She sought to
fashion a history appropriate to the national concerns and destiny of the
New South."[14]

That southern women actively defended their way of life through these
domestic sentimental fictions was a theme that Fox-Genovese returned to
again and again, insisting upon the importance of popular novels such as
Augusta Jane Evans's *Beulah* and Caroline Hentz's *The Planter's Northern
Bride*. These southern women fought ideological battles on the "battleground" of domestic fiction and were entirely aware of what was at stake in
the fight.

Seen in this light, Fox-Genovese's work sought to expand the canon to
include domestic novelists and to engage what Stephen Greenblatt dubbed
in 1982 "New Historicism." But Fox-Genovese never followed a trendy
scholarly path. If her work resembles New Historicism, it was by accident of
her own unique scholarly bent. She was by training and temperament a historian who understood that literary texts were necessarily engaged in complex cultural processes. Fox-Genovese simply and unapologetically brought
her own historical questions and her own often surprisingly "real world" concerns to the fiction she studied. These concerns remained consistent from
the beginning to the end of her career, shaping her engagement with texts
into a powerful testimony to the value of extended thought on some of the
most important questions that face us. Three prominent strands woven
throughout these pieces grow stronger as they are developed in their unique
contexts. Fox-Genovese's literary scholarship shows repeated interest, first,
in the psychological situation of the characters and/or authors; second, in
the complexity of the experiences and beliefs of southern women, a complexity best revealed by careful rhetorical analysis; and third, in the unique
problems of self-representation for African American women writers.

Fox-Genovese's formal training in psychoanalysis early in her career
shaped both the assumptions she carried with her to texts and the questions
she asked of them. Part of the reason that "Kate Chopin's Awakening" (1979)
remains so compelling is Fox-Genovese's understanding of two psychological concepts: the central importance to any woman of her own mother and
Freud's definition of primary narcissism. She thus moved beyond conventional feminist readings of Edna's suicide as an act of triumphant defiance
of—or cowardly refusal to accept—the patriarchal constriction of her freedom. Instead she showed how the novel's impressionistic method and vi-
gnette structure precludes extended reflection on social issues as it reveals

Chopin's own ambivalence toward the tension between being female as an existential reality and being female as a social reality. Through a careful reading of the novel's ending, Fox-Genovese insisted that Edna's retreat into the ocean must be read as a childlike expression of longing for a lost mother who could have loved her into maturity. Edna's notion of freedom remains narcissistic and infantile, unmoored and floating; it thereby becomes a stunning psychoanalytic indictment of northern fantasies of individual autonomy.

Fox-Genovese's interest in mothers and mothering brought her quite naturally to Toni Morrison, whose novel *Beloved* gave Fox-Genovese the opportunity to illustrate the devastation wreaked by slavery's "implacable war against motherhood."[15] In her *Unspeakable Things Unspoken: Ghosts and Memories in the Narratives of African-American Women* (1992), Fox-Genovese developed one of the theoretical convictions about autobiography that would become virtually axiomatic for her: how texts reveal the "return of the repressed" in the form of ghosts and other stand-ins. *Beloved* thus became a kind of paradigmatic text that demonstrates just how significant "unspeakable thoughts unspoken" can be, and how a scholar ignores those silences at her peril. This understanding of the return of the repressed enabled Fox-Genovese to provide one of the most satisfying readings—if not the only satisfying reading—of the ending of *Beloved,* in which Morrison repeats the line "This was not a story to pass on." While other critics flail at the irony of how a story that is clearly now in our hands is not one that should be repeated to the next generation, Fox-Genovese explained that the story that was not to be passed on was the story of the community's forgetting— the story, in other words, of the repression of the most horrible and brutal truths of slavery. Since it was this repression that brought out the ghost to begin with, only an appropriately communal "rememory" can destroy it.

The second prominent strand in Fox-Genovese's treatment of literary texts is her insistence that the lives of southern women writers represent substantial differences in experiences, beliefs, and values. But these differences do not require that we give up on writing women's literary history altogether. To the contrary, "Texas Women and the Writing of Women's History" (1993) is one of many pieces in which Fox-Genovese insisted that the only way forward for the scholar is to strike a balance between the general and the particular through critical vigilance: "Any adequate theory of women's history must simultaneously attend to similarity and difference, always asking similar to and different from whom, and in which ways."[16] It is no easy task to recognize how our own assumptions as critics might differ from the assumptions of the women we write about, but to do literary history well, we must confront our tendency to do so. We may, for example, dislike the way that many southern women easily accepted the ideology of separate spheres for men and women, but we must remember that "no determination to repudiate difference as inherently hierarchical can eradicate a past in which most women experienced their difference from men as central to their sense of self and to the rhythm of their lives."[17] Fox-Genovese insisted on the complexity of women's lives and beliefs by everywhere arguing that scholarship on southern women fails if it falls prey either to the northern abolitionist Manichaean tendency to separate good from evil, locating good in the North and evil in the South, or to the feminist tendency to favor and promote only those texts that qualify as social criticism according to an assumption that individual autonomy is the highest good.

Both Fox-Genovese's essay "Stewards of Their Culture: Southern Women Novelists as Social Critics" (1995) and her introduction to *Beulah* (1992) strongly counter the standard feminist line on what constitutes social criticism. Fox-Genovese argued that many southern women writers who were active and influential as social critics were neither critical of hierarchies in the system of slavery or patriarchy nor interested in their own individual freedom as defined by their northern counterparts. Writers such as Augusta Jane Evans, on the contrary, believed it to be their mission to defend traditional values, and, above all, "they berate Northerners, including Northern women, for abandoning scripture, the foundation of true religion, and for espousing the destructive doctrines of individualism and equality, including abolition and women's rights."[18] Fox-Genovese's critics, who take this sort of argument as proof of her conservative agenda, betray a failure to read these pieces carefully. She did not champion southern women's defense of slavery or urge facile acquiescence to their religious dogma. Instead she proved that it is a necessary part of the whole story of the South that many of its women—though racists, pietists, or bigots—were strong and intelligent in their refusal to accept northern values as God-given just because northerners thought as much. Fox-Genovese did not ignore the fact that most white southern women promoted slavery. But she repeatedly insisted that their critique of northern bourgeois individualism represented a precious baby in the dirty bathwater of slavery and racism.

The other way that Fox-Genovese's scholarship championed the complexity of the lives of individual women writers represents the final of the three strands. She consistently returned to literature by African American women to illustrate the unique issues of self-representation they evince. The articles "Slavery, Race, and the Figure of the Tragic Mulatta, or, The Ghost of Southern History in the Writing of African-American Women" (1996) and "'To Weave It into the Literature of the Country': Epic and the Fictions of African American Women" (1997) are examples of her most mature literary criticism. In "Slavery, Race, and the Figure of the Tragic Mulatta," she turns again to Harriet Jacobs, along with Francis Harper and Pauline Hopkins, to argue how difficult it was for a nineteenth-century black woman writer to discuss painful memories with candor. Since the cost of telling the true horror of slavery was so high, survivors were tempted to adopt the "manicheean vision of good and evil in which innocent victims confront evil oppressors." But merely pointing out the evils of slavery "does not tell us much about the character and humanity of those who participated in it." The hard fact that she always kept before herself as a critic is that "the experience of oppression does not inevitably transform fallible men and women into saints, any more than the exercise of domination inevitably transforms decent men and women into monsters."[19]

Elizabeth Fox-Genovese's insistence on the complexity of human experience, her sensitivity to the difficulty involved in telling the whole truth, and her refusal to let a Manichaean separation of good and evil dictate her scholarship reached their most mature expression in the essay "To Weave It into the Literature of the Country." Here she read Harriet Wilson's maverick text *Our Nig*, which not only "had no truck with the sentimental domestic pieties" of the nineteenth century, but also actively reversed them.[20] *Our Nig* is an angry and incompliant novel, and its resultant unpopularity then and today demonstrates Fox-Genovese's point about the extreme obstacles in the path of honest self-expression for black women.

Wilson's refusal to make "concessions," such as those made by Harriet Jacobs, led her to an unusually forthright description of northern white racism. Because Wilson refused to lionize northern abolitionists, Fox-Genovese concluded that many of the novel's views more closely resemble those of southern women than those of northern women. Indeed *Our Nig* would have "warmed the heart" of conservative southern white women such as Caroline Lee Hentz, not because it is proslavery (it is not), but because it refuses to flatter antislavery northerners. Instead it "forcefully suggests that the curse of racism has so infected the United States as to make the choice between sections, and even the choice between slavery and freedom, virtually meaningless."[21] The power of Fox-Genovese's argument comes from her interpretation that Wilson rejected not only racism and slavery, but also the northern domestic novelists' commitment to perfectionism, which ignores the innate evil in human nature that characterizes tragedy. Seeing evil as correctable, these northern women failed to distinguish between the evil inherent in slavery and the evil inherent in all social structures. Because of this blindness, they "dramatically narrowed the variety of human experience."[22]

It is toward this important point that the essay, and in a way Fox-Genovese's scholarship as a whole, had been moving. For Harriet Wilson to weave her own story—a story focused on northern racism—into the literature of the country is to insist that it make room for a variety of conflicting perspectives. Contrary to what Fox-Genovese's detractors might suggest, openness to conflicted readings and multiple perspectives was an intellectual ideal for her. It is in this tension, in the variety of human experience, and not in the "narrow assumptions of individualism," that one can move toward a "properly epic vision."[23]

Her viewpoint bears a remarkable similarity to that expressed by James Baldwin in his searing critique "Everybody's Protest Novel." For Baldwin both sentimental novels such as Stowe's *Uncle Tom's Cabin* and the social protest novels of Richard Wright projected a simple division of good and evil, which reinforced the very categorization of people that they were trying to fight against. Bigger Thomas, like Uncle Tom before him, must be allowed to be more than just an example of a group "or a deplorable conundrum to be explained by Science." Baldwin claimed that, "in overlooking, denying, evading his complexity—which is nothing more than the disquieting complexity of ourselves—we are diminished and we perish; only within this web of ambiguity, paradox, this hunger, danger, darkness, can we find at once ourselves and the power that will free us from ourselves."[24]

Fox-Genovese was committed to the complexity of human experience for many of these same reasons. She believed that the scholar, like the novelist, must never succumb to casting the battle as good versus evil, North versus South, or us versus them, but must enlighten all aspects of our profoundly shared human nature. And thus she concluded one of her richest analyses of that commonality by explaining the epigraph that Wilson chose for the last chapter of *Our Nig*. Fox-Genovese wrote that it was "an epigraph that ironically invoked a biblical favorite of the slaveholders—as if, once again, to demonstrate the strange and conflicted close connection between the two variants of Southern culture. She chose the words of the biblical preacher, 'Nothing new under the sun.'"[25]

Notes

1. Alan Jacobs, "Paganism and Literature," *Christianity and Literature* 56 (Summer 2007): 671.

2. Elizabeth Fox-Genovese, "Strategies and Forms of Resistance: Focus on Slave Women in the United States," in *In Resistance: Studies of African, Caribbean, and Afro-American History,* ed. Gary Y. Okihiro (Amherst: University of Massachusetts Press, 1986), 144, 148–49, 160; article reprinted in this volume, pp. 3–26.

3. Elizabeth Fox-Genovese, "To Write the Wrongs of Slavery," *Gettysburg Review* 2 (Winter 1989): 65–67; article reprinted in this volume, pp. 27–41.

4. Ibid.

5. Ibid., 64–65.

6. Elizabeth Fox-Genovese, "My Statue, My Self: Autobiographical Writings of Afro-American Women," in *The Private Self: Theory and Practice of Women's Autobiographical*

Writings, ed. Shari Benstock (Chapel Hill: University of North Carolina Press, 1988), 176–77; article reprinted in this volume, pp. 42–66.

7. Ibid., 178–79, 180–81, 184.

8. Elizabeth Fox-Genovese, "Between Individualism and Community: Autobiographies of Southern Women," in *Located Lives: Place and Idea in Southern Autobiography,* ed. J. Bill Berry (Athens: University of Georgia Press, 1990), 23, 25, 27–29, 30–31, 35; article reprinted in this volume, pp. 67–82.

9. Elizabeth Fox-Genovese, "Family and Female Identity in the Antebellum South: Sarah Gayle and Her Family," in *Joy and Sorrow: Women, Family, and Marriage in the Victorian South, 1830–1900,* ed. Carol Bleser (New York: Oxford University Press, 1991), 19, 20, 23 [article reprinted in this volume, pp. 83–104]; and Fox-Genovese, introduction to *A Blockaded Family: Life in Southern Alabama during the Civil War,* by Parthenia Antoinette Hague (Lincoln: University of Nebraska Press, 1991) x, xii, xiv; [article reprinted in this volume, pp. 105–15].

10. Elizabeth Fox-Genovese, foreword to *Parlor Ladies and Ebony Drudges: African American Women, Class, and Work in a South Carolina Community,* ed. Kibibi Voloria C. Mack (Knoxville: University of Tennessee Press, 1999), xii, xv, xviii; article reprinted in this volume, pp. 116–21.

11. Jane Tompkins, *Sensational Designs: The Cultural Work of American Fiction, 1790–1860* (New York: Oxford University Press, 1985), xi.

12. And it is adolescent girls who take these texts most intimately to heart, as Caitlin Flanagan has recently argued. The female adolescent is that "creature whose most elemental psychological needs—to be undisturbed while she works out the big questions of her life, to be hidden from view while still in plain sight, to enter profoundly into the emotional lives of others—are met precisely by the act of reading." Caitlin Flanagan, "What Girls Want" *Atlantic Monthly,* December 2008, http://www.theatlantic.com/doc/200812/twilight-vampires (accessed December 13, 2010).

13. Elizabeth Fox-Genovese, "Scarlett O'Hara: The Southern Lady as New Woman." *American Quarterly* 33, no. 4 (1981): 160; article reprinted in this volume, pp. 153–73.

14. Ibid.

15. Elizabeth Fox-Genovese, *Unspeakable Things Unspoken: Ghosts and Memories in the Narratives of African-American Women,* 1992 Elsa Goveia Memorial Lecture (Mona, Jamaica: Department of History, University of the West Indies, 1993), 11; article reprinted in this volume, pp. 174–93.

16. Elizabeth Fox-Genovese, "Texas Women and the Writing of Women's History," in *Women and Texas History: Selected Essays,* ed. Fane Downs and Nancy Baker Jones (Austin: Texas State Historical Association, 1993), 8–9; article reprinted in this volume, pp. 218–28.

17. Ibid., 9.

18. Elizabeth Fox-Genovese, "Stewards of Their Culture: Southern Women Novelists as Social Critics," in *Stepping Out of the Shadows: Alabama Women, 1819–1990,* ed. Mary Martha Thomas (Tuscaloosa: University of Alabama Press, 1995), 23; article reprinted in this volume, pp. 229–46.

19. Elizabeth Fox-Genovese, "Slavery, Race, and the Figure of the Tragic Mulatta, or, The Ghost of Southern History in the Writing of African-American Women," *Mississippi Quarterly* 49, no. 4 (1996): 794; article reprinted in this volume, pp. 247–71.

20. Elizabeth Fox-Genovese, "'To Weave It into the Literature of the Country': Epic and the Fictions of African American Women," in *Poetics of the Americas: Race, Founding,*

and Textuality, ed. Bainard Cowan and Jefferson Humphries (Baton Rouge: Louisiana State University Press, 1997), 32; article reprinted in this volume, pp. 272–85.

21. Ibid., 34.

22. Ibid., 39.

23. Ibid., 45.

24. James Baldwin, "Everybody's Protest Novel," in *Notes of a Native Son* (Boston: Beacon, 1955), 15.

25. Fox-Genovese, "To Weave It into the Literature of the Country," 45.

Elizabeth Fox-Genovese.
Courtesy of Eugene D. Genovese

Part One

Women—Making History

One

Strategies and Forms of Resistance

Focus on Slave Women in the United States

Harriet Tubman, Sojourner Truth, Linda Brent, Ellen Craft: History has preserved the names of women who resisted slavery in a variety of ways. Jane, "a mulatto woman, slave," who was indicted for the murder of her infant child, also may be taken to have resisted, albeit presumably at a high cost to herself. And her name is on record for those who are willing to seek it in the appropriate court records. Those records, like the diaries of such white women as Mary Boykin Chesnut, the narratives of slave men, and the various ex-slave narratives, also provide those who seek a poignant record of the varieties of female slave resistance.[1] Perhaps more telling yet, they bear witness to the resistance of women, whom the record keepers did not even deem worthy of being named at all: "the Rolling-house was maliciously burnt by a Negro woman of the Defts. [defendants] whereof she was Convicted . . . and Executed for it." The court was unwilling to convict the woman's master, deciding that he "is not Chargeable for the willful wrong of his servant."[2]

Such testimonies to women's opposition to enslavement, or to those who enslaved them, shed an invaluable light on the resistance of Afro-Americans as a people, as well as on slave women themselves. Not least, they help us to fill out the record of multiple forms of resistance—a subject to which I shall return. Perhaps more important yet, they demonstrate that the slaveholders, including, and indeed especially, those most deeply committed to a paternalistic ideology, recognized on some level the intentional resistance of their bondwomen: The nameless female arsonist was "malicious" and "wilful." Perhaps the slaveholders knew in their hearts that she differed only in degree from the house servant, whom they dubbed "impudent" and "uppity." But the records provide, at best, an imperfect guide to the nature, extent, and meaning of slave women's resistance to their enslavement.

The fortieth anniversary of the publication of Herbert Aptheker's pioneering study *American Negro Slave Revolts* provides an especially appropriate context in which to consider the role of slave women in the resistance of Afro-Americans to their enslavement.[3] For Aptheker, long before the emergence of women's history in its contemporary guise, insisted upon recording the presence of women among slave rebels wherever he found it. He may rank among the few historians of his generation to have understood that any people includes both men and women, and to have written history as if it resulted from the combined efforts of men and women. I can find no place in *American Negro Slave Revolts* in which women should have been included and were not.[4] If anything, Aptheker errs in the opposite direction. One suspects that at least occasionally he added "and women" following "men" because his human instinct, knowledge of the world, and commitment to women's social significance told him that women must have participated in forms of resistance, even if the records did not mention them. His willingness to credit women's contribution to the resistance of the enslaved cannot, in short, be questioned. But even his determined quest for evidence of women's participation did not unearth a plethora of forgotten female leaders of revolts; in fact, he found few specific female names. Women figure primarily as members of groups of resisters, or embodiments of specific forms of resistance. Historians of Afro-American women have recently called attention to what we might call gender-specific forms of female resistance that Aptheker did not directly address.[5] But resistance, although an essential dimension of his work, was not his main story.

That main story concerned revolts. And in telling it, Aptheker demonstrated, beyond contention, that Afro-American slaves not merely resisted degradation and dehumanization but revolted against their enslavement. Aptheker's critics have suggested that he may have exaggerated the number and significance of slave revolts, but their very differences with him have implicitly underscored his central point, namely, that some slaves, under the most adverse circumstances, engaged in armed political struggle—armed class struggle, if you prefer. The point at issue between Aptheker and these critics concerns how best to distinguish full-scale revolts from ubiquitous acts of violent resistance. The very existence of this debate confronts historians of slave women with the problem of how to interpret the role of slave women in the collective struggle of their people. For North American slave women appear not to have participated significantly in the direct planning and execution of the most explicitly political revolts of the nineteenth century, notably those of Gabriel Prosser, Denmark Vesey, and Nat Turner.[6] And women probably also did not participate in large numbers, if at all, in the smaller but explicitly military insurrections, or attempted insurrections, that punctuated the eighteenth and early nineteenth centuries.[7] Yet however we ultimately draw the line between revolt and non-insurrectionary resistance, the explicitly political and military revolts cannot be understood in isolation from the backdrop of steady resistance that could, at any moment, be both collective and violent, and in which women indisputably did not participate. Recognition of these two aspects of the struggle against slavery helps to establish a viable context for a preliminary assessment of the role of slave women in the resistance of Afro-American people.

It is impossible to discuss the specific roles of women in the general struggle of Afro-American slaves without taking account of male and female roles—gender roles—among the slaves. Gender roles, like gender relations, among the slaves remain a topic of considerable debate, and insufficient study. Scholars are slowly beginning to acknowledge that notions of what it means to be a man and what it means to be a woman, as well as the notion of appropriate relations between the two, are among the most sensitive and deeply rooted aspects of any individual's or any people's sense of identity. But to date, most of the attention to gender relations among Afro-Americans, under slavery and thereafter, has focused on discussions of family life. This ideologically charged literature has taken as its standard middle-class, Euro-American ideas of normal, in contrast to pathological, male and female roles and relations. Even at its best, and at its most appreciative of Afro-American cultural vigor, it has assumed that commitment to nuclear families and to companionate marriages under firm male leadership offers the most convincing evidence of health and stability. The Afro-Americans' struggle to defend these values under adverse conditions is presented as evidence of the slaves' successful resistance to the most brutal and dehumanizing aspects of enslavement.[8] But the discussion has not adequately assessed the perturbing problem of the extent to which these norms derived from African traditions, or the extent to which they reflected white values. Nor has it fully penetrated the yet more perturbing problem of the sources of and the links between behavior and belief: Masters could impose some forms of behavior on their slaves and encourage others, but the slaves retained considerable latitude to endow those forms that they adopted or observed with their own meanings. It remains extremely difficult to ascribe precise measures to the respective parts of African traditions and American conditions

in Afro-American practice and belief, all the more since the slaves' experience of American conditions led them to reinterpret African traditions.[9] It
remains more difficult yet to determine the extent to which slaves appropriated any of the values of American culture and, to the extent that they did,
the degree to which they modified them to conform to either their experience of enslavement or their transformed African values. If the discussion,
at this level, appears abstract, it nonetheless casts a long shadow over the
possible history of slave women in resistance and revolt. Let us consider a
concrete example: If slave women can be shown to have been decisively more
active in resistance and revolt than their white counterparts in time and
place, should their activity be attributed to the survival of African patterns
of female strength—and, if so, which ones—or to the demoralizing impact
of enslavement on male leadership and authority? For the moment, the
point is less to solve the problem than to recognize that it is highly charged.

The truth is that we have no comparative study of the role of slave
women in resistance, and no consensus about what would constitute an
appropriate comparative framework. Comparison of women's roles in the
slave revolts throughout the New World would elucidate an additional dimension of those revolts, and of the various slave systems.[10] Comparison of
the roles of slave women in revolts with the roles of women in the revolts
of other oppressed peoples and popular classes would presumably add an
important element to our understanding of the dynamics of popular rebellion in different societies, and assuredly contribute to our understanding
of women's participation in different peoples' resistance to oppression. But
this work has not yet received sustained attention. Some recent scholarship
is beginning to compare the experience of Afro-American women to that of
North American white women, but has not yet addressed specific outbreaks
of violent class struggle.[11] Nonetheless, recent work on the multiple contributions of women to war, resistance, and revolution among various peoples
at various times leaves no doubt that women have everywhere and at all
times participated in the struggles of peoples for national liberation and self-
determination. Analogous work on class struggles also reveals the ubiquity
and importance of women's contributions. In any particular struggle, women
can be found in almost any role, from leadership to armed combat to spying
to providing a variety of support services. In struggles for national or class
liberation, it is not uncommon for at least some women to depart radically
from what are taken to be normal female activities among their people. It is
uncommon, historically, for women to assume primary leadership of armed
combat, or even to engage directly in combat on a regular basis—but women
have done both. It is, in short, probably safe to say that there is no form of
insurrectionary struggle in which some women have not, at some time,

engaged. But that being said, it is also true that historically, as in the contemporary world, women are less likely than men to assume the political and
military leadership of the struggles for liberation of their people and class.[12]

Whatever women's roles in the struggles of the oppressed against their
oppression have been, they have been singularly difficult to document, especially among nonliterate peoples. Sources on the role of slave women in
resistance and revolt have proved especially sparse, and those that exist must
be recognized as themselves the product of a continuing historical struggle.
Most of the early sources are white. In assessing them, we must take account
of the blinders that white assumptions imposed on white perceptions. White
commentators may well have missed many female contributions to resistance because they did not expect them. Enslaved and oppressed peoples, as
Frantz Fanon so movingly demonstrates in "Algeria Unveiled," are quite
prepared to capitalize on the "invisibility" of their women in the interests of
a victorious struggle.[13] Many of the other sources on Afro-American slave
revolts derive from black men who were actively engaged in a total struggle.
For such men, their testimonies concerning events constituted part of that
struggle. It is not impossible that they borrowed more than the ideology of
revolution and democratic rights from the emerging Euro-American ideology of their period. It is also not impossible that they have drawn especially
on those African traditions that emphasized the leadership of men in political and military affairs. Whether drawing upon one or the other of these currents, or combining the two, black men may—consciously or unconsciously,
and for a variety of reasons—have made a political choice to prefer the leadership of men in the struggles of the enslaved.

If the nature of the sources shapes our perceptions of slave women's
contributions to resistance and revolt, the conditions of enslavement, which
were also those of struggle, shaped the historical possibilities for slave men's
and women's actual contributions to resistance and revolt. And however
much we have learned to recognize the role of slaves in setting limits to their
oppression and in shaping their own lives, the master class did establish the
conditions. Those conditions varied according to time, place, and size of
plantation, but, overall, scholars concur that they never invited the kind of
massive rebellions or establishment of maroon societies that occurred elsewhere in the Western Hemisphere.[14] I cannot in this essay begin to do justice to the impact of variations in size and location of plantations on women's
roles in resistance and revolt, although it must have been considerable. But
however much the conditions imposed by individual masters varied, they also
fell within the general structures of prevailing legal and political relations,
and of a society that can, in important respects, be viewed as a network of
households that included the decisive productive as well as reproductive

relations.[15] These general structural conditions changed significantly over time. From the perspective of slave revolts and resistance, the most important changes probably occurred toward the first third of the eighteenth century, as the fluidity and experimentation of early settlement gave way to more rigid structures that reflected the greater stability and will to ordered domination of white society, and following the wave of revolution that characterized the late eighteenth century. Both of these shifts confronted slaves with an increase in the resolution and sophistication of white society, but both—especially the second—also offered slaves new sources of collective identity and purpose as Afro-Americans. The net result can perhaps best be grasped in the tendency of nineteenth-century slave revolts to claim the explicit political purpose of realizing for Afro-Americans the promises of the new democratic ideology of individual freedom. And by the time that the slaves were claiming this message for themselves they indeed constituted a distinct Afro-American people—creoles who had become the only self-reproducing slave population in the New World.

The following preliminary discussion of the role of slave women in resistance rests on a series of working assumptions—all of which must be advanced tentatively. (1) However hard it may be to draw the lines, violent resistance and revolt should be distinguished. Revolt, to paraphrase Clausewitz, is the continuation of violent resistance by other means. (2) The relation between violent resistance and revolt changed over time, with the decisive shift occurring in the late eighteenth and early nineteenth centuries when the slaves appropriated for themselves the ideology of democratic revolution. (3) The African legacy, if difficult to identify precisely, made a central contribution to slave women's self-perceptions and hence to their patterns of resistance. (4) White culture and institutions constituted the conditions of oppression and hence shaped the patterns of resistance. (5) Although it is not uncommon that a cataclysmic struggle against oppression encourages the temporary disregard of prevailing gender roles, it is more than likely that a protracted struggle of resistance will build upon and shape the continuing life of a people, including its gender roles. In short, the resistance activities of women are likely to reflect their roles as women, as much as their commitment to resistance. Or, to put it differently, though women may fight as soldiers, they will normally resist as women. (6) Any attempt to understand the resistance of slave women as women must acknowledge the dreadful paucity of sources that testify directly to those women's self-perceptions. If we can make a preliminary attempt to identify women's patterns of behavior, we must simultaneously recognize that we have very limited evidence of the meaning that the women themselves attributed to their behavior. (7) Any assessment of slave women's resistance must make a preliminary and cautious attempt to understand the complex relation between the resistance of the individual and collective resistance and to attempt to identify the institutions and movements through which women might have contributed directly, as opposed to indirectly, to collective resistance.

The fragmentary sources and partial, if growing, scholarship on the middle passage, the early period, and other New World slave societies strongly suggest that in the early periods of enslavement women were likely to participate in nearly direct proportion to their numbers—which were fewer than those of men—in revolt and violent resistance. Certainly on the slave ships, women, whom white slavers chose to see as more docile than men, enjoyed greater freedom of movement than men and were, consequently, well positioned to play important roles. Then, as later, their occasional betrayal of revolts can at least be taken as an indication of their participation in, or proximity to, the planning of them.[16] The fragmentary evidence from the early period of settlement further suggests that arrival in the New World did not dissipate the rebelliousness many women had evinced on the middle passage. In fact, at least some women appear to have rebelled or resisted in whatever way available, whenever the opportunity offered itself or could be seized. But precise patterns remain difficult to establish. High demographic casualties among both black and white populations, as well as increasing importations of fresh Africans themselves from different peoples and states, delayed the establishment of distinct social patterns. There is no reason to doubt that during this early period, which was characterized by a constant influx of Africans and the complex class and race relations of a slave society in the making, women rejected their enslavement as wholeheartedly as men. Nor is there any special reason to believe, given the patterns of African slave trading, that women necessarily made the crossing or began life in the Americas in the company of the men of their families and communities. It is more than likely that the violent removal first from their native societies and then from Africa not merely separated women from the men of their kinship but also at least temporarily disrupted accepted patterns of relations between men and women. Many women must have confronted their enslavement as uprooted individuals. And the white society into which they were introduced may not yet have developed, or been able to implement, a fixed notion of the gender relations and roles appropriate to their new servants. With a firm eye on rapid profits, many planters proved entirely willing to exploit female slaves to the limits of their physical endurance—if not beyond—with little regard to the niceties of male and female tasks. The forms of female resistance in this early period may safely be taken to have been as varied and as violent as the complexity of the class, race, and gender relations of an emerging, frontier slave society.[17]

The increasingly cohesive slave society that emerged during the eighteenth century, especially in Virginia and South Carolina, generated considerably more information on the resistance and rebellion of slaves, just as the slaveholders manoeuvred more systematically to set about mastering and to prevent revolts by their slaves. With slaves distributed, however unevenly, throughout the colonies, slave revolts occurred throughout them as well. The records of these revolts testify to women's participation in them, and frequently to their leadership as well. There was, for example, the revolt in Louisiana in the early 1770s, after which Mariana received one hundred lashes and lost her ears for her part. Although with respect to white perceptions, it is worth noting that she received a substantially lighter punishment than did the men, Temba and Pedro, despite her apparent status as leader.[18] But women could be punished as severely as men for their roles in conspiracies, or for suspicion of having committed arson. Frequently they were burned alive.[19]

The eighteenth century witnessed the emergence of forms of violent resistance, notably arson and poison, that would characterize the entire antebellum period. Women regularly played their part, or were accused of so doing, in these activities. Peter Wood has argued that in the wake of the Stono Rebellion in South Carolina the white ruling class systematically curtailed the de facto liberties that the slaves had theretofore enjoyed. The comprehensive Negro Act of 1740 deprived slaves of those personal opportunities to which they had never been entitled, but had nonetheless seized under the frontier conditions of the early years of the colony: "freedom of movement, freedom of assembly, freedom to raise food, to earn money, to learn to read English."[20] This legislation, and above all the determination of the masters that it represented, established the ownership and discipline of slaves as a matter of class, not merely individual, responsibility. It may also have sharpened the distinction between male and female forms of resistance and revolt if only by systematizing the constraints of enslavement and thus making some forms of women's activities more visible. Or, to put it differently, it may have begun to subject female slaves to the same structural constraints that relegated white women to households and male supervision.

The case of runaways suggests that slave society hedged in women even more stringently than men. At least the scholars who have analyzed the advertisements for runaways during the eighteenth century have found far fewer women than men: Wood estimated one woman to three men during the middle decades of the century; Gerald Mullin found that 11 percent of the advertisements for runaways that specified gender were for women in Virginia between 1736 and 1801.[21] It would be rash to conclude, on the basis of this evidence, that women were intrinsically more reconciled to slavery than men. More likely, for reasons discussed below, they had more trouble in passing unobserved outside the plantation. But it is also possible that the fewer ads for female runaways also reflected masters' assumptions that a temporarily missing female had not really run away, but might only have gone to visit kin in the neighborhood. An advertisement from the *Carolina Centinel* of Newberry, North Carolina, in 1818, requested help in securing the return of a female runaway who had already been known to be absent for a considerable period of time during which she had been "harboured" by slaves on various plantations in the neighborhood.[22] Another advertisement from the *Virginia Gazette* of Williamsburg, in 1767, sought assistance in securing the return of a female slave who clearly had been anything but docile: "Hannah, about 35 years of age, had on when she went away a green plains [*sic*] petticoat, and sundry other clothes, but what sort I do not know, as she stole many from the other Negroes." Hannah was further described as having remarkable "long hair, or wool," and being "much scarified under the throat from one ear to the other," and having "many scars on her back, occasioned by whipping." The master clearly regarded Hannah as a serious runaway. "She pretends much to the religion the Negroes of late have practised, and may probably endeavor to pass for a free woman, as I understand she intended when she went away, by the Negroes in the neighbourhood." He believed that under the pretense of being a "free woman" she was heading for Carolina.[23] The two ads reflect the combination of actual conditions and masters' perceptions: A slave woman might "visit" neighboring plantations, where she would disappear among the other slaves without causing comment or provoking a search, at least initially. If she undertook serious flight, she would probably have to attempt to pass for a "free woman" in order to have a plausible reason to be abroad. To be sure, some women did run away to join groups of maroons, but probably in far fewer numbers than men, and probably with diminishing frequency as the possibilities for establishing maroon societies were eroded. Women also, like men, ran away to the British during the Revolution.[24]

The evidence from the eighteenth century remains difficult to interpret. There has been little work on slave women during the eighteenth century, and none on their roles in resistance and revolt specifically. Given the continued influx of new Africans, we can be sure that African influences played a more direct role than they would after the closing of the trade. But we lack adequate studies of the nature of those influences on gender roles and relations. Recently Afro-American and Pan-African feminists have begun to call attention to the importance of women's roles and the degree of women's authority and autonomy in African societies. They have correctly reminded us of the prevalence of matrilineality and matrifocality among West African peoples, and of the presence of queens and female leaders among them. The example of Nanny the Maroon in Jamaica has also been advanced as evidence of women's leadership in New World revolts.[25] As I have tried to suggest, the evidence from the middle passage, the early period, and the eighteenth century testifies to women's active participation in resistance and revolt. But other evidence suggests that from very early, and certainly by the time of Stono, some forms of revolt were considered primarily male affairs. No record survives, for example, of a female leader during the Stono Rebellion itself. Furthermore, scattered evidence indicates that at least some organized insurrections assumed a distinct military and masculine cast. The Stono Rebellion began with twenty black men who marched southwest toward St. Augustine with "colors flying and two drums beating." Vincent Harding emphasizes the importance that those rebellious slave men attached to their having become soldiers: "Sounding the forbidden drums, they were warriors again."[26] African history offers reason to believe that African women might fight as soldiers, but it also suggests that Africans normally viewed warfare as primarily an affair of men. It is, in short, probable that even during the early period African arrivals and Afro-Americans themselves assumed that armed insurrection constituted an essentially male activity.[27] The conditions imposed by white society, not to mention the whites' own visible commitment to male soldiers, can only have reinforced the Afro-American's indigenous tendencies to ascribe warfare to men.

As the eighteenth century gave way to the nineteenth, a series of interrelated events set the distinctive contours of antebellum slave society in the Southern states. In their various ways, the American Revolution, the French Revolution, the revolution in St. Domingue, the invention of the cotton gin, the closing of the African slave trade, and more set Southern society on the course that would lead through the development of a mature slave society to the conflagration of war with a rapidly developing industrial capitalist society. These developments established not merely the social relations within which slave resistance became endemic but also the terrain on which the great slave revolts of the period 1800–1831 would be launched, and they drew the lines within which slavery and its abolition would become national issues. Not incidentally, the same period also witnessed the consolidation of the bourgeois ideology of gender roles in general, and the distinctive Southern ideology of the lady—to be distinguished from the Northern ideology of true womanhood—in particular. Although there is scant reason to believe that Afro-American slaves grasped that ideology to their breasts, there is some reason to believe that its development had indirect consequences for the role of slave women in resistance. Assuredly, the implementation of the Southern ideal of the lady included a tendency to confine women to households and to discourage their freedom from a male "protection" that imposed special burdens and limitations on slave women.

The consolidation of North American slave society, for well-examined reasons, hedged in Afro-American slaves. The role of maroons and other groups of outlyers (runaway slaves) declined. Spontaneous violent revolts of large numbers of slaves probably also declined—although Aptheker might disagree. But the political character and self-consciousness of those revolts that did materialize were heightened. Revolt seems to have become even more a specialized political and insurrectionary male responsibility. And resistance, which became the very essence of the system, fell into some recognizable patterns. As the slaveholding class attempted to impose its own paternalistic ideology upon the enslaved, and to encourage the reproduction and expansion of the slaves, it also seems to have made a minimal effort to apply general notions of gender roles in its treatment of slaves and allocation of tasks. The gender ideology of the master class bore no organic relation to the values of the slaves themselves, although they too had their own ideas of manhood and womanhood. Moreover, with respect to their slaves, the masters clearly observed the ideology of gender difference erratically and according to their own convenience. Nonetheless, the existence of notions of gender difference and gender roles among the masters and the slaves clearly shaped the distinctive patterns of female resistance.

If we are to believe our sources, black women's resistance to slavery was much more likely to be individual than collective. The cumulative effect of individual acts of resistance did contribute decisively, as both Aptheker and Genovese, who follows him on this matter, argue, to the undermining of the system from within and to the confrontationist attitudes of the slaveholders without, but I do believe that the implications of the individual acts of resistance varied and that all must be distinguished from explicitly collective resistance. Furthermore, the characteristic forms of individual female resistance differed somewhat from those of men, perhaps because of Afro-American attitudes toward womanhood, certainly because of opportunities offered and denied by white-dominated slave society. Male and female forms of resistance differed most in those instances in which the physiological differences between the genders were most significant and in those instances in which the attitudes of the slaveholders toward gender roles most directly affected the opportunities available to the enslaved. The most difficult problem consists in identifying Afro-American attitudes toward the respective gender roles of men and women, and identifying the specific African components in those attitudes.

By the time that antebellum slave society assumed its mature form, African gender attitudes are not likely to have appeared in their original form.

Like all other aspects of Afro-American culture, African attitudes toward gender had been transformed and reinterpreted in the light of American experience—the discrete experience of the slaves as well as the possible influence of white practices and values. Obviously, male and female physiology constituted the bedrock of gender differences, and physiology did distinguish between some forms of resistance that were specific to slave men and slave women. Women's reproductive capacities offered both special opportunities for resistance and some possible deterrents against particular forms of resistance. If Afro-American attitudes toward gender began with the slaves' own interpretation of physiological differences, they also must have been shaped by the gender distinctions imposed by the conditions of life in a slave society. Whether or not the slaveholding class could influence Afro-American belief, it could assuredly influence Afro-American practice. To the extent that masters distinguished between male and female slaves—and they did in innumerable ways—male and female slaves enjoyed gender-specific opportunities for specific kinds of resistance and revolt. It seems likely that those conditions also encouraged slaves to reinterpret their African values, and perhaps slowly to include some elements of white attitudes toward gender in their own distinct emerging world view.

But let me begin with those forms of resistance that were least differentiated by gender. To the extent that slaveholders pressed women into the same kinds of heavy labor in the fields and in clearing ground as they did men, women seem to have resisted in the same ways as did men. The breaking of tools and the challenging—even the murdering—of overseers were not the monopoly of male slaves. Such sources as we have clearly demonstrate—and I shall return to the point—that female slaves took enslavement and wanton oppression personally. In 1857, a slave, David, appealed his conviction for the murder of the overseer whom he had assisted another slave, Fanny, in killing. Prior to the act, Fanny had been heard to say that she was not about to allow that overseer to mess in her affairs—and the affairs in question had nothing to do with sexual exploitation.[28] Men's and women's conspiring together to kill overseers, and indeed masters, was nothing new. In December 1774, the *Georgia Gazette* of Savannah reported the "following melancholy account, viz."

> That on Tuesday morning the 29th ult. six new Negro fellows and four wenches, belonging to Capt. Morris, killed the Overseer in the field, after which they went to the house, murdered his wife, and dangerously wounded a carpenter named Wright, also a boy who died the next day; they then proceeded to the house of Angus McIntosh, whom they likewise dangerously wounded; and being there joined by a sensible fellow,

the property of said McIntosh, they went to the house of Roderick M'Leod, wounded him very much, and killed his son, who had fired upon them on their coming up and broke the arm of the fellow who had joined them. Their leader and McIntosh's negro have been taken and burnt, and two of the wenches have returned to the plantation.[29]

The incident provides much to reflect upon. To begin with, why did the white authorities not see fit to punish the "wenches" as severely as the men? There is nothing surprising in recently arrived Africans' banding together at the point of visible oppression—labor—to strike out at their oppressors. There is also nothing surprising in the persistence of such resentment and violence against overseers, as immediate oppressors, throughout the antebellum period. But such concerted actions, which began in the fields, seem to have been less common during the nineteenth century. Furthermore, at least on large plantations, during the nineteenth century masters seem to have frequently organized men and women into different work gangs, even if the women undertook work as heavy as that of the men.[30] At this point, it is difficult to determine the precise reasons for the masters' gender-specific organization of labor gangs. It may only have reflected a desire to cut down on distractions among the slaves during work hours. It may possibly have reflected an attempt to apply the masters' own notions of male and female spheres—however imperfectly—to their slaves. But it assuredly diminished the opportunities for collective male and female resistance at the point of production. When Fanny and David acted together, they did so, as it were, after hours. But even if male and female slaves did not often engage in collective violent resistance in the fields, there is ample evidence that among field hands, especially on large plantations on which life in the quarters remained sharply separated from life in the big house, female slaves frequently resisted their enslavement in much the same ways as did male slaves.

In a crude way, we could say that female slaves resisted as laborers harsh conditions of labor and unusual abuse of the power to supervise labor. Yet even as laborers, female slaves had recourse to forms of resistance normally denied male slaves. The extent to which the slaveholders attributed social significance to the womanhood of their female slaves—the extent to which they attempted to implement gender distinctions—limited the ways in which those slave women might resist, but also offered them special opportunities for resistance. The gender relations and norms of white society made it unlikely that female slaves would be trained for most of the specialized crafts or hired out for jobs that would provide them with an excuse for mobility. Female slaves were unlikely to become carpenters, blacksmiths, masons, or coopers, or to acquire skills in comparable specialized crafts that would lead them to be hired around. And the pool of skilled craftsmen provided not merely the leadership for the most important slave revolts but also the largest number of fugitives. Even those female slaves who did receive specialized training, as cooks or seamstresses, for example, would be expected to remain not merely within plantation households but largely within houses. Since female slaves, like white women, were not expected to be abroad unaccompanied, they enjoyed far fewer opportunities for successful flight, unless they dressed as men.

Yet specialization of skills according to gender offered female slaves other opportunities for resistance. As cooks and house servants, they were in a privileged position for poisoning. And there can be no doubt that the ubiquitous fear of poison decisively contributed to exacerbating the disquiet of the slaveholding class. Plantation letters and diaries abound with references to poisonings, and testify to the uneasiness of the whites. Poison could not always be detected as the cause of death, but was frequently suspected. One slave woman poisoner, "an old sullen house negress," was identified when she complained to a fellow slave, who reported, of having misjudged the necessary amount of arsenic: "I thought my master and mistress would get enough, but it was not sufficient."[31] Another slave woman profited from her specialized position as a nurse to poison an infant and to attempt to do the same to her master. She was burned alive in Charleston, together with the man who supplied the poison.[32] These acts of resistance occurred after the South Carolinians had made a concerted attempt to curtail slaves' knowledge of and access to drugs by an addition to the Negro Act in 1751. The legislation prescribed punishment for any black who should instruct another "in the knowledge of any poisonous root, plant, herb, or other poison whatever, he or she, so offending shall upon conviction thereof suffer death as a felon." It also prohibited physicians, apothecaries, or druggists from admitting slaves to places in which drugs were kept, or allowing them to administer drugs to other slaves.[33] This kind of legislation, and the cautious spirit it reflected, may have decreased whites' mindlessly introducing slaves to the nature and use of medicinal drugs, but probably did not abolish the practice entirely. Slave women did serve as nurses on large plantations, and as midwives. It is also clear that slave women must have transmitted knowledge of poisonous herbs down through the generations. But white precautions, together with the gender conventions that assigned slave women to kitchens and to nursing, may have resulted in poisoning's becoming an increasingly female activity.

The position of slave women within the big house gave them uncommon access to the goods of the slaveholders. It is widely recognized that cooks and other house servants supplemented the diets of their near and dear from the storerooms of the masters. An occasional house servant, such as Clara, could scour the big house for bullets for a son who intended to murder his master. Clara's son succeeded. And she was convicted with him.[34]

The position of slave women within the big house further permitted them special kinds of psychological resistance, the consequences of which are almost impossible to assess. Impudence and uppitiness did constitute forms of resistance that provoked responses disproportionate to the acts. House servants proverbially tried the patience and the nerves of mistresses to whom it fell to oversee their work. Since the mistress lacked the full authority that adhered to the master of the plantation, her relations with her servants could easily lapse into a kind of personal struggle. When servants compounded sauciness and subtle disrespect with a studied cheerful resistance to accomplishing the task at hand, the mistress could rapidly find herself losing control—of herself as well as her servant. "Puttin' on ole massa" must have been, if anything, more trying in its female embodiment. In 1808, a group of South Carolinians acknowledged the undermining potential of mockery in their request to the legislature that slave apparel receive the serious attention it deserved: The citizens of Charleston argued that the dress of persons of color had become so expensive "as to tempt the slaves to dishonesty; to give them ideas not consistent with their conditions; to render them insolent to the whites, and so fond of parade and show as to [make] it extremely difficult to keep them at home." They should only be allowed to wear coarse materials. Liveries were another matter, for they, no matter how elaborate, constituted a badge of servitude. But it was necessary "to prevent the slaves from wearing silks, satins, crapes, lace muslins, and such costly stuffs, as are looked upon and considered the luxury of dress." For an orderly slave society required that "every distinction should be created between the whites and the negroes, calculated to make the latter feel the superiority of the former."[35] But slave women who worked in the big house were uniquely positioned to resist that message, to undermine the distinctions, and to make the lives of privileged mistresses an unending war of nerves.

Slave women could also take advantage of their special role as reproducers to resist various forms of labor through shamming. Although male slaves too could fake illness, female slaves could and did claim pregnancy when they were not pregnant, and claim unusual discomfort or weakness when they were pregnant. The tactic did not always work, but frequently it did, and if it undoubtedly reflected a simple desire to be relieved of labor—not to work—it also reflected a marvelous challenge to the master: You want me to reproduce as a woman, treat me as a woman. John Campbell's recent study of the treatment of pregnant slaves on George J. Kollock's Georgia plantations demonstrates that, at least in this case, the records suggest that the master did give the benefit of the doubt to pregnant slave women, especially in their third trimester, and that this latitude helps to account for the successful self-reproduction of Afro-American slaves in the antebellum South.[36] So this particular form of female resistance did more than alleviate the workload of the individual slave woman: It contributed to strengthening her people.

The relation between slave women's roles as mothers and their resistance to enslavement has generated considerable interest, albeit with contradictory conclusions. If none doubts that slave women frequently took advantage of real or claimed pregnancy to avoid labor, some have argued that they also practiced abortion and infanticide as systematic resistance to the perpetuation of the system. Court records do reveal prosecution of slave women for infanticide. And surely some cases of infanticide and numerous abortions escaped the attention of the masters and authorities. But Michael P. Johnson has recently, and convincingly, questioned whether all cases of infant death that were attributed to infanticide should have been. His discussion of the Sudden Infant Death Syndrome (SIDS) suggests that the death of slave infants by apparent smothering should be linked to their mother's labor in the fields rather than to any attempt to deprive the system of slave infants.[37] In any event, it would be difficult to argue that infanticide and abortion dealt a decisive blow to a slave society that boasted a self-reproducing and expanding slave population. And those who argue for resistance against reproduction—if it occurred with any frequency—must take into account the well-documented attachment of slave mothers to their children. It may be that some slave women practiced abortion and infanticide and that other slave women did or did not run away because of attachment to their children. But it is difficult to fit these contradictory patterns into a single explanation for female slave resistance, much less a general explanation of the significance of that resistance. We have no way of knowing whether slave women practiced abortion—and perhaps infanticide—selectively: Could they, for example, have been more likely to terminate pregnancies, if not lives, that resulted from the sexual exploitation of white men? That, indeed, would have been resistance—perhaps the primary resistance with which to counter the predatory sexuality of white men. At the present state of research, we can, at best, say only that the sexual vulnerability and reproductive capacities of slave women influenced the ways in which they resisted. We can say little about the social significance that they attached to that womanhood.[38]

The list of slave women's acts of resistance to their enslavement in particular and to the slave system in general could be extended indefinitely. Some scholars, notably Deborah Grey White and Darlene Clark Hine and Kate Wittenstein, are beginning to address that history.[39] As women, female slaves engaged in various forms of resistance associated with their sexuality and reproductive capacities. As female slaves, they especially engaged in poisoning and theft, and were much less likely than male slaves to be fugitives or even truants. Although when they did become truants, they could melt into the slave community of another plantation, which may hint at special links among women that bound slave kin and fictive kin networks. As slaves, they engaged in murder, arson, and grand larceny. However deeply their acts of individual resistance undermined the slave system, their direct contribution to political revolt appears to have been considerably less than that of men. In short, the current state of scholarship—that is, the current reading of available evidence—suggests that female slaves, for reasons closely associated with their gender, were more likely to engage in individual than collective resistance in the period following the consolidation of North American slave society and the beginnings of an Afro-American revolutionary tradition.

But this bald assessment will not do, even for a preliminary reading. The very use of the categories of "individual" and "collective" forces us to ask other questions—with full recognition that the answers will depend upon a fresh look at the sources. For a broad gap separates the random acts of individual resistance from the political and military resistance of revolt. And if we accept Aptheker's general assessment of the systematic and cumulative resistance of Afro-American people to their enslavement, we must force ourselves to identify and understand the networks and institutions through which that people forged itself as a people and supported the efforts of its most self-conscious rebels against slavery as a social system.

As Vincent Harding has especially insisted, the various records of revolts invariably make some mention of churches or funerals or religious gatherings as a backdrop for revolt itself. As we all know, there is wide acknowledgment of secret black churches and religious meetings and networks. The significance of religion in the forging of Afro-American culture can hardly be disputed.[40] But my point here is somewhat different. In my judgment, the churches and secret religious networks undoubtedly provided the institutional links between acts of individual resistance and revolts in the name of collectivity. And women were integral members of those churches and religious associations. If our sources seem not to have revealed the roles of women in continuing, collective resistance, it may be that we have not read them with the most interesting questions in mind. It seems obvious enough that those who were caught and tried for their leadership in the great revolts would not mention the networks and institutions on which their plans depended. Why sacrifice brothers and sisters needlessly? Even more, why jeopardize the future revolts of the enslaved by betraying their collective underground organizations? Long-term resistance had to have some collective focus, and its institutions and networks had to remain invisible to the oppressor. But recognizing the likelihood that such institutions and networks bound the daily lives of individuals to the most spectacular attacks against the system that oppressed them, we must also recognize the certainty of women's integral participation in them.

This recognition itself commands a further effort of research and imagination. Albert Raboteau explicitly and other scholars of Afro-American religion implicitly have minimized the importance of women's roles in the leadership of slave religion. Female religious leaders surfaced occasionally, especially in New Orleans and in conjunction with the persistence of voodoo. But slave women appear not to have become preachers and leaders of Afro-American Christianity—certainly not in large numbers. It is nonetheless difficult to believe that informal—and perhaps formal—associations of women, or sisterhoods, did not take shape in association with slave religious communities. Especially after the prohibition of separate black churches, such associations would likely have been as secret as the congregations to which they were linked. But Betty M. Kuyk's recent work on black fraternal orders in the United States opens new possibilities. For she finds that the black men's associations that took shape so rapidly during Reconstruction had roots in slavery, and beyond slavery in African culture.[41] If men's organizations, why not women's? Such gender groupings are reasonably common in societies in which gender constitutes one of the principal forms of social organization, as it did among many West African peoples. But for all the reasons advanced throughout this essay to explain the greater constraints on slave women than slave men, notably, the conditions of gender divisions within the dominant white society, should such women's organizations have existed in whatever form, they would surely have been even less visible than those of men. Deborah Grey White has been insisting on the importance of the female community of slaves in work and as the locus of female traditions of rites of passage, motherhood, and female identity.[42] It appears at least plausible that the community of female slaves generated some kind of religious sisterhood, however fragile and informal. At the least, it remains indisputable that slave women saw themselves as sisters in religion, as essential members of the religious community of slaves. To the extent that the religious community provided the context or underpinnings for the revolts, the women of that community constituted its backbone—not least because not being active members of the revolt they did not risk being cut down with their brothers, but would persist and keep the tradition alive.

The preoccupations of historians have, perhaps, mirrored the biases of antebellum white Southerners and of subsequent bourgeois ideology in missing the contributions of slave women to collective violent resistance and even insurrectionary revolts. By the same token, they may also have failed to take adequate account of the full individual opposition of slave women to their enslavement. There is a danger to which we all, including women's historians, are vulnerable in insisting upon the specific experience of women as women: We can miss the recalcitrant and determined struggle of the individual soul or consciousness against reduction to the status of thing. It has become a commonplace that slave women suffered under a double burden of enslavement as workers and as women. I should be the last to dispute that harsh truth and, indeed, shall argue shortly that its implications for the growing commitment to antislavery were decisive. But first, let me point out that, however deeply slave women themselves felt their exploitation and vulnerability as women, they also seem to have insisted, in the end, on their oppression as slaves. Despite the extensive commentary that has arisen from Judge Thomas Ruffin's celebrated decision in *State vs. Mann,* there has been almost no comment on the gender of the slave who provoked the action that led to the case. Lydia "had committed some small offence, for which the Defendant undertook to chastise her—that while in the act of so doing, the slave ran off, whereupon the Defendant called upon her to stop, which being refused, he shot at and wounded her." The Supreme Court of North Carolina acquitted the white man. In Ruffin's words: "The Power of the master must be absolute to render the submission of the slave perfect."[43] Power and submission: The conflict here is one of wills. Happily, we possess direct confirmation of a slave woman's perception of that conflict as one between the will of her master and her own.

Harriet Jacobs, who published her narrative under the name of Linda Brent, structured her entire account of her escape from slavery as a remorseless and unmediated struggle against the imposition of her master's will. Although the narrative includes much on her sexuality and her children, and her master's sexual designs upon her—so much as to have earned it a description as a modern *Pamela*—in the end everything falls by the wayside except her own refusal to accept the imposition of his will. Her womanhood accounts for many of the specific forms of her oppression, but not for her rejection of oppression. And that refusal of his will was the refusal of his power, the refusal to submit perfectly, or indeed at all. Psychologically, her struggle with her master is one with the most celebrated revolts. The object is not to ease oppression, to lighten a burden, even to protect loved ones: The object is to reject slavery.[44]

The Brent narrative is all the more remarkable for being cast in the language of Northern, sentimental domestic fiction. Brent, ably seconded by the editorial efforts of Lydia Maria Child, apparently intended to ensure the recognition of her tale by Northern, middle-class women, who were steeped in their own culture's pieties of vulnerable womanhood. But her tactical adoption of the literary conventions does not obscure the inner logic of her account, which remains not the violation of womanhood but the conflict of wills. Withal, the rhetoric of the Brent narrative has its own significance and adds a final dimension to the resistance of slave women. Northern abolitionists insisted on assessing slavery from the perspective of their own concerns. And the growing success of their opposition to the slave system depended in no small measure on their casting it as the antithesis of their own bourgeois values—presented as absolute moral standards. To their credit, they did flatly oppose enslavement. But as abolition swelled to join a more general antislavery movement, the emphasis fell increasingly upon the inherent opposition between slavery and the work ethic, slavery and initiative, slavery and democracy. In this context, the growing perception of the exploitation of slave women as a violation of the norms of true womanhood gained in importance. However deeply Northern women may have misperceived and misinterpreted the experience of slave women by imposing on them white, middle-class norms, their very misrepresentations added indispensable fuel to Northern opposition to slavery and thus, albeit ironically, added a discrete female component to that national resistance which would result in the abolition of slavery.

Notes

1. C. Vann Woodward, *Mary Chesnut's Civil War*, New Haven, 1980; Arna Bontemps (ed.), *Great Slave Narratives*, Boston, 1969; George P. Rawick (ed.), *The American Slave*, vols. 2–19, Westport, CT, 1972; and Solomon Northup, *Twelve Years a Slave*, ed. by Philip S. Foner, New York, 1970, among many.

2. Helen T. Catterall (ed.), *Judicial Cases Concerning American Slavery and the Negro*, Washington, DC, 1936, I:1, 84.

3. Herbert Aptheker, *American Negro Slave Revolts*, New York, 1943.

4. Aptheker, *Negro Slave Revolts*, e.g., 84, 89, 92, 127, 138, 148, 181, 201, 259. Aptheker does not pay special attention to women's gender-specific forms of resistance, but systematically includes them as challenges to the system.

5. Darlene Clark Hine and Kate Wittenstein, "Female Slave Resistance: The Economics of Sex," in Filomina Chioma Steady (ed.), *The Black Woman Cross-Culturally*, Cambridge, 1981, 289–300; and Gerda Lerner, "The Struggle for Survival—Day to Day Resistance," in Lerner (ed.), *Black Women in White America: A Documentary History*, New York, 1973, 27–45. Other scholars have discussed the gender-specific form of slave women's oppression, but not paid much attention to related forms of resistance; for example, Angela Y. Davis, "Reflections on the Black Woman's Role in the Community of Slaves," *Black Scholar*, 3 (December 1971), 3–15; and *Women, Race, and Class*, New York, 1981; bell hooks, *Ain't I a Woman: Black Women and Feminism*, Boston, 1981; and Jacqueline Jones, "'My Mother Was Much of a Woman': Black Women, Work, and the Family under Slavery," *Feminist Studies*, 8:2 (Summer 1982), 235–270. For women's roles in

day-to-day resistance, see Raymond A. Bauer and Alice H. Bauer, "Day to Day Resistance to Slavery," *Journal of Negro History*, 27 (October 1942), 388–419.

6. Aptheker, *Negro Slave Revolts*, and Vincent Harding, *There Is a River: The Black Struggle for Freedom in America*, New York, 1981. These general studies, like specific studies of individual revolts, simply do not mention female participants, although both Aptheker and Harding are exemplary in mentioning women in those cases in which the records even hint at their presence. See also, among many, Richard C. Wade, "The Vesey Plot: A Reconsideration," *Journal of Southern History*, 30:2 (May 1964), 143–161; Robert S. Starobin, "Denmark Vesey's Slave Conspiracy of 1822: A Study in Rebellion and Repression," in John Bracey et al. (eds.), *American Slavery: The Question of Resistance*, Belmont, CA, 1971, 142–158; William Freehling, *Prelude to Civil War: The Nullification Controversy in South Carolina, 1816–1836*, New York, 1966, 53–60; *An Account of the Late Intended Insurrection among a Portion of the Blacks of This City*, Charleston, 1822, repr. 1970; Joseph Cephas Carroll, *Slave Insurrections in the United States 1800–1865*, New York, 1938, repr. 1968; John Lofton, *Insurrection in South Carolina: The Turbulent World of Denmark Vesey*, Yellow Springs, OH, 1964; John B. Duff and Peter M. Mitchell (eds.), *The Nat Turner Rebellion: The Historical Event and the Modern Controversy*, New York; 1971; Stephen B. Oates, *The Fires of Jubilee: Nat Turner's Fierce Rebellion*, New York, 1975; and Thomas Wentworth Higginson, *Black Rebellion*, ed. by James M. McPherson, New York, 1969. For contemporaneous testimony, see John Oliver Killens (ed.), *The Trial Record of Denmark Vesey*, Boston, 1970; and Henry Irving Tragle (ed.), *The Southampton Slave Revolt of 1831*, New York, 1973.

7. Aptheker, *Negro Slave Revolts*, and Harding, *There Is a River*, like Peter Wood, *Black Majority: Negroes in Colonial South Carolina from 1670 through the Stono Rebellion*, New York, 1974, do not make a point of women's absence from these military bands, but their evidence clearly indicates that women did not belong to such bands. But women, as Aptheker and Harding show, clearly did participate in other kinds of collective risings. See Daniel Horsmanden, *The New York Conspiracy*, ed. by Thomas J. Davis, Boston, 1971.

8. Among many, see, Eugene D. Genovese, *Roll, Jordan, Roll: The World the Slaves Made*, New York, 1974; Herbert G. Gutman, *The Black Family in Slavery and Freedom, 1750–1925*, New York, 1976; John Blassingame, *The Slave Community: Plantation Life in the Antebellum South*, rev. ed., New York, 1979; Leslie Howard Owens, *This Species of Property: Slave Life and Culture in the Old South*, New York, 1976; George P. Rawick, *The American Slave: A Composite Autobiography*, 1, *From Sundown to Sunup: The Making of the Black Community*, Westport, CT, 1972; and Robert W. Fogel and Stanley L. Engerman, *Time on the Cross*, 2 vols., Boston, 1974.

9. For an excellent analysis of this process, see Sydney W. Mintz, *Caribbean Transformations*, Chicago, 1974, esp., "Afro-Caribbeana: An Introduction." See also Lawrence Levine, *Black Culture and Black Consciousness: Afro-American Folk Thought from Slavery to Freedom*, New York, 1977.

10. Steady (ed.), *Black Woman*, provides a comparative perspective on the experience of African and Afro-American women, but not on the role of women in revolts in the different New World societies. Richard Price (ed.), *Maroon Societies: Rebel Slave Communities in the Americas*, Garden City, NY, 1973, provides some information on women in different maroon societies.

11. For example, Deborah Grey White, "'Ain't I a Woman?' Female Slaves in the Antebellum South," Ph.D. dissertation, University of Illinois at Chicago Circle, 1979; and Suzanne Lebsock, "Free Black Women and the Question of Matriarchy: Petersburg, Virginia, 1784–1820," *Feminist Studies,* 8:2 (Summer 1982), 271–292. Much of the comparison between the experience of black and white women concerns the postbellum period; see, for example, Cynthia Neverdon-Morton, "The Black Woman's Struggle for Equality in the South, 1895–1925," in Sharon Harley and Rosalyn Terborg-Penn (eds.), *The Afro-American Woman: Struggles and Images,* Port Washington, NY, 1978, 43–57; and Terborg-Penn's "Discrimination against Afro-American Women in the Woman's Movement, 1830–1920," in Harley and Terborg-Penn (eds.), *The Afro-American Woman,* 17–27.

12. Carol Berkin and Clara Lovett (eds.), *Women, War, and Revolution,* New York, 1980; Stephanie Urdang, *Fighting Two Colonialisms: Women in Guinea-Bissau,* New York, 1979; Juliette Minces, "Women in Algeria," in Lois Beck and Nikki Keddie (eds.), *Women in the Muslim World,* Cambridge, 1978, 159–171; and Mangol Bayat-Philipp, "Women and Revolution in Iran, 1905–1911," in Beck and Keddie (eds.), *Women in the Muslim World,* 295–308.

13. Frantz Fanon, "Algeria Unveiled," in *A Dying Colonialism,* New York, 1965.

14. Price (ed.), *Maroon Societies*; Eugene D. Genovese, *From Rebellion to Revolution: Afro-American Slave Revolts in the Making of the Modern World,* Baton Rouge, 1979; Aptheker, *Negro Slave Revolts*; and Aptheker, "Additional Data on American Maroons," *Journal of Negro History,* 32 (October 1947), 452–460. Cf. Barbara Kopytoff, "Jamaican Maroon Political Organization: The Effects of the Treaties," *Social and Economic Studies,* 25 (June 1976), 87–105; and her "The Early Political Development of Jamaican Maroon Societies," *William and Mary Quarterly,* 35 (April 1978), 287–307; and Orlando Patterson, "Slavery and Slave Revolts: A Socio-Historical Analysis of the First Maroon War, 1655–1740," *Social and Economic Studies,* 19 (September 1970), 289–325, among many.

15. Elizabeth Fox-Genovese, "Antebellum Southern Households: A New Perspective on a Familiar Question," *Review,* 7:2 (Fall 1983), 215–253.

16. Harding, *There Is a River,* 3–23, passim; Daniel P. Mannix and Malcolm Cowley, *Black Cargoes: A History of the Atlantic Slave Trade,* New York, 1962; Basil Davidson, *The African Slave Trade,* Boston, 1961; Lorenzo Greene, "Mutiny on Slave Ships," *Phylon,* 5 (January 1944), 346–354; and Darold D. Wax, "Negro Resistance to the Early American Slave Trade," *Journal of Negro History,* 51 (January 1966), 1–15. Elizabeth Donnan, *Documents Illustrative of the Slave Trade to America,* 4 vols., New York, 1935, repr. 1965, contains many references to women's activities on the middle passage.

17. Wood, *Black Majority*; Gerald W. Mullin, *Flight and Rebellion: Slave Resistance in Eighteenth-Century Virginia,* New York, 1972; Edmund S. Morgan, *American Slavery, American Freedom: The Ordeal of Colonial Virginia,* New York, 1975, esp. 295–337; Philip Alexander Bruce, *Economic History of Virginia in the Seventeenth Century,* New York, 1895, repr. 1935, II, 57–130; James Thomas McGowan, "Creation of a Slave Society: Louisiana Plantations in the Eighteenth Century," Ph.D. dissertation, University of Rochester, 1976; Jack D. L. Holmes, "The Abortive Slave Revolt at Pointe Coupee, Louisiana, 1795," *Louisiana History,* 11 (Fall 1970), 341–362; James H. Dorman, "The Persistent Spectre: Slave Rebellion in Territorial Louisiana," *Louisiana History,* 18 (Fall 1977), 389–404; and Allan Kulikoff, *Tobacco and Slaves: The Making of Southern Cultures* [(Chapel Hill: University of North Carolina Press, 1986)].

18. Harding, *There Is a River,* 39; and Catterall (ed.), *Judicial Cases,* III, 424.

19. For example, Wood, *Black Majority,* 292; Aptheker, *Negro Slave Revolts,* 90–91, 189–190, 242, 281; and Harding, *There Is a River,* 61.

20. Wood, *Black Majority,* 324–325.

21. Ibid., 241; and Mullin, *Flight and Rebellion,* 40.

22. Ulrich B. Phillips (ed.), *Plantation and Frontier Documents, 1649–1863,* Cleveland, 1909, repr. 1965, II, 90.

23. Ibid., 93.

24. Chester W. Gregory, "Black Women in Pre-Federal America," in Mabel E. Deutrich and Virginia C. Purdy (eds.), *Clio Was a Woman,* Washington, D.C., 1980, 53–72. Benjamin Quarles, *The Negro in the American Revolution,* Chapel Hill, 1961, contains passing references to women (e.g., 27, 120–121), but pays special attention to black men's participation in the war.

25. Lucille Mathurin, *The Rebel Woman in the British West Indies during Slavery,* Kingston, 1975; Alan Tuelon, "Nanny—Maroon Chieftainess," *Caribbean Quarterly,* 19 (December 1973), 20–27; Joseph J. Williams, S.J., *The Maroons of Jamaica,* in Anthropological Series of the Boston College Graduate School, III: 4, Chestnut Hill, MA, 1938, 379–480; and Rosalyn Terborg-Penn[, "Black Women in Resistance: A Cross-Cultural Perspective," in *In Resistance: Studies in African, Caribbean, and Afro-American History,* ed. Gary Y. Okihiro (Amherst, Mass.: University of Massachusetts Press, 1986), 188–209].

26. Harding, *There Is a River,* 35.

27. Basil Davidson, *Black Mother: The Years of the African Slave Trade,* Boston, 1961, e.g., 151–152; and his *A History of West Africa to the Nineteenth Century,* with F. K. Buah and the advice of J. F. Ade Ajayi, Garden City, NY, 1966; and Paul Lovejoy, *Transformations in Slavery: A History of Slavery in Africa,* Cambridge, 1983, esp. 66–87, 108–128.

28. Catterall (ed.), *Judicial Cases,* II:1, 206–207.

29. Phillips (ed.), *Plantation and Frontier,* II, 118–119.

30. Edwin Adam Davis (ed.), *Plantation Life in the Florida Parishes of Louisiana, 1836–1846, as Reflected in the Diary of Bennet H. Barrow,* New York, 1943, throughout refers to "women" doing thus and so, frequently spinning; and Phillips (ed.), *Plantation and Frontier,* I, "Extracts from journal of the manager of Belmead Plantation, Powhaton County, Virginia, 1854," e.g., 213–214, "Women cleaning water furrows . . . ," "Women open water furrows . . . ," and "Men and Women grubbing the Land too hard frozen to plough."

31. Wood, *Black Majority,* 292.

32. Ibid.

33. Ibid., 290. See Thomas Cooper and David J. McCord (eds.), *The Statutes at Large of South Carolina,* 10 vols., Columbia, 1836–1841, VII, 422–423.

34. Catterall (ed.), *Judicial Cases,* II:1, 241–242.

35. Phillips (ed.), *Plantation and Frontier,* II, 113. The citation is from the "Memorial of the Citizens of Charleston to the Senate and House of Representatives of the State of South Carolina [Charleston 1822]."

36. John Campbell, "Work, Pregnancy, and Infant Mortality among Southern Slaves," *Journal of Interdisciplinary History,* 14:4 (Spring 1984), 793–812.

37. Hine and Wittenstein, "Female Slave Resistance"; and Michael P. Johnson, "Smothered Slave Infants: Were Slave Mothers at Fault?" *Journal of Southern History,* 47 (1981), 510–515.

38. Bauer and Bauer, "Day to Day Resistance," 50–57. Angela Davis and bell hooks (see references in note 5, above) emphasize the sexual exploitation of slave women, but do not discuss this in relation to slave women's resistance.

39. Hine and Wittenstein, "Female Slave Resistance"; and Deborah Grey White, "'Ain't I a Woman?'"; and her "Female Slaves, Sex Roles, and Status in the Antebellum Plantation South," *Journal of Family History*, 8:3 (Fall 1983), 248–261.

40. Harding, *There Is a River*, 55, but throughout; Genovese, *Roll*; and Mechal Sobel, *Trabelin' On: The Slave Journey to an Afro-Baptist Faith*, Westport, CT, 1979.

41. Albert J. Raboteau, *Slave Religion: The "Invisible Institution" in the Antebellum South*, New York, 1978, minimizes the role of women throughout, but see references on 79 and 238. Betty M. Kuyk, "The African Derivation of Black Fraternal Orders in the United States," *Comparative Studies in Society and History*, 25:4 (October 1983), 559–592. See also Bennetta Jules-Rosette, "Women in Indigenous African Cults and Churches," in Steady (ed.), *Black Woman*, 185–207, which focuses on the recent past and the contemporary period.

42. White, "Female Slaves."

43. Catterall (ed.), *Judicial Cases*, II:1, 57.

44. Linda Brent [Harriet Jacobs], *Incidents in the Life of a Slave Girl*, ed. by Lydia Maria Child, new ed. by Walter Teller, New York, 1973, orig. 1861. For the identification of Brent as Harriet Jacobs, and as her own author, see Jean Fagan Yellin, "Written by Herself: *Harriet Jacobs' Slave Narrative*," *American Literature*, 53:3 (November 1981), 479–486. The Brent narrative should be compared with that of Ellen Craft, who was no less determined, but who ran dressed as a man and in the company of her husband. See her "Running a Thousand Miles for Freedom; or, The Escape of William and Ellen Craft from Slavery," in Bontemps (ed.), *Great Slave Narratives*.

Two

To Write the Wrongs of Slavery

> And she had nothing to fall back on:
> not maleness, not whiteness, not ladyhood, not anything.
> And out of the profound desolation of her reality
> she may very well have invented herself.

> *Toni Morrison*

If, in our own time, Afro-American women's writing has taken literate Americans by storm, it has also taken them by surprise. Maya Angelou, Toni Cade Bambara, Toni Morrison, Gloria Naylor, Ntozake Shange, Rita Dove, and Alice Walker have emblazoned a brilliant path across the literary firmament, captivating a reading public that may at best have been only dimly aware of their immediate predecessors: Gwendolyn Brooks, Jessie Fauset, Zora Neale Hurston, Nella Larsen, Paule Marshall, Ann Petry, Dorothy West. Even those who were aware normally had little if any knowledge of the vibrant heritage on which Afro-American women writers were drawing. The thirty volumes of *The Schomburg Library of Nineteenth-Century Black Women Writers* figures as a milestone in our literary heritage by making accessible an essential and long neglected strand of American culture.

Normally, literary recoveries occur piecemeal, a volume or two, an author or two at a time. The cultural reappraisal of the sixties and early seventies continues to restore a great many overlooked and undervalued writers to both academic and public consciousness, with black women writers significantly among their number. Within the past decade, both Harriet Jacobs's

Incidents in the Life of a Slave Girl (1861) and Harriet Wilson's *Our Nig* (1859), respectively the first full-length narrative by a formerly enslaved black woman and the first novel by a black American, have been reissued in authoritative modern editions. Twentieth-century black women writers have also enjoyed new attention and editions. But these efforts have not been systematic. It has remained possible to read black women's writing discontinuously, to consider each remarkable new discovery as yet another wonderful exception, and to overlook the vigor of the tradition.

It is precisely because the *Schomburg Library* provides the missing context that we can now see the rich, continuous tradition of writing by black women, at once distinct from and engaged with American culture as a whole.

In the foreword included in each of the *Library*'s thirty volumes, Henry Louis Gates, Jr., the general editor, underscores the difficulties that black women have faced in being accepted as authors at all. Of course any woman will have trouble if she attempts to write in a culture that assumes that the status of author—authoritative voice—naturally belongs to men. But opponents of black women writers were not so much concerned with their womanhood as with their race. When Phillis Wheatley, the first Afro-American of either gender to publish a book, was seeking a publisher for her poems in 1773, she was subjected to an interrogation by a room full of white male Boston dignitaries. Having confirmed her ability to have written the poems, they signed an "Attestation" that was affixed by its English publisher to the volume (which no American firm would touch). As Gates points out, without the "Attestation" few would have "believed that an African could possibly have written the poetry all by herself." The experience of Harriet Jacobs is even more instructive. Although she both affixed the claim, "written by herself," to her narrative, *Incidents in the Life of a Slave Girl* (1861), and appended other testimonies to her authorship, including one by her "editor," Lydia Maria Child, until the past decade scholars have regularly claimed that the book obviously had to have been written by Child.

Even when the authorship of these works was granted, there was often an attempt—in attestations, introductions, and testimonials—to integrate their writers into the cultural mainstream. Thus the Reverend Bishop Mallalieu, in his introduction to *The Narrative of Bethany Veney: A Slave Woman* (1889)—while deploring the shame and sin of slavery—insists that, although the author "may have been born a slave . . . the pure soul that looked out of her flashing eyes was never in bondage to any miserable being calling himself her master. . . . [S]he has lived a pure and spotless life." Within the nineteenth-century cultural mainstream, of course, it was necessary to accentuate the positive and downplay the negative. And so, when the Reverend Bishop Mallalieu introduces—one year later—Mrs. Octavia V. Rogers

Albert's posthumously collected narratives of slavery, *The House of Bondage or Charlotte Brooks and Other Slaves,* he affirms that the author has known "the accursed system" but emphasizes her sense of "the joy of deliverance"; loving her race, she "would gladly have died for their enlightenment and salvation." The intent of such handling was always to accommodate the works of black women to the expectations of a white culture. Overwhelmingly, these writers are certified as chaste, pious, dutiful—as worthy embodiments of the virtues of true womanhood in the New England manner. Rarely mentioned are the spirited independence and force of character that prompted black women to write for publication.

Elizabeth Keckley presents a slightly different case. Although her memoir, *Behind the Scenes, or Thirty Years a Slave, and Four Years in the White House* (1868), was published with neither attestations nor introduction— perhaps because, as Mrs. Lincoln's dress-maker, she could count on an easier degree of acceptance—it nonetheless invokes a similar tone in its preface. Even though writing after the Civil War, Keckley assures her readers that if she has "portrayed the dark side of slavery, I have also painted the bright side. The good that I have said of human servitude should be thrown into the scales with the evil that I have said of it." She especially sought to reassure her readers that she has good and true friends in the South as well as in the North. In fact, Keckley devotes only the first three chapters of *Behind the Scenes* to her years as a slave, while emphasizing her instinctive feel for independence and status and her contempt for whites "of poor parentage." When a Mr. Bingham, the local schoolmaster and a friend of her master, proposes to whip her for some imagined offense, she responds with indignation. When he tells her to take down her dress, she "proudly, firmly" responds that she will not. "Moreover, you shall not whip me unless you prove the stronger. Nobody has a right to whip me but my own master, and nobody shall do so if I can prevent it." The pride and independence evident in Keckley's personal history served to establish her for white readers as essentially the same kind of a woman as they.

To read the *Schomburg Library* is to rediscover the nineteenth century's preoccupation with slavery and freedom, with womanhood and manhood, and—perhaps above all—with the unsuspected meaning in the links between the two. Indeed, with one important exception, the themes, rhetoric, and plots used by black women writers remarkably resemble those of their white peers—however much the underlying message may vary. From Phillis Wheatley in the 1770s to the great outpouring of the decades between the 1890 and 1910, black women's writing was overwhelmingly concerned with the demon slavery, its reality and its legacy. At the same time, these writers also engaged the other dominant themes that obsessed nineteenth-century women—most notably questions of identity, responsibility, and expectation, but also the related themes of religion, temperance, and domesticity.

Indeed, at times the attitudes of the dominant culture overpowered the specific concerns of the black writers. For example, Phillis Wheatley's poetry, which won her astonished acclaim, conformed to the white aesthetic and spiritual models of her day, thereby manifesting her own and her people's capacity for participating in polite culture. Wheatley, like many of her successors, admittedly cultivated a language alien to most blacks. But what choice did an eighteenth-century African slave woman have? To secure an audience she had to write in a language that her prospective readers (those who might buy her book) could understand. Having borrowed another people's language to ensure herself a hearing, Wheatley also borrowed their concepts, as is apparent in her poem "On being brought from AFRICA TO AMERICA":

> 'Twas mercy brought me from my *Pagan* land,
> Taught my benighted soul to understand
> That there's a God, that there's a *Saviour* too:
> Once I redemption neither sought nor knew.
> Some view our sable race with scornful eye,
> "Their colour is a diabolic die,"
> Remember, *Christians, Negros,* black as *Cain,*
> May be refin'd, and join th'angelic train.

Because of her rhetoric, many of those who read Wheatley's work in isolation dismiss it as essentially unfaithful to the black experience. Yet as John C. Shields, the editor of her Schomburg volume points out, Wheatley's reputation as little more than an accommodationist is unwarranted. In 1774, the year in which her poetry appeared, Wheatley argues in a letter to the Reverend Mr. Samson Occom that even those who shut their eyes to the rights of slaves "cannot be insensible that the divine Light is chasing away the thick Darkness which broods over the Land of Africa; and the Chaos, which has reigned so long, is converting into beautiful Order." She thus defied white Americans' views of Africa as so primitive as to be immune to history and civilization, claiming it precisely as a land of history—even if she also attributed its salvation to the gospel of Europeans. Wheatley would surely have resisted the view that her Christianity consisted only in adopted, white values. For her, as for many of her successors, Christianity figured as a powerful indication of personal worth. Religious themes predominate in her poetry, testifying to her personal concern with guidance in this world and salvation in the next, as when she prays in another poem for a "light divine" to "guide my soul, and favour my intent."

Wheatley's invocation of Christianity in effect inaugurated what would become a sustained and righteously subversive tradition among black writers of holding white people up to the implications of their beliefs. Christianity should know no distinctions of race or condition. Similarly the revolutionary ideology of individual rights should, by its own logic, extend to all. In her letter to Occom, Wheatley insists on her people's right to participate in the substance of their adopted culture. She expresses satisfaction with Occom's "highly reasonable . . . [v]indication of their natural Rights." If all peoples, including enslaved Africans, did not desire "civil and religious Liberty," why should the Israelites have sought their freedom from Egyptian bondage? Has not God Himself implanted "in every human Breast" that "Principle, which we call Love of Freedom," which is "impatient of Oppression, and pants for Deliverance"? Of course He has, and that same principle "lives in us." Wheatley's letter embodies central, and complexly interrelated, elements of the Afro-American women's literary tradition, especially a determined insistence on freedom as a universal natural right, a strong identification with Christianity, and an immersion in the rhetoric of white Americans.

Throughout the nineteenth century, Christianity enjoyed pride of place in most black women writers' work and, especially, in their self-representations. In 1835 the free, black abolitionist Maria E. Stewart presented to the First African Baptist Church and Society of Boston a collection of her "Productions." For Stewart, religion constitutes "the sure foundation on which we must build," and at the end of a brief account of her life, she insists that whatever she has done has "been done with an eye single to the glory of God and to promote the good of souls." Without friends or kin, "I stand alone in your midst, exposed to the fiery darts of the devil and to the assaults of wicked men." Withal she has faith that, should all the powers of earth and hell combine against her, she will still "trust in the Lord, and joy in the God of my salvation. For I am fully persuaded, that he will bring me off conqueror, yea, more than conqueror."

There followed in 1849 *The Religious Experience and Journal of Mrs. Jarena Lee, Giving an Account of Her Call to Preach the Gospel,* written and revised (as the title page notes) "by herself." Lee presents the entire account of her life in relation to her Christian mission: her conversion, her call to preach, and her career as "the first female preacher of the First African Methodist Episcopal Church." Throughout the century, Lee had a steady stream of successors who, like her, interpreted their lives as testimonials to the power of their God. Julia Foote, in *A Brand Plucked from the Fire: An Autobiographical Sketch* (1886), and Amanda Smith, in *An Autobiography* (1893), both proclaim their primary intent as being of service to their people. Disclaiming literary ambitions or other forms of self-promotion, each woman insists above all that the story of her life will testify to the Lord's dealings with even the least of his creatures. In this respect, each adopts a rhetoric of Christian humility owing much to the values of the prevailing white culture.

Ann Plato, writing from Hartford in 1841, also hews closely to white conventions of respectability. Eschewing discussions of slavery and association with abolitionists, Plato emphasizes religion ("the daughter of Heaven— parent of our virtues, and source of all true felicity"), education ("the great source from which nations have become civilized, industrious, respectable, and happy"), obedience to parents ("the *basis* of all order and improvement . . . not only pre-emptorily and repeatedly enjoined by Scripture but even the heathen laid great stress upon the due performance of obedience to parents and other superiors"), and similarly uplifting, non-racially-specific topics. Plato apparently sought more in demonstrating the virtues of a civilization that transcends race than in bemoaning the injustices of racial oppression. Throughout the nineteenth century, some black women authors would follow Plato's strategy, emphasizing the normal humanity that black people can share with whites.

Mrs. A. E. Johnson's novels, *Clarence and Corinne; or, God's Way* (1890) and *The Hazeley Family* (1894), both published by the American Baptist Society, similarly avoid any specific emphasis on race. Rather, both novels follow religious and domestic models in exploring situations that test moral fortitude in the small encounters of everyday life. Similarly, Emma Dunham Kelley (later Kelley-Hawkins) takes as her own, and with no special attention to race, the terrain of female adolescence delineated by Louisa May Alcott. In *Megda* (1891), her protagonist wages a protracted battle with the sin of pride and, after hard lessons, eventually finds both her true self—through conversion—and her destiny—through marrying the minister whom she had long loved but who had initially preferred one of her friends. The friend's saintly death, which opens the way to Megda's marriage with the minister, affords the decisive humbling of Megda's pride and shows her the way that she must follow. In reaching that resolution, Kelley touches upon both large and petty manifestations of pride, depicting with special care and convincing exactness Megda's difficulties in bowing her soul to God and accepting membership in His church. *Four Girls at Cottage City* (1898) explores similar themes by exposing the young women of the title to the exemplary faith and hardships of a struggling widow, Charlotte Hood.

If Kelley does not address racial issues as directly as such contemporaries as Ida B. Wells-Barnett and Anna Cooper, she does make her own contribution to the war against racism. Depicting mulatto heroines who might just as well be white, she quietly claims for her people the same sensibilities, refinement, education, and problems available to white people. Her language remarkably resembles Alcott's, as do her concerns. Like Alcott, she invokes John Bunyan's *Pilgrim's Progress* as a model for a young woman's vocational journey. And Kelley, if anything, pays more attention than Alcott to the general literate culture of middle-class Americans. Among the numerous references to religious texts and hymns, her protagonists repeatedly invoke Anglo-American high culture: an entire chapter in *Four Girls at Cottage City* is devoted to a reading of Tennyson's *Lady of Shalott,* and Megda's struggle for faith pivots in part on her reluctance to give up the theater that she loves and at which she excels. Kelley's bright, engaging, young heroine obviously found a following for *Megda,* for it was reprinted within a year of its publication. Nor is it difficult to understand why. All admirers of *Little Women* can find in *Megda* a comparably engrossing tale of how a spirited young girl finds her way to responsible womanhood.

Anyone who has read the wonderful *Journals of Charlotte Forten Grimké* needs no instruction in the depth and breadth of the culture of educated Afro-Americans. Born into the fourth free generation of a talented literary and political Philadelphia family, Charlotte Forten was privately tutored as a young woman and then sent to complete her studies in the relatively unsegregated schools of Salem. There, the precocious girl boarded with the family of Charles Lenox Redmond, leaders of an enlightened community of free blacks, and mingled with other politically and intellectually active women, sharpening both her mind and her antislavery convictions. In 1862 she journeyed south to Port Royal in order to teach freed men and women. It would be hard to find a nineteenth-century white woman's journal that more deeply reflects its author's immersion in the elite culture of her day. Absorbing and internalizing her extensive education, Forten develops a strong attachment to Great Britain as a land of culture and freedom. She delights in the sketches of "the gifted men who are the glory of Scotland—Professor Wilson, Burns, Drummond, the 'Gentle Shepherd,' Dr. Chalmers and many others." Reading Washington Irving's description of Newstead Abbey, she yearns to visit the haunts that Byron loved and that "his genius has consecrated," has "made 'sacred to genius'!" "Oh! England," she notes after studying a picture of an English church, "my heart yearns towards thee as to a loved and loving friend. I long to behold thee, to dwell in one of thy quiet homes, far from the scenes of my early childhood; far from the land, my native land—where I am hated and oppressed because God has given me a *dark skin.*"

Like so many of her sisters, Forten remains preeminently conscious of the ubiquitous iniquity of racism, of the suffering she experiences because of the color of her skin. She also remains, if anything, more conscious of the wrongs and injustice of slavery as a condition. Reading in the New Testament, she is struck by "the third verse of the last chapter of Hebrews— 'Remember them that are in bonds as bound with them.'" To her, the verse suddenly seems to mean: "*Remember the poor slave as bound with him.* How few even of those who are opposed to slavery realize this." If only more people could feel this way, the system would have to fall. The failure is one of identification—the horrendous inability of even the most well-meaning whites to recognize slaves as people like themselves.

Harriet Jacobs fully grasped the measure of that failure. Writing of her own flight from enslavement, she uses the rhetoric of Northeastern domestic fiction, striving to win the identification of potential abolitionist women with her own plight. Her narrative, *Incidents in the Life of a Slave Girl,* strains credulity at many points, primarily because of her *Pamela*-like tale of virtue defended against overwhelming odds. In recounting Linda Brent's protracted struggle with her master, Jacobs takes every pain to distinguish Linda from most slave women. Almost white, with long hair, Linda boasts a free grandmother and a father who "had more of the feelings of a freeman than is common among slaves." She herself does not even know that she is a slave until her mother's death "after six happy years of childhood had passed away." Throughout the narrative Jacobs contrasts Linda's perfectly correct English with the dialect of other slave women, thereby distancing her from the very condition that her narrative was designed to protest.

The more implausible aspects of Jacobs's narrative derive directly from the climate in which she knew herself to be writing. If slavery indeed took the heavy toll on the will and character of those who suffered under it—if it was as evil as abolitionists claimed—then how could slaves expect to meet middle-class free people on equal terms? Jacobs insists on her own equality, on her right to tell her story in the only way her readers would accept it— by demonstrating that she herself has none of the essential characteristics of the slave. Since her readers could not identify with a black slave, Jacobs makes her protagonist, in all important respects, white and free.

But not too free; Jacobs was well aware that most middle-class Northeasterners, no matter how opposed to slavery, were uneasy about claims for women's independent rights. Their dominant model of true womanhood embodied a deep commitment to the differences between women and men and favored women's domestic subordination. To be sure, advocates of women's rights were beginning to make analogies between the oppression of women within the home and the oppression of slaves, but their views had yet to win general favor. Accordingly, Jacobs makes no mention of women's possible political or individual rights, stressing instead the virtues of domestic womanhood. But beneath the surface of her words lurks a powerful contradiction, for—rhetoric of assaulted virtue and endangered motherhood notwithstanding—Jacobs is really telling a tale of the struggle of wills: "My master had power and law on his side; I had a determined will. There is might in each."

The contradiction that informs Jacobs's narrative carried powerful implications in the nineteenth century for black women in general and black women writers in particular. Slavery—and in lesser measure racism—stripped them of the protections that guaranteed the womanhood of their white counterparts. As Jacobs insists throughout her text, the law protected the womanhood of white women, the manhood of white men, and the domestic relations between white women and men. In the absence of such protection, the bonds between black women and men became—however deeply felt—mere acts of faith or will. Thus slave women were left, ultimately, on their own. Even the trappings of their womanhood fell away as they confronted the masters, from whom no male slave had the right to protect them, in solitary combat. Between the slave woman and her master, naked will faced naked will; the most important battle was not that of race or gender but that of wills.

In the view of Anna J. Cooper, the great nineteenth-century black scholar and feminist, black Americans, through no fault of their own, confronted a massive task of retraining their people, and "the ground work and starting point of its [the race's] progress upward, must be the *black woman*." To black women fell the responsibility of determining their own future and that of their people. "Only the *Black Woman* can say 'when and where I enter, in the quiet, undisputed dignity of my womanhood, without violence and without suing or special patronage, then and there the whole *Negro race enters with me.*'" Cooper's largely neglected voice proclaims in learned and theoretical terms the responsibility that black women had been taking upon themselves since before Emancipation. By the 1890s black women had long been making their mark in literature, poetry, and journalism, as Mrs. N. F. Mossell chronicles in her volume devoted to *The Work of the Afro-American Woman*. And in 1926, Hallie Q. Brown published *Homespun Heroines and Other Women of Distinction,* which contains biographies of sixty black women who had been making their mark in education, church work, club work, and many other areas of social life since the eighteenth century.

As early as 1861, Harriet Jacobs had insisted that if slavery is bad for men it is worse for women. But most black men believed that the only way to rectify the injuries to women was to strengthen black men. If black women would accept the mantle of respectability, and with it a subordinate position within orderly black homes, their men could acquire the strength to combat racism on the women's behalf. The "uplift" of the race demanded that black people display their capacity to observe the norms of white, bourgeois society. As Harriet Jacobs did through her writing, they must prove themselves "white" in taste and temperament. This conviction determined the tone of the developing Afro-American press, just as it influenced the goals of black educational and religious institutions. By the 1890s, at least some black women, whose experience had decisively differed from that of white, middle-class women, were beginning to understand the complaints and demands of the white woman's movement, even if they did not all employ the explicitly feminist rhetoric of Anna Cooper.

The most powerful and accomplished black women writers of the late nineteenth century, Frances Ellen Watkins Harper and Pauline Hopkins, turned to fiction to explore the black woman's legacy and future. Harper's best-selling novel, *Iola Leroy, or Shadows Uplifted* (1892), addresses the classic theme of the light-skinned mulatto who can pass for white. Iola Leroy, daughter of a slaveholding man and the mulatto slave woman whom he made his wife, is introduced through the eyes of slave men: "My! but she's putty. Beautiful long hair comes way down her back; putty blue eyes, an' jis' ez white ez anybody's in dis place." Reputedly a "reg'lar spitfire" whom "dey can't lead nor dribe," the Iola of this scene has just been released from her tormenting master to serve as a nurse for the Union army. But Iola, like Jacobs before her and with better reason, had spent her childhood not knowing that she was a slave: thinking he had freed and legally married her mother, her wealthy father raised her and her brother to think of themselves as white, free, and the owners of slaves. Iola discovers her true condition only after her father's unexpected, early death, when a greedy "friend" exposes her mother's condition in order to disenfranchise Iola and seize the extensive family property for himself.

Harper brilliantly depicts the free, white Iola as possessed of all the pride and fire of her class. In a particularly telling passage, she even shows her defending slavery against the arguments of her Northeastern schoolmates. The attributes of pride and determination survive her reversal of condition and reinforce Harper's underlying message that race does not account for character: either Iola came by her fierceness naturally or it was inculcated in her by her upbringing. For Harper's purposes, it does not matter which, although her depiction of other upstanding blacks forcefully suggests that she intends to underscore the lack of connection between race and character. Blacks, she allows, can be shiftless, immoral, and corrupt—but so can whites. Either God endows people with virtue or social institutions do.

Harper's complex plot includes all the improbable twists, turns, and miraculous reunions that characterize so much sentimental fiction and culminates by providing Iola with a worthy, loving, black husband and with the regathering of her larger family circle. Harper depicts Iola, who had initially been reared in the lap of white luxury, as committed to her own people, whom she chooses to serve as a teacher after the war. And despite considerable emphasis on the importance of marrying the right man and establishing a solid black community life, she also insists on Iola's independent needs as a woman. Iola explains her beliefs to her Uncle Robert: "I believe that a great amount of sin and misery springs from the weakness and inefficiency of women." Her determination to contribute to rectifying that situation prompts her to "join the great rank of breadwinners" by becoming a secretary. Her quest for employment exposes her, like so many other black people, to the unassailable walls of racism. As her mother observes, slavery may be dead, "but the spirit which animated it still lives; and I think that a reckless disregard for human life is more the outgrowth of slavery than any actual hatred of the negro."

Mrs. Leroy's statement opens a long discussion about slavery and its consequences. Iola's brother insists that the eradication of slavery is good for the whole nation. A friend, Dr. Gresham, adds that their current responsibility is to build a better future: "The great distinction between savagery and civilization is the creation and maintenance of law. A people cannot habitually trample on law and justice without retrograding toward barbarism." But the destruction of slavery has not resulted in the triumph of law: the Klan still rides the South. It is not enough, Iola insists, for a nation to build up "a great material prosperity" or to excel in literature; it must also wear "sobriety as a crown and righteousness as the girdle of her loins." This great task requires that men and women struggle together, drawing upon their respective talents and strengths.

As Harper and other black women writers at the close of the century formulated their vision they gave no quarter to the failings of white society. What world could Americans hope for if trained and talented men and women could find no employment except as menials because of the color of their skin? These writers insisted repeatedly that race explains nothing, justifies nothing. Black people are, in all essential respects, identical to white people in their inherent character, in their possibilities for greatness or degradation. Not race but slavery accounted for the miseries of black people, and slavery was the great national sin, the demon that distorted free institutions and made mockery of high purpose and pious intent. Slavery even infected the truth of the religion to which so many black women cleaved. As Harper noted in her poem, "Bible Defence of Slavery":

A reverend man, whose light should be
The guide of age and youth,
Brings to the shrine of slavery
The sacrifice of truth!

Harper's contemporary Pauline Hopkins elaborated similar themes in her series of remarkable and largely neglected novels, one of which—*Contending Forces: A Romance Illustrative of Negro Life North and South* (1900)—was published separately, while three others—*Hagar's Daughter: A Story of Southern Caste Prejudice, Winona: A Tale of Negro Life in the South and Southwest,* and *Of One Blood, or the Hidden Self*—appeared serially in the *Colored American Magazine* between 1901 and 1903. A Northerner, Hopkins devoted her life to writing and journalism, developing a powerful intellect and breadth of learning impressive by any standard. She also proved a compelling storyteller who wove her political and moral convictions into what must be recognized as a splendid body of fiction.

Hopkins's complex plots turn on the confusions and tragedies that result from unsuspected or incorrectly suspected black blood. Like Harper, she repeatedly challenges invidious assumptions about the significance of racial difference. When Hagar, who had been raised thinking herself white, is exposed to her Southern, slaveholding husband as being of African blood, she understands with anguish that the exposure will strip her of everything and leave her "to grovel and suffer the tortures of the damned. Her name gone, her pride of birth shattered at one blow! Was she, indeed, a descendant of naked black savages of the horrible African jungles?" Desperately, her bewildered mind turns upon its misery. What now were her "education, beauty, refinement"? The single fact of having black blood crushes her in humiliation.

Time and again, Hopkins returns to the question of race only to demonstrate its final and fundamental irrelevance. Her black characters live orderly, responsible lives and demonstrate intelligence and compassion, outdistancing most whites in the attributes of true civilization. Only the most unthinking prejudice, the deepest cruelty, the most flagrant greed can produce such wanton disregard for human decency. Villains embodying these base characteristics abound. Hopkins peoples her world with loathsome and decadent characters who expose, trick, and exploit people who far transcend them in worth. Like Harper, she returns time and again to the insistence that slavery, not race, accounts for the tragedy of her people. And more so even than Harper, Hopkins condemns the horrendous toll that the holding of slaves has taken on Southern conscience and character. Quietly drawing upon her great learning, she introduces historical evidence to expose the purposeful crimes of those who held slaves. "The Southerners," she insists, "were in earnest"; among them, moral considerations counted for nothing. "They dreamed of perpetuating slavery, though all history shows the decline of the system as industry, commerce, and knowledge advance." But they defied progress and civilization: "The slaveholders proposed nothing less than to reverse the currents of humanity, and to make barbarism flourish in the bosom of civilization."

Underscoring the importance of slavery as a social condition rather than as an exclusively racial phenomenon, Hopkins again unobtrusively manifests her extraordinary learning. To the slaveholders, she correctly insists, slavery represented an entire world view, related but not limited to racial prejudice. And she introduces that view's defense of slavery in the abstract through words that she ascribes to Jefferson Davis: "'The principle of slavery is in itself right, and does not depend upon difference of complexion. Make the laboring man the slave of *one* man, instead of the slave of society, and he would be far better off. Slavery, black or white, is necessary.'" Fully determined to expose Southern slaveholders and their heirs as the unreconstructed enemies of everything that American society is supposed to stand for, she borrows from an editorial in the antebellum Richmond *Enquirer*: "'Our Northern friends make a great talk about free society. We sicken of the name. What is it but a conglomeration of greasy mechanics, filthy operatives, small-fisted farmers, and moonstruck Abolitionists?'"

Any freedom worthy of the name means freedom for all—blacks as well as whites, women as well as men. In her final magazine novel, *Of One Blood,* Hopkins moves beyond domestic and sentimental conventions—although her plot and rhetoric betray some of their influence—to restore Africa as the foundation of black identity and the hope of a more just future. The plot takes her mixed-blood protagonist, Ruell Briggs, on a scientific expedition to Africa, where he miraculously stumbles upon the hidden remains of the great civilization to which he and his people are heir. The twists and turns of the central love story that parallel the African expedition eventually reveal the primary characters to be something other than they appear and, in fact, to be brother, sister, and half-brother. Hopkins thus effectively forestalls the conventional dynamic of love rewarded and turns instead to a resolution through the power and justice of a concealed African civilization that opens the possibilities of a better world. Moving into the supernatural, Hopkins shows Ruell Briggs to be the lost king of his people, recognized by them because of his magnetic ability to still a lion with his glance. In the end, Ruell returns to his people in the Hidden City and devotes himself to teaching them all that he has learned from his contact with modern culture. His abiding worry remains the inexorable advance of European nations into Africa.

Hopkins's central concern is everywhere the deceptions of race. In an authorial intrusion, she challenges her readers:

> who is clear enough in vision to decide who hath black blood and who hath it not? Can any one tell? No, not one; for in His own mysterious way He has united the white race and the black race in this new continent. By the transgression of the law He proves His own infallibility: "Of one blood have I made all nations of men to dwell upon the whole face of the earth," is as true today as when given to the inspired writers to be recorded. No man can draw the dividing line between the two races, for they are both of one blood!

At the novel's close Hopkins reiterates the message, asserting that none can pretend to judge "the handiwork of God, the Great Craftsman!" He alone has made it all—"caste prejudice, race pride, boundless wealth, scintillating intellects"—all that and more are merely "puppets in His hand, for His promises stand, and He will prove His words, 'Of one blood have I made all the races of men.'"

Hopkins—gifted writer, learned historian, and unflinching social critic—ends her novel on a religious and visionary note. But her vision rejoins that of her contemporaries and predecessors in its twin insistence on the power of faith and the dishonesty of race prejudice. She embraces matters barely hinted at by Wheatley: that Africa too belongs to history, that it may have more to honor than a white society that has betrayed its own Christian and democratic ideologies of equality. Hopkins thus joins the pan-African sensibility that would, shortly after, emerge as a full-blown movement.

As poets, essayists, autobiographers, and novelists, black women have—against staggering odds—continued to represent the legacy, values, and power of themselves and their Afro-American culture. If Africa bequeathed them an oral tradition of persisting vitality, America offered them a literate culture that they enthusiastically embraced. Their quarrel lay not with that culture itself but with white Americans' determination to exclude blacks from it or, perhaps worse, white Americans' inability to recognize blacks as fully equal participants in it.

Throughout the nineteenth century, the dominant purpose of black women writers was necessarily to wrestle down the demon slavery and the racism that it engendered. But as the century neared its close and as black communities coalesced, black women writers also turned to their rights as women among their people. When, in Frances E. W. Harper's novel, Iola Leroy's future husband asks her why she does not write the book she wants to write, she replies in words that foreshadow those of Virginia Woolf:

"I would do it, willingly, if I could; but one needs both leisure and money to make a successful book. There is material among us for the broadest comedies and the deepest tragedies, but, besides money and leisure, it needs patience, perseverance, courage, and the hand of an artist to weave it into the literature of the country."

The Schomburg Library of Black Women Writers amply demonstrates how successfully black women—frequently without money or leisure, but with patience, perseverance, courage, and artistry in abundance—have woven their works into the literature of the country. That the country has been so slow to recognize their accomplishment is the country's failure, not theirs.

Three

My Statue, My Self
Autobiographical Writings of Afro-American Women

Zora Neale Hurston, in her troubling autobiography *Dust Tracks on a Road,* unmistakably identifies the problematic relation between her private self and her self-representation: "I did not know then, as I know now, that people are prone to build a statue of the kind of person that it pleases them to be." Few people, she adds, "want to be forced to ask themselves, 'What if there is no me like my statue?' The thing to do is to grab the broom of anger and drive off the beast of fear" (34).

Hurston's statue has recently been rescued from the attics of marginal memory and received its deserved place in the museum of cultural history. But its rescuers have authenticated it in the name of values that Hurston herself might have found puzzling and perhaps would not even have entirely approved. While she might have been delighted to be acknowledged, finally, as the centerpiece of an Afro-American female literary tradition, she might also have been secretly disappointed to be acknowledged as only that. More than anything, she might have been surprised to see her multiple—and intentionally duplicitous—self-representations accepted as a progenitor of the new Afro-American female self. She might even have laughed before drawing herself up to look mean and impressive. For the rescue of Hurston's statue has been effected, at least in part, at the expense of the anger and the fear and of their consequences for the ways in which she chose publicly to represent her very private self.

The authentication of Hurston's statue cannot be divorced from the authentication of the Afro-American female literary tradition as a whole. In the search for mothers' gardens, it is both central and pivotal.[1] For Hurston, as often as not, speaks in the language of everyday use. But what are we to make of her when she does not? What, especially, do we make of the auto-biography in which she does not? Hurston continually challenges us to re-think our preconceptions, to forswear our fantasies. Attentively read, she reminds that more often than not the autobiographies of Afro-American women have been written from within the cage. Frequently they sing with the voice of freedom, but always they betray the confinement from which that freedom is wrested. Linda Brent, crouched in her grandmother's attic, knows more freedom than she knew as the prey of Dr. Flint's assaults, but the freedom of her soul cannot relieve the confinement of her body. The self, in other words, develops in opposition to, rather than as an articulation of, condition. Yet the condition remains as that against which the self is forged. And the condition, as much as the representations of self, consti-tutes an inescapable aspect of the Afro-American female literary tradition, especially of Afro-American women's autobiographies.

Hurston's statue, like that of her foremothers and successors, was fash-ioned of disparate materials. Uneasily poised between the discourses through which any writer represents the self and the conditions of gender, class, and race through which any personal experience is articulated, the statue em-bodies elements of both. But the combining of elements transforms them. Hurston does not simply "tell it like it is," does not write directly out of ex-perience. The discourses through which she works—and presumably expects to be read—shape her presentation of experience even as her specific expe-rience shapes the ways in which she locates herself in discourses.

Hurston, in fact, never explicitly describes her own statue, although inter-nal evidence suggests that she, like other female autobiographers (notably Simone de Beauvoir), had set her sights on an ideal beyond the horizon of everyday life, beyond the boundaries of her immediate community, beyond the confines of her gender.[2] For Hurston, the statue figures as the ideal for the self or, in psychoanalytic language, the ego ideal. The challenge of the autobiography, then, is to relate the ideal self to the self of everyday life— the contingent self. In Hurston's case, the statue might be said to consist primarily in a freedom from the contingent self that would permit her access as an equal to the republic of letters, the ideal interpretive community. Yet her picture of her contingent self emphasizes all the attributes that would bar her from membership in that community: her gender, her race, her identification with place. It also presents her progress towards her statue as, in large part, a succession of dependencies. Like the fool of Shakespearean drama, she fawns and flatters, reserving to herself the right to speak difficult truths that her demeanor and role appear to belie. Like the trickster of Afro-American folk culture, she speaks with a double tongue. Like the exile, she re-creates her own previous life as a function of her nostalgia. How, in the midst of this deliberate evasiveness that borders on willful duplicity, are we to locate the core of her self-representation? And how are we to locate it in relation to black women's tradition of autobiography?

A literary tradition, even an autobiographical tradition, constitutes something more than a running, unmediated account of the experience of a particular group. The coherence of such a tradition consists as much in unfolding strategies of representation as in experience itself. Some would even argue that the coherence of a tradition is only to be sought in the strategies of representation; the self is a function of discourse—a textual construct—not of experience at all. Others, including many black feminist critics, would emphasize black women's writing as personal testimony to oppression, thus emphasizing experience at the expense of text. Neither extreme will do. The coherence of black women's autobiographical discourse does incontrovertibly derive from black women's experience, although less from experience in the narrow empirical sense than from condition—the condition or interlocking structures of gender, class, and race. But it derives even more from the tension between condition and discourse, from the changing ways in which black women writers have attempted to represent a personal experience of condition through available discourses and in interaction with imagined readers.

Autobiographies of black women, each of which is necessarily personal and unique, constitute a running commentary on the collective experience of black women in the United States. They are inescapably grounded in the experience of slavery and the literary tradition of the slave narratives. Their common denominator, which establishes their integrity as a subgenre, derives not from the general categories of race or sex, but from the historical experience of being black and female in a specific society at a specific moment and over succeeding generations.[3] Black women's autobiographies resist reduction to either political or critical pieties and resist even more firmly reduction to mindless empiricism. In short, they command an attention to theory and method that respects their distinctiveness as a discourse and their relation to other discourses.

In what sense can black women's autobiographies be read as constituting a distinct discourse? Why should they not be lumped with those of black men or those of white women? Politics justifies the differentiation, but its introduction disputes what some would see as the self-referential nature of the autobiographical text. To categorize autobiographies according to the race and gender of those who write them is to acknowledge some relation, however problematical, between the text and its author and, more, between the text and its author's experience. And to acknowledge this relation is to dispute prevailing theories of the multiple deaths of the subject, the self, and the author. Much contemporary theory has found the relations between politics—understood broadly as collective human experience—and the text problematic. These autobiographies defy any apolitical reading of texts, even—perhaps especially—when they seem to invite it.

To accept the ruling pieties about double oppression will not do. Simple addition does not amount to a new theoretical category. Sex assigns black women to the same category as white women; race assigns them to the same category as black men. Both feminist and black-nationalist critics consider their particular claims prior and decisive. Neither group shows much interest in class relations in particular or social relations in general. In all fairness, sex and race more readily lend themselves to symbolization than does class, and thus they also more readily lend themselves to representation, fabulation, and myth. Sex and race more obviously define what we intuitively perceive ourselves to be: male or female, white or black. But even these basic self-perceptions are socially learned and result from acts of (re)cognition. The question thus remains: Why do we find it so much more acceptable to perceive ourselves as members of a sex or a race than as members of a gender or, even more, of a class?[4]

Americans, as a people, do not like fences. Yet as a people we have spent most of our history in raising them. Our open lands lie carved, parceled, and constructed. Our landscape features barriers. Gender and class transform sex and race into barriers, transform the forms of their exclusion into positive social values. To argue for the centrality of gender and class to any analysis of women's self-representation is not to deny the overpowering force of the racism and sexism that stalk women's experience. It is, rather, to argue that if we focus exclusively on sexism and racism we remain mired in the myths we are trying to dissipate.

In theory, it is possible to write about black women's autobiographies as so many discrete cases of the genre "autobiography." Like other autobiographers, black women construct prose portraits of themselves as histories of their lives or of the salient aspects of their lives. The special relation between the autobiographer and the final text outshines all other considerations, especially referential considerations, and reduces specific aspects of the individual history to accidents. There is no theoretical distinction to be made between Jean-Jacques Rousseau's *Confessions* and Zora Neale Hurston's *Dust Tracks*.[5]

Feminist critics, like critics of Afro-American and Third World literatures, are beginning to refuse the implied blackmail of Western, white male criticism. The death of the subject and of the author may accurately reflect the perceived crisis of Western culture and the bottomless anxieties of its most privileged subjects—the white male authors who had presumed to define it. Those subjects and those authors may, as it were, be dying, but it remains to be demonstrated that their death constitutes the collective or generic death of subject and author. There remain plenty of subjects and authors who, never having had much opportunity to write in their own names or the names of their kind much less in the name of the culture as a whole, are eager to seize the abandoned podium. The white male cultural elite has not in fact abandoned the podium; it has merely insisted that the podium cannot be claimed in the name of any particular personal experience. And it had been busily trying to convince the world that intellectual excellence requires depersonalization and abstraction. The virtuosity, born of centuries of privilege, with which these ghosts of authors make their case demands that others, who have something else to say, meet the ghost standards of pyrotechnics.[6]

Rejection of the prevailing pyrotechnics does not guarantee the replacement by something better. The theoretical challenge lies in bringing sophisticated skills to the service of a politically informed reading of texts. To read well, to read fully, is inescapably to read politically, but to foreground the politics, as if these could somehow be distinguished from the reading itself, is to render the reading suspect. Political and social considerations inform any reading, for all readers are political and social beings. To deny the applicability of political or social considerations is to take a political position. The reading of black women's autobiographies forcefully exposes the extent to which the tools of criticism are shaped by the politics that guide them. Wole Soyinka insists upon the bourgeois character of "culture"—its origins, its finality, and its instruments—but he also insists that the dismissal of all "culture" on the grounds of bourgeois contamination ends in "the destruction of all discourse" (55).

Black women's autobiography, as a category, requires justification, and justification requires classification and the delineation of principles and practices of reading.[7] The classification of black women's autobiography forces careful consideration of extratextual conditions. Some current critical tendencies reject the relevance of the extratextual and insist, in a manner reminiscent of the once New Criticism, on evaluating the text on its aesthetic merits, free of such extraneous influences as the experience of the author.

These days, evaluating the autobiographical text on its merits is further seen to expose as romanticism and humanism any concern with the self as in some way prior to the text. These views embody a sharp and understandable reaction against the more sentimental manifestations of bourgeois individualism, but they hardly provide adequate critical standards for the classification of black women's autobiography as a distinct subgenre.

To take the text on its merits legitimates Mattie Griffith's *Autobiography of a Slave Girl* as the autobiography of an Afro-American slave—which it was not. As Robert Stepto has tellingly argued, authentication of the author as author of his or her own text ranked as an important concern for the authors of slave narratives. Stepto proposes a categorization of slave narratives according to the relation between plot or narrative and legitimation in the text as a whole.[8] Although Stepto does not discuss the earliest known prose writings by Afro-American women, both Harriet Jacobs's *Incidents in the Life of a Slave Girl* and Harriet Wilson's *Our Nig* contain legitimating documentation that different readers may perceive as more or less integral parts of the texts. But both Harriet Jacobs, who wrote under a pseudonym, and Harriet Wilson, who did not, felt impelled if not obliged to provide verification of their being both themselves and worthy women. These tactical maneuvers to authenticate the black woman's authorship oblige modern readers to respect these authors' concern for the relation between their texts and their experience. They do not oblige us to take any of the history offered in the texts at face value. Rather, we should be prepared merely to accept the text as bearing some (possibly distorted) relation to reality.

The principles of classification must begin with history. Barbara Christian insists upon the significance of periodization for understanding the development of black women's fiction during the twentieth century. Gwendolyn Brooks, who organized her own autobiography around the historical sea change of the emergence of a new form of black consciousness in the 1960s, forcefully emphasizes the relation between history and consciousness. "There is indeed," she wrote in 1972 in *Report from Part One*, "a new black today. He is different from any the world has known. . . . And he is understood by no white." And, she adds: "I have hopes for myself."[9] For Christian, Brooks, and other critics of and participants in black women's culture, the relevant history concerns the coming to consciousness of Afro-Americans during the second half of the twentieth century, and perhaps the growth of American women's consciousness during the same period. The black movement and the feminist movement, with all their internal currents and tensions, have presided over the recent developments in Afro-American women's political and self-consciousness. Both have contributed to the growing emphasis on varieties of Pan-Africanism, including Pan-African feminism, and the repudiation of slavery as a significant contributor to contemporary black consciousness. In this general respect, race is taken to transcend class in the forging of Afro-American identities. Notwithstanding these long, tempestuous, and unresolvable debates, a specific case can be made for the autobiographies of black women.

Nikki Giovanni has, with special force, made the case for the relation of black women's autobiographies to changing political conditions. She attacks the assumption "that the self is not part of the body politic," insisting, "there's no separation" (Tate 62). Giovanni believes that literature, to be worthy of its claims, must reflect and seek to change reality. And the reality black people have known has left much to be desired: "It's very difficult to gauge what we have done as a people when we have been systematically subjected to the whims of other people" (Tate 63). According to Giovanni, this collective subjection to the whims of others has resulted in the alienation of black Americans from other Americans. For as black Americans "living in a foreign nation we are, as the wandering Jew, both myth and reality." Giovanni believes that black Americans will always be "strangers. But our alienation is our greatest strength" (Tate 70). She does not believe that the alienation, or the collective history that produced it, makes black experience or writing incomprehensible to others. "I have not created a totally unique, incomprehensible feat. I can understand Milton and T. S. Eliot, so the critic can understand me. That's the critic's job" (Tate 64).

Personal experience must be understood in social context. Its representation is susceptible to the critic's reading, regardless of whether he or she shares the personal experience. Giovanni rejects the claim that black writing should be the exclusive preserve of black critics—that it is qualitatively different from white writing, immune to any common principles of analysis, and thus severed from any common discourse. There is no argument about the ways in which the common discourse has treated black writing, especially the writing of black women: shamefully, outrageously, contemptuously, and silently. The argument concerns who can read black texts and the principles of the reading. For, as Soyinka said, if the denial of bourgeois culture ends in the destruction of discourse, the refusal of critical distance ends in the acceptance of an exceptionalism that portends extreme political danger. Giovanni explicitly and implicitly makes the main points: the identity of the self remains hostage to the history of the collectivity; the representation of the self in prose or verse invites the critical scrutiny of the culture. Both points undercut the myth of the unique individual and force a fresh look at the autobiographies of black women.

Selwyn R. Cudjoe, writing of Maya Angelou, has insisted that Afro-American autobiography "as a form tends to be bereft of any *excessive subjectivism* and *mindless* egotism." Rather, Afro-American autobiographies present the experience of the individual "as reflecting a much more *im-personal* condition, the autobiographical subject emerging as an almost random member of the group, selected to tell his/her tale." Accordingly, he views Afro-American autobiography as "a *public* rather than a *private* gesture[:] *me-ism* gives way to *our-ism* and superficial concerns about *individual subject* usually give way to the *collective subjection* of the group" (9). Cudjoe contends that these characteristics establish black autobiography as objective and realistic. In so arguing, he is extending significantly the tradition of the slave narratives that sought to provide living, firsthand accounts of the evils of "that demon slavery" for a Northern audience.[10]

The genre of black autobiography contains an important strand that could be subsumed under the general rubric of "report from the war zone." Brooks uses "report" in her title, *Report from Part One.* Giovanni's *Gemini* features a rather staccato, journalistic style. Both depict the author's "self" indirectly, obliquely, through reports of actions more than through discussions of states of mind. The responsibility to report on experience even more clearly shapes such autobiographies as those of Ida B. Wells and Era Bell Thompson. In their representations of a specific life, the autobiographical writings of many black women, like those of many black men, do bear witness to a collective experience—to black powers of survival and creativity as well as to white oppression. Much of the autobiographical writing of black women eschews the confessional mode—the examinations of personal motives, the searchings of the soul—that white women autobiographers so frequently adopt. Black women's autobiographies seem torn between exhibitionism and secrecy, between self-display and self-concealment. The same is true of all autobiographies, but the proportions differ from text to text, perhaps from group to group of autobiographers. And the emotions and events displayed or concealed also differ.

All autobiographers confront the problem of readers, the audience to whom their self-representation is addressed. Black female autobiographers confront the problem in especially acute form—or so their texts suggest.[11] Harriet Jacobs and Harriet Wilson seem to have assumed that most of their readers would be white abolitionists or potential abolitionists. Both, especially Harriet Jacobs, also seem to have addressed themselves especially to white, middle-class women. Neither Jacobs nor Wilson identified with those likely readers, but both sought to interest them. And in both cases, the professed reason for seeking that interest was to instruct white women in the special horrors of slavery for women and the ways in which the tentacles of slavery reached into the interstices of Northern society. Both texts reveal that their authors harbored deep bitterness toward Northern society in general and Northern white women in particular, even though they frequently expressed it indirectly. And that bitterness inescapably spills over into their imagined relations to their readers, into the ways in which they present themselves and their histories.

There is little evidence that black women autobiographers assumed that any significant number of other black women would read their work. To the extent that they have, until very recently, written for other black women, they seem to have written for younger women, for daughters, for those who would come after. Black women's autobiographies abound with evidence of or references to the love that black female autobiographers felt for and felt from their female elders: mothers, aunts, grandmothers. For the most part, those female elders are represented as rural in identification and origin, if not always in current location; immersed in folk communities; deeply religious; and the privileged custodians of the values and, especially, of the highest standards of their people. They are not necessarily literate, and those who are literate are unlikely to spend money on any books except the Bible.

From Harriet Jacobs and Harriet Wilson onward, black female autobiographers wrote to be read by those who might influence the course of public events, might pay money for their books, or might authenticate them as authors. Neither Jacobs nor Wilson wrote primarily, much less exclusively, for members of the slave community. How could they have? Subsequent black women autobiographers, many of whom have been writers or professional women, have also tended to write as much for white readers, or for black male intellectuals, as for other black women. Their focus has been changing recently with the explosion of Afro-American women's fiction in the work of Toni Morrison, Alice Walker, Ntozake Shange, Gloria Naylor, and many others.[12] But regardless of the present circumstances, it is difficult to find evidence for the emergence of a distinctive Afro-American domestic literary tradition or women's culture during the nineteenth and even the first half of the twentieth century.

Afro-American women have written of themselves as persons and as women under special conditions of colonization. In this respect, their writings cry out for comparison with those of white women. Prevailing opinion insists upon the special tradition of white American women's writing during the nineteenth and early twentieth centuries. Despite frequently sharp differences among feminist critics, there remains a general consensus that white women wrote themselves out of their domestic tradition in both senses of the phrase: they wrote from the experience, and they wrote to subvert the constraints it imposed upon them. It is not fashionable to insist upon the colonization of the imagination of white women writers, but it, too, has existed. For white women did suffer exclusion from the dominant cultural traditions and frequently from the educations and careers that provided the institutional foundations for equal participation in those traditions. That is a different problem, but it deserves mention as a way of locating the experience of black women in relation to the complexities of American culture as a system. It has been possible for feminist critics to pass briefly over white women's relation to the "high culture" of their period, in part, because of the general agreement about women's identification with literary domesticity. White women largely accepted the limitations of their sphere, sometimes turning the limitations to their advantage, and wrote either as representatives of its values, or for its other members, or both. However one assesses the value of their efforts and of their contributions (neglected, silenced) to American culture, it remains beyond dispute that they self-consciously wrote as women, as the representatives of a gender.[13]

For white American women, the self comes wrapped in gender, or rather, gender constitutes the invisible, seamless wrapping of the self. Such is the point of gender in a stable society. For in stable societies gender, in the sense of society's prescriptions for how to grow up as a man or as a woman, is inculcated in tandem with and indissolubly bound to the child's growing sense of "who I am." To be an "I" at all, to be a self, is to belong to a gender. Any society contains individuals who, for whatever reason, find their gender identification problematic. During the nineteenth and twentieth centuries, many American women began to question the attributes of or limitations on their gender. But, at least until World War II, most white American women apparently accepted their society's view of gender as in some deep way related to the persons they perceived themselves to be. For gender, understood as the social construction of sexuality, mediates between sexual identity and social identity—it binds the former to the latter and roots the latter in the former.

Under unstable social conditions, it is possible for gender, as a normative model of being male or female, to come unstuck from sexuality. Once the gaps between sexuality and gender begin to appear, men and women can begin to question whether gender flows naturally from sexuality, whether social demands on the individual are biologically determined. Gender identities derive from a system of gender relations. How to be a woman is defined in relation to how to be a man and the reverse. Neither masculinity nor femininity exists as an absolute.

In a society and culture like that of the United States, a dominant gender system or model of gender relations wrestles with various subsystems or alternate systems. But from at least the beginnings of the nineteenth century and the consolidation of the special American version of the ideology of separate spheres, the dominant model of gender relations has exercised hegemony, in part because of its importance as an alternative to class relations as a system of social classification, and in part because of its invitation to different groups of immigrants who brought with them one or another version of separate male and female spheres and a commitment to one or another form of male dominance. The hegemony of that gender system has influenced the ways in which most American women have written about themselves and their lives, and it especially has influenced their sense of their readers.

The experience and writings of Afro-American women have departed significantly from this model. For the experience of Afro-American women has left them simultaneously alienated from and bound to the dominant models in ways that sharply differentiate their experience from that of white women. There is no reason to believe that Afro-American women experienced gender as the seamless wrapping of their selves. Slavery bequeathed to Afro-American women a double view of gender relations that fully exposed the artificial or problematic aspects of gender identification. Slavery stripped black men of the social attributes of manhood in general and fatherhood in particular. As a result, black women had no satisfactory social definition of themselves as women. This social "unmanning" of the men, with its negative consequences for the women, should not be confused with the personal emasculation upon which some historians have erroneously insisted.[14] Sojourner Truth captured the contradictions in her address "Ar'n't I a Woman?" In effect Truth was insisting on her own femaleness and then querying the relation between her experience of being female and the white, middle-class experience of being a woman. She may not have put it quite that way, and she may not fully have elaborated the depths of the pain and the contradictions, but she exposed the main aspect of the problem: black slave women had suffered the pain of childbirth and the sorrow of losing children and had labored like men. Were they or were they not women?[15]

Truth's query has been widely recognized as a challenge to the possible self-satisfaction of middle-class men and women with respect to black slave women, who were not normally helped over puddles or wrapped in protective coverings. It has been recognized less widely as a challenge to assumptions about the nature of the links between femaleness and self-perception or identity in Afro-American women. Truth effectively chided white men and women for their racism—for not welcoming black women into the sisterhood of womanhood. But there is more to the story.

Truth counterposed "I"—the self—and "woman" in her hostile challenge to her white audience. Black female autobiographers have done the same, although not always with such open defiance. The tension at the heart of black women's autobiography derives in large part from the chasm between an autobiographer's intuitive sense of herself and her attitude toward her probable readers. Imagined readers shape the ways in which an autobiographer constructs the narrative of her life. Harriet Jacobs, in *Incidents in the Life of a Slave Girl*, left no doubt about the audience for whom she thought she was writing: "O, you happy free women, contrast *your* New Year's day with that of the poor bond-woman!" (14).

Jacobs wrote, at least in part, to introduce the world to the special horrors of slavery for women. To achieve her goal, she sought to touch the hearts of Northern white women and, accordingly, wrote as far as possible in their idiom. She so doggedly followed the model of sentimental domestic fiction that for a long time it was assumed that her editor, Lydia Maria Child, had written the book. Jacobs's surviving correspondence proves that she, not Child, wrote her own story, as she claimed in its subtitle: "written by herself."[16] And Jacobs's text differs significantly in tone and content from other examples of domestic fiction. In particular, her withering indictment of slavery portrays the institution as a violation of womanhood. Time and again she not merely asserts but demonstrates that if slavery is bad for men, it is worse for women. Thinking that she understands the Northern, middle-class female audience, she specifically relates the horrors of slavery for women to assaults upon female chastity and conjugal domesticity.

Linda Brent, Jacobs's self in the narrative, grows up in the shadow of her master's determination to possess her sexually. She claims to fend off his advances as an affront to her chastity. Ultimately, her determination to avoid him leads her, after her master has prohibited her sale and marriage to the free black man she loves, to accept another white man as a lover and to bear him two children. One important strand of her story concerns the ways in which she atones for this "fall" and, especially, regains the respect and love of her own daughter. In some sense Jacobs attempts to present her resistance to her master as a defense of her virtue, even though that defense leads her into a loss of "virtue" by another route. Jacobs does not fully resolve the contradictions in her behavior and principles at this level of discourse, however hard she tries. Ultimately, she throws herself on the pity—and guilt—of her readers, as she threw herself on the pity of her daughter. But Jacobs's text also invites another reading or, to put it differently, conceals another text.

Jacobs begins her narrative: "I was born a slave; but I never knew it till six years of happy childhood had passed away" (3). The claim not to have recognized one's condition—of race or of enslavement—until six or seven years of age is common among Afro-American authors.[17] For Jacobs, that opening sentence underscores the difference between condition and consciousness and thereby distances the self from the condition. But Jacobs never suggests that the condition does not, in some measure, influence the self.

She insists that her father "had more of the feelings of a freeman than is common among slaves," thereby implicitly acknowledging the difference between slavery and freedom in the development of an independent self. In the same passage she reveals how heavily slavery could weigh upon the slave's sense of manhood. On one occasion Jacobs's father and mistress both happened to call her brother at the same moment. The boy, after a moment's hesitation, went to the mistress. The father sharply reproved him: "You are *my* child . . . and when I call you, you should come immediately, if you have to pass through fire and water" (7). The father's desire to command the primary obedience of his own child flows from his feelings of being a free man and contradicts the harshest realities of slavery. Slavery stripped men of fatherhood. Even a free father could not unambiguously call his child by a slave wife his own, for the child, following the condition of the mother, remained a slave. Jacobs is, surely not by accident, depicting a spirit of manliness and an instinctive grasp of the virtues of freedom in her father as the introduction to her own story of resistance.

Jacobs's narrative embodies every conceivable element of fantasy and ambiguity. Her father and mother were mulattoes who lived in a model of conjugal domesticity. Her maternal grandmother was the daughter of a South Carolina planter who apparently has inherited the lowcountry, slaveholding elite's own sense of honor—more than could be said for her owners. Jacobs, in other words, endows herself with a pedigree of physical, mental, and moral comeliness. She is not like the other slaves among whom she lives. She has the capacity to rise above her condition. Her sense of herself in relation to the other slaves leaves something to be desired for an opponent of slavery; worse, it reflects either her assimilation of "white" values or her determination to play to the prejudices of her audience. Jacobs offers a confused picture of the relation between the identity and behavior of Afro-Americans, including herself, and the effects of slavery. If slavery is evil, it has evil consequences. If those evil consequences include a breaking of the spirit of the enslaved, then how can slaves be credited with character and will? The questions circle on and on, admitting of no easy answers. Clearly they plague Jacobs.

These difficult questions do not seriously cloud Jacobs's sense of self. They do affect her sense of how best to present that self to others, her sense of the relation between her self and her gender, and her sense of the relation between self and social condition. The awareness of white readers deeply influences the ways in which she depicts life under slavery. But under, or woven through, the discourse for the readers runs a discourse for herself. For Jacobs herself, the primary issue between her and her master was not one of virtue, chastity, sexuality, or any of the rest. It was the conflict of two wills. Having described her master's foul intentions toward her, she adds that he had told her "I was made for his use, made to obey his command in *every* thing; that I was nothing but a slave, whose will must and should surrender to his" (16). The words make her "puny" arm feel stronger than it ever had: "The war of my life had begun; and though one of God's most powerless creatures, I resolved never to be conquered. Alas, for me!" (17). The "alas for me" should not be read as regret about her determination or as any acknowledgment that such willful feelings might be inappropriate for a woman, but as a confirmation that everything that follows stems directly from her determination not to be conquered.

Jacobs's narrative of her successful flight from slavery can be read as a journey or progress from her initial state of innocence; through the mires of her struggle against her social condition; to a prolonged period of ritual, or mythic, concealment; on to the flight itself; and finally to the state of knowledge that accompanies her ultimate acquisition of freedom. The myth or metaphor of the journey to selfhood is as old as culture, although it has carried a special resonance for Western Christian, notably Protestant, culture. Jacobs, in some respects like Harriet Wilson, registers the end of the journey as a somewhat bleak dawn on a troubled landscape. Here is no pot of gold at the end of the rainbow. The accrued self-knowledge consists above all in the recognition that there is no resting place for the fugitive. The struggle for the dignity of the self persists. Insults and injuries abound in freedom as under slavery, albeit in different forms. Life remains a war. But the focused struggle of wills with the master has given way to a more generalized struggle to affirm the self in a hostile, or indifferent, environment.

Significantly, Harriet Wilson, whose narrative unfolds entirely in freedom, portrays the primary enemy as a woman rather than a man. To explore the respective cultural roles of men and women as heads of households in slave and free society would take us far afield. But the difference should be noted, not least because Wilson's enemy represents the world of female domesticity and, inescapably, underscores the possible adversarial relation between the Afro-American female autobiographer and her readers.[18] Wilson's narrative remains even more problematical as autobiography than Jacobs's, for it is cast as a fiction—and it remains, overall, far more disturbing. I can only note in passing that its structure commands close attention, especially Wilson's purpose in beginning with the story of her white mother, Mag Smith, who, as the only alternative to starvation, married a black man who loves her.

Taken together, Jacobs's and Wilson's narratives establish some important characteristics of black women's autobiographical writing. Both use the metaphor of the journey. Both betray mixed emotions toward their probable and intended (white, female) readers. Both embrace some of the rhetoric and conventions of literary domesticity even as they challenge the reigning pieties of its discourse. Both subvert the promised candor toward those readers.

The problem of readers, of those for whom one writes, persists in the autobiographical writing of black women, although it assumes a variety of forms. Writing in the late 1960s, Maya Angelou noted in an apparent aside in the first volume of her own autobiography: "If you ask a negro where he's been, he'll tell you where he's going" (86). Her observation should be appreciated in the context of Zora Neale Hurston's calling storytelling "lying"—and then offering the world her own demonstrably inaccurate autobiography.[19]

Hurston's autobiography poignantly captures the dilemmas that seemed to confront black women writers—or intellectuals—of her generation. *Dust Tracks on a Road* inimitably combines all the best and worst of Hurston's intellect and imagination. Critics and scholars have demonstrated that it does not pass muster as a factual account of her life, beginning with its inaccurate recording of her date of birth. Theoretically, that mere inaccuracy should not matter to modern critics of the text-in-itself: take the text on its merits and to hell with the facts. But Hurston's deceptions in *Dust Tracks* may exceed mere facts. She embellishes the text with a series of observations on contemporary politics and race relations that have seriously disturbed some of her most devoted would-be admirers. Finally, although Hurston wrote much more in the idiom of Afro-American culture, even of folk culture, than Jacobs or Wilson, her text does not inspire confidence in the "authenticity" of her self-revelation. In most respects, *Dust Tracks* constitutes a marvel of self-concealment. Hurston, like the storytellers on the porch whom she celebrated in *Mules and Men,* delighted in "lying."

As the single most important link between the different phases in black women's autobiographies, Hurston's autobiography commands at least a preliminary assessment.[20] Hurston should be understood as a woman who was, regarding her self-representation, concerned primarily with a "self" unconstrained by gender in particular and condition in general. Her life made her an expert on anger and fear. Determined to become a respected person, to become someone, she wrestled—not always gracefully or successfully—with the expectations of those around her. In mediating between the world of Eatonville from which she came and the worlds of Baltimore, Washington, and New York to which she moved, she functioned as a translator. In fact, Hurston used her acquired skills as an anthropologist to describe the world of her childhood. Her uncommon gift for language brought that world to life in her pages, but her obsession with self-concealment led her to veil the nature of her identification with her origins. Hurston's narrator is her statue—the amused observer she wished to become.

Hurston's autobiography singularly lacks any convincing picture of her own feelings. Her little essay on "love," which purports to convey her adult feelings toward men, reads like the amused and balanced memories of a perfectly successful individual. Men are presented as having loved her even more than she loved them. Love is portrayed as having invariably treated her well. She gives no hint of bitter disappointment, longing, or crippling loss. Maybe she suffered none, although extratextual sources invite skepticism. But the passage itself looks more like a screen than a window. There is nothing in *Dust Tracks* to suggest that Hurston trusted her readers. She never precisely identifies them, although she cultivates an arresting mixture of the urbane intellectual and the *enfant terrible*. Presumably she expected to be read by New York intellectuals, black and white. And, presumably, she was not about to trust them with her private self.

Hurston provides clues about where she wants to go, what kind of statue she wants to build. She resoundingly repudiates any possible connection between slavery and her own life or self-representation. Slavery, however unfortunate, belongs to a past that has left no relevant legacy: "I have no personal memory of those times, and no responsibility for them" (282). Above all, she fears the debilitating effects of bitterness; to be bitter is to become dependent, crippled, humiliated. She appears to have forgotten her own earlier evocation of the "broom of anger," appears not to want to explore the place of righteous anger in her responses. The purpose of the broom of anger was to sweep away fear, and she is no longer acknowledging fear. By collapsing anger into bitterness and repudiating bitterness as, in some way, an unclean emotion, she is denying the need for anger. Facing the white reader, she prefers to deny the relevance of previous oppression to her sense of herself. Just as clearly as Jacobs, she expects "you" (her reader) to be white: "So I give you all my right hand of fellowship and love. . . . In my eyesight, you lose nothing by not looking just like me. . . . Let us all be kissing-friends" (286).

Hurston also refuses to attribute any significance to race. Having been bombarded with the problem of race for years, she saw the light when she "realized that I did not have to consider any racial group as a whole. God made them duck by duck and that was the only way I could see them" (235). She learned that the color of the skin provided no measure of the person inside, even though she acerbically points out that blacks, like whites, rank blacks according to the degree of lightness of their skin. She then reminds her readers that she is of mixed race. Finally, with deep ambiguity, she asserts: "I maintain that I have been a Negro three times—a Negro baby, a Negro girl and a Negro woman." Yet she knows not what "the Negro in

America is like" (237). The Negro does not exist. Independent of its political problems—and Hurston's politics were nothing if not complex—this
statement creates considerable doubt about her identification as a woman.
If the Negro does not exist, and the only times that she has been a Negro
included the times at which she was a girl and a woman, then what? The
reader is left to complete the syllogism.

Dust Tracks constitutes only one panel in the triptych of Hurston's autobiography. The second can be found in her extraordinary novel, *Their Eyes
Were Watching God,* and the third in her collections of black folklore, notably
Mules and Men. Hurston's collections of folklore provide a way for her to
appropriate the collective history of the community to which she belongs.
Their Eyes Were Watching God, which is widely recognized as an autobiographical novel, offers her most sustained attempt to provide some representation of her own emotional life. Here, evoking the novel as an indispensable
counterpoint to *Dust Tracks,* I would emphasize one theme. In the book's
most famous passage, the protagonist Janie's grandmother says: "Honey, de
white man is de ruler of everything as fur as Ah been able tuh find out."
There may be some place "way off in de ocean" in which the black man
rules, "but we don't know nothin' but what we see." The white man throws
down his load and forces the black man to pick it up. "He pick it up because
he have to, but he don't tote it. He hand it to his womenfolks. De nigger
woman is de mule uh de world so fur as Ah can see" (29). Janie's grandmother has been praying that things will be different with her. Hurston portrays the answer to that prayer as Janie's relations with Teacake—a mutual
delight in shared sexuality.

The world that Hurston depicts in *Their Eyes Were Watching God* closely
resembles Maya Angelou's Stamps, Arkansas. Hurston does not emphasize
the oppressive weight of the neighboring white community as much as
Angelou does, but she does not shy away from its influence on the possible
conditions of black lives, even in an entirely black community. And her plot
mercilessly reveals the burdens that a legacy of slavery and racism impose on
black people. In particular she subtly, almost deceptively, offers hints of her
real feelings about what it means to be a black woman. She reveals the
extent to which the black community—or black men—have embraced the
gender conventions of white bourgeois society. Black men seek to transfer
their burdens to black women by forcing those women into domestic
corsets. A woman like Janie resists. She retains her commitment to equality
and partnership with the man she loves. Above all, she retains a commitment to the possible joy of love and sexuality. But even at her moment of
greatest success, the legacy of the social features of black manhood leads Teacake into a terrible battle. At the novel's close, which is also its beginning,

she is returning home to other black women—alone and childless, Mules. Are they metaphors or reality? Mules abound in Hurston's work. Is she inviting us to understand black women like herself as being of mixed ancestry and incapable of reproduction? Is she inviting us—as she seems to be—to recognize both the richness and the dead-endedness of black women's own traditions? To attempt a clear answer would seem to be premature, but the elements of the puzzle should not be denied.

Throughout *Dust Tracks,* Hurston provides numerous clues that her primary identification, her primary sense of herself, transcends gender. Most dramatically, in a passage reminiscent of other tales of mythic births on mythically stormy nights, she relates that at her birth her mother was unprepared and without assistance.[21] Fate intervened by sending "a white man of many acres and things" to "granny" for her mother—to fill in for the missing midwife, Aunt Judy. It is a tale of wonderful reversals: Zora was brought into the world by a man rather than a woman, by a white rather than a black. The chapter in which she relates her birth concludes with a passage about her mother's alarm that at an early age Zora manifested a clear tendency to keep on walking toward the horizon. The mother explained this behavior by blaming "a woman who was an enemy of hers" for sprinkling "'travel dust' around the doorstep the day I was born." Zora wonders at her mother's acceptance of such an explanation. "I don't know why it never occurred to her to connect my tendency with my father, who didn't have a thing on his mind but this town and the next one." She might have taken a hint from his wanderlust. "Some children are just bound to take after their fathers in spite of women's prayers" (32).

Hurston vacillates among sympathy, scorn, and amused tolerance in her discussion of the women of the black community from which she springs. She movingly depicts her grief and guilt at her own inability to carry out her dying mother's instructions due to the opposition of the other members of the black community. And she clearly links her own departure from the world of her childhood with her mother's death. She shows flashes of tenderness. But her identification with other black women remains shaky. She refuses the double role of victim and warrior that Jacobs constructs for herself. For Hurston to admit the conditions or causes of her possible victimization is to belittle herself. But her goals for herself—her statue—remain shaped by that refusal: she aspires, in some way, to transcend the constraints of group identification. By insisting on being a self independent of history, race, and gender, she comes close to insisting on being a self independent of body.

Hurston wrote under the influence of the Harlem Renaissance and the increasingly successful attempts of Afro-American men to establish a model of cultural respectability, and she wrote under the shadow of emerging professional successes for some middle-class white women. That is, she sought to carve a compelling statue for herself at a particular historical moment. Much like Harriet Jacobs, she pictured herself at war with the world in her attempt to defend her integrity. Much like Harriet Jacobs, she refused the limitations of gender and cultivated what she took to be the language of her readers only to subvert—or manipulate—their values. But where Jacobs warred with slavery, Hurston warred with a dominant bourgeois culture in which she sought acceptance as an equal. No less than Jacobs, Hurston warred with the legacy of slavery for black women. But changing times had made it difficult for her to name that war. And, unable or unwilling to name it, she spun web upon web of deception so that her statue of herself would appear to be standing in clouds.

Those who came after—especially Angelou, Giovanni, and Brooks—would find new names for the war and a new acceptance of their own black female bodies. But they would also benefit from the slow emergence of black women readers. And even they would remain at odds with the gender identifications of white society. The gap between black women and the dominant model of womanhood continues to add richness and mystery to black women's writing. The account of origins remains, at least in part, a map of "where I'm bound." The account of the black woman's self cannot be divorced from the history of that self or the history of the people among whom it took shape. It also cannot be divorced from the language through which it is represented, or from the readers of other classes and races who not only lay claim to it but who have helped to shape it. To write the account of one's self is to inscribe it in a culture that for each of us is only partially our own. For black women autobiographers, the gap between the self and the language in which it is inscribed looms especially large and remains fraught with struggle.

Above all, black women's autobiographies suggest a tension in black women's relations to various dominant discourses. Jacobs and Wilson both self-consciously sought to work within bourgeois women's domestic discourse, even as they subverted its deepest premises about the relation between the female self and gender. Their concern for discursive respectability persisted in the works of many black women from Reconstruction to the 1920s and flowered in the works of Jessie Fauset and Nella Larsen. This concern should be understood in the context of black people's struggle for respect within the confines of dominant American bourgeois conventions, even if the female embodiments of the tradition invariably, if covertly, challenged its stereotypical views of gender relations and gender identity. Hurston makes explicit two contradictory and submerged elements of that tradition: first, and most visibly, she restores funkiness and folk roots to black women's discourse; second, and no less important, she dares to articulate black women's craving for independent recognition in the republic of letters. Recent critics have reminded us that Harriet Beecher Stowe and Susan Warner deserve considerably more respect than the dominant (male) tradition chose to accord them.[22] But Hurston also had her eyes on the pinnacles of the prestigious tradition of Western letters, on Shakespeare and his canonized successors. Even her representation of black women's private selves was informed with this ambition. Her difficulty in clearly depicting her own statue resulted at least in part from the deadlock between her commitment to her roots as a black woman in a black community and her commitment to transcending all social and gender roots in her craft. In her fictional and anthropological writings, she could distance herself as artist—as translator—from the immediacy of her material. When she came to depict herself, the strategy faltered. How could she bear to lay bare that private self for which the canon allowed no position of respect? Nevertheless, the best clue to the essence of that private self lies in the troubling autobiography, which, more than all the other writings, reveals the struggles that wracked the self, even if it does not directly testify to them—does not, as it were, confess.

Few have written more movingly or with greater anger of the toll extracted by cultural colonization than Frantz Fanon. Fanon, in particular, walked the narrow boundary between recording the dreadful impact of specific instances of colonization and raising the concept of colonization to the status of a metaphor for the dependent status of all subgroups in a dominant culture. The autobiographies of Afro-American women similarly delineate a specific history of colonization and offer a compelling metaphor for the human spirit's dependency on the communities and forms of expression to which it belongs. Black women like Jacobs and Wilson insisted on their right to an independent self under conditions in which they could counterpoise the self to enslavement. Since emancipation, black women have been torn between their independent relation to the dominant culture and their people's relation to it. In complex ways, their self-perceptions retain a characteristically uneasy relation to the wrappings of gender. Is the black woman writer first a self, a solitary statue? Or is she first a woman—and if so, in relation to whom? No dilemma could more clearly expose the condition of any self as hostage to society, politics, and language.

Notes

1. See Walker, *In Search of Our Mothers' Gardens*. On new directions in black feminist criticism, see Smith; McDowell.

2. See Miller.

3. Black women's "autobiographies," as used here, includes some autobiographical fiction as well as formal autobiographies, both streams of which have sources in a rich oral Afro-American culture.

4. I am using *gender* to mean the social construction of sexuality.

5. For my own views on autobiography as a genre, see Fox-Genovese, *Autobiography of Du Pont de Nemours*, 38–51. Among the many other recent works on autobiography, see Olney, *Autobiography*; Weintraub; Lejeune; Gunn; Stone; and—for a review of recent critical trends—Lang, "Autobiography in the Aftermath of Romanticism."

6. The quintessential statement of the position remains Michel Foucault, "Qu'est-ce un auteur?" For a feminist defense of deconstruction in terms of the Third World, see Spivak, "'Draupadi,'" but for a defense of the claims of gender and race, see her "Politics of Interpretation."

7. On the general problem of black women's autobiography, see Blackburn.

8. See Stepto. This article was apparently reprinted in the Davis collection from Stepto's *From Behind the Veil: A Study of Afro-American Narrative* (Urbana: University of Illinois Press, 1979).

9. Brooks's autobiography should be read in conjunction with her autobiographical novel, *Maud Martha*. See also Washington; Christian, *Black Literature and Literary Theory* and *Black Feminist Criticism*.

10. The phrase "demon slavery" is from Harriet Wilson, *Our Nig*.

11. See Tompkins, *Reader-Response Criticism*; Flynn and Schweickart, *Gender and Reading*.

12. See Christian, *Black Women Novelists*, for a preliminary periodization. For a sharp assessment of the relation between one black novelist and her readers, see Harris.

13. The work on white women's writing, in sharp contrast to that on black women's writing, has grown extensive. Among many, see Baym, Kelley, and Kolodny.

14. See Elkins, in particular. Elkins has not significantly revised his position in the two subsequent editions of *Slavery*. See, for instance, Lane. For alternate views on the effect of slavery on Afro-American men, see Harding and Genovese.

15. For a recent overview of women's position under slavery, see White.

16. See Yellin, "Texts and Contexts" and "Written by Herself." Henceforth, Yellin's edition of *Incidents* will be the standard, but it did not appear in time for me to use it in this essay. For Jacobs's account of her experience and authorship, see her correspondence in the Post family papers, University of Rochester Library. Dorothy Sterling has reprinted some of Jacobs's letters in her excellent anthology, *We Are Your Sisters*. On the general tradition of the slave narrative, see, among many, Starling; Sekora and Turner; Olney, "'I Was Born'"; Baker; and Davis, "The Slave Narrative." As a rule, treatments of slave narratives take little or no account of any female perception, in part because so few women either escaped or wrote narratives.

17. See, among many, Hurston's *Their Eyes Were Watching God*: "Ah was wid dem white chillun so much till Ah didn't know Ah wuzn't white till Ah was round six years old" (21).

18. See Gates's introduction to *Our Nig*. He offers a preliminary exploration of the role of white women in the novel but does not discuss the problem of Wilson's attitude toward her readers. For a fuller discussion of the differences between women's roles in Northern and Southern households, see Fox-Genovese, *Within the Plantation Household*.

19. On the facts of Hurston's life and the variants of the text, see Hemenway's introduction to *Dust Tracks*; see also his comprehensive study of her life and work, *Zora Neale*

Hurston. For a composite picture of Hurston culled from her own writings, see Walker, *I Love Myself When I Am Laughing.* See also Walker's essay on Hurston in *In Search of Our Mothers' Gardens;* Johnson, "Metaphor, Metonymy, and Voice"; Hurston, *Tell My Horse.*

20. On the successive phases of Afro-American women's writing, see McCaskill. The generation of Afro-American women writers that preceded Hurston, including Frances Ellen Watkins Harper, Amanda Smith, Julia Foote, Elizabeth Keckley, and Bethany Veney, focused on racial uplift and on proving the respectability of Afro-American womanhood.

21. Black women writers' use of African and Western myths deserves more attention than it has yet received. Angelou, for example, in *Gather Together in My Name,* reworks the Persephone myth for her own purposes. Jacobs, in the account of her period of concealment and flight, draws on African mythology. Gates's concept of the "signifying monkey" opens the discussion but does not pay special attention to the blending of cultures in Afro-American women's imaginations (see his "The 'Blackness of Blackness'" and *The Signifying Monkey*). For a sensitive discussion of Afro-American culture, see Levine.

22. See Tompkins; and Ann Douglas's introduction to Stowe.

Works Cited

Angelou, Maya. *I Know Why the Caged Bird Sings.* New York: Random House, 1969.
———. *Gather Together in My Name.* New York: Random House, 1974.
Baker, Houston A., Jr. "Autobiographical Acts and the Voice of the Southern Slave." In Davis, 242–61.
Baym, Nina. *Woman's Fiction: A Guide to Novels by and about Women in America, 1820–1870.* Ithaca: Cornell University Press, 1978.
Blackburn, Regina. "In Search of the Black Female Self: African-American Women's Autobiographies and Ethnicity." In Jelinek, 133–48.
Brooks, Gwendolyn. *Maud Martha.* Boston: Atlantic Monthly Press, 1953.
———. *Report from Part One.* Detroit: Broadside Press, 1972.
Christian, Barbara. *Black Feminist Criticism: Perspectives on Black Women Writers.* New York: Pergamon Press, 1985.
———. *Black Women Novelists: The Development of a Tradition, 1892–1976.* Westport: Greenwood Press, 1980.
———. *Perspectives on Black Women Writers.* New York: Pergamon Press, 1985.
Cudjoe, Selwyn R. "Maya Angelou and the Autobiographical Statement." In Evans, 6–24.
Davis, Charles T. "The Slave Narrative: First Major Art Form in an Emerging Black Tradition." In Davis and Gates, 83–119.
———. *Black Is the Color of the Cosmos: Essays on Afro-American Literature and Culture, 1942–1981.* Ed. Henry Louis Gates. New York: Garland Publishing, 1982.
Davis, Charles T., and Henry Louis Gates, eds. *The Slave's Narrative.* New York: Oxford University Press, 1985.
Elkins, Stanley. *Slavery: A Problem in American Institutional and Intellectual Life.* Chicago: University of Chicago Press, 1959.
Evans, Mari. *Black Women Writers (1950–1980).* Garden City: Anchor Books, 1984.
Flynn, Elizabeth A., and Patrocinio P. Schweickart. *Gender and Reading: Essays on Readers, Texts, and Contexts.* Baltimore: Johns Hopkins University Press, 1986.
Foucault, Michel. "Qu'est-ce un auteur?" *Bulletin de la Société Française de Philosophie* 63.3 (1969): 75–104.

Fox-Genovese, Elizabeth, *Within the Plantation Household: Black and White Women of the Old South*. Chapel Hill: University of North Carolina Press, 1988.

————, ed. and trans. *The Autobiography of Du Pont de Nemours*. Wilmington: Scholarly Resources Press, 1984.

Gates, Henry Louis, Jr. "The 'Blackness of Blackness': A Critique of the Sign and the Signifying Monkey." *Critical Inquiry* 9.4 (1983): 685–724.

————, ed. *Black Literature and Literary Theory*. New York: Methuen, 1984.

Genovese, Eugene D. *Roll, Jordan, Roll: The World the Slaves Made*. New York: Pantheon, 1974.

Gilbert, Olive, comp. *Narrative of Sojourner Truth: A Bondswoman of Olden Time*. 1878. New York: Arno Press, 1968.

Giovanni, Nikki. *Gemini: An Extended Autobiographical Statement on My First Twenty-Five Years of Being a Black Poet*. Indianapolis: Bobbs-Merrill, 1971.

Griffiths, Mattie. *Autobiography of a Female Slave*. 1857. Miami: Mnemosyne, 1969.

Gunn, Janet Varner. *Autobiography: Toward a Poetics of Experience*. Philadelphia: University of Pennsylvania Press, 1982.

Harding, Vincent. *There Is a River: The Black Struggle for Freedom in America*. New York: Harcourt Brace Jovanovich, 1981.

Harris, Trudier. "On *The Color Purple*, Stereotypes, and Silence." *Black American Literarture Forum* 18.4 (1984): 155–61.

Hemenway, Robert. *Zora Neale Hurston: A Literary Biography*. Urbana: University of Illinois Press, 1977.

Hurston, Zora Neale. *Dust Tracks on a Road: An Autobiography*. 1942. Ed. Robert Hemenway. 2d ed. Urbana: University of Illinois Press, 1984.

————. *Mules and Men*. 1935. New York: Harper and Row, 1970.

————. *Tell My Horse*. 1938. Berkeley: Turtle Island, 1981.

————. *Their Eyes Were Watching God*. 1937. Urbana: University of Illinois Press, 1978.

Jacobs, Harriet [Linda Brent]. *Incidents in the Life of a Slave Girl, Written by Herself*. Ed. Lydia Maria Child. 1861. New ed. Walter Teller. New York: Harcourt Brace Jovanovich, 1973.

————. *Incidents in the Life of a Slave Girl, Written by Herself*. Ed. Jean Fagan Yellin. Cambridge: Harvard University Press, 1987.

Jelinek, Estelle, ed. *Women's Autobiography: Essays in Criticism*. Bloomington: Indiana University Press, 1980.

Johnson, Barbara. "Metaphor, Metonymy and Voice in *Their Eyes Were Watching God*." In Gates, *Black Literature* 205–20.

Kelley, Mary. *Private Woman, Public Stage: Literary Domesticity in Nineteenth-Century America*. New York: Oxford University Press, 1984.

Kolodny, Annette. *The Land Before Her: Fantasy and Experience of the American Frontiers, 1630–1860*. Chapel Hill: University of North Carolina Press, 1984.

Lane, Ann J., ed. *The Debate over Slavery: Stanley Elkins and His Critics*. Urbana: University of Illinois Press, 1971.

Lang, Candace. "Autobiography in the Aftermath of Romanticism." *Diacritics* 12 (Winter 1982): 2–16.

Lejeune, Philippe. *Le pacte autobiographique*. Paris: Editions du Seuil, 1975.

Levine, Lawrence W. *Black Culture and Black Consciousness: Afro-American Folk Thought from Slavery to Freedom*. New York: Oxford University Press, 1977.

McCaskill, Barbara. "Eternity for Telling: Topological Traditions in Afro-American Women's Literature." Ph.D. diss., Emory University, 1988.

McConnell-Ginet, Sally, Ruth Borker, and Nelly Furman, eds. *Women and Language in Literature and Society.* New York: Praeger, 1980.

McDowell, Deborah E. "New Directions for Black Feminist Criticism." In Showalter, 186–99.

Miller, Nancy K. "Women's Autobiography in France: For a Dialectics of Identification." In McConnell-Ginet et al., 258–73.

Olney, James. *Autobiography: Essays Theoretical and Critical.* Princeton: Princeton University Press, 1980.

_____. "'I Was Born': Slave Narratives, Their Status as Autobiography and as Literature." In Davis and Gates, 148–75.

Sekora, John, and Darwin T. Turner, eds. *The Art of Slave Narrative.* Macomb: Western Illinois University Press, 1982.

Showalter, Elaine, ed. *The New Feminist Criticism: Essays on Women, Literature, and Theory.* New York: Pantheon, 1985.

Smith, Barbara. "Toward a Black Feminist Criticism." In Showalter, 168–85.

Soyinka, Wole. "The Critic and Society: Barthes, Leftocracy and Other Mythologies." In Gates, *Black Literature* 27–58.

Spivak, Gayatri Chakravorty. "'Drapaudi' by Mahasveta Devi." *Critical Inquiry* 8.2 (1981): 381–402.

Starling, Marion Wilson. *The Slave Narrative: Its Place in American History.* Boston: G. K. Hall, 1981.

Stepto, Robert Burns. "I Rose and Found My Voice: Narration, Authentication, and Authorial Control in Four Slave Narratives." In Davis and Gates, 225–41.

Sterling, Dorothy, ed. *We Are Your Sisters: Black Women in the Nineteenth Century.* New York: Norton, 1984.

Stone, Albert E. *Autobiographical Occasions and Original Acts.* Philadelphia: University of Pennsylvania Press, 1982.

Stowe, Harriet Beecher. *Uncle Tom's Cabin or, Life among the Lowly.* 1852. New York: Penguin, 1981.

Tate, Claudia, ed. *Black Women Writers at Work.* New York: Continuum, 1983.

Thompson, Era Bell. *American Daughter.* Rev. ed. Chicago: University of Chicago Press, 1967.

Tompkins, Jane P., ed. *Reader-Response Criticism: From Formalism to Post-Structuralism.* Baltimore: Johns Hopkins University, Press, 1980.

_____. *Sensational Designs: The Cultural Work of American Fiction, 1790–1860.* New York: Oxford University Press, 1985.

Walker, Alice. *In Search of Our Mothers' Gardens: Womanist Prose.* New York: Harcourt Brace Jovanovich, 1983.

_____. "Looking for Zora." In Walker, *In Search of Our Mother's Gardens.*

_____. "Zora Neale Hurston: A Cautionary Tale and a Partisan Review." In Walker, *In Search of Our Mothers' Gardens.*

_____, ed. *I Love Myself When I Am Laughing . . . and Then Again When I Am Looking Mean and Impressive: A Zora Neale Hurston Reader.* Old Westbury: Feminist Press, 1979.

Washington, Mary Helen. "'Taming All That Anger Down': Rage and Silence in Gwendolyn Brooks' *Maud Martha.*" In Gates, *Black Literature* 249–62.

Weintraub, Karl H. *The Value of the Individual: Self and Circumstance in Autobiography.* Chicago: University of Chicago Press, 1978.

Wells, Ida B. *The Autobiography of Ida B. Wells.* Ed. Alfred M. Duster. Chicago: University of Chicago Press, 1970.

White, Deborah G. *Ar'n't I a Woman: Female Slaves in the Plantation South.* New York: Norton, 1985.

Wilson, Harriet E. *Our Nig: Or, Stretches from the Life of a Free Black, in a Two-Story White House, North. Showing That Slavery's Shadows Fall Even There. By "Our Nig."* Ed. Henry Louis Gates. New York: Vintage, 1983.

Yellin, Jean Fagan. "Texts and Contexts of Harriet Jacobs' *Incidents in the Life of a Slave Girl: Written by Herself.*" In Davis and Gates, 262–82.

_____. "Written by Herself: *Harriet Jacobs' Slave Narrative.*" *American Literature* 53.3 (1981): 479–86.

Four

Between Individualism and Community
Autobiographies of Southern Women

Individualism figures as the very stuff of autobiography, at least in its most characteristic modern guise, for autobiography takes as its subject the chronicle of the self understood as essentially different from all other selves. I am not claiming that I am better or worse than any other man, only that I am different from all others, insisted Jean-Jacques Rousseau, arguably the first modern autobiographer, in his powerfully influential *Confessions.* The modern bourgeois culture that spawned autobiography as an endlessly fascinating genre took individualism as given. Contrarily, community figured preeminently as a form of nostalgia. As Raymond Williams has argued, bourgeois culture, beginning with romanticism, has regularly juxtaposed notions of community, especially pastoral harmony, to the capitalist market that constituted its mainspring. In Williams's view, the vision of the country as a retreat from the competition and strife of the city amounted to a myth that was engendered by and depended upon the dynamism of the city, which it only superficially opposed. Community and individualism could, in most instances, be substituted for Williams's country and city, with community's being understood as the nostalgia that trailed the central commitment to individualism.[1]

Conservatives have attempted to endow the myth of community with some semblance of reality, although frequently with chilling political implications. The conservative sociologist Ferdinand Tönnies drew the line sharply when he explicitly juxtaposed *Gemeinschaft* to *Gesellschaft,* arguing that the former embodied all the affective principles that the latter, instrumental modern society, denied.[2] The Southern conservative tradition, notably represented by Allen Tate and the Agrarians, followed a similar spirit in arguing that the South embodied the last true community in the Western world precisely because it continued to combat the corrosive tendencies of individualism.[3] For these and other conservatives, the individual should, ideally, be understood as subordinate to and even constituted by the community to which he or she belonged. But they, like the bourgeois and radical thinkers they opposed, failed to provide a clear guide to the actual relations between individual and community in modern culture.

Contemporary studies of autobiography remain by and large silent on this problem. Modern autobiographies have so successfully privileged the self as the subject of its own history that its indebtedness to community remains largely unexamined. To be sure, autobiographers may nostalgically evoke the community—frequently rural or ethnic—of their youths, but rarely do they credit those communities with decisive roles in their adult identities. Almost invariably, autobiographers write as exiles from the worlds of their childhood. The language and experience that prompt them to write of that world derive from what they have done since they left it. Not infrequently, and very understandably, they emphasize what they believe made them unique, what permitted them to leave the world of their childhood behind. As a result, the self that figures in their pages emphasizes the unique qualities that endow it with interest for their potential readers.

Today, the most heated theoretical debates in the study of autobiography concern the status of the self that is the subject of autobiography—notably, whether it should be viewed as in some way absolute, or pretextual, or as essentially textual, a product of the act of writing. In principle, these debates could apply as well to female autobiographers as to male, unless one chooses to argue that the male self exists through writing whereas the female self is in some way essential, or pretextual—or the reverse. Thus, short of accepting an essential difference between male and female autobiographers, it would seem that feminist criticism is condemned to address the nature of the (gendered) autobiographical self. Yet recent debates in feminist theory, which have underscored the problematic status of women's autobiography in general, have especially focused on the anxiety of women's self-representation within the confines of an androcentric culture. For women, it is generally agreed, the very autobiographical act remains inherently conflicted, for in writing autobiographies, women are, as Sidonie Smith has reminded us, caught in a "doubled subjectivity" as at once protagonists and narrators of their own stories.[4]

Nancy Miller has made the case with special force. Since, she argues, the dominant discourse has been resolutely male, women who attempt to represent themselves within that discourse confront the almost insurmountable difficulty of writing authoritatively within a discourse that casts them as object. To be sure, the condition obtains for all women's writing, but it becomes especially constraining in the case of autobiography—the case in which women attempt an unmediated representation of self. Susan Friedman, in contrast, argues that women autobiographers write differently, experience their selves differently, than men. For women, the self exists through merging with others rather than through differentiating itself from them, exists in relation to community rather than separate from it. But no more than others is Friedman referring to specific communities. She is referring to a psychological propensity presumably common to all women in all times and places. In this respect, feminist theory has remained closely tied to the assumptions and debates of male autobiographical theory by implicitly considering women primarily as individuals, albeit possibly different kinds of individuals.[5]

The problems of the female autobiographical self have been complicated by the intrusion of psychoanalytic, notably Lacanian, theory into poststructuralist theory, for psychoanalytic theory, in spite of or perhaps because of its unyielding androcentrism, has at least offered feminist critics a position from which to defend the essential difference between men and women as writing subjects. Lacanian theory has led Jane Gallop, among others, to argue that women who seek to represent their selves in writing confront a "patriarchal" language. Susan Friedman, following Nancy Chodorow, has attempted to turn the disadvantages of androcentric psychoanalytic theory to the advantage of female autobiographers. Both positions share the same weakness, namely, that women's writing in some way results directly from their biological condition as women. From this theoretical perspective, it makes little difference whether a woman is French or American, rich or poor, white or black: she writes out of her inescapable femaleness.[6]

The concern with fundamental difference grounded in biology has led very different kinds of feminist critics to treat women's biology as the material basis of female experience. This tactic has reinforced the tendency to focus either on women's autobiographical writing in general or on the writings of specific women autobiographers. Yet women, like men, belong to specific communities—nations, classes, races—that shape their relations as women to the dominant male culture. Women's autobiography, even more than women's writing in general, challenges us to understand the complexity of women's writing as simultaneously shaped by their specific experience as women among their people and by their specific access to dominant cultural discourses, which may or may not be those of their own people.

In practice, feminist critics have normally moved from considerations of the general category of female autobiography directly to the texts of specific women autobiographers without paying particular attention to identifiable groups of women autobiographers, although that pattern is beginning to shift. Essays have recently appeared on the autobiographies of Afro-American women, French women, Native American women, Quebecois women, lesbian women, and "privileged" British and American women. But even these essays have not especially attended to the specific communities to which these women belonged.[7] In other words, the discussions of indiviualism and community in women's autobiographies remain strangely abstracted from women's historical and social condition. The most sophisticated arguments address the women autobiographers' relations to the dominant male discourse of their culture but take little account of the historical and social dimensions of the women's experiences. Yet without explicit attention to women's social and historical locations within specific communities, we are in danger of claiming that the only significant aspect of women's autobiographies derives from their biology. As Nancy Miller has written, arguing that autobiography is as much a mode of reading as a mode of writing, "The historical truth of a woman writer's life lies in the reader's grasp of her intratext: the body of her writing and not the writing of her body."[8]

One of the most fruitful results of the debates about the nature of autobiography as a genre (if it can be at least provisionally accepted as one) has been the attempt to link the emergence of modern autobiography to the emergence of bourgeois individualism. This position, as developed, for example, by Philippe Lejeune and Georges Gusdorf, seeks to distinguish between self-representation in its various forms and autobiography in particular, holding that autobiography embodies a characteristic attitude toward the self that can be differentiated from previous attitudes toward it.[9] The position rests on the assumption that modern autobiography depends upon the emergence of a view of the self as an end in itself—a view of the self as the internal consciousness of that objective entity, the individual. Since the bourgeois individualism that promoted the emergence of autobiography continues to dominate theoretical discussions of autobiography, it is perhaps less clear than it should be that even the apparently ahistorical individual is also the product of a specific community or communities. In other words, all autobiographies result from the efforts of an individual to interpret his or her self in relation to community. Both the myth of the essential self and the myth of the textual self obscure the historical dimension of any self.

To argue for the historical contingency of both the male and the female self does not imply that men and women experienced historical conditions in the same way. Modern individualism did not open the same possibilities for women as it did for men. Indeed, it could reasonably be argued that modern male individualism relegated women to the supporting roles of mother, wife, and daughter. Yet because modern individualism claimed the status of a comprehensive ideology, it, however unintentionally, offered women a discourse through which they might also view themselves as individuals. The difficulty for women, upon which so many feminist critics have commented, has lain in writing of themselves as individuals under cultural or discursive conditions in which the models of individual excellence have been male and the models of female excellence have been circumscribed by specific gender roles. These conditions have strengthened the feminist temptation to consider all women, independent of nation, race, and class, through the prism of those roles, as if the roles were indeed as invariable as the universalist ideology of individualism sought to present them. Yet close attention to women autobiographers' self-representations does reveal differences.

The autobiographical writings of Southern women, black as well as white, dramatically illustrate the advantages of considering women's autobiography in historical perspective, although I readily admit that in choosing Southern women I am stacking the deck. Early-nineteenth-century Southern women, black and white, differed from their bourgeois counterparts in the North and in western Europe in belonging to a modern slave society. That membership decisively marked their perceptions of themselves and, despite radical differences in their experiences, bound them to a common history. Even after the abolition of slavery and the defeat of the South, Southern women remained uncommonly concerned with the history of their region as an aspect of their own identities. For many generations, no Southern woman autobiographer wrote of her self without explicit reference to social and historical conditions. And even a woman as engaged with modernism and committed to the idea of the self as Ellen Glasgow allowed in her autobiography that, although she had resolved "to write of the universal, not of the provincial in human nature," she "knew my part of the South, and I had looked deep enough within and far enough without to learn something of human beings and their substance." She believed that she and other writers wrote better "when we write of places we know, and of a background with which we are familiar."[10]

Both black and white Southern women autobiographers have struggled with the same problems of female self-representation through dominant male discourses. But they have done so under conditions in which race, class, and regional identification have played as important a role as gender in their self-representations. In the Old South, slavery effectively discouraged both white and black Southern women from any form of public self-representation—white women because of the constraints of respectability, black women because of the constraints of being unlettered. White women, especially slaveholding women, did in fact write personal narratives; they simply did not publish them and normally did not even write them as autobiographies. Characteristically, white slaveholding women kept journals or diaries, which they wrote for the benefit of their children, especially their daughters, and in which they primarily attempted to take stock of their selves and their souls. Occasionally, a slaveholding woman (for example, Eliza Clitherall) would write an autobiography to summarize the events of her life up to the moment of starting to keep a diary. Occasionally, a slaveholding woman (for example, Sarah Gayle) would include in her journal a representation of herself as she envisioned herself as having been. Most slaveholding women came closest to self-conscious self-representation in their investigations of the state of their souls.[11]

Most slaveholding women's personal narratives differ from autobiographies in following the course of a life as it unfolded rather than in interpreting the life as a whole from the vantage point of a particular personal and historical moment. They nonetheless embody a concern with self as the focus of the narrative, and a concern with bridging the gap between private (female) experience and public (male) discourse. Slaveholding women regularly drew upon the texts of "high culture" to express their own sentiments, beliefs, and aspirations. And they frequently constructed self-representations grounded in an ideal of personal honor informed by high standards of individual excellence. But even when most concerned with their own status as individuals, they understood the individual as grounded in ties of community—ties of class and race, of kinship and culture. They thought of themselves as particular kinds of individuals—women, of course, but also privileged, white Southerners—whose individuality derived its meaning from membership in specific social groups. But their sense of their relations to the communities cannot easily be understood simply as a case of women's permeable ego boundaries, their general tendency to merge with rather than to differentiate themselves from others. Rather, their sense of those relations had more to do with a concept of delegation, of themselves as distinct representatives of a community.

Significantly, the first autobiographical writing published by a Southern woman was written by a former slave and was published in the North. Harriet Jacobs's *Incidents in the Life of a Slave Girl*, notwithstanding its status as a slave narrative and notwithstanding Jacobs's use of a fictional persona, Linda Brent, to mask her own identity, has strong claims to being regarded as an autobiography. Written in the first person and explicitly from the perspective of a particular historical moment—Brent's acquisition of freedom—*Incidents* begins with childhood and represents the developing self-consciousness of a female self. Although the account of an escape from slavery, *Incidents* adopts the idiom of Northern, white, middle-class domestic fiction, thus inscribing itself in a discourse foreign to the experience of its author and protagonist. The conventions of domestic fiction led Jacobs to emphasize the wrongs of slavery as primarily an assault upon female virtue and motherhood. In this spirit, she attempted to represent her self as seeking above all to conform to the roles deemed appropriate for the women of her intended audience. But despite her best efforts, *Incidents* above all represents the "unfeminine" tenacity, determination, and isolation of its protagonist. *Incidents* thus betrays a deep fissure between the cultural expectations of the dominant bourgeois discourse of womanhood and the identity, or self, of the former slave woman who brazenly insisted that her narrative was indeed "written by herself."

Jacobs's autobiography can, from one perspective, be read as an example of women's difficulty in representing the personal female self within the dominant discourse, but it cannot be read as only that. And it assuredly cannot be read as an example of women's propensity to represent the personal female self in relation to others. *Incidents* forcefully, if sometimes covertly, proclaims a fierce quest for independence and self-determination. The protagonist's refusal to subject her will to that of her master engages her in a lonely struggle in which she casts off all ties to secure her freedom. To establish herself for her readers as a person worthy of respect, she distanced herself from the condition of slavery, emphasizing the paleness of her skin and her father's instinctive feelings of freedom. The realities of Southern slavery (and Northern racism) powerfully inform Jacobs's narrative but not her self-representation. Her autobiography can only be understood as the product of specific historical conditions that would deny her any self-possession. But in struggling against those conditions, she claims a self more independent from the restrictions of gender than was possible for most women of her time. Jacobs's juxtaposition of her naked will against that of her master, like her tendency to repudiate the identity of a slave, comes closer than most female self-representations to an assertion of an essential self. Yet Jacobs, in the act of reaching for an essential self, searingly testifies to the historical condition she was determined to write herself out of.

After the war, when increasing numbers of elite Southern women turned to publication, a significant group did in fact publish autobiographies or, perhaps more accurately, memoirs. The great majority of these authors focused on their early lives during slavery times, on the upheavals of the war years, and on the changed conditions of their lives after the war. Many insisted that they had always been hostile to slavery, thus providing evidence for those who would see slaveholding women as much the unwilling victims of the slaveholding regime as were their black slaves. Others were more candid in admitting the sense of loss that followed in the wake of defeat. But whatever position they adopted vis-à-vis the ancien régime, they all foregrounded the society to which they belonged and cast their personal stories as primarily representative of the experience of their region. Even those, such as Elizabeth Meriwether, who claimed to have always been opposed to slavery, emphasized the history of their region, thus underscoring the roots of self in community. Many Southern women's personal narratives from the late nineteenth and early twentieth centuries may thus, at least in part, be classified as memoirs rather than as autobiographies in the strict sense.[12]

It would nonetheless be rash to dismiss entirely the element of autobiography—of self-representation—that motivated and informed Southern women's accounts of their experiences of slavery, war, and recovery. In accounts that they explicitly wrote for publication, many Southern women claimed the authority of the writing self. They may, in many instances, have veiled their intentions under disclaimers of any unfeminine or subversive intent. They may have insisted that they wrote in the interests not of self-display but of testifying to the experience of their community. But they did, disclaimers notwithstanding, assume the public mantle of witness. And in witnessing to the experience of their community, they insisted upon their right to speak in its name. Thus, even when they did not foreground the development of the female self, they did publicly represent it. They simply were more likely to emphasize the self as Southern—whether typical or atypical—than as female.

Katharine DuPre Lumpkin, writing in 1946 as a white Southern woman who had sharply repudiated many of the values of her region, cast her autobiography as an assessment of the historical legacy that had shaped her.[13] Eschewing a confessional mode, Lumpkin wrote little, if at all, of her personal feelings. Her autobiography begins not with her birth or her childhood but with her slaveholding great-grandfather, William Lumpkin. The title of her first chapter, "Of Bondage to Slavery," identifies her people's history as the fount of her own identity. From the perspective of feminist criticism, it would be easy to argue that the anxiety of representing her self through a dominant male discourse had effectively silenced Lumpkin. But *The Making of a Southerner* contains no evidence of anxiety. Its very style testifies to a sure authorial presence, to her strong sense of herself as an individual. Much like Jacobs, if for different reasons, Lumpkin possessed a determined will. That will drove her north to define and consolidate her independent identity. Yet when years later she came to write her autobiography, she represented her self as above all the product of history.

Lumpkin begins "Of Bondage to Slavery" with an account of her great-grandfather, William Lumpkin, a man of many children, slaves, and acres, and progresses to her grandfather, who inherited his possessions and his authority. Deftly adopting the male slaveholder's perspective, she details the buildings and activities of his plantation, the members of his household, and the responsibilities that weighed upon his shoulders. Toward the end of the chapter, her perspective shifts. Grandfather, she notes, "did not have to bear his burden of management unaided. He was fortunate in having a slave who carried on his mighty shoulders a substantial share of the heavy load" (30). The penultimate section of the chapter depicts the responsibilities that devolved upon the slave, Jerry, emphasizing how heavily Grandfather Lumpkin depended upon him to influence and keep order among the other slaves. Jerry, the religious head of the slave community, reprimanded fellow slaves who were "neglectful of their duty toward the master." But he was also "their stay, whose mighty frame and steady spirit were the staff on which they leaned when trouble and sorrow overtook them—as it could overtake slaves" (34). Jerry buried the dead and baptized the living. "My grandparents," Lumpkin comments with devastating irony, "were not alone in seeing in Jerry's influence an exceedingly valuable possession" (34). But even Jerry had one weakness: he could not read.

Each Sunday Jerry would come up to the big house so that her grandmother could read him a chapter from the Bible. The reading completed, she would return the Bible, which she had given to him at his request, and he would depart. The same afternoon, he would rise before his slave congregation, open the Bible at the place Grandmother marked, and from his lips would pour "the entire chapter his mistress had read aloud to him in the morning. He would 'read' it word for word and from it take his text and preach his sermon" (35).

In the final section of this chapter, Lumpkin writes of her father's tenth birthday, his coming of age as "young master." On that day, his father called all the slaves together, telling them simply, "'This is your young master'" (36). And then the slaves, who had known him since his infancy, came one by one to make their curtsies or bows. Young Will had known what to expect. "It had been the same for his father before him and his grandfather" (37). But he enjoyed his new status for only five years, the better part of which were dominated by the war. "Nevertheless until the very end he went on expecting to be even as his father had been" (44). Lumpkin concludes the chapter by observing that the way of life of the Southern gentleman left a special stamp upon the men who lived it, "but more particularly in a special way it stamped their sons, who were reared to expect it and then saw it snatched away" (44).

In book 2, "Uprooted," Lumpkin writes of the trauma of war and defeat for the men of her family and other white Southerners. Her childhood, like that of so many others, was shaped by tales of Negro "'uppitiness,' 'sassiness,' molestation of whites" (86). They were told bitterly of Reconstruction, when true Southerners were ruled by scalawags and carpetbaggers. "And to be ruled by Negroes! Ruled by black men! To have those born in the womb of slavery, those children of dark ignorance and lowest race, as they were spoken of, put in office over white men! The slave ruling over the master!" (87). For white Southerners, there was no other side to the story, no possibility of seeing different views. There was only the disaster, injustice, and outrage that only white supremacy could counter.

Lumpkin, born into this world of defeat and uncertainty, lived in three different houses in the first three years of her life. Daughter of an uprooted slaveholder, she was reared on the dream that one day they would find a good plantation and begin to recover the old way of life. In the midst of uncertainty, her mother, like other Southern mothers, did her best to keep up appearances, with "her silk dress that rustled, bonnet or hat touched with velvet ribbon, dainty black shoes, and black kid gloves" (106). But the moorings for the life they were defending had passed beyond recall. The places in which Lumpkin lived as a girl were each "just another house . . . only another house, as I thought of it then, from which we would inevitably move on" (108).

Lumpkin implicitly draws a sharp contrast between the impermanency of her family's residences, the uncertainty of their material situation, and the permanence and certainty of their beliefs. Between them, she suggests, both the uncertainty and the certainty established the core of her identity. "In the case of my particular generation, it seems that we first learned both behavior and belief at a time when those around us were peculiarly disturbed." She was (she informs us in book 3, "A Child Inherits a Lost Cause," more than halfway through her autobiography) "born in 'ninety-seven" (128). Her father's struggles on behalf of white supremacy nonetheless provided a constant center to her youth. As the children reached the "club-forming age," they "had a Ku Klux Klan" (136). In a debate at school, possible only because the class included one Yankee boy to take the opposing side, she defended white supremacy.

> Of course I told of our history and how the South had been saved by the courage of our fathers—we always told this. Probably I told of the Invisible Empire—we often did. Obviously, I recited all the arguments we had for Negro inferiority, and that this was why he must never be allowed to "rise out of his place." My peroration comes back to me in

so many words, and how I advanced it with resounding fervor amidst a burst of applause from all the children in the room but my opponent: ". . . and the Bible says that they shall be hewers of wood and drawers of water forever!" (137)

Lumpkin deploys pronouns with virtuosity, variously using "he," "we," and "I" to represent the threads of her own identity. "He" represents her inherited identity, appropriately privileging the masculine cast of slavehold-ing values. "We" represents the identity of her generation as heirs to former slaveholding parents. "I" represents the emerging consciousness of self as capable of judging the inherited and collective aspects of her identity. After describing how she had absorbed the vocabulary of white supremacy and racism in her high chair, Lumpkin notes that she herself learned to speak it even before she understood what it meant. "Of course I did come to com-prehend. When I did, it was a sharp awakening. This was mere chance" (130). One morning she heard the sounds of a ferocious beating, the victim of which, she knew, could not be one of the children, for even their corpo-ral punishment was administered with some dignity. She edged carefully over to peer through the kitchen window and witnessed a severe thrashing that was being administered to "our little black cook": "I could see her writhing under the blows of a descending stick wielded by the white master of the house. I could see her face distorted with fear and agony and his with stern rage. I could see her twisting and turning as she tried to free herself from his grasp. I could hear her screams, as I was certain they could be heard for blocks" (132). The repeated use of "I" forcefully underscores the dawn-ing of her independent consciousness, from the perspective of which her father becomes objectified as "the white master of the house." At the time of the beating, Lumpkin's independent consciousness remains a flicker that could be snuffed with the assurance that the cook had been beaten because she had been "impudent" to her mistress, had "answered her back." And, underscoring her younger self's retreat into the comfort of community val-ues, Lumpkin notes, "It was not the custom for Southern white gentlemen to thrash their cooks, not by the early 1900's. But it was not heinous. We did not think so. It had once been right not so many years before" (132).

When Lumpkin was almost twelve, her family moved to a farm in a poor section of Richland County. "None of us called the place Father had selected 'plantation'" (151). Even she could understand that two hundred acres did not justify the term. However, poor by antebellum Lumpkin standards, the place was rich in comparison with those of their neighbors. The sense of the surrounding poverty led Lumpkin to think of the years on the farm as her "Sojourn in the Sand Hills." Her interactions with the local white children, who lived with a poverty she had associated only with blacks, led her to a new sense of her self. Her clothing was different; her lunches were different; and "there was the matter of manners" (158). The other children accused her of putting on airs, but, then, her knowledge and especially her sense of religion were different. In the end, these differences, which were those of class, resulted "in a sort of ignominious isolation from the people around us whom once I almost felt I had come to know" (173). They also resulted in that distance on one's community known as self-consciousness. Looking back on the experience, she nonetheless thought that something "was begun out there in the Sand Hills" (182). Something, which she had not entirely recognized at the time, "apparently had been taken away." That something was the glamour of the family history, of the old plantation that in her experience had been revealed as only a farm. Why, Lumpkin the autobiographer reflected, "would not the old picture be blurred by the insertion of this new one, in which Negro laborers came and went as strangers, among whom were no counterparts of the slave names so familiar in one's family annals" (182)?

The Sand Hills stay had also, she thought in retrospect, provoked the beginnings of her religious skepticism, which college accelerated. In the place of the God of wrath with whom she had been reared, college offered her a God of love who could be followed, in whose name one could work to transform the world. The message "went on soaking into my consciousness for a year without any peculiarly eruptive consequences. But then it came." And it came in the form of the Word made flesh, an idea she had accepted with no suspicion of what it might mean: "It had not remotely occurred to me what this might be thought to mean" (189). The Word made flesh meant that she, a Southern white woman, would be spoken to on Christianity and the race problem by a Southern black woman, whom she would be expected to call Miss Arthur.

Foreboding gripped Lumpkin and her friends: it was unthinkable. "*Jane* Arthur," perhaps, "*Miss* Arthur," never. "We had known and forgotten tens of thousands of Negro Marys and Janes. But never a '*Miss* Arthur.' How forget a '*Miss* Arthur'?" (189). But how could they refuse? They dared not. And, afterward, "I found the heavens had not fallen, nor the earth parted asunder to swallow us up in this unheard of transgression" (192–93). The event brought Lumpkin another flicker of consciousness as she listened to Miss Arthur. "If I should close my eyes, would I know whether she was white or Negro?" (192). Remembering the touch of exhilaration that accompanied the indefinable sense of discomfort that informed her memories of the event, Lumpkin evokes the biblical story of the man in the Book of Samuel who had defied the law by touching the sacred tabernacle of Jehovah. She had, by thinking that nothing essential distinguished Miss Arthur from a white woman, touched the "tabernacle of our sacred racial beliefs" (193). "I had reached out my hand for an instant and let my finger-tips brush it. I had done it, and nothing, not the slightest thing had happened" (193).

Lumpkin's fleeting vision of what she calls a new heaven preceded her complementary vision of a new earth in which she began to learn, concretely, that her inherited beliefs might not be accurate. Why, she queries in her final chapter, did she take this course? Could she not have better found the personal certainty that she sought in following in the ways of her forebears? "We may call it chance. We may speak of the mysterious chemistry of individuality" (238). Perhaps the very ideals of her childhood had shaped her course, enjoining her sternly to do her duty. Whatever the reason, once her eyes had been opened there was no turning back. Pressing forward, she learned that the South embodied in her family's sense of its history had been something more than that myth allowed—had included many whites who did not own slaves and many blacks who were not slaves. She learned that beyond her immediate community there was another South in which she could anchor her identity. "As it came about, it was this different South that in the end drew me towards my refashioning, even as my Old South receded ever farther into history" (239).

Writing of herself as a Southerner, Lumpkin never explicitly emphasizes her gender. She sharply emphasizes the centrality of the master—of male dominance—in the Old South and even its persistence into the New South. But she does not cast her own struggle as one to escape male dominance in particular—or, rather, since everything she comes to oppose is represented by men, she does not cast her struggle for individuality in a female discourse. In a deep sense, she does not represent her identity as a woman as central to her efforts to come to terms with her past and to chart a new course. And even when she succeeds in charting that course, she brings it back to the South of which she feels herself a part.

Not all Southern women autobiographers match Lumpkin's historical and sociological imagination. Nor, as many feminist critics have noted, do all women autobiographers match her determination to represent the development of her self. It is, in fact, tempting to argue that Lumpkin's explicit attention to the historical and sociological conditions of her self permits her to adopt the strong authorial position that she does. Like other women autobiographers, Lumpkin maintains a discreet silence on her sexuality; even more than many others, she eschews any hint of personal confession. *The Making of a Southerner,* like all autobiographies, including the most exhibitionist, contains its silences. But the silences do not weaken Lumpkin's representation of her self. And the evocation of history, for all its apparent impersonality, strengthens it by delineating the ties that bind any individual to her community.

Black Southern women autobiographers have shared the history that Lumpkin emphasizes in her autobiography, however differently they experienced it. And, like their white counterparts, they have forged their representations of self in response to it. Zora Neale Hurston and Maya Angelou, in very different ways, followed Harriet Jacobs's lead in writing of Southern childhoods from the perspective of the North and for a predominantly Northern audience.[14] But in part because of a difference of generation, Hurston and Angelou followed different strategies in representing those Southern roots. Hurston, writing in the 1940s and intent upon distancing her self from the fetters of the past, tended to transform Southern black history into myth or folktale, thereby denying its consequences for her self. Angelou, writing at the end of the 1960s and benefiting from the militant struggle for civil rights, carefully detailed the community from which she sprang, openly acknowledging its roots in slavery. Hurston, seeking to establish her identity as a member of the republic of letters, denied the significance of all boundaries of race, gender, or class, as if in fear that they would compromise the worth of her self. Angelou accepted the boundaries, trusting that her ability to celebrate and simultaneously to transcend them would validate her self.[15]

In her life as in her work, Angelou represents the dawning of a new generation in which the female legacy and quality of a woman's self have been gaining new attention. In this sense, she properly belongs to the generations that have been developing the feminist theory through which we scrutinize previous women's writings. Lumpkin and Hurston were more reticent about their experiences and identities as women, but their reticence should not be taken as evidence of the fragility of their sense of self. To the contrary, both, as women, have insisted upon the strength and integrity of self. Lumpkin, in insisting more than once that chance may account for the specific way in which her self developed, is reaching for a language to explain the uniqueness of a self that is also a product of its community and history. Hurston, in drawing upon the mythic events and personal visions that shaped her unique self, is doing the same. Both have something in common with Ellen Glasgow, who begins her autobiography not with the South but with her own dawning consciousness.

> I see the firelight, but I do not know it is firelight. I hear singing, but I do not recognize my mother's voice, nor any voice, nor any singing. I feel myself moved to and fro, rocked in my mother's arms, only I do not know that I am myself, or that I am lulled to sleep with a murmur, with a rhythm, a pause, a caress. All this I learn afterwards. All this is attached, long afterwards, to my earliest remembered sensation. (3)

Glasgow, focusing sharply on the "I" of self and consciousness, none-theless underscores the relation between that self and community. Without community, the self of sensation would have no words through which to claim its identity. Her "I" cannot even know that it is her self without the help of those who subsequently give her words. In *The Woman Within*, Glas-gow also writes of the specifics of her Southern childhood, and although she recognizes the importance of history for her sense of self, she emphasizes the influence of the past less than does Lumpkin. But as a woman writer, Glasgow, like Hurston, reaches for a self that transcends the limiting claims of gender, race, and class.

Like other women autobiographers, Southern women, black and white, have wrestled with the claims of individualism and community in their self-representations, but they have not normally seen those claims as incom-patible. To be a woman has meant, for most, to be a woman among their people, within the specific communities that defined their womanhood. In the measure that Southern women autobiographers have also reached for an essential self, they have viewed it as shedding gender together with other historical or material contingencies. The self of will—the will to resist oppres-sion, the will to claim a place in the republic of letters—emerges from their representations as pure individual energy, talent, or chance. In this respect, they have insisted upon pushing the claims of individualism to their logical conclusion, where they meet the Christian vision of the soul. In contrast, most have understood the gendered self as above all historical—as the prod-uct of race, class, and region.

Notes

1. Raymond Williams, *The Country and the City* (New York: Harper and Row, 1973).
2. Ferdinand Tönnies, *Gemeinschaft und Gesellschaft: Grundbegriffe de Reinen Soci-ologie* (Leipzig, 1887).
3. Twelve Southerners, *I'll Take My Stand: The South and the Agrarian Tradition* (New York: Harper, 1930).
4. Sidonie Smith, *A Poetics of Women's Autobiography* (Bloomington: Indiana Uni-versity Press, 1988), 17.
5. Nancy K. Miller, "Women's Autobiography in France: For a Dialectics of Identi-fication," in *Women and Language in Literature and Society,* ed. Sally McConnell-Ginet, Ruth Borker, and Nelly Furman (New York: Praeger, 1980), pp. 258–73; Susan Stanford Friedman, "Women's Autobiographical Selves: Theory and Practice," in *The Private Self: Theory and Practice of Women's Autobiographical Writings,* ed. Shari Benstock (Chapel Hill: University of North Carolina Press, 1988), 34–62.
6. Jane Gallop, *The Daughter's Seduction: Feminism and Psychoanalysis* (Ithaca, N.Y.: Cornell University Press, 1982); Friedman, "Women's Autobiographical Selves"; Nancy Chodorow, *The Reproduction of Mothering* (Berkeley: University of California Press, 1976).
7. Elizabeth Fox-Genovese, "My Statue, My Self: Autobiographical Writings of Afro-American Women," in *The Private Self* [reprinted in this volume, pp. 42–66]; Nancy K.

Miller, "Writing Fictions: Women's Autobiography in France," in *Life/Lines: Theorizing Women's Autobiography,* ed. Bella Brodzki and Celeste Schenck (Ithaca, N.Y.: Cornell University Press, 1988)[, 45–61]; Carolyn G. Heilbrun, "Non-Autobiographies of 'Privileged' Women: England and America," in ibid., 62–76; Helen Carr, "In Other Words: Native American Women's Autobiography," in ibid., 131–53; Mary Jean Green, "Structures of Liberation: Female Experience and Autobiographical Form in Quebec," in ibid., 189–99; Biddy Martin, "Lesbian Identity and Autobiographical Difference[s]," in ibid., 77–103.

8. Miller, "Writing Fictions," 61.

9. Philippe Lejeune, *Le Pacte autobiographique* (Paris: Le Seuil, 1975); Georges Gusdorf, "Conditions and Limits of Autobiography," in *Autobiography: Essays Theoretical and Critical,* ed. James Olney (Princeton N.J.: Princeton University Press, 1980), pp. 24–48.

10. Ellen Glasgow, *The Woman Within* (New York: Harcourt, Brace and Company, 1954), 129–30. Page numbers for quotations from this work hereafter appear in the text.

11. For a general discussion of the self-representations of slaveholding women and specific references to their manuscript narratives, see Elizabeth Fox-Genovese, *Within the Plantation Household: Black and White Women of the Old South* (Chapel Hill: University of North Carolina Press, 1988).

12. Elizabeth Avery Meriwether, *Recollections of Ninety-two Years, 1824–1916* (Nashville: Tennessee Historical Commission, 1958).

13. Katharine DuPre Lumpkin, *The Making of a Southerner* (New York: Alfred Knopf, 1946; reprint, Athens: University of Georgia Press, 1981). Page numbers for quotations from this work appear in the text.

14. Zora Neale Hurston, *Dust Tracks on a Road: An Autobiography,* ed. Robert E. Hemenway, 2d ed. (Urbana: University of Illinois Press, 1984); Maya Angelou, *I Know Why the Caged Bird Sings* (New York: Random House, 1969).

15. For a fuller development of these arguments, see Elizabeth Fox-Genovese, "Myth and History: Discourse of Origins in Zora Neale Hurston and Maya Angelou," *Black American Literature Review* 24, no. 2 (Summer 1990), 221–235. See also Nellie Y. McKay's fine discussion of Hurston's *Dust Tracks,* "Race, Gender, and Cultural Context in Zora Neale Hurston's *Dust Tracks on a Road,*" in *Life/Lines: Theorizing Women's Autobiography,* ed. Bella Brodzki and Celeste Schenck (Ithaca, N.Y.: Cornell University Press, 1988), 175–88.

Five

Family and Female Identity
in the Antebellum South
Sarah Gayle and Her Family

In March of 1820 Sarah Furman Haynsworth wrote to her granddaughter, Sarah Ann Haynsworth Gayle, to congratulate her on her marriage and to offer some advice. In particular, she advised her "not to take your maxims for the regulation of your conduct from the popular writing, such as are found in Romances and Plays, but from the unerring word of sacred truth, which abundantly and minutely instructs in the relative duties."[1] If her granddaughter would act with a "sincere and humble regard to divine instruction, and pray for that wisdom which is from above to illumine and direct you," she would surely achieve "such happiness as can be well expected in this imperfect World." We need, Sarah Haynesworth insisted, associating herself with her granddaughter in the station of wife, a share of prudence "to retain the esteem and affections of our husbands," who should be treated "with at least as much good manners as other people." In return for "a meek, quiet, obliging, affectionate and virtuous conduct" women can count on retaining "the love and esteem of our husbands, when youth & beauty are fled." In contrast, a woman's "turbulent, ill natured, willful, disobliging" behavior can be guaranteed to "alienate and wean [husbands] from us."[2]

Sarah Haynsworth trusted her granddaughter to forgive her for "embarquing so much on this head," but "the subject is important, and you are dear to me." Above all, it would give her pleasure to know that her granddaughter was happy.[3] In writing to mark her granddaughter's coming of age as a wife, Sarah Haynsworth was underscoring the ties that she believed bound successive generations of women of one family together and provided the necessary foundations for building a new family. She was also implicitly evoking the core aspects of a woman's identity as the member of interlocking families. Sarah Haynsworth's letter calls attention to the links between prescription and experience, between language and behavior, in female identity as she understood it. She takes for granted that Sarah Gayle would have read and been influenced by romances and plays but begs her to put them aside as she embarks upon her new married estate. She cogently reminds her that henceforth her happiness will, above all, depend upon the success with which she realizes her role as wife. A deep sense of family as the primary influence upon a woman's identity informs the advice that the grandmother felt obliged to tender to the new bride. Although Sarah Gayle's relations as daughter and granddaughter would continue to influence her identity, they would now lose priority to her relations as wife.

Sarah Haynsworth's advice to Sarah Gayle doubtless resembles the advice that innumerable other early nineteenth-century grandmothers would have offered at the time of a darling granddaughter's wedding. In truth, her professed values do not differ significantly from those which, according to Laurel Thatcher Ulrich, governed the lives of the women of northern New England during the late seventeenth and early eighteenth centuries. The words of Sarah Haynsworth, who had lived through the Revolution, also evoke the values of that republican motherhood which, as Linda Kerber has shown, took shape in the war's aftermath as an attempt to prescribe appropriate roles for women in the new world of male individualism.[4] There is, in short, nothing about Sarah Haynsworth's letter, considered abstractly rather than in context, to mark it as distinctively Southern. But Sarah Gayle, in her attempt to follow the spirit of the letter during the fourteen years before her death, fashioned a mature identity that marked her understanding of its message as essentially Southern.

Sarah Gayle had been born in Sumter County, South Carolina, in 1804. As an adult, she continued to treasure memories of her family's journey to Alabama Territory in 1810, still frontier country and not yet a state, although she also regretted the separation from her kin in South Carolina. Judge Wood Furman, the father of her grandmother, Sarah Furman Haynsworth, had signed the South Carolina "Declaration of Rights"; Richard Furman, her grandmother's brother, was the Baptist minister for whom Furman University was named. The parents of John Gayle, whom Sarah Haynsworth Gayle married in 1820, had also migrated from South Carolina to Alabama at the beginning of the nineteenth century. The Gayles, like the Furmans, the Haynsworths, and the kin of Sarah Gayle's mother, the Pringles, had actively supported the patriot side during the Revolution. During Sarah Gayle's girlhood in Claiborne, in Monroe County, Alabama, her parents and the Gayles had become friends. In 1815, after graduation from South Carolina College, John Gayle, who had been born in 1792, read law with Judge Abner S. Lipscomb at St. Stephens, Alabama. In 1818, he joined his parents in Claiborne, where he established a law practice and met Sarah Haynsworth, whom he married a year later. The bride was a few months before her sixteenth birthday; the groom, twenty-eight.[5]

During the next few years, John Gayle pursued his law practice and began to make a career in Alabama politics. In 1818, President Monroe appointed him to the first Council of the Alabama Territory; the year after, he was elected solicitor of the Alabama circuit court; and in 1822, he was elected to the state legislature from Monroe County. Since the demands of law and politics kept John Gayle frequently away from home, he determined to settle in Greensboro, in Greene County, which provided a more central location and permitted him more time at home. After living there for a few years, John Gayle, in 1826, bought a house for his family and in 1828 resigned his judgeship so as to remain at home. The Greensboro in which Sarah Gayle lived as a young wife and mother bore the traces of its frontier status. Retaining a strong rural cast, it featured muddy roads and its share of disorderly residents. But by 1826, it could also claim a hotel, a tailor's shop, five stores, and a law office, as well as the possibility of attending Methodist, Baptist, and Presbyterian services. More important, it boasted a settled population, among whom Sarah Gayle found many women friends who provided companionship and assistance during John Gayle's frequent absences. Greensboro also provided John Gayle with a new political base from which he was elected to another term in the state legislature (during which he was chosen speaker of the House) and, in 1831, to the governorship.[6]

By the time that John Gayle became governor, he and Sarah Gayle had been married eleven years and had four living children—Sarah, Matthew, Amelia, and Mary Reese. In 1832, they had a son, Richard, and in 1835 another daughter, Maria. Much of Sarah Gayle's life was given over to the bearing and rearing of her six children, although she always enjoyed considerable assistance from slaves. Hetty, Mary Ann, and especially Rose, all of whom had belonged to her parents, helped to supervise and care for the children, permitting Sarah Gayle the freedom to attend church, visit with her friends, and write her journals and letters.[7] In 1833, at the beginning of

John Gayle's second term as governor, Sarah Gayle moved with the children to Tuscaloosa to meet the requirements of the new law that mandated the residence of the governor's wife in the capital. At the end of that term, she and the children returned to Greensboro to await what the Gayles expected would be a permanent move to Mobile. In the early summer of 1835, John Gayle left on a trip to investigate the possibilities of speculation in newly opened Indian lands in northern Alabama, and during his absence, Sarah Gayle died suddenly of tetanus following dental work. In many respects, her brief life of thirty-one years superficially resembled that of innumerable other American women, but in other essential ways, it differed significantly, as did her sense of her own identity.

At the heart of the experience that distinguished Sarah Gayle's life and identity from those of contemporary northeastern or Western European women lay the social relations of the slave society of the South. For as early as 1820, indeed earlier, Southerners were developing a worldview grounded in the life of rural households that remained centers of production as well as reproduction and that, for slaveholders like the Haynsworths and the Gayles, included slaves among household members. In attempting to explain this world and its values, as well as to rear children to perpetuate them, Southerners developed a distinct ideology of hierarchy and particularism that owed much to the heritage they shared with their Northern counterparts, but also embodied significant differences. Southerners never remained immune to the influences of bourgeois culture, but in absorbing new currents of thought— from the celebration of republican motherhood and companionate marriage to the appreciation of Romanticism—they carefully selected and adapted them to fit their own circumstances.[8]

Among the various facets of this emerging Southern worldview, the concept of womanhood and identity of women especially challenges the imagination. Bourgeois society, from which Southern society was attempting to distinguish itself, remained notoriously conservative on the woman question. Scholars have carefully detailed the innumerable ways in which bourgeois women suffered continuing exclusion from the full benefits of individualism, lived under the dominance of men, and struggled against massive cultural odds to construct independent roles and identities for themselves. The early proponents of women's rights remained noteworthy exceptions and were frequently associated with a variety of radical political movements. Even among those who argued for enlarged roles and possibilities for women, many did so in the name of women's rights as women, combining their demands with an insistence upon women's special nature and domestic vocation. The case of female identity thus offers an especially arresting example of the complex ways in which antebellum Southerners were in but not of a larger capitalist world upon which their households depended but from which they sought to differentiate themselves. For even if practice remained conservative in the North as in the South, in the North capitalism and individualism were increasingly undermining conservative practice; whereas in the South, slavery was reinforcing and reshaping it.[9]

The concept of family—of women's relations to and places in families—illuminates the similarities and the differences. In practice and in imagination, the idea of family bound antebellum white Southerners together by providing a compelling representation of enduring and natural ties among individuals. Family figured as a central metaphor for Southern society as a whole—for the personal and social relations through which individuals defined their identities and understood their lives. Women, especially, relied upon family membership to define their identities, for they normally did not have access to other, more abstract roles that would offer competing sources of identity. Men also emphasized family as an important source of identity, but they enjoyed other opportunities, notably as citizens but also through specialized occupations. Men's multiple identities underscored their special position as heads of families in which relations among members were not equal. Southerners, especially, relied upon the metaphor of family to cover a variety of relations, notably networks of kin, but also black slaves. Thus, the slaveholders' ubiquitous phrase, "our family, white and black," emphasized the persistence of the metaphor of family as an appropriate representation for various social relations.

Family membership defined a Southern woman's place in the world, as family roles articulated her deepest sense of herself in her immediate circle. There is every reason to believe that the pervasive sense of female self as predominantly a matter of family membership informed the lives of non-slaveholding as well as slaveholding rural women, but the direct evidence for their most intimate sense of themselves as women remains sparse.[10] Slaveholding women, who have left more direct evidence of their personal responses, certainly understood the female self as primarily the product of family relations. In this essential respect, the majority of slaveholding women differed from those bourgeois women who were beginning to define a sense of self in the abstract and to find ways of claiming for themselves the status of individual, and they even differed from those who were beginning to speak of women's public rights and responsibilities as women. In this respect, too, they were conforming to more traditional American and European notions of female identity as grounded in a web of relations, of which family membership was the most important.

Southern politicians, educators, and, especially, clergymen regularly reminded women of their primary responsibility to identify with their families.

Religious and secular proslavery theorists alike forcefully insisted that all social relations—notably those of slavery—depended upon and were grounded
in the natural and divinely sanctioned subordination of women to men.[11]
But in so insisting, they very much resembled the proverbial lady who "doth
protest too much." For, disclaimers notwithstanding, they were themselves
unavoidably infected with the virus of a radical individualism that had been
sweeping Western culture at least since the eighteenth century. Their cherished vision of hierarchy and particularism, of which women and slaves
constituted the primary embodiments, thus contained a strong measure of
defensiveness. They were not simply propounding an accepted view of the
world as it was; they were attempting to construct a solid bulwark against a
rising wave of disorderly social change.

Antebellum Southerners lived, and knew themselves to live, in a world
that was increasingly challenging their most cherished values and social relations. In dangerous times, the family provided an especially attractive defense
against the forces of change, not least because it apparently embodied human beings' most natural relations. As a metaphor, family privileged organic
over contractual relations, community over individual self-interest, harmony
over conflict, but the very notion of family, most dearly cherished by Southerners, owed a considerable debt to the cultural and ideological currents that
most directly threatened their sense of a proper, hierarchical social order.
When slaveholding women embraced the sense of themselves as preeminently members of families, they were frequently borrowing from a language
or rhetoric of family that primarily derived from the emerging bourgeois
discourse of domesticity, companionate marriage, and attentive motherhood.[12] But even as they selectively borrowed words and ideas, they were
applying them to what they understood to be women's place in a modern
slave society.

Sarah Gayle, like many others, albeit in her own way, continuously
attempted to take stock of her own identity in relation to those whom she
loved, with whom she lived, and in interaction with whom she forged her
sense of self. The rich, if discontinuous, journal that she kept from 1827 until
her death in 1835 provides striking, if incomplete, testimony to the ways in
which she constructed and interpreted her self as the articulation of her
place in interlocking families.[13] Perhaps most striking is that she addressed
her most intimate recorded self-investigations to her children, especially her
daughters. Marveling early in her first journal that so physically unattractive
a woman as Miss Bates could be the friend of Mrs. Chambers, she reminds
herself "that personal attractions are not indispensable to the forming of
friendships" and explicitly enjoins her daughters, "I would have you my darling girls early impressed with the belief for it is a fact which experience will

ultimately teach you."[14] Yet she could not entirely banish her regrets about the deterioration of her own looks or her fear that she might not continue to appear beautiful in the eyes of her husband. She worried about the example such superficial concerns might set for her daughters:

> But in acknowledging this weakness, I forget that you, my daughters, may read these pages as the only means of learning the disposition of a parent who may have left you. Be it so—to you, I wish to be unveiled, that if I possess anything worthy to be adopted you may do it and if anything which out [*sic*] to be shunned it be a warning tho' you should say "it is *my mother's* frailty."[15]

If her words testify to the ways in which she understands her self in relation to her daughters and attempts to anchor her various feelings in her role as mother, they also betray her continuing preoccupation with death. At some time, be it sooner or later, she will exist only in the memories of those she has loved, notably her family. In reminding herself of her future identity as memory, Sarah Gayle draws upon her own devotion to those whom she has loved and who have died. Throughout her journal, she regularly returns to death—sometimes her own, sometimes that of another. For her sense of self depends heavily on continuity across generations and beyond the grave, on the ways in which she has internalized the love and examples of others, especially her parents. Recollecting her girlhood, she writes:

> so it is—my father, my mother, my idolizing mother—my friends, Amelia & Sara, my good tutor—all are buried—yet I am happy—the recollection of them has no bitterness in it—it only melts me, courses all that is good in my nature, makes me turn, with the more intense delight, to the good yet left, and with subdued hope to the moment, when those I possess and those I have lost will be secured to me, *forever* & *ever*.[16]

In such moments, Sarah Gayle expresses her confidence that she has indeed accepted the loss of those she loved by merging them in her own identity. She sees her identity as the product of her relations with others. She also takes seriously her responsibility for perpetuating the memories of those she has lost. Names, especially, signify continuities. She names her oldest son for her husband's father; her oldest daughter for herself, her mother, and her grandmother. Younger daughters receive the names of especially cherished friends; her younger son, that of her own father. She notes, after a visit, that Mrs. Erwin, like herself, "finds in 'auld lang syne' a sweet and inexhaustible theme."[17] But Mrs. Erwin's husband will not consent to her naming the new infant after her bosom friend Caroline Feemster. Sarah Gayle condemns his attitude as entirely ungenerous, for has he not brought his wife "away from her family & friends to a land of strangers, where she finds much to regret without any prospect of having it supplied"? Under such conditions, how can he deny her "the simple but to her inestimable privilege of perpetuating the names of those she loves in her own children"?[18] Every day of her life Sarah Gayle has reason to congratulate herself that Mr. Gayle has behaved so differently.

Concern with death frequently leads Sarah Gayle to worry about her children's futures and the likelihood of being reunited in heaven with all of those she has lost. Thus, she asks herself what will become of her "little flock": "Will they live, will I live, will their father[,] the corner stone of our happiness?"[19] At least her baby who never breathed in this world is safe, "is now a child of Paradise." But what of her mother? "I should go mad, if I did not believe that she the excellent, the honorable, the true, the *all* that was good, had not received the reward."[20] And what of herself? Each confinement renews her fears about her own possible death. And what of her children if something happens to her? She is determined that they not have a stepmother, determined that they not be deprived of those maternal connections which alone can ensure the proper development of their characters.[21]

Past, present, and future imperceptibly merge in Sarah Gayle's developing identity. As she matures, the past in particular plays an increasingly important role in her sense of who she is. In 1828, at twenty-four, she reproaches herself for dwelling upon her outrage that the husband of one of her closest friends had remarried immediately after the friend's death. "I am very foolish to care anything for the matter, but I become more and more unwilling that any I used to know and with whom I used to be on terms of intimacy should be strangers now."[22] Her outrage suggests how easily she could project her fears about her own possible death into the death of her friend. From that perspective, she resents the husband who so quickly could forget his wife. Yet she also wishes to retain her personal relation with him, if only because they have known each other for so long. She admits that she values "old friends, old scenes[,] everything I knew in early life, with something like romance."[23]

Even as she cherishes the memories of previous times, she insists that she is "willing to accept the pleasures proper to my time of life, or rather to the size of my family[,] for I am but just twenty-four."[24] Perhaps no bliss could be compared to that she experienced when she was fifteen, but "now when my children are playing around me—and their father's head is on my knee, & his arms clasped in fondness around me—I look back to my days of girlish happiness as to a dream, sweet indeed, but which must not be compared to the quiet sober reality."[25]

The bliss of Sarah Gayle's fifteenth year, as she remembers it, consisted in watching the gallants of the country arrive at her father's house. She seems in this passage to be evoking the bliss of adolescence and of her brief life as a belle, which she no longer regrets exchanging for the more sober contentment of marriage and motherhood. Her own emerging identity as a mother leads her to reevaluate aspects of her youth, especially her feelings for her mother. Vowing to attend to her father's grave as a "mark of respect & affection," she admits that she has never so much as placed a rosebush beside her mother's grave. She has not been able to go to it, but she never thinks of it "without a gush of tenderness, more gratifying to her, if she knew it, a thousand thousand times more precious than the bloom of roses & the kissing of willow-boughs."[26] Each passing year makes her more conscious of the loss of her mother, whom she never valued as she should have. Now she recognizes her excellence and recognizes that "when she died I lost one who loved me with a more enduring, a more indulgent boundless affection, than any one else ever did or can[—]more than almost any other mother ever cherished for a faulty child."[27]

At times, Sarah Gayle worries that although she loved her mother, she did not love her as her mother loved her. She now feels as if she "could never be happy again, because she went down to her grave without knowing, how was she to know, when I was ignorant myself?"[28] Now she knows how much gratitude and admiration her mother deserved and cherishes all memories of her, deprecating "as an evil every thing like forgetting her person, her manners, habits & high virtues."[29] And Sarah Gayle delights to think that as soon as her daughters are old enough, she will describe her mother to them and encourage them to imitate her. At the same time, she is also probably thinking of how she hopes her daughters will love and remember their own mother.

She continues to cherish her mother as a standard for womanly excellence and, by implication, for her own identity. Finding herself unduly critical of Mrs. P.'s wearing a veil, which is really becoming to the features of fifteen but hardly those of fifty, she allows that she herself has doubtless been influenced by her mother's ideas. For her mother wore her raven hair parted on her forehead and nothing but a plain cap and bonnet. But then, nothing of her countenance should have been veiled. Her black eyes, which "expressed her true inborn nobleness," could "sparkle with indignation, with pleasure or with hope—but oh! how eloquently did their gentle glance speak to the heart of her child."[30] The fears that plague Sarah Gayle during her pregnancies, especially, lead her to think of her mother to whom she was wont to turn confidently with her complaints and unspeakable fears.

In Sarah Gayle's memory, her mother always counseled wisely, reproved mildly, and participated feelingly. There was no agony, she believes, that her mother would not gladly have borne for her. At the time, she barely noticed these "evidences of affection," but now "they rise upon my recollection & I think of them as they deserve."[31] Now she knows that her mother would have risked her life for her, could never have survived had anything happened to her. "I have wept bitter, bitter tears, when I recall'd the unkindness of my conduct towards her many times."[32] She does not think that she was "undutiful or rebellious," but her "temper was quick and did not well brook control." Her father's lessons, she now believes, pushed her toward "independence," and "too great carelessness for the opinions of others" made her "hardheaded."[33] But then, she reminds herself, she did love her mother, who especially had her entire confidence in matters of courtship and who preferred John Gayle for her daughter's husband. She recalls how devotedly she nursed her mother during her last illness and how, in recognition, her mother called her "my guardian angel."

The deep identification between mother and daughter in itself hardly marks slaveholding women as different from bourgeois women. To the contrary, psychologists, for whom bourgeois women constitute primary subjects, forcefully insist upon the importance of that identification for women's sense of self.[34] There are, nonetheless, reasons for which the identification would have been especially strong for antebellum Southern women who, as girls, spent most of their time in their mothers' company and who could be expected to lead lives that closely replicated those of their mothers. Demographic patterns reinforced the special identification between Southern mothers and daughters, for Southern women, who continued to marry younger than their Northern counterparts, would be close in age to their mothers and thus, to borrow Sarah Gayle's words, be their companions, friends, and sisters as well as their daughters.[35] Under these conditions, Southern women like Sarah Gayle went to their marriages more as girls than as mature women, and they remained closely tied to their mothers. Sarah Gayle's journals suggest that she, at least, transferred many of her feelings for her mother directly to her husband, looking to him for a quasi-maternal love and understanding.

Sarah Gayle assuredly viewed her marriage as the foundation of her mature identity. By temporarily taking the perspective of the man who marries a young girl such as she had been, she finds a way of presenting her personal feelings as the general case. She writes that a man cannot but be happy when a lovely young woman gives her heart into his keeping and by her language and conduct says, "from this moment henceforth, I acknowledge none but you as my protector in the wide, wide world, upon no arm will I lean but yours, while buoyed up by prosperity; in adversity, no head but thine, shall be pillowed upon this bosom, while I whisper, that the vial of bitterness cannot be emptied, if thy sustaining love be spared to me."[36] At the wedding of a young friend, she thinks back on her own wedding. Her emotions overpower her as, significantly, she thinks in one breath of her husband, her father, her mother. As the ceremony progressed, she "was more and more sensible of the importance of the act which was then receiving an unchangeable seal. None but a wife could know what she wished."[37] The ceremony evoked powerful contradictory feelings, first tears and then an unaccountable fit of laughing. But when the bride left with her husband, there were tears again, and "warm wishes rose for her, going, as she was, from the very bosom of her parents to the somewhat uncertain welcome of strangers."[38] The experience of others teaches Sarah Gayle that marriage in truth harbors dangers as well as joy and protection.

One Sunday, Mr. Hillhouse, the Presbyterian minister, "delivered a more touching sermon than I ever heard him pronounce. He told us he intended with the permission of the heads of the families to meet with them at their firesides and carry on there what might come less warmly & nearly from the pulpit."[39] She is sure he will not be excluded from theirs. She also thinks that she could "discover the domestic histories of those who were affected at various parts of the discourse." The woman who was sitting in front of her, for example, "shrunk as if from a probe, at the picture of the unhappiness of many who to observers are cheerful enough."[40] Sarah Gayle did not have to look far to discover the source of her grief. The husband who was sitting next to her was "a bloated victim of intemperance" whose character was "blackened by infidelities." Surely, Christian faith offered such a woman more than anything earth had to offer. Another woman, Mrs. Bell, almost suffocated with her emotions, and Sarah Gayle recalled that she had, lying at home, a beautiful daughter who had been suffering for two years with a fatal disease. Yet another, Mrs. Thurman, also attended to the sermon with particular care. Again, Sarah Gayle could understand the reason. "I had met *her* husband, staggering from the grog-shop to the home which should be approached alone by a man with sober & sacred and tender feeling. Is there a fate like hers?"[41] Surely, none could suffer more than the woman who "gave her destiny up to him, and far from shedding on it the light of his grateful affection, he forgets he has it in his keeping, while draining the bottle or seeking the vulgar amusement of the shuffleboard!" Such a betrayal of trust erodes a woman's very identity. "No wonder her cheeks have become pale and her appearance careless—what inducement has she to adorn her body, when the worm is gnawing within? None, None."[42]

Reading a set of lectures that acutely explored the relation between public and private virtue, Sarah Gayle thinks that the author "ably discourses on the pernicious effects of infidelity upon the public morals and the public good, while like most men the agony of the wife's outraged heart sinks into comparative insignificance!"[43] And what is a wife to do under such circumstances? She herself can form but the faintest idea of such misery, but what she can imagine is dreadful enough "—the bare supposition that Providence could make such a fate the punishment of my sins, would if followed up put me beside myself." The longer she is married,

> the more intense and single is my love for my husband and sometimes when he is gone & I am melancholy, I ask myself, can he still place first in his heart & his thoughts, the faded being who is changed in all but her feelings, who has nothing of youth of beauty of talent not even the poor charm of manner to fascinate?[44]

Happily, John Gayle's presence banishes such questions, which she believes wiser not to dwell on.

Some women defame the identity of wife and mother. When Mrs. Dann's two-day-old infant is reported to be dying, Sarah Gayle cannot but think that its death might be a blessing, if only by removing the evidence of the mother's shame. But she is surprised at Mrs. Dann's want of feeling, having expected her at least to show "the instinctive parental love in which even brutes seem her superior." Mrs. Dann also has a daughter of about five years who can be expected to follow in her mother's steps. Sarah Gayle knows that all of the women of that family are "of bad character," and Mrs. Dann herself "a young handsome & unblushing prostitute." The possible causes of such a career trouble Sarah Gayle, who suspects that the first cause might indeed be slight, perhaps "an incautious word a light and unmeaning look—imprudence first placed the curse upon them—believing *all* lost, they became careless & callous—gave birth to unfortunate children whose fathers dared not lay their hand upon them, and say 'it is mine.'" She cannot imagine how such parents will be able to stand with "such children before the Judgment seat of a holy God."[45] Beneath her moral outrage lurks the conviction that mothers decisively shape the identities of their daughters.

Sarah Gayle, drawing upon the example of her own mother, holds the highest standards for women and takes strong exception to the behavior of her sister-in-law Lucinda, who attempted to transact some matters of business, although Mr. Gayle had attempted to persuade her not to. But Lucinda's efforts, as was to be expected, availed nothing, for "no gentleman would consent to transact business of importance with a lady whose husband was fully capable of attending to it himself." Lucinda should have known that it "is a real misfortune for her thus to meddle in affairs to which women are generally strangers, for it not only mortifies her friends, but after she has failed leaves her to be laughed at." Sarah Gayle could love her sister-in-law dearly if only she had more "straight forward honesty." But Lucinda's failings should not be minimized, for: "my dear children tho a few good qualities may be liked you can never be respected & honored unless you possess that high sense of honor which will lead you at all risks to speak & act the true & the right."[46] In this example, she explicitly links her standards of female honor to the acceptance of prescribed female roles.

By a clear train of association, these reflections on Lucinda's weakness of character lead Sarah Gayle directly into a discussion of what she is doing about her own children's education. She has started Matt with Mr. Hall but fears that Matt, being small, will be overlooked among the larger boys. Meanwhile, Mrs. Potts, whose school Sarah had been attending, has moved to the upper end of the village, too far away for Sarah to walk. Worse, on such a walk, Sarah "will be liable to hear, & see so much I would be grieved for her to hear, that I would almost prefer her staying at home and learning nothing."[47]

The very next day, Matt again reminds Sarah Gayle of her responsibilities as the educator of her children by asking her a series of difficult questions, beginning with, "when was General Washington born?" then, "when was God born?" and finally, "what is a sinner?" She replies that bad men were sinners, "that all were sinners," and then names the sins of anger, theft, lying. Matt protests, "But Mah you get angry, and that is sin, and the sinner can't go to Heaven." She replies that she was sorry for it, and God forgave her. But Matt insists, "'you get mad again and keep getting so.'"[48] At that point, she finds herself at a loss. Matt, undaunted, moves on to ask if angels were sons of God. And what about the Devil? Matt persists with his questions, all equally puzzling to her. And addressing him directly, she writes of her hope that his spirit of inquiry would lead him, at a mature age, to investigate these matters more thoroughly for himself.[49]

The burden of overseeing Matt's education plagues Sarah Gayle throughout her life, forcefully reminding her of the differences between male and female identity. She especially worries about his growing interest in guns. "I never saw a child so devoted to his gun, and I have many apprehensive moments lest he should do injury, perhaps a terrible one, to man or beast."[50] But should she take his gun from him? Would she not push him towards other, less innocent, amusements? Without his gun to occupy him, might he not take to the street or, worse, to the billiard room? There he might contract habits "of a nature to destroy his future usefulness and my happiness as a mother. A mere chance of accident is much preferable to such a fear."[51] In truth, she has only the most imperfect knowledge of the male vices that worry her, for she has always been sheltered from them. She is fully capable of appreciating and admiring Matt's masculinity, viewing him at the age of twelve on his return from one hunting expedition as a painter might have seen him: "His countenance flushed to the deepest red, his eyes flashing and sparkling, teeth white as ivory, his hair dishevelled but pushed back, shot bag hung around him, his gun in one hand, while he held the two 'coons upon his shoulder with the other."[52] But as he grows up, she increasingly views him as a man—as fundamentally different from herself. He thus evokes her deepest and contradictory feelings about men, who may be either women's protectors or their abusers.

For Sarah Gayle, the responsibilities of educating male and female children underscore different aspects of her own identity. Throughout her journal, she reveals a certain confidence in her dealings with her daughters. Here and there, doubts creep in and frustrations arise. Amelia proves willful and unmanageable, however bright and delightful. Sarah offers less reason for concern, consistently proving herself to be the most reliable and responsible of girls. But Matt poses entirely different problems, especially as he moves steadily toward such distinctly male interests as hunting and as he begins to make possibly undesirable companions outside of the household. On one frightful occasion, when a horse almost ran away with him and she was powerless to intervene, she was prompted to reflect on the implications of his danger and possible death. The experience led her to explore in her journal the difference in her feelings for him and her daughters:

> and if he had been kill'd happiness would not have visited my heart again. I love my daughters very dearly do I love them, and all that is amiable & good, intelligent & lovely would I have them, but all I possess of ambition, pride & the hope that steps over the threshold of home all such is centered in him, and if Death had crushed them, I should have mourned as Rachel.[53]

Obviously, such feelings could also plague bourgeois women who lived in a world that sought to bind women closely to a female sphere. Southern and bourgeois women alike lived with a steady stream of injunctions about their responsibilities as mothers. Both were heir to the ideology of motherhood that held women preeminently responsible for early childhood education.[54] But Southern patterns of child rearing adapted a common prescriptive literature to a distinct reality in which Southern mothers, especially slave-holding mothers, performed different tasks as mothers than their Northeastern sisters. Rarely, for example, did Southern women assume complete, or even primary, responsibility for the material care of their small children, including nursing. In this, as in so much else, all of their efforts were seconded or even superseded by the efforts of slave women.

Southern women of all classes were much less likely than Northeastern women to send their children to school at an early age, if only because they lacked schools to send them to. Slaveholding women in particular would commonly assume primary responsibility, not merely for the early training of their children's characters, but also for their early formal instruction. In the case of daughters, especially as in Sarah Gayle's case in the semi-frontier conditions engendered by plantation slavery, they might continue that instruction for years or share it with a tutor. Only when it came time to send girls away to school would their fathers assume primary responsibility. Fathers might take over the education of boys much earlier, except in cases in which, like John Gayle's, they were often away from home and could not do so systematically. In any event, boys were commonly sent to such schools as were available at a younger age than girls.[55]

The ideals of Southern women like Sarah Gayle for themselves as mothers, which lay at the core of their identities, had less to do with tasks than with a way of being in the world. Sarah Gayle intertwines her thoughts about her mother, her daughters, and herself with her basic thoughts about character, including religion. Even when concerned with the most abstract qualities of character that presumably applied to men as well as women, she commonly insists that for men these things are different. Even when she reproaches women with abstract failures of character, she ties those failures to their roles within families as mothers, wives, and daughters. Similarly, she expresses her continuing preoccupation with religion as an articulation of identity in relation to her family. Her feelings as a mother, especially, overcome her when she reflects on conversion and her hopes for her own children. Salvation, above all, promises the prospect of being permanently reunited with those she has loved, of reconstituting her household in heaven.[56]

The overlapping of family and household occurs in Sarah Gayle's self-representations when she writes of her slaves, who, although in significantly lesser ways than whites, also helped to anchor her identity as the member of interlocking families. In 1828, when she had been thinking about her parents, she notes that "Old Granny will soon close her earthly career." Granny was about eighty or ninety and "has been in my family since my mother's first marriage."[57] And she enjoins herself not to forget old Granddaddy, who toward the end of his life loved to sit in the door and listen to her read the parts of the Bible that he most remembered. Their names, she reminds herself, were Roger and Nanny, although "the other appeleatives [*sic*] alone were used."[58]

Other slaves, notably Hampton and Hetty and even, on occasion, her favorite, Mike, provoke angry outbursts for their recalcitrance in effecting her wishes.[59] But as soon as the heat of anger has passed, she forces herself to be honest. The fault lies as much with her as with them, if not more. Her mother had known how to manage servants properly—to exact obedience and to render justice. She does not and does no better with the children than with the servants. On a bad day, she notes that the children are troublesome, "but it is because my management is so faulty. When they misbehave my temper is terribly in my way, and I fail in attempts to reason, expostulate, entreat or command with necessary calmness."[60] Her difficulties with servants and children reinforce her sense of inadequacy. "Several of the negroes have been sick—all mending. My children are half-wild from their liberty."[61] Yet, however "perplexing" she finds the management of her children and however "lamentably deficient" she finds herself "in the art of governing them," she thanks "Heaven that I possess these to give my life some object and my body, mind and affections some employment, in my sort of widowhood."[62]

In wrestling with her own conflicting feelings and her frequent bouts of depression, Sarah Gayle attempts to cope with the "causes of disquiet peculiar to the mother and mistress of a family."[63] The phrase, "mother and mistress of a family," captures the essence of Sarah Gayle's mature identity, albeit one with which she continues to struggle, especially in John Gayle's absence. Loneliness and her own inadequacy continually threaten to engulf her spirits. "In spite of the size of my family," she writes, "many is the unpleasant moment, when such a feeling of loneliness and desolation comes over me, that I shut my eyes in hopelessness."[64] At the worst, she feels no disposition even to read or write. Thinking of the books she would like to read or the journal in which she would like to write, she sadly acknowledges that "I absolutely lack energy to send a servant for one, or to open the drawer, which has the other."[65] Time and again, her preoccupation with her own identity leads her back to her rearing of her children. "I fear I am lamentably deficient in that patient, calm firmness, without which a mother cannot properly manage her children."[66] Thus, she sees her personal identity as imperceptibly merging with her identity as a mother.

Worrying that her children "are far from improving as I desire" and alarmed at the "numerous rumors concerning the slaves," she nonetheless knows that the problem derives not from "what is *about* me," but from "the unsettled state of my mind and temper[.] I am deeply sensible the error is in them, and in solitude and silence I make a thousand resolutions, quickly broken[,] of amendment—they vanish before the first trial." And once again, she determines "to make a more vigorous effort for the sake of my children. . . ."[67] In one moment of depression, she writes of her intense longing again to see old Sheldon (her father's place), to see in reality the scenes that remain so fresh in her memory. "What a creature of happiness and mirth I was then—how young, how caressed, how worshiped by a father who was proud of me and a mother who lived in my life alone." Into that enchanted world and her young existence came "the revolution in my affections, the breaking up of old, and the forming of new and most ecstatic ties." Now she can only thank the "Fountain of Light . . . that this period of unmixed felicity has been mine, and that sometimes when I am wearied and lonely, and it may be *murmuring*, I may look back to it, and feel invigorated to pace on in the even and unvaried line of duty, which extends itself before me."[68]

Sarah Gayle's juxtaposition of the "unmixed felicity" of her youth and the "unvaried line of duty" of her present and future permits speculation that she harbored conflicting feelings about her adult situation as wife and mother. She indisputably had her bad moments and her flares of temper, but she never so much as hints that she did not love her husband. To the contrary, she repeatedly and convincingly writes of her deep and abiding love for him, implicitly associating him with her mother as her most important source of happiness and security. His long absences, nonetheless, left her in charge of children and servants whom she frequently found difficult to govern, thus confronting her with her own angers and limitations. Indeed, the presence of servants in her household and metaphoric family forced her, more than bourgeois women, to accept the austere, adult responsibilities of governance. But those responsibilities did not lead her, as some bourgeois women were being led by the logic of their society, beyond the home, much less to identify with an abstract identity as an individual. Instead, they forced her back upon her own identity as defined by her family membership. The evangelical virtues that she sporadically attempted to cultivate remained preeminently particular, not abstract, virtues—the virtues of her station, not those of the individual in general.

Like other women, in all times and places, Sarah Gayle frequently found the demands of adulthood trying and sought escape, if only in fantasy. Her quests to escape her burdens did not, however, lead her into overt rebellion against her situation. Doubtless, her frequent comments upon the unhappy marriages of others and the viciousness, brutality, and simple irresponsibility of some men can be read as covert protests against male privilege and its abuses. Similarly, her recurring lassitude and depression can be interpreted as an unconscious protest against what some part of her viewed as her crushing responsibilities. But we have no evidence that she saw her life that way. We do have evidence that she remained psychologically bound to her family of origin and to her own life as a cherished daughter. And in periods of depression, she would commonly turn to those memories, as other women have turned to other fantasies to ease distress. She also turned to those memories, much as her grandmother (whose letter must be read in its Southern context) had recommended, as the foundation for a mature identity that she embraced. For like other Southern women, she belonged to a world that encouraged women to find their primary identities in the roles and relations of families.

In 1859, Augusta Jane Evans published a novel, *Beulah,* in which she attempted to explore the implications of individualism for Southern women. After a protracted exploration of her protagonist's progress toward philosophical skepticism, personal independence, and public authorship, she resolved the plot by having Beulah regain her faith, marry her guardian, and accept her ordained role as wife.[69] Although Evans does not especially dwell on Southern social relations, notably slavery, the novel's conclusion forcefully endorses the superiority of Southern over Northern ways. Evans scrupulously exposes the ways in which the logic of bourgeois thought undermines family and religion. Her account of Beulah's travails appealed to many Northern readers, for whom women's roles and identities remained a necessary bastion of conservatism, women's subordination to men the best protection against unacceptable egalitarianism. But Evans intended something more than a mere prescription for female duty. Beulah, in finally embracing her identity as a woman, was embracing a view of her identity as defined by Southern society and articulated by its own peculiar family roles. And tellingly, in order to start Beulah on her misguided quest for independence, Evans represents her as an orphan. Only by her gradual ability to reclaim herself within the family relations specific to the slaveholding South could she consolidate her identity.

Notes

1. Sarah Furman Haynsworth to Sarah Ann Haynsworth Gayle, 28 Mar. 1820, Gayle Papers, Library of the City of Mobile; also in Alabama Department of Archives and History.

2. Ibid.

3. Ibid.

4. Laurel Thatcher Ulrich, *Good Wives: Image and Reality in the Lives of Women in Northern New England, 1650–1750* (New York: Oxford Univ. Press, 1982); Linda K. Kerber, *Women of the Republic: Intellect and Ideology in Revolutionary America* (Chapel Hill: Univ. of North Carolina Press, 1980).

5. "Sarah Haynsworth Gayle and Her Journal," Alabama Department of Archives and History, Montgomery, Alabama. This account was written by one of Sarah Gayle's descendants for the family. See also "John Gayle," *Dictionary of American Biography,* 20 vols., Allen Johnson and Dumas Malone, eds. (New York: Charles Scribner's Sons, 1928–36), vol. 7, 197–98; and Mary Tabb Johnston with Elizabeth Johnston Lipscomb, *Amelia Gayle Gorgas: A Biography* (University: Univ. of Alabama Press, 1978). Sarah Gayle's recollections of the journey from South Carolina to Alabama can be found in Sarah Haynsworth Gayle, Diary, William Stanley Hoole Special Collections, Amelia Gayle

Gorgas Library, Univ. of Alabama (henceforth *Diary*). For other discussions of the early migration to Alabama, see Weymouth T. Jordan, *Hugh Davis and His Alabama Plantation* (University: Univ. of Alabama Press, 1948); Ray Mathis, *John Horry Dent: South Carolina Aristocrat on the Alabama Frontier* (University: Univ. of Alabama Press, 1979); J. Mills Thornton, III, *Politics and Power in a Slave Society: Alabama, 1800–1860* (Baton Rouge: Louisiana State Univ. Press, 1978).

6. On Greensboro, see William E. W. Yerby and Mabel Yerby Lawson, *History of Greensboro, Alabama, from Its Earliest Settlement,* 2nd ed. (Northport, Ala.: Colonial Press, 1963). See also "John Gayle," *Dictionary of American Biography; Diary*; and Sarah Ann (Haynsworth) Gayle, Journal, Bayne and Gayle Family Papers, Southern Historical Collection, University of North Carolina at Chapel Hill (henceforth *Journal*).

7. Johnston and Lipscomb, pp. 1–9 passim; Elizabeth Fox-Genovese, *Within the Plantation Household: Black and White Women of the Old South* (Chapel Hill: Univ. of North Carolina Press, 1988), 1–28 passim.

8. For a fuller elaboration of this argument, see Fox-Genovese, *Within the Plantation Household.* For a contrasting interpretation that stresses the extent to which Southern slaveholders accepted the emerging values of bourgeois individualism beginning in the mid-eighteenth century, see Daniel Blake Smith, *Inside the Great House: Planter Family Life in Eighteenth-Century Chesapeake Society* (Ithaca: Cornell Univ. Press, 1980), and his "Autonomy and Affection: Parents and Children in Eighteenth-Century Chesapeake Families," in N. Ray Hiner and Joseph M. Hawes, eds., *Growing Up in America: Children in Historical Perspective* (Urbana: Univ. of Illinois Press, 1985), 45–58; and for the nineteenth century, see Jane Turner Censer, *North Carolina Planters and Their Children, 1800–1860* (Baton Rouge: Louisiana State Univ. Press, 1984).

9. For an elaboration of the argument, see Fox-Genovese, *Within the Plantation Household.* See also Linda K. Kerber, "Separate Spheres, Female Worlds, Woman's Place: The Rhetoric of Women's History," *Journal of American History* 75 (June 1988): 9–39; Jeanne Boydston, Mary Kelley, and Anne Margolis, *The Limits of Sisterhood: The Beecher Sisters on Women's Rights and Woman's Sphere* (Chapel Hill: Univ. of North Carolina Press, 1988); and Mary Kelley, *Private Woman, Public Stage: Literary Domesticity in Nineteenth-Century America* (New York: Oxford Univ. Press, 1984).

10. The best evidence for the familial identification of non-slaveholding women lies in religious history: sermons and, especially, church records.

11. See, especially, Thomas Roderick Dew, "Influence of Slavery on the Condition of the Female Sex," in *Review of the Debate in the Virginia Legislature of 1831 and 1832* (1832; repr. Westport, Conn.: Greenwood Press, 1970), 35–38, and his "Dissertation on the Characteristic Differences between the Sexes, and on the Position and Influence of Woman in Society," *Southern Literary Messenger* 1 (July, Aug. 1835): 621–32, 672–91; H[ershel]. V. Johnson, *Address by the Hon. H. V. Johnson, at the Commencement Exercises of the Wesleyan Female College, Macon, Georgia, on the 14th of July, 1853* (Macon: Georgia Telegraph Print, 1853); Charles Colcock Jones, *The Glory of Woman Is the Fear of the Lord* (Philadelphia: William S. Martien, 1847); William Harper, *Memoir on Slavery, Read before the Society for the Advancement of Learning at Its Annual Meeting in Columbia, 1837* (Charleston, S.C., 1838); John Fletcher, *Studies on Slavery, in Easy Lessons* (1852; repr. Miami: Mnemosyne, 1965); Frederick A. Ross, *Slavery Ordained of God* (1857; repr. Miami: Mnemosyne, 1969). And for a general development of the argument, see Eugene D. Genovese, "'Our Family, White and Black': Family and Household in the Southern Slaveholders' World View," in Carol Bleser, ed. *In Joy and in Sorrow: Women,*

Family, and Marriage in the Victorian South (New York: Oxford University Press, 1991), 69–87.

12. Elizabeth Fox-Genovese and Eugene D. Genovese, *Fruits of Merchant Capital: Slavery and Bourgeois Property in the Rise and Expansion of Capitalism* (New York: Oxford Univ. Press, 1983), ch. 11. See also Elizabeth Fox-Genovese, "Women in the Age of Enlightenment," in Renate Bridenthal, Claudia Koonz, and Susan Mosher Stuard, eds., *Becoming Visible: Women in European History,* 2nd ed. (Boston: Houghton Mifflin, 1987); Elizabeth Fox-Genovese, "Introduction," in Samia Spencer, ed., *French Women in the Age of Enlightenment* (Bloomington: Indiana Univ. Press, 1985); Smith, *Inside the Great House*; Anne L. Kuhn, *The Mother's Role in Childhood Education: New England Concepts, 1830–1860* (New Haven: Yale Univ. Press, 1947); Mary Sumner Benson, *Women in Eighteenth-Century America: A Study in Opinion and Social Usage* (New York: Columbia Univ. Press, 1935); Sylvia D. Hoffert, *Private Matters: American Attitudes toward Childbearing and Infant Nurture in the Urban North, 1800–1860* (Urbana: Univ. of Illinois Press, 1989).

13. For Sarah Gayle's papers, see Bayne and Gayle Family Papers, esp. the journal (1829–1835) and correspondence (1820) of Sarah A. (Haynsworth) Gayle, Southern Historical Collection, Univ. of North Carolina at Chapel Hill (henceforth SHC); the Gayle and Crawford Family Papers, SHC; and Sarah Haynsworth Gayle Diary (1827–1831), Hoole Special Collections, Univ. of Alabama (henceforth HSC). Citations will be to *Journal* and *Diary* respectively.

14. *Diary,* 10 Sept. 1828, HSC.

15. Ibid.

16. *Diary,* Thursday morning, n.d., 1828, HSC.

17. *Diary,* Monday, 22 [Sept.] 1828, HSC.

18. *Diary,* Saturday, 20 [Sept.] 1828, HSC.

19. Ibid.

20. Ibid.

21. Sarah Gayle to John Gayle, 19 May 1831, SHC.

22. *Diary,* 19 Feb. 1828, HSC.

23. Ibid.

24. *Diary,* 23 Feb. 1828, HSC.

25. Ibid.

26. *Diary,* 7 Mar. 1828, HSC.

27. Ibid. Her mother, Ann Haynsworth, died in 1822 at the age of 42.

28. *Diary,* 7 Mar. 1828, HSC.

29. Ibid.

30. *Diary,* 17 Apr. 1828, HSC.

31. *Diary,* 21 Apr. 1828, HSC.

32. Ibid.

33. Ibid.

34. See, for example, Nancy Chodorow, *The Reproduction of Mothering* (Berkeley: Univ. of California Press, 1978).

35. On the relations between mothers and daughters, see Fox-Genovese, *Within the Plantation Household.* On the age of wealthy Alabama women at marriage (significantly lower than wealthy Bostonian women), see Ann Williams Boucher, "Wealthy Planter Families in Nineteenth-Century Alabama" (Ph.D. dissertation, Univ. of Connecticut, 1978), esp. ch. 2; and on the general propensity of slaveholding women to marry younger than their Northern counterparts, Catherine Clinton, *The Plantation Mistress: Woman's*

World in the Old South (New York: Pantheon Books, 1982). We do not, in fact, have enough systematic studies of either age at marriage or fertility of slaveholding women throughout the antebellum South to evoke scientific precision, but the private papers of slaveholding women strongly suggest that young women were commonly marrying around, or slightly before, the age of twenty through 1860, when the age of marriage for Northeastern women had risen to twenty-four or twenty-five. Similarly, the fertility of slaveholding women seems not to have dropped as rapidly as that of Northeastern women, although among white Southern women there may have been significant variation according to class and region. On the general problem of the "demographic transition," see Robert V. Wells, "Family History and Demographic Transition," in Hiner and Hawes, eds., *Growing Up in America*, pp. 61–77.

36. *Diary,* 1827, date unclear, HSC.

37. *Diary,* 16 Dec. 1827, HSC.

38. *Diary,* 23 Dec. 1827, HSC.

39. *Diary,* 2 Dec. 1827, HSC.

40. Ibid.

41. Ibid.

42. Ibid.

43. *Diary,* 12 Jan. 1828, HSC.

44. Ibid.

45. *Diary,* 8 Mar. 1828, HSC.

46. *Diary,* 15 Jan. 1828, HSC.

47. Ibid.

48. *Diary,* 18 Jan. 1828, HSC.

49. Ibid.

50. *Journal,* 17 Nov. 1832, HSC.

51. Ibid.

52. Ibid.

53. *Diary,* 30 Dec. 1830, HSC.

54. See, e.g., Kuhn, *The Mother's Role in Childhood Education*; Benson, *Women in Eighteenth-Century America*; Hoffert, *Private Matters.*

55. Although education for slaveholding women improved considerably toward the end of the antebellum period, attendance at school typically remained brief, normally no more than a year or two. Especially during the later part of the period, young girls might episodically attend such schools as were available near their homes, but they continued to receive much of their education from their mothers and, when available, a governess or a tutor. See Catherine Clinton, "Equally Their Due: The Education of the Planter Daughter in the Early Republic," *Journal of the Early Republic* 2 (Spring 1982): 39–60; Steven M. Stowe, "City, County, and the Feminine Voice," in Michael O'Brien and David Moltke-Hansen, eds., *Intellectual Life in Antebellum Charleston* (Knoxville: Univ. of Tennessee Press, 1986), 295–325, and his "The Not-So-Cloistered Academy: Elite Women's Education and Family Feeling in the Old South," in Walter J. Fraser, Jr., R. Frank Saunders, Jr., and Jon Wakelyn, eds. *The Web of Southern Social Relations: Women, Family, and Education* (Athens: Univ. of Georgia Press, 1985), 90–106.

56. See, e.g., *Journal,* 31 June 1832, 2 July 1832, SHC. She dwells with increasing frequency on religion as she and her children get older, in part, no doubt, because of her own fears of death; in part because of her concern that her children have an adequate religious grounding with which to face the temptations of adolescence.

57. *Diary,* 7 Mar. 1828, HSC.

58. Ibid.

59. For a fuller discussion of Sarah Gayle's relations with her slaves, see *Within the Plantation Household,* pp. 20–27, and *Journal* and letters to John Gayle, 1833–35, SHC.

60. *Diary,* 15 Aug. 1830, HSC.

61. *Diary,* 5 July 1831, HSC.

62. *Diary,* 20 Nov. 1830, HSC.

63. *Diary,* 30 Oct. 1831, HSC.

64. *Diary,* Saturday night, n.d., Sept. 1830, HSC.

65. *Diary,* 30 Oct. 1831, HSC.

66. *Journal,* 13 July 1833, HSC.

67. *Diary,* 30 Oct. 1831, HSC.

68. *Diary,* Sunday n.d., Apr. 1831, HSC.

69. Augusta J. Wilson, *Beulah. A Novel* (Atlanta: Evans, Martin and Hoyt Co., 1887; first ed., 1859).

Six

Introduction to *A Blockaded Family*

Countless memoirs testify to the upheaval that the Civil War effected in the lives of Southern women, mostly those of the slaveholding class who, either during or after the war, wrote of their experiences of grief, shock, and deprivation. From Appomattox to the present, many have emphasized women's passionate devotion to the cause—their heroic sacrifices and subsequent bitterness.[1] William Faulkner epitomized this view in *Absalom, Absalom!*, where he represented Mr. Compson as saying, "Years ago we in the South made our women into ladies. Then the War came and made the ladies into ghosts. So what else can we do, being gentlemen, but listen to them being ghosts?"[2] According to this widely accepted view, the war stripped Southern women of wealth, slaves, material comfort, and, above all, the leisure necessary to fulfilling the role of lady. But in so doing it only reinforced the intensity of their identification with their region and its traditional values.[3]

However great women's disaffection in the final years of the war itself, their subsequent accounts of it suggest that even the humiliation of defeat did not seriously undermine their loyalty to their region, and probably strengthened it. The rash of Southern women's diaries and memoirs published during the fifty years after 1865 read overwhelmingly like the seedbed of the nostalgic plantation novels in the manner of Thomas Nelson Page and his successors. Diary-keeping was nothing new for Southern women. Innumerable antebellum Southern women had kept diaries and journals or even written memoirs but rarely published them. Normally, they wrote in a tone

Introduction to *A Blockaded Family: Life in Southern Alabama during the Civil War*, by Parthenia Antoinette Hague, ix–xxviii. Lincoln: University of Nebraska Press, 1991. Copyright 1991 by the University of Alabama Press. All rights reserved. Used by permission of the current copyright holder, University of Alabama Press.

that clearly reflected their primary purpose of leaving an account of their lives—and frequently their souls—for their daughters or other kin.[4]

After the war, the tone of the diaries, journals, and memoirs shifted dramatically. In the first instance, many of the diarists and memorialists were writing explicitly for publication, frequently out of the desire to make some money to contribute to depleted family fortunes.[5] In the second, the vast majority of them were also writing to justify themselves and their region to the Northern readers, who still accounted for the majority of book buyers. These writings contributed mightily to the "moonlight and magnolia" view of slavery, as they did to the sanctification of the memory of the "lost cause" and "our boys in grey." In the most romanticized versions of this tradition, gracious ladies and dashing cavaliers frequent white columned mansions set among lush grounds. Happy, attentive slaves respond eagerly to the least wish of paternalistic slaveholders. Modern cynicism has stripped this image of much of its glamor, insisting upon the crude conditions that prevailed throughout much of the slaveholding South, insisting above all upon the slaves' resistance to their own enslavement and commitment to freedom. Many have even argued that elite Southern women themselves should be counted among the secret opponents of the system. Neither the myth nor the demystification serves well.

Parthenia Antoinette (Vardaman) Hague may or may not have ranked among the ladies of the slaveholding elite by birth. Born November 29, 1838, to Thomas Butts and Emily Adeline (Evans) Vardaman, she grew up in Hamilton, in Harris County, Georgia, and completed her education at Hamilton Academy.[6] She says nothing specific about the size of her father's household, or the number of slaves he owned, but he appears to have been a modestly successful, if not large, slaveholder, who served as high sheriff of Harris County.[7] And, as a girl, Parthenia certainly had some acquaintance with substantial slaveholding, for Harris County lay securely in the Georgia piedmont plantation district and included 7,166 whites and 6,972 blacks. The town of Hamilton, near which the family lived, was, like so many other Southern towns, very small, with a population of only four hundred.[8]

Parthenia grew up as the second child and the oldest daughter in a large family of eleven children, although she here refers only to her three brothers who fought in the war.[9] After completing her education, presumably in the late 1850s, she moved to Alabama, where she would live during and after the war, to teach in a school near Hurtville. There, she lived in the wealthy plantation district near Eufala with an apparently prosperous slaveholding family.

A Blockaded Family testifies to considerable literary accomplishment that reflects both family background and education, although we cannot be sure that she was as accomplished in the early 1860s as she was at the time she wrote. She was both cultured and well read, although she may not have read everything to which she refers until after the time about which she is writing. *A Blockaded Family* abounds with references to Christianity and the Bible, which suggest that Hague, like many other Southern women, took her faith seriously and turned to it for explanations of the most dramatic events in human affairs. She attended the Mount Olive Baptist Church in Harris County with her family and may well have been a member. Her specific religious attitudes and church affiliation during the years of the blockade remain unclear, but she seems to have been reared in a strong Protestant tradition and her frequent biblical quotations apparently derive from early habits of Bible reading.[10] By the time she wrote *A Blockaded Family*, she identified closely with a nostalgic, elite postbellum view of antebellum life and values.

Hague laces her account with lavish descriptions of the beauty of the Southern countryside. Her rhetorical strategy links her account to the work of innumerable Southern women novelists, notably that of Augusta Evans Wilson.[11] She dwells lovingly upon the beauties of the trees, of the Spanish moss peculiar to the region, the soft aroma of the pines, the flowers, the fruits, and much more; and she carefully associates the feelings of the people with whom she sympathizes with nature in all its abundance. In a similar spirit, she associates the outbreak of war with a fierce, gathering storm. While returning to Alabama by train in 1861, she saw through the window "the dark green gloom of the almost unbroken forest, the low wail of the wind in the tops of the pines, the lowering dark clouds dimly outlined through the shaded vista." This prospect burdened her heart with a great sorrow, exacerbated by "the faraway mutterings of thunder." The moaning of the wind fell upon her ears like the wail of a banshee. "All seemed to presage some dire affliction" (see p. 6).

However sympathetic and romantic, Parthenia Hague's views of the harmony of antebellum slaveholding society do not rest on a glossy picture of luxurious living. Early in her account she describes the house of her "generous employer" as "in every respect the characteristic Southern home, with its wide halls, long and broad colonnade, large and airy rooms, the yard a park in itself, fruits and flowers abounding" (p. 13). Writing of the war, she focuses primarily on the prevalence of suffering and material hardship, although her detailed chronicle suggests a high antebellum standard of living. As an author, she manifests a strong determination to justify the ways and values of the South to Northern readers. She wants her readers to appreciate what Southerners suffered; even more she wants them to understand Southerners' motivations and virtues. Although she evokes some of the familiar themes of Southern gallantry and graciousness, and although she paints the most conventionally rosy picture imaginable of the happy relations between slaveholders and slaves, she focuses above all on the virtues of ingenuity, industry, and patriotism.

Hague devotes the largest part of her memoir to minute descriptions of the ways in which she and the other members of the household coped with the deepening scarcities that resulted from the blockade. As a result, she offers an extraordinarily detailed picture of household production—a topic that many antebellum women diarists passed over lightly.[12] Her memoir thus provides a rare glimpse, from a woman's perspective, of the full activities of a slaveholding household.[13] Possibly her own background made her more willing to accept and understand extensive domestic production than more elite slaveholding women, who had rarely, if ever, actually worked at it themselves. But if experience had prepared her to grasp a wide range of productive activities—and we do not know that it did—conviction almost certainly fueled her commitment to describing it in such appreciative detail.

Hague especially sought to underscore the inventiveness and industry of her compatriots, who had demonstrated their ability to survive under extreme adversity. With a telling rhetorical flourish, she claims that if instead of being hedged in by the blockade, they had been surrounded by "a wall as thick and high as the great Chinese Wall," they would not "suffer intolerable inconvenience, but live as happily as Adam and Eve in the Garden of Eden before they tasted the forbidden fruit" (p. 110). Having given up luxuries, and even simple comforts, they were, with the crudest of resources, proving their ability to feed and clothe the people of the South. "We felt all the more pride," she notes, "when we remembered that at the beginning of hostilities we were unprepared in almost every essential necessary to the existence of our Confederacy; yet now, the best part of two years had gone, and the South was holding her own" (p. 111).

The analogy to the Garden of Eve figures as one of her many reminders of the essential innocence of the Southerners in a conflict she portrays as forced upon them. Upon first hearing word of Georgia's secession—"my native State, one of the original thirteen of revolutionary fame"—she confesses that she felt a certain sadness. No one, she periodically insists, loved the Union more than she. But almost immediately, an unpleasant recollection "rushed to mind, which caused me to think that perhaps, after all, secession was not so very bad." She remembered a temperance lecturer from New England who, having been warmly received and welcomed, betrayed the trust of his unsuspecting hosts. No one thought that "his one sole purpose was to make a secret survey of our county, to ascertain which settlements were most densely populated with slaves, for the already maturing uprising of the blacks against the whites" (p. 4).

No, the Southern white people cannot fairly be blamed either for forsaking the Union or for the war. No less than the Northerners did they love the Union, but who can fail to understand that "when a political party, with no love in its heart for the Southern white people, came into power, a party, which we believed felt that the people of the South were fit only for the pikes hidden at Harper's Ferry, we should have cried out, 'What part have we in David? to your tents, O Israel'" (pp. 3–4).

Writing years after the fact, she cheers herself with the reflection that their "deeds and intentions have one great Judge, who will say, 'Neither do I condemn thee'" (p. 4). And, in conclusion, Hague returns to the theme. Today, she insists, the people of the South are loyal to the Union, loyal to the very fibers of their beings. "Accepting all the decisions of the war, we have built and planted anew amid the ruins left by the army who were the conquerors" (p. 176). They may still be poor, but believe themselves to be destined by God "to a brilliant career of prosperity and glory" (p. 176).

In building their future, Southerners will be able to draw on the virtues that sustained them through the war and blockade: industry, ingenuity, determination, and good cheer. Hague's account of the range and intricacy of household production during the war retains great intrinsic interest as a source of information on the kinds of goods white Southerners considered necessary and on the materials and skills that were available locally. It also serves as a running testimony to Southern character. Before the war "there were none, even the wealthiest, who had not been taught that labor was honorable, and who had very clear ideas of how work must be done." The advent of disaster found none of them "wanting in any of the qualities necessary for our changed circumstances" (p. 14).

From Lincoln's initial proclamation of the naval blockade of the Confederacy on 19 April 1861 until the fall of Mobile on 23 August 1864, South Alabama felt the growing pinch. Given the long range of coast to be cordoned and the initial weakness of the Northern navy, the blockade did not immediately take maximum effect, although as early as the summer of 1861 Southerners were complaining of its effects.[14] But in September 1861 Northern forces took possession of Ship Island, which lies halfway between Mobile and New Orleans, and by the summer of 1862 most of the Southern ports were closed. Thus, although the battle of Mobile Bay did not occur until August 1864, South Alabama spent the years of the war effectively cut off from its normal markets and sources of supplies.

Until the outbreak of war, South Alabama, where, Hague insists, cotton indeed had been king, had depended upon the North for "almost everything eaten and worn" (p. 15). In South Alabama in particular, even the cultivation of cereals had been rare. Overnight, so it seemed, everything changed and people throughout the South "put hands to the plow" (p. 16). Our planters, she notes, "set about in earnest to grow wheat, rye, rice, oats, corn, peas, pumpkins, and ground peas" not to mention the "chufa," a thing she had never heard of before (p. 17). Here, as elsewhere throughout her account, Hague engages in something of a sleight of hand. It is safe to assume, especially during the years before emancipation, that large planters like her generous host no more set their hands to the plow after the beginning of the war than they had before it. It is also safe to assume that throughout much of the lower South—although less on large plantations that lay close to water transport—many households cultivated many crops besides cotton and were reasonably accustomed to providing for a sizeable share of their own basic foodstuffs.[15]

The shift imposed by war and blockade was, nonetheless, dramatic, and the wealthier the planter the greater it was likely to have been. In passing, Hague notes her amazement at one day finding a woman, whose husband and sons were away in the army, doing her own threshing. "There she sat, a sheaf of wheat held with both hands, and with this she was vigorously belaboring the barrel, at every stroke a shower of wheat-grains raining down upon quilts and coverlets" (p. 23). Hague's surprise reflects her own experience. Women of slaveholding households might never have witnessed threshing and assuredly would not have threshed themselves before the war; even during the war they almost certainly were not called upon to thresh. But the woman whose behavior so astounded Hague lived in a small cottage, appears to have owned no slaves, had undoubtedly seen threshing before the war, and may, conceivably, have helped with it herself.

The women of the slaveholding household within which Hague lived were never called upon to thresh, but they did rapidly turn their hands to a wide range of tasks of which they presumably had no previous experience. An excellent observer, Hague carefully details the wide range of new activities undertaken within the slaveholding household. Her extensive list of goods that had previously been purchased and were now produced within the household, or for which homemade substitutes were developed, includes agricultural products such as goobers, bolted meal, candles, coffee, tea, starch, castor oil, quinine, opium, and bicarbonate of soda. The members of the household also engaged in extensive domestic production: tanning, weaving, carding, spinning, dyeing, sewing, knitting, hat-making.

Clearly Hague paid surprisingly close attention to a large number of activities, but she reserves her most meticulous descriptions for the various aspects of textile production in which she participated directly. From the very beginning of the blockade, she writes, sewing machines fell into disuse because they could not accommodate the homemade thread upon which the household was forced to rely. Under the new conditions, household textile production had to provide for all of the members of the household, white as well as black. The white ladies who presumably had been accustomed only to fine sewing now had to turn their skills to spinning, carding, weaving, and dyeing if they were to have anything new to wear at all. In addition, Hague insists, they had to provide for the needs of the slaves.

Hague takes visible pride in the skills that she and the other white women developed. She proudly and lovingly describes their spinning, their selection of natural dyes, their experimentation with weaving, and their ultimate ability to produce a pretty plaid or striped homespun. Finding even the most attractive homespun too warm for the steamy Southern months, they improvised a way to make a simple muslin. They knitted and crocheted slippers and shoes as well as shawls, gloves, capes, sacques, and hoods. They learned to make palmetto hats from straw. The appearance in the local store of an unexpected shipment of calico and leather slippers poignantly reminds them of the limitations of their efforts, but her pride in what they did accomplish does not flag.

Throughout, Hague stresses the novelty of their work and their pleasure in newly developed skills. But her enthusiasm for the white women's accomplishments probably obscures a longstanding tradition of household textile work. It is doubtful that the household would have had the tools—wheels, looms—of textile production at the outbreak of hostilities if some household members had not been using them all along. The narratives of former slaves and the day-books of planters from throughout the South strongly suggest that, in most slaveholding households during the entire antebellum period, slave women were regularly spinning, carding, and weaving. The evidence also suggests that many slave women had a sophisticated knowledge of dyes, which they used primarily in making their families' Sunday clothes.[16]

Many slaveholding women had their own textile skills, primarily in fine, light sewing and in the cutting of the material for the slaves' clothes, but few had much knowledge of spinning and weaving. The cloth for their clothing was purchased. Suddenly confronted with the necessity to produce cloth for their own clothing, or do without new clothing, slaveholding women turned to slave women for instruction in skills that they had never expected to need. That Hague never mentions such instruction does not mean that it did not occur. Just as her reference to planters' putting their hands to the plow obscures the labor of the slaves who did the actual field work, so her reference to slaveholding women's textile work probably obscures the role of slave women in introducing them to new skills.

A complex combination of antebellum proslavery thought and postbellum racism permeates *A Blockaded Family.* From the initial pages, Hague leaves no doubt that she views slavery as a benevolent social system. During her return to Alabama at the beginning of the narrative, a severe storm forces her to stay over in Hurtville, where she is graciously welcomed into the home of a former school friend, Winnie. During her stay, she fondly remembers, she had occasion to witness the marriage of "one of the negro girls of the house." The memory includes the image of herself sitting on the colonnade with Winnie, "flowers scattered all around, our laps and hands full," twining "the wreath for the negro girl, the bride elect for the evening." When the moment finally came for the bride to dress, Winnie "pulled off her own watch and chain, together with her bracelets, and with these further adorned the bride," who was then married in the house in which she had been raised "almost from her cradle" (p. 8). The supper that followed and that had been prepared under the direct supervision of the mistress of the house "would have been pleasing to the taste of an epicure" (p. 9).

The chain of memory leads Hague from the wedding back to an earlier occasion on which Uncle Sol Mitchell, "a member and preacher in good standing in the Mount Olive Church" in Harris County, preached to the congregation with never a shadow of objection from any of the whites who were present. All joined with special effort in the singing and, remembering how, at his invitation, they knelt together to pray, she avows herself "very sure I have never knelt with more humble devotion and reverence than on that same Sabbath morning" (p. 11).

Today, it is easy to dismiss such claims and self-serving platitudes, designed to justify blatant racism and oppression. Many modern readers have found it easy to conflate such justifications of slavery with the unrealistically glamorized image of antebellum Southern society and to dismiss both out of hand. *A Blockaded Family* assuredly offers scant grounds for questioning Hague's racism. Wondering about the speed with which Southerners adapted to the great changes thrust upon them, she explains their success by reminding herself (and her readers) "that the Southerners who were so reduced and so compelled to rely entirely upon their own resources belonged to the Anglo-Saxon race, a race which, despite all prating about 'race equality,' has civilized America" (p. 97).

Racism notwithstanding, she insists upon the whites' acute sense of responsibility to the blacks who fell to their charge. The world she paints is one in which all members know and accept their place. To the slaves accrue the duties of loyalty and service; to the slaveholders accrue the complementary duties of care and protection. "During the war when bacon was very scarce," she insists, "it often happened that the white household would deny themselves meat to eat, so as to give it to the slaves, as they had to toil in the field" (p. 120). Nor, throughout the ordeal, would the slaveholders ever let their slaves want for proper clothing.

If such assertions try a modern reader's credulity, they should nonetheless be taken less as the measure of actual practice than as testimonials to the slaveholding ideal. Hague assuredly knew that the ideal was as likely to be observed in the breach as in the practice. The shortages that prevailed during the war affected the slaves as much as or more than the whites. By the time that Hague was writing in the late 1880s, an increasingly virulent racism was replacing whatever remained of the slaveholders' paternalistic ideals. That racism arose from the ashes of defeat and economic ruin and throve even as the signs of an emerging "new South" began to make themselves felt. Defeat and recovery alike imposed their own strains upon Southern society, increasingly dividing Southerners among themselves.

The myth of moonlight and magnolias, to which Hague in many ways contributes, sought to establish a specific version of the Southern past as the common legacy of all. Hague hints at this element of Southern unity when she writes that the war drew Southerners of all ranks into "a closer union, a tenderer feeling of humanity linking us all together, both rich and poor; from the princely planter, who could scarce get off his wide domains in a day's ride, and who could count his slaves by the thousand, down to the humble tenants of the log-cabin on rented or leased land" (pp. 107–8).

Hindsight may here have led Hague into an overly rosy picture. In many respects, Southern unity proved remarkable, but, as the war went badly, fissures inevitably appeared. The pressures on the yeomanry especially increased as men found that the wives and daughters they had left were frequently unable to get in the crop and began to go hungry. Resentment raged in many quarters against wealthy planters' ability to buy replacements for military service. Experiencing the war from within the relative security of a wealthy slaveholding household, Hague may have confused the travails of putting up with shortages and homemade substitutes with absolute want. Quite possibly, the yeoman women whose threshing she observed would have seen things in a different light. Certainly the many slaves who deserted their masters as soon as the opportunity arose did.

A Blockaded Family unmistakably reflects the concerns of a white Southern woman in the period in which it was written and, in this respect, offers another valuable testimonial to the ways in which white Southern women constructed an ideal of Southern regional identity on the basis of a specific memory of the war. At the same time, it offers an extraordinarily detailed and accurate account of the household production that assumed a growing place in Southern life during the war. In combining these two strands, Hague skillfully constructs an image of elite Southern whites as, in essential ways, very much like their Northern peers: industrious, resourceful, devoted to their families, and loyal to the Union.

The dire affliction that Hague chronicles tested and chastened the Southern people, but never broke their spirit. *A Blockaded Family* quietly, but firmly, defends the Southern position in the war, from secession to the treatment of prisoners. It no less firmly holds some Northerners accountable for the pain that both sides suffered. And it implicitly suggests that the restored Union must embody a large measure of the resourcefulness and virtue that carried the Southerners so gallantly through their ordeal.

Notes

1. For the most recent comprehensive account, see George Rable, *Civil Wars: Women and the Crisis of Southern Nationalism* (Urbana: University of Illinois Press, 1989).

2. William Faulkner, *Absalom, Absalom!* (New York: Modern Library, 1936), p. 12.

3. Recently, Drew Faust has argued that the progress of the war ultimately stripped them of even that identification, turning them into bitter internal enemies. Faust, like others, emphasizing the immense human loss and the toll of material scarcity, concludes that by the final years of the war women had had enough and wanted peace at any cost. Drew Faust, "Altars of Sacrifice: Confederate Women and the Narratives of War," *Journal of American History* 76 (March 1990): 1200–28.

4. See Elizabeth Fox-Genovese, *Within the Plantation Household: Black and White Women of the Old South* (Chapel Hill: University of North Carolina Press, 1988).

5. See, for example, Elisabeth Muhlenfeld's fine biography, *Mary Boykin Chesnut: A Biography* (Baton Rouge: Louisiana State University Press, 1981).

6. Thomas McAdory Owen, *History of Alabama and Dictionary of Alabama Biography*, 4 vols., vol III (Chicago: S. J. Clarke Publishing Co., 1921), 720.

7. His position as high sheriff provides no necessary indication of the extent of his slaveholding. I am assuming that had he been a very large slaveholder she would not have taken a position as a teacher and had he been a non-slaveholder she would probably not have attended the academy.

8. George White, *Statistics of the State of Georgia* . . . (Savannah: W. Thorne Williams, 1849; reprint, Spartanburg, S.C.: Reprint Co., 1972), 317–20.

9. Letter from Parthenia Antoinette Hague to her niece, Emily, 10 September 1904, in the private possession of one of her descendants, Erin A. Muths.

10. Elizabeth Fox-Genovese, "Religion in the Lives of Slaveholding Women of the Antebellum South," in *That Gentle Strength: Historical Perspectives on Women in Christianity*, ed. Lynda L. Coon, Katherine J. Haldane, and Elisabeth W. Sommer (Charlottesville: University Press of Virginia, 1990), pp. 207–29. For a general discussion of religion in the lives of Southern women, see Jean E. Friedman, *The Enclosed Garden: Women and Community in the Evangelical South, 1830–1900* (Chapel Hill: University of North Carolina Press, 1985).

11. See, especially, Augusta J. Evans, *Beulah. A Novel* (Atlanta, 1887; first ed., 1859).

12. See Fox-Genovese, *Within the Plantation Household*.

13. For antebellum accounts, see, among many, W. Emerson Wilson, ed., *Plantation Life at Rose Hill: The Diaries of Martha Ogle Forman, 1814–1845* (Wilmington, Del.:

Scholarly Resources, 1976); and Mary Steele Ferrand Henderson Journal, John Steele Henderson Papers, Southern Historical Collection, University of North Carolina Library.

14. See C. Vann Woodward, ed., *Mary Chesnut's Civil War* (New Haven, Conn.: Yale University Press, 1981), p. 101.

15. Fox-Genovese, *Within the Plantation Household*; Sam Bowers Hilliard, *Hog Meat and Hoe Cake: Food Supply in the Old South, 1840–1860* (Carbondale, Ill.: Southern Illinois University Press, 1972); Eugene D. Genovese, *The Political Economy of Slavery: Studies in the Economy and Society of the Old South* (New York: Pantheon Books, 1965).

16. See Fox-Genovese, *Within the Plantation Household*.

Seven

Foreword to *Parlor Ladies* and *Ebony Drudges*

Throughout history, the everyday lives of ordinary women have provided the glue that holds families, communities, and societies together. Until recently, however, most historians virtually ignored these lives, presumably on the grounds that they have been so unremarkable as to defy sustained attention or comment. It is as if historians, focusing upon the drama of war, politics, and social struggles, simply did not "see" the women who always and everywhere have formed the bedrock of social life. During the past few decades, social historians and women's historians have done much to rectify this neglect. Indeed, much recent historical scholarship has tended to reverse former priorities and to privilege the experience of such previously marginalized groups as women, blacks, and working people. The proliferation of women's and African American history has directed our attention to a wealth of new information, experiences, and questions. This work establishes a context for Kibibi Voloria Mack's engaging exploration of the working lives of the black women of Orangeburg, South Carolina. But *Parlor Ladies and Ebony Drudges* does not simply fill in another piece of the mosaic that women's historians have been assembling. Raising new questions, it offers a fresh perspective on the history of African American women and invites us to follow new paths of inquiry.

In these pages, we meet an arresting group of Southern black women who fashioned lives, nurtured families, and built communities within the

Foreword to *Parlor Ladies and Ebony Drudges: African American Women, Class, and Work in a South Carolina Community,* edited by Kibibi Voloria C. Mack, xiii–xviii. Knoxville: University of Tennessee Press, 1999. Copyright 1999 by the University of Tennessee Press. All rights reserved. Used by permission of the publisher.

frequently draconian constraints of the Jim Crow South. On Mack's showing, work—hard work—runs like a unifying thread through many black women's lives, for work most of them did labor. But, as she unflinchingly insists, not all. In the wake of the Civil War and Reconstruction, an African American elite emerged in Orangeburg, as in other cities, and its women did not share the fate of their less-privileged sisters. Not only did they not work themselves, but they had servants to relieve them of the household labor that figured so prominently in most women's lives. Labor, Mack nonetheless insists, defined most black women's lives, and it ranked high among their— and other African Americans'—contributions to the development of their city, their region, and the country as a whole. From the earliest slave ship landings in the seventeenth century until the present, black people have labored in the service of their own people and others, virtually in every occupation and at every conceivable task. Until the end of the Civil War, the vast majority lived in legal bondage and labored under coercion. Even after emancipation, the majority continued to labor under coercion—or as much coercion as the laws of the market, tenancy, share-cropping, and segregation could impose upon them. The command, coercion, and extortion of black labor has cast a long shadow over African American history, and historians have, perforce, regularly paid black labor its due. Dr. W. E. B. Du Bois himself established the model and set the tone, organizing and directing a series of pathbreaking monographs on Southern black labor, which culminated in his own monumental *Black Reconstruction in America*.

Du Bois especially, if somewhat romantically, underscored the centrality of black women's labor to the life of their people. Most memorably, in *Darkwater: Voices from Within the Veil*, he wrote, "As I look about me today in this veiled world of mine, despite the noisier and more spectacular advance of my brothers, I instinctively feel and know that it is the five million women of my race who really count. . . . If we have today, as seems likely, over a billion dollars of accumulated goods, who shall say how much of it has been wrung from the hearts of servant girls and washerwomen and women toilers in the fields? As makers of two million homes these women are today seeking in marvelous ways to show forth our strength and beauty and our conception of the truth." Labor, Du Bois insisted time and again, constituted the very fabric of black women's lives; labor underwrote their irreplaceable contributions to their families, communities, and people. These "black women toil and toil hard," and in proportionately larger numbers than their white "sisters"—"over half of the colored female population as against a fifth in the case of white women." They "are a group of workers, fighting for their daily bread like men; independent and approaching economic freedom!" Although the emergence of women's history focused new attention upon women's work in general, the work of African American women in particular remained largely in shadow, not least because of the apparent paucity of sources. Studies published since the 1980s have gradually brought black women's work into sharper relief, but much of this scholarship has primarily attended to their work in the rural South, during and after slavery. That women's work was unremitting and hard cannot be doubted. Much of it, especially work in the fields of others, tore black women from the work for their own families, which both they and their husbands and children strongly preferred. Following the tone set by Du Bois, these studies have gradually brought a picture of rural black women's lives and labor into focus. But the lives of urban black women, especially those whose class position freed them from obligatory work, has largely remained in shadow. Only slowly and intermittently have a few historians begun to illuminate the lives and work of women in cities and towns, including those of nurses, teachers, librarians, and social workers. Here, Darlene Clark Hine and Stephanie Shaw have opened promising new lines of inquiry even as they have broadened our understanding of the intricate tapestry of black women's work.

In *Parlor Ladies and Ebony Drudges,* Mack clarifies and impressively deepens this understanding by exploring the work and working lives of black women in a New South Carolina city between 1880 and 1940. Above all, she locates the black women of a small Southern city within an intricate social network that not merely distinguished between blacks and whites, but among blacks themselves according to the complex calculus of class. Mack divides the black women of Orangeburg into three main social classes: working class, middle class, and upper class. Not surprisingly, the vast majority of Orangeburg's African American women belonged to the working class, and work dominated and structured their lives, primarily in agricultural and domestic employment. Middle-class women, in contrast, had more opportunity to work in their own homes even when they were working for wages, and the women of the small upper-class elite did not typically have to work at all. In evoking women's experience and perceptions of their work, Mack draws heavily upon interviews with women from the Orangeburg African American community, and her use of the women's voices and perceptions endows her account with a compelling immediacy. These oral histories and interviews also illuminate the women's own perceptions of the social stratification of the black community, even as they help to explain the women's goals for themselves and their children.

Mack explicitly disclaims any intention of providing a full socioeconomic analysis of Orangeburg's African American community, insisting that her primary commitment is to bring the experience of individuals to life. Yet, in so doing, she simultaneously brings to life the dynamics of class relations and the cultural norms that informed and structured them. Color, she frequently reminds us, played a decisive role in the articulation of class position. For, in the absence of evidence to the contrary, it was widely assumed that the lighter a person's skin and the straighter their hair, the more likely they were to belong to the elite. Indeed, in the interest of consolidating the external representation of social status, elite men as well as women were known to pursue products and treatments that would "improve" both the texture of their hair and the color of their skin. A woman's ability to pass the fabled "brown bag test" (to have a complexion no darker than a brown paper bag) did not alone guarantee her access to the upper class, but an inability to pass that test would seriously cripple her prospects of making the "best" possible marriage and might even result in some loss in social status. Most women's status did primarily depend upon family connection: the status of the woman's family of origin and of the husband with whom she started her own family. In the world of Orangeburg, an upper-class woman might never marry, but most who did not continued to live with one or another family member rather than on their own. Unmarried women's tendency to reside with family implicitly underscores the importance of family relations and community sensibilities in defining a woman's status, for many—perhaps most—of the women who remained single were capable of supporting themselves. Thus the decision to live within the web of the family apparently had more to do with social and cultural than economic considerations.

The social and cultural dimensions of class figure prominently in the lives of all of Orangeburg's African American women. Mack skillfully draws out the threads of these social and cultural sensibilities, weaving them into an arresting, if sometimes disconcerting, picture of women's role in the formation and perpetuation of the black community. In the case of religion, for example, she shows that while the mass of working women belonged to Baptist and Pentecostal churches, the women of the upper class strongly favored the Episcopalian, AME, or Presbyterian churches. Indeed, she reports one unkind speculation that the women of the African American elite would have preferred to endure segregated seating in an acceptably fashionable church rather than rub shoulders with their less-affluent brothers and sisters among the Baptists.

Social distinctions in church membership and religious observance are assuredly not unique to the African American community: white folks have cultivated them since time immemorial. But Mack's forthright evocation of them, like her forthright evocation of the preoccupation with color as a social marker, serves an important purpose. For if Mack occasionally betrays a hint of impatience with the pretensions of the elite, she also displays a nuanced understanding of their motivations. This was an elite that over-whelmingly depended for its status upon the income of the male head of the household and, in almost all instances, that income depended upon the man's earnings from an occupation or profession. Or, to put the matter differently, this was not an elite that enjoyed the security of substantial inherited wealth. Elite status was not given but had to be re-created continually and sustained by work. Under these conditions, it was understandable—if not admirable—that those who had worked their way to the top would use all of the resources at their command to sustain their position.

Among those resources, none seems to have ranked higher than education. Orangeburg's African American elite placed a high value upon education, which it not merely viewed as a mark of distinction, but exploited as an important buttress of its own position. Mack illuminates the ways in which Claflin University served as a reservoir of opportunity for elite African Americans, who increasingly monopolized the opportunities it afforded. For if Claflin provided affluent African Americans with an advanced education, it also provided them with professional employment (and attendant salaries) and, over time, with private primary and secondary education for their children. Not until 1937 did Orangeburg provide a public high school that black people could attend, which meant that the large majority of Orangeburg's blacks, who could not dream of private school for their children, had to forgo all prospect of secondary education. This situation further strengthened the elite's grip on its privileged status and enhanced its ability to deflect aspiring members from its ranks.

These conditions may help to explain why a majority of working-class African American women tended to discourage educational aspirations in their own children. But their lack of interest in pushing their children toward educational attainments also reflected severe economic constraints. Like many working people throughout the country, especially recent immigrants, they knew that their family could not give up the economic contribution of any one of its members. In their eyes, paid work trumped education every time, and as soon as a child was old enough to earn a wage, he or she should do so. The prospects and priorities of middle-class African Americans predictably fell between these two extremes and varied according to a myriad of accidents and external circumstances. Members of the middle class could reasonably aspire to more education and greater stability and respectability than their working-class brothers and sisters, but in the essential respect of women's work, their experience more closely resembled that of the working class than of the elite. The women of Orangeburg's African American middle class worked out of necessity, and without their work their families would have had no hope of sustaining their middle-class status. But unlike their working-class sisters, middle-class women did not typically work in the fields or in the homes of other people. And although some remained close to domestic labor, working in their own homes as seamstresses or laundresses, others moved into a variety of white- and pink-collar occupations. Mack brings us the voices of women from all of these groups as well as those of many of their descendants. Their accounts of their working lives evoke the rich texture of their experience, including hardships and disappointments, and readers will come away from this book with a new appreciation of African American women's humor, vitality, and courage. The book as a whole, however, does not invite complacent romanticization. For, as Mack firmly reminds us, the relations among African American women of different classes do not suggest an all-encompassing sisterhood. Women played an important part in the differentiation among social classes and in the defense of social stratification. Perhaps more than anything, Mack demonstrates that the ultimate respect for African American women requires us to view their history with the same combination of admiration and criticism with which we view the history of any other group of women. If women indeed provide the glue of families, communities, and societies, they deserve their fair share of credit for the bad as well as the good that those groups have wrought. This thoughtful and illuminating book ushers us into a world and a dimension of women's experience that has too long remained shrouded and even unsuspected. It introduces us to the texture of African American women's lives in a small Southern city and to the values and allegiances that endowed those lives with purpose and meaning. Kibibi Voloria Mack's evocation of these lives decisively broadens our understanding of African American women's history to which it makes a valuable and welcome contribution. More, it gently challenges us to expand and deepen our understanding of American women's history.

Part Two

Women—Redefining
Southern Culture

Eight

Kate Chopin's Awakening

Recent critical attention has taught us to read Kate Chopin's *The Awakening* as a courageous and honest statement about unfolding female sexuality, as a searing critique of woman's place in patriarchal bourgeois society, as a female version of that realism embodied in the works of Theodore Dreiser. We have been encouraged to recognize Edna Pontellier as a martyr to repressive social codes, and her creator as no less one. The currents of modern feminism and the freer attitudes towards female sexuality have been quick to welcome Chopin and her ill-fated heroine as sister-victims to dominant male attitudes of possession that cast women as property and mothers but permit them no space for personal independence. Judith Fryer has even celebrated Edna as the quintessential new woman who "*chooses* to die" and her suicide as "part of her awakening, the ultimate act of free will."[1]

These feminist and liberationist readings have not prevailed without some modification. Psychological insights have been mustered to suggest the conflict between "*eros* and *thanatos*" that pervades the novel, to highlight the "motherlessness" captured in one of the two narrative stances, and to suggest the tension between the role models proffered by Mlle. Reisz and Mme. Ratignolle respectively. But even the subtlest and most intelligent of these readings has not fully captured the contradictions that inform—indeed constitute—the structure and dynamic of the novel.[2]

The Awakening (1899) presents a brief twenty-eight-year-old married woman's discovery of love and sexual passion and her rebellion against the marital codes and institutions of her society.[3] The first fifty of the novel's one hundred and twenty pages are set in Grand Isle, a summer resort for comfortable New Orleans residents. The remainder of the novel, with the exception of the last chapter—a return to Grand Isle—is set in New Orleans. During the period in Grand Isle, Edna Pontellier, wife of Leonce Pontellier and mother of two young sons, falls in love with Robert Lebrun, unmarried son of the proprietress of the resort and resident cavalier. Edna also learns to swim. Upon her return to New Orleans, she embarks upon a disengagement from her previous life as the respectable wife of a prosperous Creole businessman. Her progressive steps—including regular cultivation of her painting, taking a lover, and moving out of her husband's house—lead to greater self-confidence and independence in the living of her life but do not assuage or supersede her love for Robert. His return from Mexico, whence he had gone on business to escape Edna's dawning love, triggers an emotional crisis that leads her to return to Grand Isle and to swim to her death.

On this bare frame, Chopin hangs a complex tapestry of interlocking threads. She depicts Edna's relationships with other women—most important her friend the "mother-woman" Adele Ratignolle and the pianist Mlle. Reisz, but also Robert's mother, Mme. Lebrun, and a faster set of socially dubious matrons—and a number of men, including Edna's father, Mr. Ratignolle, Dr. Mandelet, Robert's wild brother Victor, and Edna's lover Alcée Arobin. She also sketches Edna's past, identifying her two living sisters, Margaret and Janet, and barely evoking her mother who died in Edna's youth. Where precision of detail is called for, she fills in the origins, cultural attitudes, and speech patterns of the characters. Thus, her sure touch firmly establishes the particularities of the various social groups among the New Orleans Creoles and delineates Edna's own more Northern and Puritanical—specifically Kentucky—roots. Edna, the "American," emerges as something of an outsider in a world the social codes and attitudes of which remain learned, rather than instinctive, to her.

The point of *The Awakening* lies in its ending. Edna's suicide organizes everything that precedes it. But that retroactive perspective does not suffice to explain the suicide. From what does Edna's self-destruction arise? At what point does it become inevitable? Why did Chopin settle upon that particular outcome? Is Fryer justified in labeling the suicide an "act of free will" and discerning in it a manifestation of independence? Could Chopin, herself a Catholic, be expected to equate suicide with triumph or maturity? Conversely, can the suicide be dismissed as the defeat of a weak spirit? Or be understood as the iniquitous price an oppressive society extracts for the least fluttering of female selfhood? Do the causes of the suicide lie in Edna's character and are they, thus, given from the opening of the tale, or do they emerge from the actions and interactions of the plot? At what level of time and plot can the suicide best be understood and explained? And what narrative, metaphoric, or psychological truth does it serve?

These questions do not permit easy answers, but the answers selected govern the reading of the novel as a whole. In my judgment, the suicide must be understood on the two levels of accidental temporal sequence and necessary psychological permanence. The suicide provides the pivot for a double reading of Chopin's text: readings with and without knowledge of the ending. The technique of over-privileging the ending derived from Chopin's practice as a writer of short stories. In moving to the novel, she never relinquished that practice which permitted her to set forth an ambiguous truth about the human condition. She specialized in calling attention to the disjuncture between appearance and reality. Particularly in *The Awakening*, however, she refused a decisive choice between the claims of appearance and reality. In her work, the appearance normally includes social institutions as well as the surface of events, whereas the reality remains the preserve of the personal or subjective consciousness. The two readings meet in the ending that binds their respective narrative structures, even though it fails to resolve the contradictions between them. For the ending stands in lieu of both the authorial judgment and the invitation to confessional identification that Chopin eschews. Edna's suicide articulates the implicit contradiction at the core of *The Awakening* by highlighting the antinomies upon which the novel rests. In choosing that ending, moreover, Chopin assuredly intended to call attention to the paradoxical character of her narrative even if she could not bring the deepest contradictions to the surface.

The Awakening owes its position of respect in American letters as much to its style as to its theme. Yet a profound contradiction separates style from theme. Chopin's narrative structure and technique effectively neutralize the emotional impact of her subject. In a complex fashion, she has objectified the personal and subjectified the impersonal in such a way as to create a deadlock or stasis at the core of her work. The deadlock rests on a pervasive system of antinomies that extends from the title—and the original, reluctantly abandoned title—through the personalities of the characters to the details of described behavior and setting. The antinomies, moreover, in their very profusion, function, like sunlight glancing off water, as both signs of and distractions from the underlying currents.

Initially, Kate Chopin attained her modest, but solid, literary reputation on the basis of her short stories. As a respected local colorist, she published in such magazines as *Century, The Atlantic,* and *Vogue,* and brought out her collection, *Bayou Folk*. Her first novel, *At Fault* (1890), was privately published and commands little interest today.[4] The short stories, however, combined a telling eye for regional detail and a fine ear for local patterns of speech with a sense of the dramatic or surprise denouement in plot. And, from her very first efforts, her plots played with the possibilities and

vicissitudes of female lives. Her preoccupation with female sexuality, freedom, and consciousness—in a word, selfhood—well antedates the drafting of
The Awakening.

Stylistically, as well as structurally, Chopin's stories betrayed a strong
European influence, particularly the influence of Maupassant whom she
read voraciously and translated. Indeed, Cyrille Arnavon, in introducing the
French translation of *The Awakening,* reproaches the mechanical manifestation of that indebtedness: "One gets the impression of a story told back-
wards, hinging on the last word."[5] In the stories, Chopin demonstrates a
naturalist sensitivity to detail of character and situation. She develops a
deceptively limpid and translucent prose. But, in a disconcerting manner,
she de-familiarizes the very intimacy and coziness she has established by the
trick of the ending. The procedure seems designed to drain the potentially
shocking material of any vital sense of meaning or motivation. The shock
derives as much from the experience of reversal of the signs, or signifiers, as
from recognition of the signified. In this respect, the authorial voice, in
story after story, separates character from plot. The action, recognition, or
resolution of the ending bears no necessary affective relationship to that
which preceded it. Or the ending so changes the reader's experience of the
text as to impose a totally new reading which coexists, rather than merges,
with its predecessor.

This strategy can, and frequently does, work reasonably well for the stories. Their brief compass permits a circularity in which the change from
beginning to end turns not upon development, but rather upon a shift in
angle of vision that can afford the illusion of recognition. The regional
specificity contributes, moreover, an effective distancing mechanism. The
play of dialect and local color spins a pleasing web of strangeness that simultaneously permits the innocent introduction of potentially shocking ideas
and lowers the requirements for developmental verisimilitude. The disjuncture between the body of the story and its conclusion further contributes to
this innocence of distance. The characters can be real—more real than convention would normally permit—and yet so other as to defy identification.
In particular, the strategy permitted Chopin to evoke the most radical and
subversive views about women without ever endowing those views with the
situational or psychological weight that would permit their recognition.
Anger, passion, tragedy flit through these tales, but more as functions of
plot than character. Like shadows playing in a sunny glade, they are not reg-
istered as signs of an impending storm, but as mere facets of the prevailing
brightness. Thus Chopin neutralized her genuine awareness of the tortured
complexities of the human soul. Her stories mobilized the knowledge of good
and evil, but never in such a way as to invite judgment or identification.

Chopin's stylistic strengths merge with her limitations. The many commentators who have noted the French influence on her work have emphasized her realism. Not merely do they call attention to her affiliation to Maupassant and Merimée, but they regularly compare *The Awakening* to Flaubert's *Madame Bovary*. And her talent for meticulous attention to the psychological or physical detail would seem to confirm this judgment. Realism alone, however, does not suffice to describe Chopin's style. For her realism blends disconcertingly with a symbolist sensibility. The detail invariably refers beyond itself to some larger meaning: It stands for something as much as it stands by itself.

This tendency towards symbolic realism emerges full-blown in *The Awakening,* which sets forth a network of imagery that promises an inner significance for each of its signs. Yet the signs contradict each other at least as much as they contribute to some coherent underlying meaning. Like the stories, the novel exists as a function of its predetermined—or rather preestablished—but hidden ending. But that ending constitutes a conventional paradox rather than a dramatic or emotional necessity. Unless one accepts a Darwinian determinism whereby the end was written in the beginning—genetically encoded as it were—one has difficulty in discerning the novel's dynamic. In refusing judgment of her heroine, Chopin also forecloses identification with her. In presenting Edna as a violator of prevailing social codes, she shuns a close examination of the real content of those codes. Her symbolic realism evokes the social texture in which the individual lives as a kind of fate or destiny, rather than as a set of social relations. Chopin has a keen eye for social institutions, but she conflates the institutional conditions of women's lives with the stories of individual women. In the telling, she blurs her judgment of the society as it impinges on the individual and of the individual who fails to conform to social norms. As sensitive to the specificity of detail as Flaubert, Dickens, or even Zola, Chopin nonetheless evokes detail more to symbolize society as entity than to evoke society as process. Her tactic precludes precisely that reflection on the social conditions of female existence which her novel would seem to address.

In its symbolic realism, *The Awakening* strongly resembles the stories that it never really moves beyond. The contradiction between that development or process one would look for in a novel and the simple revelation that one can accept in a story lies at the center of *The Awakening*. The distancing inherent in Chopin's style presents Edna's experience as a simple manifestation of nature, yet the conclusion of the novel, as well as a series of observations along the way, suggest psychological and social conflicts never fully dramatized or developed. Chopin ultimately relies far more on vignettes—a loosely connected sequence of tableaux—than upon a narrative of process.

The title, *The Awakening*, points to the contradictions on which the novel rests: Does Edna awaken or does she go to sleep? Is death an awakening, or does sexual awakening necessarily result in death? Critics have called attention to the ubiquitous references to sleep and dreaming in the novel. For the moment, however, the point is the intentional paradox of the title, which evokes not merely the conflicting readings of Edna's story, but Chopin's attitude toward it.

Before settling on *The Awakening*, Chopin had entitled her work *A Solitary Soul*. And even after adopting the second title, she retained the first— rather than crossing it out as was her wont after such a substitution—perhaps intending to use it as a sub-title.[6] Whatever her reasons for finally taking *The Awakening*, the move from the first to the second title reflects a progression in cloaking one of the central contradictions in the novel. For "solitary" necessarily refers to its contrary, "social." Soul, moreover, suggests body or being. By naming the locus of solitude—the soul—even while playing with the derivative use of soul for person—altogether in keeping with the "folk" of her short story collection—the original title retained at least the illusion of a relationship between the signifiers and that being signified. *A Solitary Soul* would have been an illusive and evocative title, would have teased and played with the notion of veiled meaning. But *The Awakening* moves decisively closer to what I have called symbolic realism by transforming the— already ambiguous—references to persons into the apparently more specific, but actually more abstracted reference to an action. *The Awakening*, in other words, ensconces metaphor as the governing principle of the novel. And it, thereby, deflects attention from "who" to "what."

The "who" of the solitary soul should not be over-hastily abandoned. For that who—and her complexities—remains central to *The Awakening*. Solitary obviously evokes loneliness, but also being alone. Presumably the title, affixed to the novel we know, would force the question of Edna's solitary state. The title might lead to a reading that emphasized solitude as the cause of her death. The solitude would, at least superficially, have to be understood as spiritual. It would also have to be associated with the loss of Robert. It could not, reasonably, be understood as general abandonment or isolation. The social institutions that Edna finds so constricting, and that are sometimes taken to have strangled her freedom, have, in fact, adapted to her need for space. Nor could the title, unambiguously, be read as a condition imposed by others. In other words, one could not easily accept it—in conjunction with the plot—as a sign of Edna's having been driven to her death.

Among other things, Edna's story constitutes a deliberate attempt to free herself from the social networks of her life. To the extent that she becomes solitary, she does so by choice and enjoys the results. She, after all, rejects her Tuesday afternoons at home by absenting herself. And Chopin shows her taking delight in her first solitary dinner at home after Leonce's departure on a business trip: "The cook, placed upon her mettle, served a delicious repast—a luscious tenderloin broiled *à point*. The wine tasted good; the *marron glacé* seemed to be just what she wanted. It was so pleasant, too, to dine in a comfortable *peignoir*." During the meal, she thinks "sentimentally" of her husband and children, talking "intimately" to her little dog. After dinner, she sits reading Emerson in the library—and the prophet of transcendental self-realization soon has her dozing off. "After a refreshing bath, Edna went to bed. And as she snuggled comfortably beneath the eiderdown a sense of restfulness invaded her, such as she had not known before" (955–56). So much for solitariness—understood as being alone—as the cause of death, unless death be understood as simple restfulness.

The passage is discretely brilliant—as so many in Chopin's work are. The early description of the dinner refers directly back to a dinner at the same table shared with her husband. He found everything unsatisfactory and went off to dine at his club, having berated Edna for her inability to manage her cook well enough to produce an adequate meal. Edna, left alone, rather than succumbing to the unhappiness that had overwhelmed her on prior enactments of the recurrent domestic scene, finished her dinner. She then retired to her room, where she tore her handkerchief to shreds, stripped off her wedding ring, which she attempted to crush with her stamping heel, and finally shattered a glass vase upon the tiles of the hearth. As for the ring, "her small boot heel did not make an indenture, not a mark upon the glittering little circlet" (934).

A maid, hearing the noise, came to inquire as to the matter and to offer assistance. Edna explained that the vase had fallen and the cleaning up could wait until morning. The maid demurred, worrying that Edna might step on the debris and get some of the glass in her feet. In picking up the broken pieces, she found Edna's ring. "Edna held out her hand, and taking the ring, slipped it upon her finger" (935).

The reference to the ring echoes the opening chapter of the novel and Edna's initial appearance. She enters as a bobbing sunshade in the gaze of her husband Leonce. As the sunshade approaches him, it is seen to protect the heads of Edna and Robert Lebrun. Mr. Pontellier greets his wife with a reproach: "'You are burnt beyond recognition,' he added, looking at his wife as one looks at a valuable piece of personal property which has suffered some damage." Edna merely holds up her "strong, shapely hands . . . which reminded her of her rings, which she had given to her husband before leaving for the beach. She silently reached out to him, and he, understanding, took the rings from his vest pocket and dropped them into her open palm" (882).

The passage laconically captures the contradictions that riddle Edna's marriage. Bound to a man who looks upon her as a valuable piece of property, she shares with him an understanding that requires no words. Trapped in an oppressive institution, she can shed its chains—her rings—to go off to the beach with a single young man. The ring she tramples in her bedroom in the later scene thus represents not merely external constraint, but the ties of understanding, the institutionally-sanctioned space of freedom, a shared life anchored in an instinctive communication. The Pontellier marriage rests on a communication not so different from that which Chopin emphasizes in describing the Ratignolle marriage. Edna's solitariness of soul is far from total. And her progress toward solitude throughout the novel derives from her own intentional actions. But the solitude she seeks and welcomes may not be isomorphic with the solitariness that prompts her to her final swim. Or does that swim simply constitute the ultimate quest for solitude? Chopin never provides a clear guide to how the reader should experience Edna's death, although the closing paragraphs of the novel elide the judgment and the identification that, in sharp, unmediated form, Chopin so determinedly avoids.

In one of its possible readings, *The Awakening* offers a sharp critique of marriage as an institution. The critique, however, remains circumscribed—or ambiguous—in important ways. For Chopin does heed the complex relations between institutions as structures and the living that is their embodiment: the office of the priesthood as against the sin of its mortal agent. The accuracy of Chopin's attention to detail—her faithful re-creation of specific social and regional patterns—can veil her interest in structural similarity. Thus, despite Chopin's underscoring of the cultural differences between Edna's Presbyterian father and her Creole husband, the attentive reader can easily discern the similarities that unite the two men. In a pervasive counterpoint, the specificities and universalities jostle each other in such a way as to mute the clarity of Chopin's voice.

From the novel's opening, we know that Leonce Pontellier looks upon his wife as a valuable piece of personal property. The observation recurs. We also know that the mild and generous Leonce expects his wife to fit his every convenience. We know further that he—perhaps unfairly—criticizes her raising of their two small sons, even as we are told that the boys do not run to their mother for comfort as other children do—Chopin's unmistakable underscoring of the absence of an affective mother-child bond. We are never certain if Leonce understands this emotional vacuum, or if he is merely picking at formalities, or if his criticism of behavior reflects an unconscious knowledge of Edna's psychological distance. We do know that he indulges in a casual highhandness in his treatment of her. Thus, when he comes back

late at Grand Isle and she is sleeping, he awakens her to tell her some trivial stories from his evening. When the dinner does not suit him, he goes to
eat at his club. In fact, he frequently goes to eat at his club or to spend the
evening there. And when Mme. Ratignolle ventures to call his regular absence a pity, Edna looks blank and wonders what they would have to say to
each other should he spend his evenings at home. Finally, when Edna informs Leonce, absent on a protracted business trip, that she is moving out
of their house into a small cottage around the corner, he responds by
arranging to have their home totally redecorated and having the papers
carry a story to that effect. Thus, he assures the propriety of appearances:
Heaven forbid that the New Orleans business community should suspect
that he was in financial trouble. That the New Orleans community wonder
about his relations with his wife apparently concerns him less—and assuredly
does not bring him home to explore her motives.

As for Edna's father, he accuses Leonce of being far too lenient with her:
"Authority, coercion are what is needed. Put your foot down good and hard;
the only way to manage a wife. Take my word for it" (954). And, in a direct
narrative intervention, Chopin notes: "The Colonel was perhaps unaware
that he had coerced his own wife into her grave. Mr. Pontellier had a vague
suspicion of it which he thought needless to mention that late in the day"
(ibid.).

Beyond their differences of temperament, age, and background, these two
men share the conviction that it is their given right to rule over the women
of their families. Their tactics vary, but in their sense of women as dependent, as property, and as reflections of themselves rather than fellow human
beings, they are as one. Chopin is at her best in allowing Pontellier to serve
as critic of the father-in-law he essentially resembles. Or does he? For beyond
Chopin's irony lies the haunting question: Does Leonce, or Leonce as the
representative of bourgeois marriage, drive Edna to her death? If Chopin is
merciless in her feminist reaction to the residually patriarchal institutions of
her society, her treatment of women's reaction to that society is far more
nuanced and complex than a narrow, if politically engaged, feminist polemic.

In important respects, *The Awakening* may be read as a variant of the female
bildungsroman or novel of female initiation.[7] But it cannot neatly be fit to
either model. The ending, which overshadows the rest of the novel, inescapably shapes our assessment of the text. Chopin, moreover, remains simultaneously preoccupied with the tension between female destiny as a truth of
nature and female destiny as a social truth. Her open critique of male privilege and power is shadowed by a more tentative and ambiguous exploration
of female influence over other women. If *The Awakening* sets forth a quest

for a possible female identity, it remains nuanced in its evaluation of the decisive forces that shape such an identity. And, as it plays with male and female influences, so does it weave a complex pattern of progression and regression in the course of the woman who seeks to escape the institutional context of female life.

Unlike many other novels, *The Awakening* does not present marriage as the external symbol of female identity formation. From the early days of the novel, marriage had figured as a conventional resolution of the female quest for self. If many novelists, both male and female, had oversentimentalized marriage or refused to look at the real price it extracted from women, some who accepted the convention had, nonetheless, understood that marriage must be taken to unite the natural and social, the subjective yearnings and objective possibilities of female existence. Female adolescence, in one novel after another, constitutes a quest for self or a struggle to assume willingly the appropriate social role that invariably ends in marriage. The emphasis falls not on the inescapable limitations of female destiny, but rather on the female's active choice of her particular destiny. Romantic love may constitute a myth, but it also functions as the codifier of female aspiration, desire, and even self-assertion. And, within the conventional possibilities of the novel, female love normally ended in marriage or death.

By the time Chopin wrote *The Awakening*, the constitutive assumptions of this tradition were being widely questioned. She had not merely read the major European realist and naturalist novelists, but had shown serious interest in Darwin, Schopenhauer, and many others preoccupied with the deep strains of struggle and tragedy inherent to the human condition. In notable respects, *The Awakening* belongs to the same sensibility that generated Ibsen's plays—especially, but not only, *A Doll's House*. For if *The Awakening* shares with *A Doll's House* a profound concern with the self-experience and self-representation of women in patriarchal marriages, it also resonates with the complex picture of female psychology that informs *Hedda Gabler*. It is impossible to read Edna's story as the simple victory of patriarchy over a fragile female soul—or, it is impossible so to read it unless one understands patriarchy as an exceptionally complex set of social and psychological relations that depend upon the complicity of women.

Ruth Sullivan and Stewart Smith have called attention to the double narrative stance that governs *The Awakening*.[8] They are particularly sensitive to the pervasive voice of "motherlessness." In my judgment, Edna's immature emotional neediness cannot easily be exaggerated: The voice of that neediness provides an important counterpoint to the voice of self-conscious rebellion against constricting institutions. Various psychoanalytic schools concur in recognizing the ocean as a maternal symbol. It is, accordingly, relatively noncontroversial to suggest that Edna returns, at the novel's close, to the maternal womb for that repose and nurture she cannot find in the human world. Smith and Sullivan trace the imagery of food and sleep that evoke this maternal dimension throughout the novel. Their attention to this component of Edna's unconscious motivation elucidates a central dynamic of the novel as a whole and provides an indispensable corrective to more unidimensional readings.

Recognizing Edna's quest for mothering does not, however, negate the reality of Edna's quest for a more mature self-determination. In fact, the two movements toward identity work in tandem throughout the novel and, in some measure, converge in the quality of adolescent longing that characterizes Edna's notion of genuine love. Some might choose to read the ending as the resolution of the conflict between the two attempts at self-formation. But to settle for such a neat package means to sacrifice some of the tension and density of Chopin's work. The problem of narrative stance itself remains more intractable, even disorderly, than the recognition of two narratives would suggest.

The most important characteristic of the narrative mode of *The Awakening* may well be the virtual absence of Edna's own voice. To be sure, she speaks, even in the first person. But her speech occurs in conversation with other characters. For all the emphasis on her solitude, she indulges in few monologues, and Chopin gives us precious little direct access to her thoughts. Where her thoughts are reported, they are commonly reported in a spare economical prose that does little more than name extremely complex reactions. The reader has little access to Edna's motivations, nor to their overdetermination. Thus, in a much quoted passage: "Despondency had come upon her there in the wakeful night, and had never lifted" (999). I do not mean that Chopin fails in painting Edna's state of mind, but rather that she paints it in the sparest of brush strokes, refusing the luxuriant detail that would draw a reader into participation.

Chopin herself, as author and narrator, frequently undercuts or substantively modifies Edna's account of herself. As a totality, Chopin's narrative strategy forecloses direct identification with Edna. Even when she appears to take her most seriously, Chopin maintains a skeptical distance. At the same time, Chopin maintains a comparable distance from any judgment of Edna's actions. The narrative mode of *The Awakening* has a strangely ambiguous and inconclusive cast. This willed distance challenges us to explore the sexual structure and identities of *The Awakening* better to apprehend Chopin's attitude towards her protagonist.

Normally, Chopin's narrative voice is embedded in a simple reportage that both carries the external actions of the plot and alludes to psychological states and motivations. Thus, at one point at Grand Isle, Robert invites Edna to go bathing. "'Oh, no,' she answered with a tone of indecision. 'I'm tired; I think not.' Her glance wandered from his face away toward the Gulf, whose sonorous murmur reached her like a loving but imperative entreaty" (892). The passage beautifully illustrates Chopin's narrative strategy. We are not privy to Edna's feelings of indecisiveness. We are told only that her tone carried indecision. We cannot even be sure that the tenor of the tone existed apart from Robert's hearing of it. Then, however, she admits to being tired and says she thinks she will not bathe. The "thinks" indeed conveys indecision. She then turns toward the Gulf, which is linked to Robert's face. All at once, it is not clear whether Robert or the murmur of the ocean proffers the "loving but imperative entreaty." Clearly, the two converge in her mind, as do love and imperium. Robert, or the water, or both, or some older love they reactivate exercise a seduction or compulsion for her. The new feelings that are troubling Edna manifestly have their roots deep in her unconscious.

The chapter that follows this scene is less than a page in length and is entirely given over to Chopin's voice. "Edna Pontellier," it begins, "could not have told why, wishing to go to the beach with Robert, she should in the first place have declined, and in the second place have followed in obedience to one of the two contradictory impulses which impelled her" (893). Edna does not understand her own motivations, but we are to understand that she was vacillating between two impulses, one of which—not Robert— she obeyed. Chopin then informs us that a light was beginning to dawn within Edna, but that it dawned dimly and bewildered her. The light, moreover, forbade the very way it was illuminating. Confusion and contradiction are shown to pervade Edna's "awakening." And Chopin subtly establishes her own omniscience and externality by her use of "at that early period," which implies knowledge of the full story—hence, of the ending. Knowledge of the end, however, merely underscores the irony in Chopin's account that "at that early period" the light bewildered Edna and "moved her to dreams, to thoughtfulness, to shadowy anguish which had overcome her . . ." (893).

From this admission of knowledge, Chopin progresses to apparently unmediated didacticism: "In short, Mrs. Pontellier was beginning to realize her position in the universe as a human being, and to recognize her relations as an individual to the world within and about her. This may seem like a ponderous weight of wisdom to descend upon the soul of a young woman of twenty-eight—perhaps more wisdom than the Holy Ghost is usually pleased to vouchsafe to any woman" (893). The crux of *The Awakening* lies embedded in this passage: Does Edna, indeed, recognize those nuggets of knowledge Chopin attributes to her? Does Chopin believe that she does? The ironic distance re-established with the reference to the Holy Ghost permits doubt. But then, that very irony contains its own—like the nests of Chinese boxes—for Chopin surely does not associate herself with the notion that little knowledge is vouchsafed to any woman.

The paragraph about realization and recognition is cast almost in a masculine mode, almost in the factual or scientific mode. This tone further sharpens the ironic reference to the Holy Ghost: clear certainty—male logic—would not have been based on knowledge vouchsafed by a spirit in Chopin's day. But institutionalized religion itself had been a male preserve and had provided much of the rhetoric and rationalization of female inferiority. Chopin's polysemy thus manages to convey an ironic stance on masculine attitudes towards women. Her succeeding paragraph adopts a more female voice—an understanding, mature, almost maternal female voice: "But the beginning of things, of a world especially, is necessarily vague, tangled, chaotic, and exceedingly disturbing. How few of us ever emerge from such a beginning! How many souls perish in its tumult!" (893). Her tone conveys both reassurance and comfort for Edna and that identification with her that an older woman can offer a younger one.

And finally the chapter concludes with two more brief paragraphs:

The voice of the sea is seductive; never ceasing, whispering, clamoring, murmuring, inviting the soul to wander for a spell in abysses of solitude; to lose itself in mazes of inward contemplation.

The voice of the sea speaks to the soul. The touch of the sea is sensuous, enfolding the body in its soft, close embrace. (893)

The first of the paragraphs moves one step closer to identification with Edna and to participation in the pull of the sea, solitude, inward contemplation. The use of "for a spell," however, maintains some distance both by setting temporal limits—not forever—and by allowing the double meaning of "spell" precisely to undercut those limits by its inherent irony. If, in one reading, a moment of retreat rather than a permanent loss of self is at issue, in the other, the very self is lost by falling under a spell.

The final paragraph progresses to complete identification with Edna's state of mind, captured by the use of the present tense of the verb "to be." But an ultimate narrative distance may remain: For where Edna's voice equates soul and body, the narrative structures of the novel separate them. This very tension serves to forestall both judgment and identification. Only in the ending—and in the bosom of the sea—do the two converge.

Indisputably, Edna's awakening consists, at least partially, in her growing rejection of the prescribed social role of woman, namely the acquiescent creature of her designated lord and guardian. Edna's first appearance as an intrusion on her husband's vision seemingly underscores this perspective. Chopin, however, weakens her own focus on this patriarchal dominion by having the possessive glance fall upon Edna while sharing the intimacy of her sunshade with a male attendant. To be sure, the licensing of a mild flirtation might indicate the strength of the patriarchal system rather than its weakness. But Chopin further whittles away at the foundations of male supremacy by placing Leonce himself within an unambiguously domestic space, the Lebrun compound owned and run by Madame Lebrun. Mr. Pontellier was disturbed in his newspaper reading by the clamour of a parrot. "He had been seated before the door of the main house. The parrot and the mockingbird were the property of Madame Lebrun, and they had the right to make all the noise they wished. Mr. Pontellier had the privilege of quitting their society when they ceased to be entertaining" (881). He retreats, accordingly, to the cottage occupied for the summer by his wife and children. He is merely down for a weekend visit. The cottages are connected to the main house, in which everyone eats together, by a bridge. The newspaper is a day old. Grand Isle is clearly established as its own world, different from that of hot news, market reports, and the other concerns of the masculine, public space.

If *The Awakening* begins with a domestic space carved out from the masculine world, it ends with an oceanic maternal space that negates the entire world. The point, however, is to seize the dynamic of Edna's progress from one space to the other. Chopin leaves no doubt that the world as it is affords numerous models of female being and numerous opportunities for female self-assertion. Edna's problem results from the ways in which those models and opportunities fail, or fail to satisfy, her. Women are at least as important to her as are men. But the narrative of Edna's relations with and dependence upon other women pursues a more subterranean course than does that of her infatuation with Robert and her rebellion against the social structures she sees as incarnated by her husband.

The Awakening is densely peopled with socially adapted women. And the social requires underscoring. Madame Lebrun, Madame Ratignolle, Mlle. Reisz, Mrs. Highcamp, Mrs. Merriman, the shadowy and sinister lady in black, even Edna's sisters, all live. They have all found a social space adequate to their existence. As has the briefly-mentioned Miss Mayblount who, "no longer in her teens . . . looked at the world through lorgnettes and with the keenest interest. It was thought and said that she was an intellectual; it was said of her that she wrote under a *nom de guerre*" (970). And she came to Edna's farewell/coming-out party with a male companion, Mr. Gouvernail, whose name suggests that Miss Mayblount had shared her unconventional, but apparently stable, existence not with some patriarchal governor, but with one whose modest function was to serve as a rudder.

The point is that the patriarchal world depicted in *The Awakening* provides considerable space for a variety of female being. Men may set the public terms of female existence, but they do not seem capable of crushing the female spirit. Chopin even hints at Edna's unconscious awareness of these complexities when she has her dream "of Mr. Highcamp playing the piano at the entrance of a music store on Canal Street, while his wife was saying to Alcée Arobin, as they boarded an Esplanade streetcar: 'What a pity that so much talent has been neglected! but I must go'" (958). In other words, Chopin is exploring a complex interaction between men and women, between public and private spaces, in the construction of personal—but especially female—identity. Commentators frequently call attention to the passage in which Edna reflects, "'By all the codes which I am acquainted with, I am a devilishly wicked specimen of the sex. But some way I can't convince myself that I am. I must think about it'" (966). Edna's words to Alcée Arobin are taken to attest her lack of guilt for her unsanctioned behavior. But they can also be taken to mean that the codes allow for considerable personal variation and that Edna has difficulty feeling her subjectivity as a function of a social role.

From the beginning, Edna has difficulty in understanding the claims of the social code and its permissiveness. Chopin makes sure the reader understands that Robert regularly indulged in flirtations with the women of Grand Isle—that was his function. Indeed, the summer before Edna's awakening, Robert had devoted his attentions to Madame Ratignolle—that most happily married of married ladies. For a single man so to entertain and squire his mother's female guests fell within accepted procedure. Hence, Leonce's calm acceptance of Robert's presence beneath his wife's sunshade. Edna departed from convention not in dallying with Robert, but in taking him seriously. But even her manner of taking him seriously violated protocol. Had she merely wanted a lover, her choice should have fallen—as it eventually did—upon a man like Alcée Arobin, a *demi-mondain* and something of a *roué*. To be sure, such an affair would test the latitude of the code and risk reprisal, but Alcée would have been the correct choice for the role. Edna, however, seeks in Robert some nameless, ineffable, haunting love. That love, not her actions—and infinitely more than any of her actions—brings her to the final watery embrace. The growing need for that particular romantic love cannot be reduced to Edna's revolt against patriarchal institutions. The longing that ultimately consumes her has its roots deep in her childhood—as Chopin clearly indicates.

Following the brief chapter, discussed above, that closes with the voice, touch, and embrace of the sea, Chopin devotes an unusually long chapter to Mrs. Pontellier and Madame Ratignolle. She begins with the observation that for Edna, sharing confidences had been "hitherto contrary to her nature." The possibility that nature, in the sense of fundamental being, might change bears attention, but Chopin's main point is that even as a child Edna had "lived her own small life all within herself." Early on, "she had apprehended instinctively the dual life—that outward existence which conforms, the inward life which questions" (893). The summer at Grand Isle, however, had seen the mantle of her reserve begin to loosen. In Edna's gradual opening up, there "may have been—there must have been—influences both subtle and apparent, working in their several ways to induce her to do this; but the most obvious was the influence of Adele Ratignolle" (894).

The remainder of the chapter sets forth almost all of what we learn of Edna's early life. In particular, Edna recalls walking through a meadow in Kentucky on a summer day. The sight of the water, the hot wind "made me think—without any connection that I can trace—of a summer day in Kentucky, of a meadow that seemed as big as the ocean to the very little girl walking through the grass, which was higher than her waist. She threw out her arms as if swimming when she walked, beating the tall grass as one strikes out in water. Oh, I see the connection now!" (896). But whatever connections she sees, she misses that of Adele's warm maternal presence. In the succeeding paragraphs, we are told, as commentators have noted, that Edna was running away from prayers—the Presbyterianism of her father; that her sunbonnet blocked her view; and that her early loves included "a dignified and sad-eyed cavalry officer," a young man already engaged to another and to whom Edna knew herself to be nothing, and a great tragedian—whose picture could safely be hung on her wall without evoking comment. All of these loves are spoken of as dreams and infatuations that gradually merge into fate and grand passion.

But the passage that describes the girl in the meadow deserves attention for other reasons as well. In recalling it, Edna, who had been speaking in the first person, schizophrenically recalls not "I," but "the little girl." We are never told exactly when her mother died, except that it was when "they were quite young." But the memory of the meadow is presented as belonging affectively to the little girl she was, rather than to herself. The reader is permitted to speculate about what might have caused the dissociation. The other important point about the chapter is that Edna's memories emerge in the context of her extraordinarily sensual and seductive interchange with Adele Ratignolle. Nowhere else in the novel do descriptions of physical seductiveness and sensuality assume such importance or merit such detail.*

---

*[EF-G] The only other comparably sensual scene is that of the dinner party Edna gives to celebrate her departure from her husband's house and her twenty-ninth birthday. But

"The excessive physical charm of the Creole had first attracted" Edna, who was sensuously susceptible to beauty. The two women set out for the beach "arm in arm, under the huge white sunshade." Significantly, Edna had persuaded her friend to leave the children at home. Chopin describes the physical presence and dress of both women with care. Having no intention of bathing, they had come to the beach "to be alone and near the water." They settle down upon a rug, leaning against two huge pillows. "Madame Ratignolle removed her veil. . . . Edna removed her collar and opened her dress at the throat. She took the fan from Madame Ratignolle and began to fan both herself and her companion" (895). The reference to the sunshade covering them both echoes the opening scene in which Robert and Edna shared the shade. Now the two women install themselves in intimate privacy. In this setting, Edna remembers her past. After speaking of the meadow, she "broke off, turning her quick eyes upon Madame Ratignolle and leaning forward a little so as to bring her face quite close to that of her companion, 'sometimes I feel this summer as if I were walking through the green meadow again; idly, aimlessly, unthinking and unguided'" (897). Madame Ratignolle responds by covering Edna's hand with her own. "Seeing that the hand was not withdrawn, she clasped it firmly and warmly. She even stroked it a little, fondly, with the other hand, murmuring in an undertone, 'Pauvre chérie'" (897).

Edna finds Adele's action confusing, "but she soon lent herself readily to the Creole's gentle caress" (897). Edna's childhood had not prepared her for outward expressions of affection. She had quarreled with or been distant from her sisters. And her mother had died. And her closest friends had all been the self-contained type, particularly her best friend with whom she had participated in long, intellectual discussions. And then Chopin introduces the recollections of Edna's early loves: "Edna had often wondered at one propensity which sometimes had inwardly disturbed her without causing any outward show or manifestation on her part" (897). The sequence commands scrupulous attention. The meadow is associated with feeling unguided (motherless?). That memory leads to the mention of the mother's death. But the mention fades into the passing flow, without foregrounding: It remains a simple fact in contradistinction to the emotion invoked elsewhere. And the emotion seems especially displaced, following the internal logic of the narrative, to the impossible loves. And the emotion, like the

---

the sensuality evoked at the party is explicitly induced by wine, food, and setting. It, too, depends upon a kind of intoxication, but is altogether less intimate than the scene with Mme. Ratignolle. The two scenes should probably be understood as structurally and psychologically juxtaposed: day vs. night, sun vs. candles, and so forth.

memories, is called forth by the warm embrace of Adele Ratignolle's presence and undivided attention.

The chapter concludes with a brief review of Edna's marriage and her attitudes towards her husband and children. The narrative voice is indirect. It remains unclear whether the words encode Edna's speech to Adele—reported indirectly—or her own thoughts, or Chopin's account of her. The point of view falls among all three possibilities, or draws, intermittently, upon all three. The substance, however, identifies Edna's marriage to Leonce as an "accident," motivated in part by her illusion that they shared a sympathy of taste and thought and in part by the opposition of her father and her sister Margaret. Gradually, however, realities took over and Edna "grew fond of her husband, realizing with some unaccountable satisfaction that no trace of passion or excessive and fictitious warmth colored her affection, thereby threatening its dissolution" (898). And, as for her children, she was fond of them "in an uneven, impulsive way" (898). Edna did not actually tell all this to Madame Ratignolle, but "a good part of it escaped her. She had put her head down on Madame Ratignolle's shoulder. She was flushed and felt intoxicated with the sound of her own voice and the unaccustomed taste of candor. It muddled her like wine, or like a first breath of freedom" (899).

The *tête à tête* ends with the arrival of Robert and the Pontellier and Ratignolle children. The structural unification of Robert and the children highlights the nexus of motherlove around which the chapter revolves. For Edna's love for Robert derives from the same internal place from which her love for her children would have come had her female self been nurtured and knit up. The love of Madame Ratignolle clears a space for her memories of girlhood and adolescence. The flowering of her normally suppressed self under the warmth of the friendly touch and gaze reveals the depth of her need. Chopin surely meant that of all the influences working on Edna that summer, the influence of Madame Ratignolle was probably the most important. For Edna had grown to womanhood without a mother, without a focus of identification and a source of nurturance. The "motherlessness" colors many of her responses, particularly her love for Robert, which belongs to the same part of herself as those other impossible loves of her youth. They are loves that partake of, even as they mask, the longing for the lost mother. They are loves tinged with the kiss of death, for the mother's death shaped Edna's subsequent expectations of true love as necessarily ending in dissolution. In this context, freedom, for Edna, is like a quaff of wine—a headiness, an intoxication—rather than like the staff and substance of life.

If Madame Ratignolle can rouse Edna's senses, loosen her memories, and soothe her spirit, she cannot replace the mothering that Edna missed. By the middle of the novel when Edna, having returned to New Orleans, goes to visit the Ratignolles, she is prepared to reject outright the model of life presented by her friend.

> Edna felt depressed rather than soothed after leaving them. The little glimpse of domestic harmony which had been offered her, gave her no regret, no longing. It was not a condition of life which fitted her, and she could see in it but an appalling and hopeless ennui. She was moved by a kind of commiseration for Madame Ratignolle,—a pity for that colorless existence which never uplifted its possessor beyond the region of blind contentment, in which no moment of anguish ever visited her soul, in which she would never have the taste of life's delirium. Edna vaguely wondered what she meant by "life's delirium." It had crossed her thought like some unsought, extraneous impression. (938)

Yet Edna had gone to Madame Ratignolle, among other things, to elicit her friend's opinion of her paintings. And, knowing the opinion worthless from a professional standpoint, she had lapped up the praise bestowed with a "feeling which bordered on complacency" (937). And, to her surprise, she found the dinner, to which she had been spontaneously invited, "a delicious repast, simple, choice, and in every way satisfying." She also discovered Mr. Ratignolle to be an animated, informed, and interesting conversationalist. As to the marriage: "The Ratignolles understood each other perfectly. If ever the fusion of two human beings into one has been accomplished on this sphere it was surely in their union" (938).

Edna's reaction to this domestic bliss resembles that of the Romantics to bourgeois culture, or even that of an adolescent to mature, adult pleasures. The "life's delirium" that Edna seeks, but cannot define, must be something more than the perfect marriage, something more than the maximum possible union between two individuals. Must it then be the submersion of one individual into another? Must it be something totally uncorrupted by human institutions? And, if it must, can it be anything but death? Chopin answers these questions only with her ending which itself remains ambiguous.

Edna can no more be dismissed as a rebellious or emotionally insatiable adolescent than can the Romantic notion of love be reduced to adolescent fantasies. But, this strand of Edna's personality surfaces in conjunction with her visit to Madame Ratignolle precisely because it is tied to her lost mother, as is her inability to accept a female identity as child-bearer or mother.

The concluding chapters of the novel encompass Robert's reunion with Edna and the wrecking of their love on the contingencies of the real world. Their relationship unfolds in a series of domestic spaces and appears largely governed by female rather than patriarchal power. Upon Robert's return, they first meet, apparently by accident, in the rooms of Mlle. Reisz. They next stumble upon each other at an out-of-the-way garden restaurant to which both were wont to come, unbeknownst to the other, for a retreat from the outside world. The restaurant is a classic domestic space, hidden from the public view, secured from the bustle of the streets, and presided over by a nurturing Creole who serves up simple, sustaining food, especially milk. They then return together to Edna's pigeon house, where they confess the love that dawned the previous summer at Grand Isle.

Robert avows his having departed for Mexico to fight his love for Edna and having spent his stay "thinking of you all the time and longing for you" (992). She interrupts to reproach his not having written. He rejoins: "Something put into my head that you cared for me and I lost my senses. I forgot everything but a wild dream of your some way becoming my wife." Incredulous, she repeats: "Your wife!" He insists that, had she cared, religion, loyalty and all the rest would have given way. Edna sees it differently. Has he forgotten that she is the wife of Leonce Pontellier? If marriage is on the table, she belongs to a man of parts who will not easily watch his rights, or those of the order they represent, give way. But, in any event, marriage is the last thing she has in mind:

> "You have been a very, very foolish boy, wasting your time dreaming of impossible things when you speak of Mr. Pontellier setting me free! I am no longer one of Mr. Pontellier's possessions to dispose of or not. I give myself where I choose. If he were to say, 'Here, Robert, take her and be happy; she is yours,' I should laugh at you both." (992)

To be sure, Edna is somewhat less than candid in her attitude toward the patriarchal world in which she lives. Just as Robert fantasizes true passion as marriage—not the possession of Edna so much as replacing her husband— so Edna, for all her genuine revolt, remains tied in subtle ways to the prevailing social relations of her culture. Thus, in an extraordinary touch, Chopin depicts her presiding over the sensuous dinner party she gives before quitting Leonce's house for her pigeon house, wearing the sensational diamond that Leonce had just sent her for her twenty-ninth birthday. Wearing the diamond in her hair, like a diadem.

Robert is so tied to the idea of marriage as the realization of love that he cannot grasp Edna's meaning—and does not even suspect his own unconscious motivation. Just as he is pressing her as to what she meant about no longer being one of Mr. Pontellier's possessions, Madame Ratignolle's servant arrives to announce that her mistress has been taken ill and requires Edna's presence. In fact, Madame Ratignolle is about to give birth to yet another child, and Edna had promised to be with her during the delivery.

Edna leaves and upon her return Robert had departed, leaving a note: "I love you. Good-by—because I love you" (997). The following morning, having slept not a wink, Edna goes down to Grand Isle, to the ocean.

In the scenes between Edna's departure and her return, she assists Madame Ratignolle at the birth and has a conversation with the wise family doctor, Mandelet. The experience of the birth shocks Edna. The normally warm and complacent Adele had become querulous and fretful, reproaching her husband and the doctor for their failures in attention to her. Pain and fear unravel her normally generous personality. Edna wishes she were not there but does not leave. "With an inward agony, with a flaming, outspoken revolt against the ways of Nature, she witnessed the scene of torture" (995). And, when it is over and she is leaving, Adele, sensing her preoccupation with Robert, whispered: "'Think of the children, Edna. Oh think of the children! Remember them!'" (995).

Out in the open air, Edna, still dazed, encounters Dr. Mandelet and allows him to walk her home. He, too, senses her trouble, of which Leonce had spoken to him shortly after their return from Grand Isle. Leonce had not understood the causes of Edna's restlessness, but the good doctor had immediately suspected another man. Now, he reproaches the selfishness that led Adele to insist upon the presence of her most impressionable friend at such a time. But Edna answers with indifference: "'I don't know that it matters after all. One has to think of the children some time or other; the sooner the better'" (995). And then she rambles on about not permitting herself to be forced to do things she does not want. "'Nobody has any right— except the children, perhaps. . . .'" And the doctor, instinctively grasping her meaning: "'The trouble is . . . that youth is given up to illusions. It seems to be a provision of Nature; a decoy to secure mothers for the race. And Nature takes no account of moral consequences, or arbitrary conditions which we create, and which we feel obliged to maintain at any cost'" (996).

Edna answers by saying that the years gone by seem like a dream and by wondering if it would not be better to continue to dream: "'But to wake up and find—oh! well! perhaps it is better to wake up after all, even to suffer, rather than to remain a dupe to illusions all one's life.'" And her thoughts move on to Robert, to the moment of passion she intends to spend with him, to the transcendent joy of the complete possession of the loved one. Adele's whispering voice comes back, reminding her to think of the children. Tomorrow she would think of the children, not tonight. "To-morrow would be time enough to think of everything" (997).

In these final chapters, Chopin weaves together the themes of the novel. The children, in particular, assume ever greater importance as the inescapable link that binds Edna to the norms and institutions of her society. But Chopin also ties the children to Nature, to the essence of womanhood. Edna rebels not merely against the social constraints of a female identity but against the natural ones. She revolts against being a woman. In a sense, Chopin reverses the convention that led men like G. B. Shaw to paint women as the snare that trapped men in civilization, and shows women as the prey of the civilizing process. But, in this perspective, the joy that Edna expects from consummating her love for Robert cannot be taken to mean her realization as a woman. The love that will satisfy her soul lies on the borderland of death, of self-oblivion.

From early in the novel, Chopin establishes that Edna is not one of the "mother-women," not one of those female creatures who live only for and through husbands and children. Critics frequently applaud that dimension of Edna's personality as proof of her incipient independence, her willingness to live for herself. Chopin doubtless intended Edna's rejection of motherhood as a totally self-determining vocation to express her own impatience with women's internalization of the social restrictions under which they lived. Thus, when Edna affirms that she would sacrifice everything for her children—money, her life, whatever—but not the essential, she surely speaks for a serious criticism of an overly-sentimentalized view of motherhood. Chopin does not leave matters there. Motherhood cannot be reduced to a social convention, however much society attempts to do so. Motherhood also has something to do with bringing forth life—an experience that Chopin herself supremely valued—and with accepting one's place in the succession of generations. Edna never received that nurture from her own mother that would have permitted her to nurture others and then move on. She remains tied to an unsatisfied maternal longing that forces her either to subordinate herself to, or to divorce herself from, her own children. Chopin embeds her critique of women's social subordination in the complexities of Edna's personal immaturity.

The love Edna seeks transcends any social possibility. Had she been content to settle for a satisfying, sensuous affair, she could have been satisfied with a relationship such as that she had with Alcée. Chopin presents that affair as rousing and meeting Edna's sensual needs. Had she sought self-realization through her work, she could have pursued her increasingly successful career. Hardly a great artist, Edna nonetheless was succeeding in selling her paintings and in taking pleasure in the mastery of her craft. The needs that drive her, however, spring from deeper sources and seem to permit no assuaging short of delirium. And Chopin clearly indicates that the love for Robert derives in large part from the repressed longing for the mother who died before helping Edna to become a woman.

The disturbing and sinister figure of Mlle. Reisz haunts Edna's story much as the woman in black haunts the steps of the young lovers in the early scenes at Grand Isle. Mlle. Reisz fills a complex function in the novel. Her role as counterpart to Madame Ratignolle is highlighted by the juxtaposition between the white of Madame Lebrun and the black of the other lady in the opening sections of the book. As Madame Ratignolle is married, beautiful, sensual, fair, and beneficently maternal, Mlle. Reisz is single, homely, ascetic, dark, and malevolently maternal. As an artist, Mlle. Reisz stands for the possibility of female independence. Her life may be austere and frugal, but it is her own. And her unappealing external frame harbors a rare musical talent. Her music, indeed, seduces and entwines Edna, blending into, even as it seems to articulate, the nameless, shapeless longing that consumes and fires Edna's soul.

Mlle. Reisz first appears at Grand Isle where she is called upon to play for the assembled guests. Her performance draws together the threads of the transformation that Edna is beginning to undergo. Having always loved the music of the pianist, in particular her rendition of a Chopin *Impromptu,* Edna finds herself participating in it in a new way. Previously, the pianist's playing had evoked pictures in her mind: One piece, which Edna privately named "Solitude," brought into her imagination the picture of a man "standing beside a desolate rock on the seashore. He was naked. His attitude was one of hopeless resignation as he looked toward a distant bird winging its flight away from him." At the novel's close, Edna herself, perched on the edge of the ocean, will shed her clothing and re-create this picture. On this particular evening, however, she waited in vain for the pictures to materialize. "She saw no pictures of solitude, of hope, of longing, or of despair. But the very passions themselves were aroused within her soul, swaying it, lashing it, as the waves daily beat upon her splendid body. She trembled, she was choking, and the tears blinded her" (906).

Thenceforth, the dour little pianist is closely associated with Edna's passion for Robert. After her return to the city, Edna goes in search of Mlle. Reisz, for whom no one seems to have an address. Eventually, she finds her through Madame Lebrun. Having found her in a small set of rooms at the top of a building, she begs permission to return often to hear Mlle. Reisz's playing. As Arnavon pointed out, Mlle. Reisz's rooms are the only space in the novel from which one looks out over the quays and warehouses of New Orleans: Her vision encompasses the business life of the city.[9] But Edna goes not for what lies outside the rooms but for what they contain. The music becomes her drug, her potion. And her favorite theme is that of Isolde. Chopin's treatment of music as romantic love potion prefigures that of Thomas Mann, even as it echoes Schopenhauer.

The female space of Mlle. Reisz includes none of the normal womanly attributes. Significantly, she must go out to eat or to bring in food. No material nurturance here. But for spiritual nurturance, she offers not merely music but talk of Robert and—wonder of wonders—letters from Robert over which Edna can cry as she listens to the strains of the piano. Mlle. Reisz is a seductress. Appearing to offer Edna that which she most craves, she contributes to binding her to a hopeless passion. She casts a spell as surely as any evil fairy from an ancient tale. If Madame Ratignolle stimulates and lures Edna with her warm, embracing body, Mlle. Reisz winds the threads of her power around Edna's soul. Robert writes to Mlle. Reisz, Mlle. Reisz turns his letters over to Edna. She mediates their love and, in mediating, encourages it in the paths of fantasy, longing, and that soul-engulfing death of drugged escape.

Mlle. Reisz embodies the themes of *eros* and *thanatos* to which Cynthia Wolff has called attention.[10] And, like Wagnerian music, she casts a spell, drawing Edna into the net of her own infantile longings. In this respect, she fills the role of the bad mother, binding Edna to her by mobilizing Edna's weaknesses. At the same time, she offers one of the few models of an independent woman. But as a model of female independence she lacks appeal. It is possible to understand her as stealing the children of others as a revenge for her own childlessness. And the children over whom she establishes her sway both lack parents of their own sex: Edna has lost her mother and Robert his father. Indeed, Chopin has Edna believe that Robert was the favorite child of Madame Lebrun, only to be disabused by Mlle. Reisz: "Mademoiselle laughed maliciously. 'Her favorite son! Oh dear! Who could have been imposing such a tale upon you? Aline Lebrun lives for Victor, and for Victor alone. She has spoiled him into the worthless creature he is. She worships him and the ground he walks on'" (930). Edna cannot even recognize the dynamics of parental love.

Madame Ratignolle and Mlle. Reisz offer Edna two models of female being. They also offer her two modes of motherhood, both partial. Their limitations, however, have not interfered with their own social existence. Both have adapted to the world in which they live. Edna can accept neither of their roles as adequate to her needs. Moreover, from neither can she draw the sustenance she so deeply craves. Both women bear the firm imprint of the patriarchal structures of their society. And Chopin should not be read as offering either as an ideal solution to female needs. Yet Chopin remains profoundly ambiguous about their strengths and weaknesses relative to those of Edna.

In refusing the roles presented by Madame Ratignolle and Mlle. Reisz, Edna is left without a guide or a charted path. She does indeed face a sea of grass in which she can see no markers. Chopin portrays her awakening as a clear-eyed recognition of the constricting social system that imprisons women within such partial roles. At the same time, Chopin insists that, in Edna's case, the awakening led not to life, but to death. And the way to death lay back through Edna's adolescence toward the abyss of need and longing left by her mother's death. The sequence of infatuations and loves, of which Robert constituted the last, merely masked the deeper insatiable love, forever foreclosed by that premature death. In an extraordinary gambit, Fryer, in arguing for Edna's suicide as an act of free will, cites the entire concluding paragraphs of the novel, with the exception of a few critical sentences.[11] The final paragraph begins: "She looked into the distance, and the old terror flamed up for an instant, then sank again" (1000). It concludes: "There was the hum of bees, and the musky odor of pinks filled the air" (1000). Fryer separates the two sentences, which she quotes, with dots, thus omitting: "Edna heard her father's voice and her sister Margaret's. She heard the barking of an old dog that was chained to the sycamore tree. The spurs of the cavalry officer clanged as he walked across the porch" (1000). The excised sentences address precisely the human context of Edna's suicide. The notion of terror is associated with the voices of her father and the sister who assumed her mother's role, and with the barking of a chained dog. Then follows the critical sentence about the cavalry officer who constituted the first of her infatuations/loves. Edna's mother is not mentioned. The structural substitution seems incontrovertible.

Edna's quest for her mother through a sequence of impossible and unattainable loves lies at the core of *The Awakening*, but does not exhaust its subject matter. The theme of longing and regression coexists throughout with the serious critique of bourgeois patriarchalism. For reasons of her own, however, Chopin resists either the clear editorial judgment or the clear invitation to an identification with Edna that would permit a firm statement about the message of the novel. Antinomies balance each other so neatly that the center remains deadlocked. The possible reasons for this strategy are numerous and most likely reinforce rather than compete with each other.

Although Chopin's personal biography cannot be advanced as an interpretive key to the text, personal motivations may have contributed to the complex and unresolved structure of the text. Taking the ending as central, we may ask from what perspective could the ending be read as satisfying. And one answer is from Chopin's personal perspective. It requires no extraordinary effort to recognize important bits of Chopin herself in Mlle. Reisz, Madame Ratignolle, and Edna. A successful writer, who had been very happily married, mother of six children, by all accounts content in her life, Chopin had also lost her husband and the mother with whom she had been unusually intimate.[12] In writing *The Awakening,* Chopin may easily have been killing off a part of herself—a residual adolescent dependency—even as she played with criticizing a society that had, by and large, treated her well.

Whether or not some such motivation prompted Chopin's writing of her novel, the novel assuredly sets forth a series of conflicts between individual female identity and social structure that it never elucidates. In *The Awakening,* Chopin offers the reader a range of clues about Edna's preoccupation with and repression of the loss of her mother. In this respect, Chopin adopts a splendidly clever strategy. She tells a story of a young woman who awakens to the injustices of her society and to her own sexuality, who rebels against patriarchal restrictions, and who attempts to realize her inner being through sensuality, love, and art. The tale should be a straightforward indictment of a society's treatment of women. But Chopin laces this account with unmistakable indications that her heroine suffered from unusual psychological weaknesses. And she musters a galaxy of women who adapt perfectly well to the unjust social order in a variety of different roles. Suddenly, the indictment of the social system becomes an individual case history—and the case history of an aberrant individual at that. We are dealing with personal pathology—with a proclaimed "outsider"—not with social or sexual injustice at all. But Chopin cannot bring herself to undercut the feminist thrust of her novel entirely: She simply weds it indissolubly to the portrait of a psychological regression. The two narratives must be read together, for the grounds for choosing one rather than the other do not exist.

The narrative voices of *The Awakening* are, respectively, institutional and personal voices. Edna's subjective experience provides the critique of social institutions; the reality of social institutions provides the critique of Edna's subjectivity. In this way, Chopin avoids a fully candid look at the interrelations between the personal and the institutional. Chopin was a genuinely institutional and essentially conservative person herself, even if one deeply aware of the hypocrisies and waste attached to social forms.[13] She was not likely to let a searching critique lead her to conclude that the social order of the bourgeois South required the institutional subordination of women. Nor would she have been comfortable with the view that the freedom of women dictated the substantial reform of prevailing social institutions. The spirit of rebellion burned within her, but did not dominate her life. By wedding that restlessness to female adolescence she simultaneously tied it to the roles, both positive and negative, passed on from mothers to daughters and denuded it of social import. In *The Awakening,* she explored her own knowledge that a person who wished to be free could not aspire to become a woman—in the sense that her society constructed womanhood—and that a girl who wanted to become a woman had to kill her deepest wishes to be free.

Chopin accepted the institutional compromise and, in so doing, had to tie the impulse to freedom to the longings, fantasies, and loves of early adolescence—to a state of mind that could and should be outgrown with the assumption of natural and social womanhood. Her position resembled that of those slaveholders who flourished between the Revolution and the nullification controversy: Deploring slavery, they nonetheless cherished a Southern way of life that depended upon slavery for its continued existence. Thus Chopin, deploring the subordination of women, cherished a society for which challenging the prevailing sexual division of labor would have challenged the foundations of the social structure.

Notes

1. Per Seyersted & Emily Toth, *A Kate Chopin Miscellany* (Oslo and Natchitoches, 1979), 212–61, contains a complete bibliography of writings on Kate Chopin through 1979. Kate Chopin, *The Awakening*, ed. Margaret Culley (New York, 1976), 143–228, contains selected critical materials. Judith Fryer, *The Faces of Eve* (Oxford, London, New York, 1976), 242–57. See also Per Seyersted, *Kate Chopin: A Critical Biography* (Baton Rouge, 1969); Larzer Ziff, *The American 1890s: Life and Times of a Lost Generation* (New York, 1966), 296–305; Gladys W. Milliner, "The Tragic Imperative: *The Awakening* and *The Bell Jar*," *Mary Wollstonecraft Newsletter* 2 (December 1973), 21–26; Clement Eaton, "Breaking a Path for the Liberation of Women in the South," *Georgia Review* 128 (Summer 1974), 187–99; Jacqueline Berke, "Kate Chopin's Call to a Larger 'Awakening,'" *Kate Chopin Newsletter* 1 (Winter 1975–1976), 1–5; Joyce Ruddel Ladenson, "Paths to Suicide: Rebellion Against Victorian Womanhood in Kate Chopin's *The Awakening*," *Intellect* 104 (July–August 1975), 52–55; Emily Toth, "The Independent Woman and 'Free' Love," *Massachusetts Review* 16 (Autumn 1975), 647–64, and her "Kate Chopin's *The Awakening* as Feminist Criticism," *Louisiana Studies* 15 (Fall 1976), 241–51; Otis B. Wheeler, "The Five Awakenings of Edna Pontellier," *Southern Review* 11 (January 1975), 118–28.

2. Cynthia Griffin Wolff, "Thanatos and Eros: Kate Chopin's *The Awakening*," *American Quarterly* 25 (October 1973), 449–71; Peggy Skaggs, "Three Tragic Figures in Kate Chopin's *The Awakening*," *Louisiana Studies* 13 (Winter 1974), 345–64.

3. All references will be to *The Complete Works of Kate Chopin*, ed. Per Seyersted (Baton Rouge, 1969), vol. II, 881–1000.

4. See Seyersted, *Kate Chopin*; Daniel Rankin, *Kate Chopin and Her Creole Stories* (Philadelphia, 1932). Cf. Thomas Bonner Jr. "Kate Chopin's *At Fault* and *The Awakening*: A Study in Structure," *Markham Review* 7 (Fall 1977), 10–15; Bernard J. Koloski, "The Structure of Kate Chopin's *At Fault*," *Studies in American Fiction* 3 (Spring 1975), 89–94.

5. Cyrille Arnavon, "Introduction" to Kate Chopin, *Edna* (Paris, 1953), repr. in *A Kate Chopin Miscellany*. See also, Thomas Bonner Jr., "Kate Chopin's European Consciousness," *American Literary Realism* 8 (Summer 1975), 281–84; Pamela Gaude, "Kate Chopin's 'The Storm': A Study of Maupassant's Influence," *Kate Chopin Newsletter* 1

(Fall 1975), 1–6; Eliane Jasenas, "The French Influence in Kate Chopin's *The Awakening*," *Kate Chopin Newsletter* 2 (Spring 1976), 6; Cyrille Arnavon, "Les Debuts du roman realiste american et l'influence française," *Romanciers Americains Contemporains,* ed. Henri Kerst (Paris, 1946), 9–42.

6. See Per Seyersted, *Kate Chopin,* and his note to the text of the novel in *Collected Works,* 1032.

7. Cf. Elaine Ginsberg, "The Female Initiation Theme in American Fiction," *Studies in American Fiction* 3 (Spring 1975), 27–37, and Patricia Meyer Spacks, *The Female Imagination* (New York, 1975).

8. Ruth Sullivan and Stewart Smith, "Narrative Stance in Kate Chopin's *The Awakening*," *Studies in American Fiction* 1 (Spring 1973), 62–75.

9. Arnavon, "Introduction" to *Edna, Miscellany,* 177.

10. Wolff, "Eros and Thanatos," *loc. cit.*

11. Fryer, *Faces of Eve,* 244.

12. Seyersted, *Kate Chopin*; Rankin, *Kate Chopin*; Seyersted, *Miscellany,* 47–99.

13. Ibid.

Nine

Scarlett O'Hara

The Southern Lady as New Woman

If *Gone With the Wind* has become something of an American classic, it has done so as much by its popular appeal as by any aesthetic merit. The components of its record-breaking success include all the classic ingredients of popular romance wrapped in the irresistible trappings of historical adventure and glamour—the hurtling saga of sectional catastrophe and rebirth, the nostalgia for a lost civilization, the green Irish eyes of a captivating and unruly Miss, and the languorous, steel-sprung dynamism of her Rhett Butler. But, if the novel fails to transcend its indebtedness to popular culture and to a sentimental female tradition, it nonetheless betrays a complexity that distinguishes it from the standard mass-market historical melodrama.[1]

The extraordinary overnight success of *Gone With the Wind* testifies to the immediacy with which it engaged the American imagination. Critical acclaim, which likened it to *Vanity Fair* and *War and Peace,* as well as popular sales, rapidly established the saga of Scarlett O'Hara as a significant addition to the national culture.[2] Scarlett and her world entered the mainstream of American life, thereby incorporating the Old South, its beauties and its travails, firmly into the prevailing myth of the American past. In this respect, *Gone With the Wind* celebrated, even as it contributed to, the restoration of the South to the nation and the nation to the South.

Like so many spontaneous cultural manifestations, the appearance of *Gone With the Wind* had been carefully engineered. In the 1930s the American public was showing a taste for historical fiction and Southern fiction.

When Harold Latham acquired the manuscript for Macmillan in 1935, he was on a trip through the South looking for Southern material—looking, in fact, for *Gone With the Wind,* had he only known it existed.[3] So Mitchell's novel fit into the demand of a popular sensibility that, as Warren Susman has argued, had taken a conservative turn. The American people, in Susman's view,

> entered an era of depression and war somehow aware of a culture in crisis, already at the outset in search of a satisfactory American Way of Life, fascinated by the idea of culture itself, with a sense of some need for a kind of commitment in a world somehow between eras.[4]

The first World War looms as the critical experience of cultural transformation. There was an element of strain and unreality in the prosperity and "liberation" of the twenties—a glossing over of problems unresolved. This link between the war and the two postwar decades provided the context for the drafting and reception of *Gone With the Wind.* Its compelling dynamism derived as much from its implicit engagement with the America of the 1920s as from its outward concern with the Civil War and Reconstruction. Never just another historical romance of magnolias and moonlight, *Gone With the Wind* grappled with the nature of the New South, with twentieth-century problems of social change and tension, and with the dilemmas of female identity in the modern world.

The story of Scarlett O'Hara, which opens and closes the novel and organizes the intervening flood of historical cataclysm, drew countless readers through the collapse of one civilization and the birth of another. Scarlett engaged a special identification from her readers by simultaneously mobilizing and obscuring the tensions of female being and passion that plagued Mitchell and her contemporaries. The appeal of *Gone With the Wind* has proved so broad and enduring as to defy any single explanation. Surely every female reader will always cherish her own Scarlett. And the novel's attraction for men can be traced to Rhett's special qualities, in particular that tough and ferocious romanticism so reminiscent of Hemingway's heroes or Humphrey Bogart's roles. Yet any possible explanation of the novel's appeal should take account of Mitchell's special ability to render Scarlett's experience at once immediate and distant. Holding a careful line between mystification and autobiographical realism, Mitchell casts Scarlett's tale neither as a gothic fantasy nor as a portrait of the modern woman. Instead, Mitchell chooses to wed Scarlett to the death and rebirth of the South, but she also uses that historical specificity to veil altogether contemporary concerns. *Gone With the Wind,* in short, rests on a series of displacements that both bind the reader with an illusion of psychological immediacy and mask the immediacy of social issues. Mitchell's decision to weigh equally Scarlett and the agony of social upheaval, the individual and historical process, forces us to consider both strands of the novel together, however complex the reading.

Like any text, *Gone With the Wind* must be taken on its own terms, as a discrete entity with rules, logic, and meaning of its own. Yet, also like any text, it must be read in full historical and cultural context. We gain nothing from insisting on a radical purity that severs the text entirely from its production and reception, from the motivations—open and buried—of its author, or from the predispositions of its readers. The full complexity of Margaret Mitchell's personal relation to her novel exceeds the scope of this essay, but no reading of the novel should dismiss the relation as insignificant. Mitchell, who had not assumed her own adult female identity without detours, wrote a single novel that, whatever its scope and range of compelling characters, focused upon a female adolescent's passage to womanhood. And her account of Scarlett's passage raises all the questions of female identity, role, and sexuality that figured in American consciousness during the first three decades of the twentieth century.[5]

If Mitchell did not write the *bildungsroman* of a twentieth-century Southern female adolescence and young womanhood, she nonetheless understood female being as historically specific.[6] By displacing Scarlett's career historically while simultaneously confronting her with contemporary dilemmas, she relies upon history and social conventions to complete the silences she leaves in her exploration of female identity, just as she relies upon them to contain, in however contradictory a fashion, the painful and confusing desires of the female self. Indeed, by emphasizing history and social order, which she merges with the idea of civilization, she obscures the measure of her personal rebellion against prescribed female roles. In *Gone With the Wind*, she offers a rationalization of middle-class American values, especially white middle-class social domination. Yet the rationalization depends on establishing a historical pedigree for a national ruling class in a period of advanced capitalism and perceived social change. This rationalization, moreover, is laced with veiled challenges to the prevailing gender system, even as it proclaims that gender system as the cornerstone of social order. At its core lies a psychological exploration of the place of women within the ruling class and of the tensions between their subjective desires and their assigned, objective role.

Mitchell invests Scarlett with the conscious and unconscious conflicts that inform the transition from explosive and tense girlhood to socially-determined womanhood under conditions in which that transition is open to reinterpretation. By casting the dilemmas of her own generation in the context of the Civil War, Mitchell prohibited an autobiographical reading of her text. She intended to distance herself from the most pressing emotional conflicts, to protect herself as well as her privacy from curious readers. The one-to-one relationship between Mitchell and Scarlett, even if it could be established, matters little, and is certainly less important than the kind of female identity that attracted so many female readers. The point, after all, is less to understand the personal case history of Margaret Mitchell than to understand its mediation through a fictional character that responded to the fantasies of so many American women. Only in this sense does the 1920s substratum that underlies the Civil War foreground become significant. But, in this sense, it matters that the roots of *Gone With the Wind* lie in the imagination and experience of a woman who came to maturity with, as she frequently insisted, the generation of flappers.

Born in 1900, Margaret Mitchell lived most of her life in the Atlanta of the New South. The preliminary biographical materials available and her own *Gone With the Wind Letters* portray a young woman torn by the claims of family traditions, conventional behavior, an independent career, and a strong streak of social and sexual rebellion. Her correspondence exudes contradictions in her self-perception—or, better, her preferred self-presentation—which can only be captured by that generally misused term, ambivalence. Her epistolary style reminds one of nothing so much as her own descriptions of Scarlett: "She knew how to smile so that her dimples leaped, how to walk pigeon-toed so her wide hoop skirts swayed entrancingly, how to look up into a man's face and then drop her eyes and bat the lids rapidly so that she seemed a-tremble with gentle emotion. Most of all she learned how to conceal from men a sharp intelligence beneath a face as sweet and bland as a baby's" (59).[7] Or, "At sixteen, thanks to Mammy and Ellen, she looked sweet, charming and giddy, but she was, in reality, self-willed, vain and obstinate. She had the easily stirred passions of her Irish father and nothing except the thinnest veneer of her mother's unselfish and forbearing nature" (59). Although Scarlett has nothing but contempt for the simpering girls who live out the prescriptions of Southern ladyhood, she nevertheless adopts the conventions when she wants to attract men.

Although *Gone With the Wind* cannot be reduced to a simple reading of Scarlett O'Hara as Margaret Mitchell, bits of Mitchell's attitudes can be found scattered among various characters, and Scarlett herself does contain attributes which Mitchell possessed. Mitchell's psychological complexities emerge from the structure of the novel as a whole, from the interactions among characters and their allotted rewards or punishments. Mitchell's own ambivalence becomes clearest in the gaps that separate the affects with which she invests a character—the sympathy or admiration she makes the character invite—and the destiny she assigns to the character. The historical setting further permits Mitchell both to distance her readers from the psychological drama and to bind them to it. For she uses history as a specific series of events—a drama in its own right—and as a common, nostalgic memory of a lost agrarian world.

Hers was the last generation to grow up with minimal exposure to the new cultures of radio and film. Her experience of vicariously living the histories of grandparents, parents, and communities through the telling and retelling of tales must have been common throughout the country. "I was about ten years old," she wrote, "before I learned that the war hadn't ended shortly before I was born."[8] In the South, the stories of fathers and the lullabies of mothers ensured a widespread and living engagement with the events of the Civil War and Reconstruction; similarly, elsewhere, historical events and interpretations probably became intertwined with the personal identities of many Americans. But, given the emergence of a national industrial and indeed corporate economy, that familial and local identity was becoming more a private and less a public matter. In this respect Mitchell wrote for a generation that increasingly recognized regional identities as distinct, yet in some sense interchangeable, strands in a national history. Even the special legacy of Southerners was becoming ever less a source of divisiveness and defensiveness under the influence of the proponents of the New South Creed.[9] The arrival of Woodrow Wilson in the White House opened a new stage in the vindication of Southern concerns: with him came the racial segregation of public buildings and his personal endorsement of D. W. Griffith's racist film, *Birth of a Nation*.

As social commentary, *Gone With the Wind* moves between a historical treatment of the 1860s and general statements about civilization as a universal category. But the oscillation between the particular and the general invites contemporary identification. To the extent that the readers' identification bridges the past and present, the statements about society proffered by the novel function as commentaries on contemporary problems. Mitchell's psychological realism, however complex, ensures the appeal of her work far more than does her faithful depiction of social types. It is the combination of contemporary psychological power and historical verisimilitude that commands attention. For Mitchell's accuracy and realism of detail can be compatible with a number of conflicting, broad patterns. To put it differently, the precision in detail does not necessarily tell us anything about the argument, commitments, or world view which the detail is marshalled to serve. What did Mitchell hope to accomplish in telling the tale of Scarlett O'Hara, and in writing a novel of the Civil War and Reconstruction?

The historical setting of *Gone With the Wind* cannot be reduced to a simple displacement of Mitchell's era, for that era, the 1920s, required special historical foundations.[10] For Mitchell, the New South, of which she was trying to make sense as a setting for female life, needed to be understood in the mainstream of American life. The middle-class values which were being challenged by the ferment of the 1920s had to be anchored in a national culture, not limited to sectional idiosyncracies. In *Gone With the Wind* Mitchell reread Southern history through a prism of conservative progressivism. If she indeed effected a certain displacement from the 1920s to the earlier period, she did so not to jettison it entirely, nor to reduce it to a simple case study of the present, but literally to reconstruct it. She sought to fashion a history appropriate to the national concerns and destiny of the New South.

Gone With the Wind as a whole transforms a particular regional past into a generalized national past. In this respect, it contributes to integrating Southern history into national history even as it reestablishes the South, with all its idiosyncracies, as an only slightly special case of an inclusive national destiny. Mitchell's antebellum South manifests features characteristic of the nation as a whole. Even prior to the war, the cavalier tradition is shown as infused with the blood of Irish immigrants. As W. J. Cash does in *The Mind of the South,* Mitchell emphasizes the assimilation of the various gradations of the white elite—specifically excluding poor "white trash"—into a rural precursor of the industrial middle class.[11]

Throughout the novel, Mitchell explicitly underscores her interest in the rise of Atlanta and the emergence of a business culture in the South. She returns regularly to the excitement and importance of Atlanta as a raw, growing, bustling city, the outgrowth of the railroads. She directly points to the similarities between Atlanta and Scarlett: "Atlanta was of [Scarlett's] own generation, crude with the crudities of youth and as headstrong and impetuous as herself. . . . " The two were roughly the same age and grew up together. During Scarlett's first seventeen years, Atlanta developed from a stake in the ground into a "thriving small city of ten thousand that was the center of attention for the whole state. The older quieter cities were wont to look upon the bustling new town with the sensations of a hen which has hatched a duckling." The maternal reference should be noted. In the eyes of the staid Georgia towns, Atlanta had little to recommend it save some railroads "and a bunch of mighty pushy people. . . . Scarlett always liked Atlanta for the very same reasons that made Savannah, Augusta, and Macon condemn it. Like herself, the town was a mixture of the old and the new in Georgia, in which the old often came off second best in its conflicts with the self-willed and vigorous new" (141–43).

Atlanta, not the "old days," emerges as the victor in *Gone With the Wind.* Tara, which initially figures as a dynamic, frontier plantation—the locus of vitality—ends as a place of retreat. In the early pages of the novel, Gerald

O'Hara confidently points to the land as the only reliable source of wealth. Even during the war, Scarlett recalls and echoes his view. But by the war's end, Scarlett must turn to the city to raise the money to pay the taxes on Tara. And the section of the novel devoted to Reconstruction takes place in the city. When, at the conclusion, Scarlett thinks of returning to Tara, she thinks only of a temporary refuge. With only the slightest exaggeration, it could appear as the typical house in the country to which busy city-dwellers repair for rest and refreshment. In this sense, it blends imaginatively with those New England farm houses that had also once encompassed productive labor. In Mitchell's rendition, the Civil War becomes a national turning point in the transition from rural to urban civilization. And this reading permits her to incorporate the South into a shared national drama.

This vision of Atlanta as symbol of a general urban vitality conflates the destiny of the city with the defense of middle-class values. Mitchell reserves her endorsement for an enterprising, indigenous, Southern bourgeoisie— for those who can adapt to the times without sacrificing the essence of their values. Her merciless depiction of the Yankees as rapacious, dishonest, political parasites identifies them as predators, not true capitalists. Yankees are those who manipulate and stir up Negroes and poor whites. She reserves her rage for those who came South to milk the victim. She never denies the possibility of honest Yankee businessmen, comparable to their Southern counterparts. But she does intend to make the country as a whole understand "what the South endured in the days of Civil War and Reconstruction."[12]

Atlanta stands for the dynamism of the New South. At the core of the novel lies Mitchell's fascination with the way in which a new world emerges from the ashes of the old. Time and again, she returns to the problem of a dying civilization in confrontation with one being born. How, she asks, does one make money from the collapse of a society? Who makes the money? How does one survive, adapt, and prosper in the wake of a major social upheaval? Historically, economically, and socially, Atlanta provides the lynchpin of *Gone With the Wind*. By the novel's close, all of the major characters have tied their destinies to that of the city. Similarly, the character of Scarlett provides the novel's identificatory core. For against the collapse of the Old South and the birth of the New, the novel chronicles Scarlett's coming of age—her painful assumption of the burdens of Southern womanhood. The historical cataclysm, however, transforms Scarlett's saga from the account of establishing a personal identity as a woman into an investigation of how to become—or whether to become—a lady.

The terms "woman" and "lady" evoke mature female identity, but in different forms. "Woman" suggests at once a more inclusive and more private female nature, whereas "lady" evokes the public representation of that nature. To be a lady is to have a public presence, to accept a public responsibility. But the essence of that presence and that responsibility consists in recognizing and maintaining a sexual division of labor that relegates any proper woman to the private sphere. No lady would admit that she, and not her husband, ran the plantation. No lady would admit to being hungry in public. No lady would admit to sexual desire or pleasure.

In Mitchell's account, the Civil War and Reconstruction forced the issue of how one remains a lady under new historical conditions. Changing times permit and even require new modes of behavior. At the same time, no society would survive did not its female members internalize certain standards and responsibilities. In *Gone With the Wind* the special case of appropriate female behavior and values in the collapse of a civilization is overdetermined by the private drama of a girl who grows to womanhood under tumultuous conditions. Mitchell provides ample evidence that Scarlett would have had trouble with or without the war. But without the war, social structures and norms would have provided a corset for her unruly impulses. It is Mammy who embodies those shattered structures and norms and who struggles in vain to tighten the laces of the corset.

> What a young miss could do and what she could not do were as different as black and white in Mammy's mind; there was no middle ground of deportment between. Suellen and Carreen were clay in her powerful hands and harkened respectfully to most of her warnings. But it had always been a struggle to teach Scarlett that most of her natural impulses were unladylike. Mammy's victories over Scarlett were hard-won and represented a guile unknown to the white mind (76–77).

Scarlett stands apart in *Gone With the Wind,* not merely because she is the central character, but because for her alone among the female characters do the years of the war and its aftermath render problematical the question of appropriate gender role—the definition of being, the aspiration to become, a lady. Any understanding of Scarlett's personality must take account of the other characters who, by responding to the pressures of the times, relate to her and provide both the context and the measuring stick for her responses. Mitchell once claimed that her novel had been written entirely "through Scarlett's eyes. What she understood was written down; what she did not understand—and there were many things beyond her comprehension— they were left to the reader's imagination."[13] Mitchell's claim will not withstand even a cursory reading of her text. Possibly, she believed that she had written from Scarlett's point of view. But if so, she confused her own identification with Scarlett and had trouble differentiating her function as presentor of Scarlett's vision from her function as commentator on Scarlett. In any event, whatever the source of Mitchell's ambivalence about sexuality, gender identity, and gender role, it reaches schizophrenic proportions. Her relationship with Scarlett, her own creature, exemplifies her dilemma of identification and judgment.

Scarlett O'Hara is not beautiful. Neither is she a lady, although in her idiosyncratic way, she sentimentally aspires to be one, providing that it does not cost too much. Her adored mother Ellen had been a lady; Melanie Hamilton Wilkes is a lady; Aunt Pittypat Hamilton, Mrs. Merriwether, Mrs. Meade, India Wilkes, and the other Atlanta worthies pride themselves on being ladies. Her sisters, Suellen and Carreen, suffering like Scarlett from Ellen's saintly distance, are pale shadows of ladies. Belle Watling, to be sure, is not a lady, but the classic whore with a heart of gold, a shrewd and successful business woman in her own right, has a far deeper sense than Scarlett of the essential qualities that informed true ladyhood. But however splendid her personal qualities, the code cannot admit her as a lady. Scarlett, for her part, has no time for irrelevant niceties, and no understanding of the deeper meanings. Raw like the burgeoning city of Atlanta, determined and grasping like her Irish immigrant forebearers, Scarlett has never been nice and, with the advent of the war, commits herself wholeheartedly to surviving. Scarlett's survival tactics include marriage without love hastily entered into for spiteful reasons, manslaughter, the theft of her sister's fiancé, flagrant disregard of proper female behavior to the point of risking the lives of her own menfolk, and the mindless sacrifice of her husband's life. The same arsenal houses such lesser sins as dancing while in mourning, offering herself for cold cash to pay the taxes on Tara, parading around town while pregnant, flaunting a disconcerting talent for business, and otherwise violating all accepted conventions that defined the Southern lady. In Scarlett's judgment, the Yankees, in all other respects so despicable, were right "on this matter. It took money to be a lady" (610). The times, the grim days of the war and Reconstruction, demanded harsh stratagems of those who would survive them. Survival assured, the times would permit the resumption of ladylike graces. Let others retain, at the risk of destruction, the inner sense of being ladies, or assume the mask, whatever their inner feelings of despair. She was different. And "she knew she would never feel like a lady again until her table was weighted with silver and crystal and smoking with rich food, until her own horses and carriages stood in her stables, until black hands and not white took the cotton from Tara" (609).

Mitchell makes scant effort to redeem Scarlett from the stark self-interest and greed of her chronicled behavior. On the contrary, from the opening pages of the novel in which upland Georgia basks in the glow of antebellum serenity, she establishes the fundamental contours of Scarlett's grasping personality. The self-conscious manipulation with which Scarlett pursues her prey foreshadows precisely the resources she will muster in her pursuit of financial security during Reconstruction. Her marriage to Rhett Butler and the ensuing hold on material security do not suffice to transform her into a real lady. But then Scarlett lacks any vital understanding of what it is to be one.

Through Scarlett, Mitchell exposes the hypocrisy of being a lady or a gentleman. Time and again, she shows Scarlett chafing under the constraints of correct behavior and utterance. No one, in Scarlett's view, could believe the phrases that govern polite interchange. Repeatedly, she mentally dismisses Melanie as "mealy-mouthed." Yet Mitchell also shows Scarlett raging because Rhett cannot be counted on to be a gentleman. In the scene of the charity bazaar in Atlanta, Scarlett worries that Rhett cannot be trusted to observe the gentleman's code and keep his mouth shut. A few pages later, during the same scene, Scarlett flares up at the hypocrisy of required ladylike conduct. Finally, in the name of the Cause, Rhett bids for Scarlett as his partner to lead the opening reel. Scarlett, aching to dance, furious at the imprisonment of her mourning, joins him, feet tapping "like castanets," green eyes flashing. This one scene captures all the contradictions of Mitchell's attitudes. For the codes against which Scarlett rebels also provide her protection: she festers at their demands, but fears a world that will not provide her the respect the codes are designed to ensure. If she does not always wish to meet the requirements of being a lady, she should not wish to be treated as one.

Mitchell thus remains ambivalent about Scarlett's difficulties. She regularly calls attention to Scarlett's natural vibrancy. "There was no one to tell Scarlett that her own personality, frighteningly vital though it was, was more attractive than any masquerade she might adopt. Had she been told, she would have been pleased but unbelieving. And the civilization of which she was a part would have been unbelieving too, for at no time before or since, had so low a premium been placed on female naturalness" (80). Here, Mitchell seems to hold civilization responsible for repressing healthy and attractive female vitality, but her novel as a whole offers a more complex reading of the relation between female vitality and civilization. Vitality serves as a code word for sexuality, and Mitchell harbored conflicting attitudes towards the proper relation between sexuality, gender identity, and gender role.

Her confusion on this matter endows the novel with a complexity that transcends Scarlett's stereotypical features. For indisputably, if in an occasionally perverse way, Scarlett invites identification. The dynamics of that identification turn upon Scarlett's proximity to young bourgeois women of the twenties and thirties. Her career raises questions of appropriate female behavior in a changing world. Her internal life reverberates with overtones of the early twentieth-century crisis in the bourgeois family and the received notions of fitting female behavior.[14] Much of the force of the novel as an affirmation of acceptable, middle-class social attitudes depends upon Scarlett's psychological plausibility. Scarlett herself is caught in a war between the socially ordained role into which she is expected to fit and her own natural impulses. The war in Scarlett, as perhaps in Mitchell herself, is fierce, for she lacks that solid bridge between the two—a strong identity as a woman—which might permit her to weather the storms of social change. But the acceptance of herself as a woman, Mitchell implies, would have required a resilient identification with another woman, presumably her mother, that would have nurtured her initiation into female sexuality and generativity.

As Scarlett herself comes to understand at the close of the novel, the only women she has ever loved and respected are her mother and Melanie. Tellingly, Scarlett omits Mammy from this company despite compelling claims. As Rhett (who along with Ashley represents the voice of objective judgment) categorically affirms, both Ellen and Melanie were genuinely great ladies. Scarlett's tragedy lies in her inability to understand the meaning of being a lady. Scarlett is correct in her criticisms of the hypocrisies of the pseudo-ladies, although even here, she underestimates their strengths. Surviving the war and its aftermath calls for more than forms of gentility. Scarlett fails to realize that the prevailing etiquette represents a social effort to codify, institutionalize, and reproduce the deeper qualities of the lady and the fabric of an entire society. Having never grasped the depth and meaning of the informing spirit, she confuses it with its forms. So deeply does she miss the point, that until the moment of Melanie's death she remains unaware that Melanie believes in the words she uses and the standards she observes, and that those words and standards derive from strength rather than weakness. Only at Melanie's deathbed does she recognize that Melanie too would have killed the Yankee who threatened them—or would have died in the attempt.

Ellen and Melanie are presented as attractive and admirable, albeit highly self-disciplined and possibly repressed. The interpretation adopted depends upon one's angle of vision and the relative weight accorded to Scarlett's perceptions, as against an independent reading that derives from the actions and words of the characters themselves. Thus, Scarlett reveres Ellen even though the reader has ample evidence that Ellen may have failed decisively as a mother. Ellen's most direct address to Scarlett comes in the form of a letter, written as soon as Ellen receives word of Scarlett's shameless dancing at the Atlanta charity bazaar. That letter, with its cold feelings, could have been written by any one of the Atlanta worthies. Melanie, on the same occasion, insists on believing the best of Scarlett and defends her. Yet Scarlett persists 'in seeing Melanie as pale, fragile, and lacking in womanly warmth and charm—in a word, asexual. The reader, however, having seen Melanie's plain face flare into beauty with the passion of her love for Ashley, has every reason to appreciate her special strength. Both Melanie and Ellen lack that raw undisciplined sexuality that pulsates in Scarlett herself, but Mitchell makes less than clear whether she regards sexuality as a male or female trait. Time and again, she links Scarlett's exuberance to her paternal inheritance. She establishes Scarlett's early preference for the activities of boys over those of girls. She proclaims Scarlett's repugnance for and failure at motherhood. Although she leaves no doubt about Scarlett's attractiveness to men, she links Scarlett's success as a belle to her unseemly ambition.

Mitchell remains preoccupied with those features of being a lady that survive social upheaval. If the role of lady is constructed and carries serious responsibilities, how much of that role can be taken to persist through change? Or, to put it differently, does being a lady possess an essence that remains constant as manners change? The sections of the novel that describe Scarlett's early forays into the world of business betray what could be interpreted as a strong feminist approval of the self-reliance, business skills, and survival abilities of the heroine. By Mitchell's day, the South had a tradition of resilient women who, with or without their menfolk, had seen their families through the difficult postbellum decades and had reestablished family fortunes. Scarlett's economic success need not have contravened her standing as a lady. Scarlett runs into trouble not for adapting to new times, nor for displaying a vigorous individualism, but for transgressing those boundaries at which individualism becomes greed and adaptation a threat to any viable social order. For Mitchell, those limits seem to have come with the employment of convicts, the systematic betrayal of business's own standards of probity, and female intrusion—however inadvertent—into the political domain. But if Mitchell shows Scarlett's irresponsible actions as bearing heavy consequences, she does not show Scarlett experiencing pain or guilt as a result of them. The social dimensions of superego sanctions are delineated, but Scarlett has not internalized them. Her own responses remain determined by whether she gets what she wants: at the center of Scarlett, the apparent woman, lingers a demanding and frightened child. In presenting Scarlett as emotionally immature and willful, Mitchell validates the legitimacy of social constraints on female lives. In presenting Scarlett as so personally immune to the normal emotional responsibilities for her socially inappropriate behavior, Mitchell questions the psychological foundations for socially prescribed roles. She remains, in short, deadlocked on the social possibilities for and the social legitimacy of the free expression of female nature.

Mitchell's strategy highlights a gap between the desire and its object, between the act and its emotional resonance. The formal account of Scarlett's actions and behavior is shadowed by unstated psychological considerations. The central flaw in Scarlett's character, the source of her egoism, derives from the relationship with her mother that purportedly furnishes her standards of being a lady. All explicit references to Ellen in the novel, including Scarlett's own, are positive. Yet all indirect evidence suggests that Scarlett never attained that psychological identification with her mother that would have provided the bedrock for becoming her mother's successor. At the center of the novel, at the end of the devastating road back from the destruction of Atlanta, falls Ellen's death. For Scarlett, that road "that was to end in Ellen's arms" ended in a "blank wall," in "a dead end." Scarlett had believed that she was fleeing to "the protection of her mother's love wrapped about her like an eiderdown quilt." With Ellen dead, the hope of that love had vanished. From her despair and abandonment, Scarlett wrests the determination to survive. Somewhere "along the road to Tara, she had left her girlhood behind her." The scene that marks her assumption of womanhood ends with her vow: "as God is my witness, I'm never going to be hungry again" (418). That night, she first dreams what is to become her recurrent nightmare, of being lost in the fog. On this occasion, Melanie comes to her bedside. Later in the novel, Rhett would comfort her, promising to feed and spoil her like a treasured child. But she still passes on to Bonnie, her daughter, a fear of the dark.

The first appearance of the dream underscores the psychological dimension of her fight against hunger. The scene in the fields of Tara conflates, in a manner that persists throughout the novel, the elements of ladyhood that derive from social structure and those that derive from intrapsychic identification—especially from the mother-daughter relationship. Scarlett's willfulness, graspingness, and jealousy of other women, including her own sisters, have been present from the opening pages. Her admiration of and love for her mother have also been there. But her mother emerges as distant and preoccupied, as having never recovered from an early passion, as having little of her emotional substance to give to those she so dutifully cares for. Scarlett germinated the need for love and nurture from her childhood. The crisis of her adulthood consolidates a persisting need. The social and historical circumstances of that crisis merely determine the form and intensity of her adult behavior. The underlying longing remains to be wrapped in the quilt of her mother's love. The hunger she determines to appease harks back to a longstanding unconscious feeling of deprivation.

Richard King has recently argued, in *A Southern Renaissance,* that the Southern family romance, which "placed the father-son relationship at its center," left only the role of mother to the white woman who, as mistress of the plantation, was to care for the "wants and needs of her family both white and black." In King's view, this "queen of the home" was denied erotic appeal and, in "extreme form," was "stripped of any emotional nurturing attributes at all. Eventually, she came to assume a quasi-Virgin Mary role. . . ." Interestingly, Mitchell does state that Scarlett perceives her mother as the Virgin Mary. But she also provides the reader with information that supports a more complex interpretation.[15]

Ellen Robillard O'Hara had, as an adolescent, experienced an intense passion for a young cousin whom her family prevented her from marrying. After his death, in a bar room brawl in New Orleans, the young Ellen cried all night and then dried her tears and closed her heart. Her marriage to Gerald O'Hara is presented simply as an alternative to entering a convent for the rest of her life. This renunciation of her own passionate self crippled Ellen's ability to provide nurture to her own daughters and bequeathed, at least to Scarlett, contradictory attitudes toward men as objects of sexual and emotional desire. On the surface, Mitchell affirms Ellen's goodness and Scarlett's love for her. But Mitchell also shows that Scarlett managed to hide much of her impetuous, passionate self from Ellen, that in crucial ways Ellen did not know—perhaps did not want to know—Scarlett. Mitchell also informs us that Ellen had never told Scarlett that "desire and attainment were two different matters" (73). These clues and others invite the reader to criticize Ellen from Scarlett's perspective, much in the manner that Lillian Smith would criticize her own mother. Yet they do not commit Mitchell to an open critique of the mother's (her own mother's) failure vis à vis the daughter.[16]

If Ellen's death forces Scarlett to assume a womanhood for which she is not emotionally prepared, Melanie's death, at the novel's close, provides her with an opportunity to relive and rework that earlier loss. The parallels between Ellen and Melanie are deep and numerous. Most important, however, in psychological terms, is Melanie's marriage to Ashley, whom Scarlett loves. Scarlett's failure to understand the nature of Ashley and Melanie's love for each other, her attempt to fathom the secrets of that love through reading Melanie's letters from Ashley, her resentment of Melanie in the face of Melanie's maternally unselfish love for her, all evoke the attitudes of a female Oedipal crisis, of an adolescent girl who loves her father and hates her mother. Melanie and Ashley permit Mitchell to explore that crisis because they are not Scarlett's parents. Yet the emotional logic of the situation forces the reader to take it as evidence of Mitchell's using Melanie as a double for Ellen. And whatever Scarlett's conscious feelings, her relationship with Melanie permits her to come to terms with her ambivalent feelings about her mother. Only at Melanie's deathbed does Scarlett begin to see clearly, to arrive at

some measure of self-understanding. Only at Melanie's death does she recognize the true object of longing in her recurring nightmare of cold and
hunger. Throughout the novel we are told that Scarlett loves Ellen; as the
novel progresses, we come to know that Melanie loves Scarlett. That love,
as Rhett asserts, may indeed be Scarlett's cross, but it may also be her salvation. For at the end, the loss of Rhett may have to be weighted against her
recognizing Rhett as the object of her desire.[17]

Ellen had endowed Scarlett, the child, with a hunger for herself, a longing for maternal love. That longing colors Scarlett's choice of men. Both
consciously and unconsciously, Scarlett perceives Ashley Wilkes to be cut
from the same cloth as Ellen. Aristocratic and self-controlled, he possesses
self-knowledge and acts according to principles that she cannot fathom.
Until the final scenes of the novel, Scarlett misunderstands and misevaluates
Ashley: she understands neither his strength nor his weakness, least of all
does she understand his love for Melanie, or that his love could coexist with
an altogether different love for herself. In comparable fashion, Scarlett mis-
perceives Rhett: only in the final pages of the novel does she recognize her
love for him (although the reader has known of that love since the early sections of the novel on the war years in Atlanta), but by then she has (apparently) lost him. Scarlett's woeful inability to fathom her own desires or those
of the men in her life has its roots in her inability to arrive at a mature female
identity—to become a woman. Or so Mitchell would seem to be suggesting. Scarlett fails to integrate her needs and her desires, her understanding
of love—the longing of romantic love—with her sexual feelings. There are
persisting hints that Scarlett, the erstwhile tomboy, would, on some level,
prefer to be a man. Mitchell never fully resolves these tensions. For although
she allows Scarlett a clearer perception of herself and her desires, she deprives
her of the objects of that desire. In the end, Scarlett has only herself. Even
Tara will provide only a temporary retreat, not a full life.

Mitchell's ambivalent attitudes towards female sexuality, gender identity,
and gender role—desire, womanhood, and ladyhood—informed her own
life, as well as the life of her heroine. The discrete components of this ambivalence include uncertainty as to whether sexuality is compatible with
womanhood, mixed feelings about motherhood and its relationship to sexuality, and the possibility for wedding female individualism to ladyhood.
The core of Scarlett's dilemma remains whether she can transform her need
for her mother into love for a man and children. And this basic psycho-
dynamic pattern is faithful to an increasingly typical early twentieth-century
pattern. Ellen could be read as a positive rendition of Philip Wylie's
"Momism." Gerald O'Hara could qualify as the absent father. Scarlett herself could be recast as a 1920s flapper.[18] Mitchell mediates, rather than invites,

these transpositions. But the compelling popularity of her novel may have turned on her readers' effecting the identifications for themselves. Even the resonances that bind contemporary identifications to the historical plot do not clarify Mitchell's own attitudes toward the appropriate meaning and responsibilities of womanhood and ladyhood, especially toward female destiny relative to that of men.

Historians such as Anne Firor Scott and A. Elizabeth Taylor have demonstrated the interdependence of the position of Southern women and the Southern social system as a whole, and have argued that Southern women themselves criticized Southern patriarchy.[19] Mitchell understands these arguments, but on the surface, her own critique is more narrowly focused on men as men and is more indirect in its expression. For Mitchell does not so much criticize men as display their weaknesses and, too often, kill them off. At the same time, she endows men with the objective view of history and the nature of civilization. Despite the constant juxtaposition of Rhett and Ashley in Scarlett's mind, Mitchell presents them as one in their grasp of historical process. Thus, even as individual men fall by the wayside, men as a group emerge as the custodians of objective knowledge. The problem is to identify Mitchell's own ultimate attitude toward the claims of female independence. That problem is complicated by her play with transsexual identifications: "But Scarlett, child of Gerald, found the road to ladyhood hard" (58). Ellen's early passion suggests that sexuality cannot simply be classified as masculine. Mitchell nonetheless underscores Scarlett's inheritance from her unruly Irish father and portrays raw sexuality as masculine and inherently dominating—to wit, the famous scene in which a drunken Rhett carries Scarlett off to bed. Mitchell also considers the relations between sexuality and generativity problematical: Scarlett miscarries the baby conceived in her and Rhett's mutual passion; Ellen, reproducing without passion, lost all of her sons; Melanie dies in childbirth; Bonnie, beloved of both Scarlett and Rhett, dies perhaps as a result of her inherited Irish recklessness, perhaps as a result of her father's delight in her unladylike high spirits, perhaps as a result of the Oedipal confusions that inform Scarlett's own life, perhaps in testimony to Scarlett and Rhett's failed communication—their inability to reproduce.

Any of these readings is compatible with one or another female critique of patriarchy and the toll it exacted from women. Any is compatible with a severe judgment on women who rebel against their ordained role. Mitchell, like Scott and Taylor, stresses the interdependence of female role and social system. If she, consciously or not, resented the constraints that the role of lady imposed on women, she remained attached to the class basis of the social system—to the class and race relations within which that role was essential.

But Mitchell's strategy is complicated by her interest in social change and her commitment to establishing the Old South as a special case of a general national past. Her treatment of the Old South brilliantly blends a nostalgia for a lost social order, a more stable agrarian world, with a specific evocation of Southern culture. She eschews any defense of slavery as a coherent social system in favor of evoking a harmonious agricultural order reminiscent of that evoked in *I'll Take My Stand*.[20] Her early discussion of Tara, resting upon a detailed rendition of upland Georgia, establishes the specificity of time and place, but none of the description bears any relation to the slave system. Mitchell brings her readers to accept a particular world without including any of the social features that structure it. By this marvelous sleight of hand, she invites a national audience to accept the old South as a direct antecedent of its own American civilization. The lost antebellum civilization is validated for the South even as it is absorbed into the loss of an earlier American order.

Similarly, Mitchell recast Southern slavery to conform to a national class system. Her attitudes toward blacks resemble those of Howard Odum in their social Darwinism and in "the racist transformation of social 'facts' into natural givens." Yet, as Odum did in his later works, Mitchell also allows for the development of a black leadership under white guidance. Her attitudes remain contradictory, all the more because she draws upon black characters to provide psychologically revealing doubles of whites, but she is wedded to conservative class and racial attitudes. Her attitudes toward contemporary issues shape her depiction of slavery which, in her treatment, disappears as a coherent social system.[21]

Mitchell distinguishes between house and field slaves. In an authorial intervention, she explains that "the house negroes and yard negroes" despised "these lowly blacks." For the position of the house slaves rested upon merit and effort. "Just as Ellen had done, other plantation mistresses throughout the South had put the pickanninies through courses of training and elimination to select the best of them for the positions of greater responsibility. Those consigned to the fields were the ones least willing or able to learn, the least energetic, the least honest and trustworthy, the most vicious and brutish. And now this class, the lowest in the black social order, was making life a misery for the South" (654). Mitchell here echoes the prevailing capitalist ideology of work, schooling, and the promotion of merit, tempered by a harsh attitude toward crime.

Mitchell also describes even the good, deserving blacks as "monkey-faced" and "child-like." The former fieldhands, whom the Yankees had so irresponsibly promoted to positions of responsibility, "conducted themselves as creatures of small intelligence might naturally be expected to do. Like monkeys or small children turned loose among treasured objects whose value is beyond their comprehension, they ran wild—either from perverse pleasure in destruction or simply because of their ignorance." Not naturally malicious, they were, "as a class, childlike in mentality . . ." (654). Mitchell thus combines racism as a justification for black subordination with a commitment to individual betterment through the work ethic. Blacks, she believes, can rise in the social ladder to the extent that they accept and profit from the tutelage of their white betters.

Mitchell cannot resist some nostalgic pronouncements on the ties binding the black and white family, but her star characters in this category—Mammy, Uncle Peter, Sam, and, with special reservations, Prissy—all relate to the white family as individuals rather than as members of families of their own. And the personal loyalties that transcend class and racial lines all have roots in the lost agrarian civilization. When the blacks remain true to those roots and reject their chance for independence, they fare well and even have the freedom to chastise their masters. The moment they cut loose from the restraining bonds, their inferiority becomes a crippling disadvantage. By thus substituting racism for slavery as the basis for domination, Mitchell endorses precisely the process that historically established the grounds for a reconciliation between the North and the South.

Mitchell's harsh attitude towards blacks collectively does not prevent her from valuing individual blacks on the basis of their personal attributes. Mammy especially, but also Uncle Peter, Sam, and even Prissy are shown as genuine characters in their own right. Mitchell in fact uses them as psychological doubles for important white characters. Uncle Peter functions as a double for Ashley and, beyond him, for the white gentlemen of the antebellum South. Uncle Peter embodies all the manners, bearing, and respect for convention that purportedly characterized the antebellum aristocracy. From this perspective, Uncle Peter's finicky timidity reflects on Ashley and alerts the reader to those weaknesses which Scarlett refuses to see, or at least to interpret correctly. Sam, in contrast, throws into relief the solidity and dependability that underlie Rhett's unconventional and disturbing surface behavior. Prissy illuminates Scarlett's own failure to achieve an internal sense of female generativity: "Laws, Mis Scarlett, I doan know nothing 'bout birthin babies." And, in this case, since Prissy has claimed to have precisely that knowledge, her failure underscores the gap between Scarlett's external appearance as a grown woman and her internal identity as a needy child.

In this context, Mammy plays the most complex role of all. The life of the character almost escapes Mitchell's control, and assuredly escapes Mitchell's racist convictions. For Mammy, the compelling double for Ellen, comes close to providing Scarlett with everything that Ellen could not.

Mammy's knowledge of Scarlett and her acceptance of her could have provided the foundations for Scarlett's gender identity. Mammy neither sees nor experiences any contradictions between understanding Scarlett and loving or forgiving her. Lacing Scarlett into her corset, forcing her to eat before a barbecue so she will not disgrace herself by eating at it, are to Mammy the unavoidable requirements of correct behavior. Scarlett's recalcitrance elicits disciplinary action but not condemnation. Mammy could have molded Scarlett into a lady, precisely because Mammy would have felt no need to repudiate Scarlett the needy child and the sensual woman. Ellen, having repudiated those qualities in herself, could not afford to recognize them in Scarlett and, therefore, could not help her deal with them. Mammy, swishing proudly in her red petticoat, knows as much about sexuality as Belle Watling. Mammy also knows that you wear your red satin where it does not show. But if Mitchell could, consciously, allow Mammy to lay bare Ellen's failures as a woman and as a mother, she could not surmount her class and racial attitudes in order to allow Mammy's knowing nurture to provide Scarlett's maternal identification. Herein, perhaps, lies her most devastating, if unintended, condemnation of the values she sought to support.

Gone With the Wind originated in and spoke to a particular moment in American culture. Its very status as a novel, straddling the worlds of elite and mass culture, captured the dilemma of a bourgeois society that struggled to preserve its own values against internal rebellion and to engage the allegiance of a broad and heterogeneous popular base. Not unlike the new languages of radio, film, and advertising, it appeared to offer Americans an image of themselves at once specific enough to invite identification and general enough to encompass national diversity.[22] Mitchell's re-creation of the 1860s, so faithful in its historical detail, bound the destruction of an ordered world to the birth of modern America. Structurally equated as the two great opportunities for making a fortune, the building-up and breaking-up of civilizations emerge as cyclical recurrences in human affairs. That philosophical distance in no way detracts from the poignancy and drama of the carefully documented tale. Nor does it ever soar to encompass the full range of human destinies. Rather, it subsumes a purportedly traditional society under the aegis of bourgeois norms. And this fusion, in turn, promises the persistence of those norms in a world that is outstripping its original social base.

No one more compellingly portrayed the relation between the past and the future of the nation and the South than Mitchell. But, for her, the binding up of wounds required a shared bourgeois ethic and could ill afford the luxury of mourning a "feudal" past. Under the bourgeois rubric, the nation could be understood as the destiny of the South, and the South as a generalized, rural, national past. Perhaps it is a final, fitting irony that the magnetic core of Mitchell's vision of a revitalized bourgeois order lay in the unconscious life of a most disorderly girl.

Notes

1. The problem of genre merits particular attention with respect to *Gone With the Wind*, but transcends the scope of this essay. As a novel, *Gone With the Wind* falls somewhere between the great bourgeois novels and recent mass-market melodramas or gothics, and blends features of all. Less programmatic, at once historically more accurate and psychologically more complex than the classic melodrama, it nonetheless approaches the melodrama in that its "universal moral order validates current social attitudes." And, like the social melodrama, it basically affirms a connection between traditional middle-class domestic morality and "the operative principles of the cosmos." See John G. Cawelti, *Adventure, Mystery, and Romance* (Chicago: Univ. of Chicago Press, 1976), on these questions of genre. *Gone With the Wind* also owes much to the tradition of the historical novel analyzed by Georg Lukacs, *The Historical Novel* (Boston: Beacon Press, 1963).

2. David O. Selznick's spectacular film only extended its impact. Among many, see Roland Flamini, *Scarlett, Rhett, and a Cast of Thousands: The Filming of* Gone With the Wind (New York: Collier, 1975); and Jack Temple Kirby, *Media-Made Dixie: The South in the American Imagination* (Baton Rouge: Louisiana State Univ. Press, 1978).

3. Finis Farr, *Margaret Mitchell of Atlanta* (New York: Avon, 1974), 110–13. See also Richard Gray, *The Literature of Memory: Modern Writers of the American South* (Baltimore: Johns Hopkins Univ. Press, 1977), 93, 151.

4. Introd., in Warren Susman, ed., *Culture and Commitment, 1929–1945* (New York: George Braziller, 1973); and his "The Thirties," in Stanley Coben and Lorman Ratner, eds., *The Development of an American Culture* (Englewood Cliffs, N.J.: Prentice-Hall, 1970)[, 179–218].

5. Among many, see James McGovern, "The American Woman's Pre–World War I Freedom in Manners and Morals," *Journal of American History,* 55 (1968), 315–33; Estelle Freedman, "The New Woman: Changing Views of Women in the 1920's," *Journal of American History,* 61 (1974), 372–93; Gerald E. Critoph, "The Flapper and Her Critics," in Carol V. R. George, ed., *Remember the Ladies: Essays in Honor of Nelson Manfred Blake* (Syracuse, N.Y.: Univ. of Syracuse Press, 1975).

6. Cf. Dawson Gaillard, "*Gone With the Wind* as Bildungsroman, or Why Did Rhett Butler Really Leave Scarlett O'Hara?" *Georgia Review,* 28 (1974), 9–18.

7. Farr, *Margaret Mitchell,* is the most comprehensive treatment available. See also, *Atlanta Historical Bulletin: Margaret Mitchell Memorial Issue,* 9 (1950); Robert L. Grover, "Margaret Mitchell, The Lady From Atlanta," *Georgia Historical Quarterly,* 52 (1968), 53–69; and Richard Harwell, ed., *Margaret Mitchell's* Gone With the Wind *Letters, 1936–1949* (New York: Macmillan, 1976). All references to *Gone With the Wind* will be to the first edition (New York: Macmillan, 1936).

8. Harwell, ed., *Letters,* 3.

9. Paul Gaston, *The New South Creed: A Study in Southern Mythmaking* (New York: Knopf, 1970). See also Michael O'Brien, *The Idea of the American South, 1920–1941* (Baltimore: Johns Hopkins Univ. Press, 1979); Daniel Aaron, *The Unwritten War: American Writers and the Civil War* (New York: Oxford Univ. Press, 1973); and Gray, *Literature of Memory.*

10. Mitchell's work may, in this respect, be compared to that of Ulrich Bonnell Phillips, *Life and Labor in the Old South* (1929; rpt. Boston: Little, Brown, 1963). See also Eugene D. Genovese, "Ulrich Bonnell Phillips: Two Studies," in his *In Red and Black: Marxian Explorations in Southern and Afro-American History* (New York: Pantheon, 1968), 259–98.

11. Cash, *The Mind of the South* (New York: Knopf, 1941). Mitchell recognized the similarity between her views and those of Cash and warmly praised his book when it appeared.

12. Harwell, ed., *Letters,* 57.

13. Ibid., 41.

14. See, *inter alia,* John C. Burnham, "The Progressive Era Revolution in American Attitudes toward Sex," *Journal of American History,* 59 (1973), 885–908; and references in note 5 above. For changing Southern attitudes, see John Ruoff, *Southern Womanhood, 1865–1920: An Intellectual and Cultural Study* (Ann Arbor: Univ. Microfilms, 1980); Anne Firor Scott, "The 'New Woman' in the New South," *South Atlantic Quarterly,* 65 (1962), 473–83. Cf. Ellen Glasgow, *In This Our Life* (New York: Grosset and Dunlap, 1941).

15. King, *A Southern Renaissance: The Cultural Awakening of the American South, 1930–1955* (New York: Oxford Univ. Press, 1980), 35.

16. Lillian Smith, *Killers of the Dream,* rev. ed. (New York: Norton, 1961).

17. This reading suggests that the years between the death of Ellen and that of Melanie constitute, in part, an extended period of mourning for Scarlett. See Sigmund Freud, "Mourning and Melancholia," in James Strachey, ed., *The Standard Edition of the Complete Psychological Works of Sigmund Freud, 1914–1916* (London: Hogarth Press, 1957), XIV, 243–58. For the general problems of female psychological development, see J. Chasseguet-Smirgel, et al., *Female Sexuality* (Ann Arbor: Univ. of Michigan Press, 1970); Harold P. Blum, ed., *Female Psychology: Contemporary Psychoanalytic Views* (New York: International Universities Press, 1977).

18. Philip Wylie, *A Generation of Vipers* (New York: Rinehart, 1942).

19. Scott, "Women's Perspective on the Patriarchy in the 1850's," *Journal of American History,* 61 (1974)[: 52–64]; Taylor, "The Last Phase of the Woman Suffrage Movement in Georgia," *Georgia Historical Quarterly,* 43 (1959), 11–28.

20. Twelve Southerners, *I'll Take My Stand: The South and the Agrarian Tradition* (New York: Harper and Brothers, 1930).

21. Odum, *The Social and Mental Traits of the Negro* (New York: Columbia Univ. Press, 1910), 52 ff.; and King, *Southern Renaissance,* 41.

22. For example, see Lary May, *Screening Out the Past* (New York: Oxford Univ. Press, 1980).

Ten

Unspeakable Things Unspoken

Ghosts and Memories in the Narratives
of African-American Women

> Everybody knew what she was called, but nobody anywhere knew
> her name. Disremembered and unaccounted for, she cannot be lost
> because no one is looking for her, and even if they were, how can they
> call her if they don't know her name? Although she has claim, she is
> not claimed. . . .
> It was not a story to pass on. . . .
> So they forgot her. Like an unpleasant dream during a troubling
> sleep. . . .
> This was not a story to pass on.

The concluding pages of Toni Morrison's novel *Beloved,* from which these
words are taken, evoke the difficulty of telling the story of women's experience of slavery—of the cost of slavery for enslaved mothers and their children.[1] Beloved, the ghost of the murdered, "crawling already?" baby, remains
not lost, but disremembered and unaccounted for, because no one is even
looking for her. The story of her murder by her own mother, which implicated slavery in its entirety, including the other members of the community
of slaves, was not one that anyone—black or white, slave or free—chose to
tell. So they forgot. And their forgetting, even more than the original event,
becomes a story that cannot be passed on.

*Unspeakable Things Unspoken: Ghosts and Memories in the Narratives of African-American
Women.* 1992 Elsa Goveia Memorial Lecture. Mona, Jamaica: Department of History, University of the West Indies, 1993. Copyright 1992 by the Department of History, the University of the West Indies, Mona. All rights reserved. Used by permission of the publisher.

The woman's story of slavery has challenged historians no less than it has challenged novelists and autobiographers. Since the nineteenth century it has been common to assert that slavery was necessarily worse for women than for men, since they were subjected to special brutality and indignity on account of their sex. In general, however, historians have primarily focused upon the injustice and indignities of slavery for men. Those who defended the freedom of labor, soil, and men readily identified the enslavement of men as a violation of the fundamental principles of individualism to which they were committed.[2] It was not that historians have lacked sympathy for the violation of women's sexuality, but that many have found it difficult to write of it from a subjective perspective—from the "inside."

The recent historians who have devoted most attention to understanding the history of African-American slaves in the United States have written, in large measure, from a commitment to documenting and representing the strength and vitality of slave culture.[3] They have, accordingly, emphasized the slaves' commitment to marriage and family. At the extreme, Robert Fogel and Stanley Engerman have even argued that the slaves developed and enforced a sense of family loyalty and sexual morality that remarkably resembled the values of their masters.[4] The recent debates among these and other historians have primarily concerned the respective elements of African and American culture that the slaves forged under adversity.

Yet more recently, scholars such as Deborah White, who have focused explicitly on the experience of slave women, have more directly emphasized the sexual exploitation of slave women by white men, notably their masters. Yet even as White exposed and deplored the abuse of slave women's sexuality, she especially argued that the experience of slavery, combined with African traditions, led African-American women to develop a greater sense of autonomy and independence than their white contemporaries.[5] Thus even she did not explore the possible consequences of sexual exploitation for slave women's minds and hearts, much less their relations with the other members of the slave community.

While working on *Within the Plantation Household,* I came increasingly to believe that slavery had taken a higher toll upon the sexual relations of African-American men and women than most of us were prepared to face. With this matter, even more than with others, the evidence tended to be oblique, veiled, indirect. Through the disguises and reticences, it nonetheless seemed to me that there lurked a troubling story. Countless slave infants may indeed have died from Sudden Infant Death Syndrome, from disease, and from inadequate supplies of maternal milk, but some undetermined number also fell victim to infanticide. No less disturbing, it seemed clear that the sexual exploitation of black women by white men might poison those women's relations with the men of their own people who might, in all too human a fashion, turn their rage against the victim. As a result, in any given instance, the most violent abusers of slave women's sexuality might be black rather than white men.

Given the paucity of direct evidence and my wish to respect the reticence of others, and perhaps even succumbing to a measure of cowardice, I decided to avoid extensive discussions of sexuality. African-American slave women had not left extensive accounts of their objective lives, and I was loath to probe their silence. My decision was bolstered by the knowledge that even when those, like Harriet Jacobs, who had written of their personal experience, had written of extra-marital sexual relations and of sexual exploitation, they had refrained from exposing what must have been the most painful aspect of their experience—their own dehumanization. For, from a woman's perspective, the worst of sexual exploitation is never simply that "he" desired me and (perhaps violently) overpowered my resistance: The worst of sexual exploitation is that "he" treated me as a thing—not as a unique object of his desire, but as an indifferent object of his lust.

The appearance of Toni Morrison's novel *Beloved*, just as I was completing my own book provided welcome assurance that I was not alone in what I thought I was discerning in the fragmentary sources. It further confirmed my deepest sense that if slavery had indeed been the oppressive system most of us believed it to have been, those who endured it could not have emerged unscathed. Notwithstanding my having had formal psychoanalytic training and the high value I place upon the insights that psychoanalysis can contribute to the understanding of history and culture, I have always recoiled from—more properly resented—the mechanical use of psychoanalytic theory that treats other people as intellectual fodder for the analytic mind— that makes complex and sometimes troubled lives and motivations conform to someone else's rigid model. But my sense of the complexity of slave women's experience and of the extraordinary mixture of courage and frailty, anger and love their survival entailed continued to haunt me.

Recent years have brought thoughtful new attempts to map and circumscribe the activities of slave women and their central role with the community of slaves.[6] But even now, with more than a century of distance, it remains difficult, perhaps impossible, to recapture the subjective story of slave women's experience. In rare instances, as in the case of *Beloved*, fiction can powerfully supplement elusive psychological "facts." And so I turned to *Beloved* for a plausible, if imaginative, representation of the feelings of some women who endured slavery and, like Sethe, continued to bear its scars. Even more I turned to *Beloved* as itself a source for another history, namely the history of the elusiveness of women's experience of slavery until our own time. For *Beloved* is less the story that could not be passed on—the story that was impossible to tell—than it is the story of how the story that could not be passed on was forgotten and, to borrow from psychoanalytic language, the reasons for which it was repressed.

Although slave women, like slave men, suffered oppression as laborers, some of their coerced labor permitted them to develop skills and expertise in which they could take the pride of craft, and even hard monotonous labor, which did not, did not necessarily inflict lasting scars on their sense of themselves.[7] But as women—as sexual partners and mothers—they confronted a constant threat. The culture of domesticity and separate spheres that prevailed in the non-slave, and even in modified form in the slave, states during the mid-nineteenth century emphasized women's purity as sexual beings and their selfless devotion as mothers. No less important, it steadfastly repudiated women's sexual passion and, perhaps even more, their anger.[8]

African cultures were generally less obsessive about women's sexual purity, although they did favor marital fidelity, but they placed high value upon children and upon women's roles as mothers. So even if African-American slave women were not normally predisposed to take the cult of sexual purity very seriously and even if their circumstances too frequently permitted their observing it, they were strongly predisposed to take their roles as mothers and their responsibilities to their children as seriously as their circumstances permitted. And the sources movingly attest that they took the separation of a mother from one or more of her children as a slaveholder's ultimate violation both of the system's professed values and of his minimal responsibilities.

Before emancipation, the majority of slave women, being illiterate, had virtually no opportunity to write of their outrage at the violation of their sexuality and, especially, their motherhood. In the measure that committed free white women wrote of it for them, they invariably wrote in their own idiom of domesticity.[9] We know, from occasional accounts in the narratives of former slaves, that they spoke of their outrage to each other. But the narratives collected during the 1930s from those who had been children during slavery times could only tell of the outrage at a generational remove. And, as the African-American community reconstructed itself following the Civil War, it too tended to adopt the idiom of domesticity, perhaps less out of conviction than as a defense of respectability and a wish to hide their scars from the curiosity of outsiders.[10]

All of the stories we tell depend heavily upon the ways in which stories have previously been told. Not surprisingly, the story of baby-killing has had limited possibilities. Most commonly, it has taken the form of a cautionary tale, closely associated with the horrors of war. That evil men kill babies serves to underscore their malignant overreaching of the boundaries of civilized existence. Think of King Herod. And if men who kill babies in the public arena evoke horror, how much more so do women who kill them under the veil of domestic privacy? And if women in general, what of mothers in particular?[11] Medea has not been easy to inscribe in conventional images of motherhood.

All cultures have valued motherhood, but nineteenth-century bourgeois culture raised it to unprecedented heights of sentimentality and thus made it especially difficult for women to tell stories about its dangers and conflicts. Bourgeois idealization of mothers' natural inclinations for nurture and self-sacrifice virtually prohibited women from writing realistically of motherhood from a subjective stance. Or, to put it differently, the sanctity that shrouded the conventions of motherhood virtually dictated that women would have to embrace prescribed motherly feelings when writing of their own emotions and experience. Occasionally, a female author would touch upon a woman's possible resentment of, or failure at, motherhood by including an explicitly bad mother, but this projection would not include an empathetic exploration of the unfortunate woman's feelings. More frequently, one might write an orphaned girl whose situation would permit an indirect exploration of women's feelings about motherhood.[12]

As for motherhood, so for sexuality. It is difficult to find a proper nineteenth-century woman who wrote forthrightly of desiring sexual relations. To be sure, bourgeois women's limited experience narrowed the topics of which they could write with authority. But even more than women's limited experience, because women did, felt, and especially knew many more things than they were acknowledged as doing, feeling, and knowing, the conventions of women's narratives hedged women in. Thus even the most daring women writers found it difficult, if not impossible, to explore those aspects of women's subjective experience that frontally challenged narrative conventions of womanhood.

That the experience of female slaves openly mocked the conventions was not lost on all white women. During the late antebellum period, many American women, notably Harriet Beecher Stowe and Harriet Jacobs, began to insist that slavery indeed extracted an especially heavy price from women— that the evils of slavery ran so deep as to threaten the most sacred domestic bonds and virtues. In *Incidents in the Life of a Slave Girl*, Harriet Jacobs unambiguously insisted that if slavery is terrible for men, "it is far more terrible for women. Superadded to the burden common to all, *they* have wrongs, and sufferings, and mortifications peculiarly their own" (p. 77).[13]

Jacobs has primarily, and deservedly, been appreciated for her brave and perhaps unique account of slavery from a woman's perspective.[14] Jacobs, possibly following Stowe's example, left her readers no doubt that she was indicting slavery as a social system. Not least, she insisted, the evil of slavery made it impossible to judge a slave woman by the standards to which free women were held—"the slave woman ought not to be judged by the same standard as others" (p. 56). Yet even Jacobs never unambiguously stated that slavery made it impossible for women to be good mothers. In her narrative, she tried to expose the aspects of slavery that made it impossible for slave women to conform to prevailing standards, but she remained reticent about slave women's personal motivations. Attentive readers can easily recognize that the anger instilled by her personal experience frequently threatens to explode her narrative, but only indirectly and without ever fully disrupting the conventions within which she deemed it prudent to write.

Accepting the dominant discourse of womanhood and motherhood as normative, Jacobs, who candidly admitted to having had children by a man to whom she was not married, attempted to justify her actions as the product of her inescapable circumstances. Thus *Incidents,* which superficially accepts Northeastern, middle-class female norms and simply asks forgiveness for her inability to conform to them, on another level suggests that the norms entirely miss the realities of slave women's experience. Jacobs' anger obviously derived from her outrage at a social system the logic of which was to reduce a woman to a thing—from her own refusal to be treated as a thing. But it may also have derived from her recognition that there was no way that she could candidly tell her story, for there was no way that she could publicly admit to having been treated like a thing.

In acknowledging the impossibility of telling her real story, Jacobs presumably made a calculated judgment about the expectations of her prospective readers, shrewdly determining that it was better to meet those expectations than not to be read at all. And she assuredly could not have expected a sympathetic reading—perhaps not any reading at all—had she not respected the most cherished myths of those she hoped to reach. By the time Jacobs published *Incidents,* anti-slavery women, like Stowe herself, were insisting that slavery's greatest evil lay in its violation of domestic relations. But, by the same stroke, anti-slavery women had also ensconced their own standards of motherhood and womanly virtue as the ultimate justification for opposition to slavery.

Stowe had mapped the imaginative universe into which Jacobs apparently felt obliged to write her own story. The strength of Stowe's vision lay in her uncompromising insistence that, as the systematization of absolute power, slavery corrupted everyone it touched—made it impossible for anyone to be a good person. Jacobs unquestionably concurred in Stowe's indictment, but nonetheless found it impossible to press her understanding to its bitterest and most naked conclusions. It is not difficult, as I have argued elsewhere, to demonstrate that Jacobs' text may more profitably be read as the account of her direct contest with the power of her master than as the remorseful confession of her fall from virtue.[15] But even as she permits us to doubt that the protection of womanly virtue ranks as her primary concern, she attempts to strengthen free white women's identification with her feelings of motherhood.

The hard truth is that there are feelings that Jacobs could not share with her readers and maintain their identification and respect. Notwithstanding her evocation of the support and assistance that her protagonist, Linda Brent, received from other women, she tellingly distances her from the mass of slave women whose plight she purportedly embodied. Jacobs thus represents Linda Brent and the members of her immediate family as speaking in the purest English, while representing other slaves as speaking in dialect. For similar reasons, she relegates her harshest examples of slaveholders' brutality, notably the sexual exploitation of slave women, to cases of which Linda Brent has heard, but has not personally experienced. Jacobs never shows Linda as beaten or raped, as dirty or disfigured. She never describes her as scantily clad or even as calloused. The scratches she receives derive from the difficulties of her escape, not from the degradation of her everyday life. Above all, the persecution she endures never seriously compromises her membership in a recognizable narrative, never pushes her literally beyond the pale of civilized discourse.

For understandable reasons, Jacobs sought the identification of her readers, sought to convince them to accept her as a woman like themselves. No wonder then that she introduces the worst specific abuses of slavery as reports rather than as subjective experiences. How could she have been expected to do otherwise? If rather than representing Linda Brent—and by implication herself—as the object of corrupt male desire, she had represented her as the victim of indiscriminate lust, she would have reduced her to that status as thing to which the logic of chattel slavery pointed. And she would, thereby, have decisively undercut her own claims of empathy and respect. Worse, to do so would have forced her to acknowledge that, through the eyes of Dr. Flint, Linda Brent was little more than an animal—one occasion, among many, for the casual satisfaction of his lust.

Accordingly, Jacobs' protagonist, Linda Brent, experiences little that an unfortunate free white protagonist might not have experienced, and, in the measure that she does, the experience remains abstract.[16] Even when slavery exposes Linda Brent to the threat of separation from her children, loss of the power to determine their fates, and even the possibility of their being sold away from her, her role as mother remains intact. She conveys the assaults that might easily have been taken to compromise her identity as mother in the most conventional bourgeois idiom. Thus Jacobs, even as she harshly indicts slavery for its violation of the minimal norms of womanhood, especially motherhood, sustains the prevailing fictions about women's innate feelings of virtue and mother love. She cannot bring herself to represent the full corruption of slavery lest that attempted representation erase her entirely from an acceptable plot. Her goal remains to indict slavery for its violation of womanly virtue and motherhood, while leaving the identity of the virtuous woman and mother intact. In Jacobs' account, slavery prohibits slave women from behaving as they would want to behave, but does not penetrate, much less permanently scar, the inner reaches of their hearts and minds.

Tellingly, Jacobs represents Linda Brent as revering the memory of her own mother, whom she barely knew. "When I was six years old, my mother died; and then, by the talk around me, I learned that I was a slave" (p. 6). Everyone spoke warmly of her mother, "who had been a slave merely in name, but in nature was noble and womanly" (p. 7). When, years later, Linda Brent enters the church for the baptism of her children, "recollections of my mother came over me, and I felt subdued in spirit" (p. 78).[17] Subsequently, at the moment of her flight, Linda Brent visits her mother's grave. "I had," she remembers, "received my mother's blessing when she died; and in many an hour of tribulation I had seemed to hear her voice, sometimes chiding me, sometimes whispering loving words into my wounded heart" (p. 90). And it grieves her to think that "when I am gone from my children they cannot remember me with such entire satisfaction as I remembered my mother" (p. 90).

It seems likely that Jacobs has reshaped Linda Brent's memories of her mother for narrative purposes, although a child who loses her mother at six may well not remember much. More important, such comforting memories serve the important mission of sustaining the ideal of motherhood among a people whose circumstances frequently threatened the reality. The interviews with former slaves collected during the 1930s abound with recollections of mothers, which, for painfully obvious reasons, significantly outnumber those of fathers. Many of those who had been children during the final years of slavery fondly remembered their mothers' skills as cooks or weavers, specific acts of kindness, or their general devotion to their children. Many others allowed that they could not remember their mothers, who had died or run off when the children were young.[18] As best we can tell, most slaves had a strong bias in favor of emphasizing the strength of mothers' love for their children under what were too often dishearteningly difficult circumstances.

Thus from the midst of shattered families and in the absence of legal protection for the most basic family ties, slaves and former slaves fashioned a collective memory of the resilience and devotion of mothers. But whatever the accuracy of the memory in individual cases, its collective version coexisted with the unsettling knowledge that slavery could lead individual women to behave in ways that might indeed be considered unmotherly. The former slave Lou Smith recalled that her mother had told her of a woman whose master had sold her first three children before they were three years old. It broke her heart that she was not allowed to keep them and, after the birth of her fourth child, she determined to forestall its sale herself. "She just studied all the time about how she would have to give it up," and decided that she would not. So one day she "got up and give it something out of a bottle and pretty soon it was dead."[19] At what may be presumed to have been devastating cost to herself, that slave mother had enforced her right to define herself as mother, not as breeder.

Orlando Patterson has argued that the essence of enslavement lies in condemning those who suffer it to social death. Slavery severs the ties that bind people into society, effectively leaving isolated individuals to fend for themselves. Slavery denies the enslaved the right to establish and enforce social identities, including family identities, and also minimizes their possibilities, which is not exactly the same thing as doing so.[20] We know that in the Americas the latitude that slaves enjoyed or seized to sustain their own families and communities varied considerably from one slave society to another. As a rule, the greater the ratio of slaves to free people, and the greater the ratio of blacks to whites (again, not exactly the same thing), the stronger the elements of African culture remained and the greater the opportunities that slaves enjoyed to sustain de facto community relations, including marriages.[21] But even under the most favorable conditions, the absence of legally sanctioned marriage left the sexuality and motherhood of slave women vulnerable.

The inherent violence of slavery in this regard appears to have been most intense and most fraught with contradiction in the slave society of the Southern United States. For there, the ratio of blacks to whites was lowest, the rate of reproduction was highest, the survival of African culture was most precarious, and the influence of bourgeois culture was greatest. Consider the implications of this situation. By the first quarter of the nineteenth century, slave importations had virtually ceased, many slaves had embraced aspects of Protestant Christianity, and African-American reproduction was steadily increasing. Increasingly for the slaves of the Southern United States, such marriage as was possible embodied bourgeois rather than African norms, which slaveholders as well as slaves sought to promote. The self-respect and Christian concerns of Southern slaveholders as a class depended heavily on promoting the idea of slave marriage, even when economic fluctuations or simple convenience might lead any given slaveholder to break up marriages by sale. Similarly, the self-respect of Southern slaveholders precluded a crass view of slave women as mere breeders, although we know that many valued the natural increase of their slaves for economic reasons.

Both slaveholders and slaves had their own reasons to promote a version of the bourgeois ideal of domesticity and motherhood for African-American slaves. Both also knew that the reality remained so fragile as frequently to look like a hypocritical fiction. The precise blend of black African and white bourgeois values in the slaves' minds and identities will always remain elusive. But the evidence is strong that throughout the first six decades of the nineteenth century the force of the bourgeois ideals of marriage and motherhood steadily grew. It is at least clear that following the Civil War innumerable former slaves struggled mightily to ensure those ideals for themselves, which suggests that they had, in important ways, claimed them as their own. Clearly, this commitment to the ideals informed the way in which Harriet Jacobs wrote of a woman's experience of slavery. No less clearly, the commitment deterred her from a forthright subjective description of the most horrendous costs of slavery for a woman whom the realities of slavery continuously exposed to being stripped of all the conventional attributes of domesticity and motherhood.

More than a century after the appearance of *Incidents in the Life of a Slave Girl,* Toni Morrison, in *Beloved,* explicitly reopened the discussion of how to tell the story of women's experience of slavery. Gone is the gentility that dominates the tone of *Incidents.* None of the former slaves whose stories make up the novel speak in the conventions of domestic fiction, or even in standard English. Drawing upon reference, images, and figures of speech that derive from Southern black culture as Morrison envisions it, their words evoke a distinct social, cultural, and material universe. In sharp contrast to *Incidents, Beloved* anchors the experience of the slave mother in the horrifyingly tangible indignities of slavery. It is as if the examples of abuse from which Jacobs had so carefully distanced Linda Brent had come to life. No longer things that happen to others, the atrocities that slavery can perpetrate have become things that happen to you or me.

As a novel rather than a confessional narrative, *Beloved* does not present the harrowing events that occurred at 124 Bluestone Road or the history of the house's inhabitants through a single consciousness, but rather successively shows various characters' perceptions of them.[22] In the end, *Beloved* figures less as the story of a former slave woman who killed her own child than as the story of a community's rememory (to borrow Morrison's word) of that killing and of the events that led up to it, and, especially, of the ways of telling unspeakable things. *Beloved* is a novel about personal and collective history. Like *Incidents, Beloved* embodies an attempt to come to terms with the legacy of slavery, or, to put it differently, the attempt of former slaves finally to break slavery's shackles. But where *Incidents* had preserved the mantle of bourgeois discretion, thus effectively neutralizing the very horrors it sought to mobilize opposition against, *Beloved* lays the horrors bare, inviting readers to confront the ways in which slavery ate into the consciousness of all of those it touched.

Although the narrative of *Beloved* is infinitely complex, the story is chillingly simple. It is the story of a group of slaves who had, in the 1850s, lived on the Sweet Home plantation in Kentucky. When the slaveholder, Mr. Garner, had died, Sweet Home had been bought by Schoolteacher, who rapidly made life for the slaves intolerable. Eventually, the main character, Sethe, young mother of three and expecting a fourth, escapes to join her mother-in-law, Baby Suggs, in Cincinnati. En route, she gives birth to the child, a girl whom she names Denver. Some time after her arrival at Baby Suggs' house at 124 Bluestone Road, Schoolteacher appears with a small band of men (the four horsemen) to reclaim his property. Sethe, recognizing his hat, flees to the woodshed, kills her oldest daughter, and is about to kill the other children when Stamp Paid, another former slave, stops her.

Such is the prehistory of the events of the novel, which begin in the early 1870s, when Paul D, another former Sweet Home slave, arrives at 124. Just as he and Sethe begin to build a free love, Beloved, who is apparently the ghost of Sethe's oldest daughter, arrives and turns all of their lives inside out. The novel concludes with Beloved's departure, and Sethe's acceptance by her world—Denver, the women of the black community, and Paul D, who gently tells her, "'me and you, we got more yesterday than anybody. We need some kind of tomorrow.'" And then insists, "'You your best thing, Sethe. You are'" (p. 273).[23]

The core of *Beloved* lies in Sethe's murder of her cherished, "crawling already?" baby—the still nursing, not-yet-two-year-old girl, for whom she had braved nearly inconceivable horrors in order to provide the milk of her own breasts, which the baby needed to survive. "Why I did it. How if I hadn't killed her she would have died and that is something I could not bear to happen to her" (p. 200). Throughout *Beloved*, Morrison returns time and again to slavery's implacable war against motherhood. Baby Suggs bore eight children and was stripped of them all—"four taken, four chased, and all, I expect, worrying somebody's house into evil" (p. 5). Approaching death, she can remember only that her first-born loved the burned bottom of bread. "Can you beat that? Eight children and that's all I remember" (p. 5).

Sethe reproaches her own mother for never having let her be a daughter. A daughter is what she wanted to be "and would have been if my ma'am had been able to get out of the rice long enough before they hanged her and let me be one" (p. 203). Sethe's ma'am had had the bit so many times that she always smiled, but Sethe "never saw her own smile" (p. 203). Eventually she was caught and hanged, but Sethe did not know why or what she was doing. She could not have been running. "Because she was my ma'am and nobody's ma'am would run off and leave her daughter would she?" (p. 203). But then how would Sethe know about a ma'am who had only suckled her daughter for a week or two and then left her in the yard with a one-armed woman who had to nurse the white babies first and frequently did not have enough left over for Sethe? "There was no nursing milk to call my own" (p. 200). She would never allow that to happen to any daughter of hers. Beloved had to understand that Sethe had cut her own daughter's throat precisely to ensure that she could be a daughter—that Sethe could be a mother.

The figure of Sethe, standing in the woodshed, dripping with the blood of the murdered baby girl, whose body she will not relinquish, offering her blood-dripping nipple to the surviving infant, challenges any recognizable image of motherhood. Schoolteacher, the leader of the four white horsemen, who have come to return her to slavery, sees only "a nigger woman holding a blood-soaked child to her chest with one hand and an infant by the heels in the other." Never turning to look at the invaders, "she simply swung the baby toward the wall planks, missed and tried to connect a second time," while two bleeding boys lay in the sawdust at her feet (p. 149). Schoolteacher, who was not looking for a mother, saw none. He saw nothing there to claim at all. He saw only a woman gone wild, "due to the mishandling of the nephew who'd overbeat her and made her cut and run"—the same nephew, although Schoolteacher does not see the connection, who had, back at Sweet Home, held her down and stolen the milk she was saving for her baby girl (p. 149). Schoolteacher had tried. He "had chastised the nephew, telling him to think—just think—what would his own horse do if you beat it past the point of education. Or Chipper, or Samson. Suppose you beat the hounds past that point that away" (p. 149).

Small wonder that Schoolteacher, seeing Sethe as a breeder, a skillful ironer of shirts, a maker of excellent ink, cannot understand her motivations. For him she is a domesticated animal to be handled and if mishandled should be expected to go wild. It would not cross his mind that her excesses could result from the violation of her humanity and the denial of her mother's love. Paul D, who had his own knowledge of the worst that slavery had to offer, who had known Sethe at Sweet Home, and who had loved her there and at 124, is another matter. Confronted by Stamp Paid with the newspaper account of Sethe's action, Paul D refuses to believe that the woman who killed her baby could be Sethe. "That ain't her mouth" (p. 154). "You forgetting," Paul D told Stamp Paid, "I knew her before . . . back in Kentucky. When she was a girl. . . . I been knowing her a long time. And I can tell you for sure: this ain't her mouth. May look like it, but it ain't" (p. 158). And Stamp Paid himself, looking at the "sweet conviction" in Paul D's eyes, almost wonders if it really happened, if eighteen years ago, "while he and Baby Suggs were looking the wrong way, a pretty little slave girl had recognized a hat, and split to the woodshed to kill her children" (p. 158).

Paul D never asks Sethe directly if she killed her baby, he merely confronts her with the newspaper clipping, implicitly asking her to tell him that the woman it describes is not she. Showing it to her, he smiles, ready for her to "burst out laughing at the joke—the mix-up of her face put where some other colored woman's ought to be" (p. 161). It may have been his smile or "the ever-ready love she saw in his eyes" that made her try to explain. Her trying led her back to Sweet Home, about which she did not have to tell him, and to what he may not have known, "what it was like for me to get away from there" (p. 161). For the getting away was her own doing. "Me having to look out. Me using my own head" (p. 162). And it was also more, "It was a kind of selfishness I never knew nothing about before. It felt good. Good and right" (p. 162). It was a selfishness that allowed her to love her children more than she ever had before. "Or maybe I couldn't love em proper in Kentucky because they wasn't mine to love." When she got to Ohio, a free woman, "there wasn't nobody in the world I couldn't love if I wanted to" (p. 162).

That Paul D could understand all too well. For him, slavery had meant the necessity to protect yourself and love small. Under slavery, you picked "the tiniest stars out of the sky to own" so that your love would not be competing with that of the men who owned the guns. "Brass blades, salamanders, spiders, woodpeckers, beetles, a kingdom of ants. Anything bigger wouldn't do. A woman, a child, a brother—a big love like that would split you wide open in Alfred, Georgia." Oh yes, Paul D "knew exactly what she meant: to get to a place where you could love anything you chose—not to need permission for desire—well, now, *that* was freedom" (p. 162). Threatened with the loss of that freedom, Sethe explained to Paul D, "I took and put my babies where they'd be safe" (p. 163). The "safe" shakes Paul D, who knows it is precisely what 124 was lacking when he had arrived, who thought he had made it safe, and who thought that if Sethe her own self had not it was because she could not.

Sethe's definition of her murder as assuring her baby's safety shows Paul D how wrong he has been. "This here Sethe was new. . . . This here Sethe talked about love like any other woman; talked about baby clothes like any other woman, but what she meant could cleave the bone. This here Sethe talked about safety with a handsaw. This here new Sethe didn't know where the world stopped and she began" (p. 164). All of a sudden, Paul D could see what Stamp Paid had wanted him to see: "More important than what Sethe had done was what she claimed. It scared him" (p. 164). Paul D tells Sethe that her love is too thick, that what she did didn't work. It did work, Sethe counters. How, Paul D queries, can she calculate that? Both her boys have run off, one of her girls is dead, and the other will not leave the yard. "They ain't at Sweet Home. Schoolteacher ain't got em" (p. 165). Maybe, Paul D responds, there is worse. "It ain't my job to know what's worse. It's my job to know what is and to keep them away from what I know is terrible. I did that" (p. 165). But what she did, Paul D insists, is wrong; there could have been some other way. And when she asks what way, without stopping to think, he rejoins, "You got two feet, Sethe, not four" (p. 165).

No more than Schoolteacher, can Paul D understand Sethe's motivations and, to the extent that he can understand something, he ultimately shares Schoolteacher's view of Sethe's deed as the deed of an animal. In his eyes, Sethe's desperate act of claiming her motherhood, her children, and her love for them shatters the boundaries between self and other, between self and the world. What Sethe sees as her ultimate act of self-definition, Paul D can only see as an act of madness. Frightened like her sons, Howard and Buglar, who survived her murderous attack but ran away from home as soon as they were old enough, he leaves, leaving 124 to Sethe, Denver, and Beloved and the three women to each other. Stamp Paid, having suffered the pain of knocking and not gaining entrance, left 124 to its own devices and the women inside it "free at last to be what they liked, see whatever they saw and say whatever was on their minds." But behind the freedom of their words, which Stamp Paid could recognize if not decipher, lurked their thoughts, "unspeakable thoughts, unspoken" (p. 199).

From the start of the novel, we know that 124 is inhabited by the ghost of a murdered baby. No sooner than Paul D reappears after eighteen years, bathes Sethe's scarred back and moves into her bed, takes Sethe and Denver to the carnival, and begins to rebuild a family at 124, does Beloved herself reappear as a material presence. Entrancing, demanding, seductive, Beloved gradually wreaks her revenge by consuming Sethe's life—by confronting Sethe with a love as totally demanding as that which led Sethe to kill her baby. Beloved, the ghost-become-presence, defies any neat interpretation. But complexities notwithstanding, she must in part be understood as a narrative device that Morrison saw as necessary to telling the story she wanted to tell. Beloved embodies some essential residue of the experience of all the other characters, embodies the parts of the story that still cannot be told—the unspeakable thoughts unspoken.

For Sethe, Beloved is the daughter who has come back to her. "She mine. See. She come back to me of her own free will and I don't have to explain a thing" (p. 200). Beloved is the child to whom she can tell of Sweet Home, to whom she can talk of the things that Denver does not want to hear. For Denver Beloved, "is my sister. I swallowed her blood right along with my mother's milk. . . . Ever since I was little she was my company and she helped me wait for my daddy." Denver loves her mother, but knows "she killed one of her own daughters, and tender as she is with me, I'm scared of her because of it" (p. 205). Denver knows that there is something in her mother "that makes it all right to kill her own." And she constantly fears that "the thing that happened that made it all right for my mother to kill my sister could happen again" (p. 205). Denver does not know and does not want to know what that thing might be. She only knows that it comes from outside 124, and so she never leaves the house, carefully watching over the years "so it can't happen again and my mother won't have to kill me too" (p. 165). More frightening yet, maybe "the thing that makes it all right to kill her children" is still in her mother (p. 206).

The ghost of the victim—the name on the tombstone of the victim—of an infanticide prompted by too-thick love, Beloved is the custodian of the story that was not to be passed on. Her arrival at 124 signals her refusal to lay it down and get on with things. Nothing can be laid down or got on with until the story is told. The story belongs to no one person but to them all—the folks from Sweet Home who made it to 124. Baby Suggs feared that the murder had occurred because of the Sweet Home escapees' too-great arrogance about their freedom. Twenty days after Sethe's safe arrival, Baby Suggs had given a party for ninety people who "ate so well, and laughed so much, it made them angry" (p. 136). So when they awoke the next morning the odor of their disapproval at what they took to be Baby Suggs' overstepping hung in the air, masking the odor of the "dark and coming thing" that was the four horsemen in pursuit of Sethe (p. 138). Had it not been for the party, Baby Suggs worried, might they not have recognized the threat soon enough to take steps to avert it?

Baby Suggs' worries link Sethe's infanticide to the free black community. Sethe's and Paul D's memories link it to Sweet Home and, beyond Sweet Home, to slavery as a social system. For Paul D fully corroborates Sethe's fragmented account of life at Sweet Home, demonstrating that we should not mistrust her memories. It was that bad. In fact, under Schoolteacher, it was so bad as to cast doubt upon their belief that it had really been any better under the Garners. The issue is not a good or a bad master. The issue is slavery. And a slavery that leaves the definition of men to the good will of a master, rather than to the identity of the men themselves, is also a slavery that destroys the definition of women—especially mothers. Sethe, having barely known her own mother and lacking the companionship of other women, knew nothing of the practices of mothering. But by the time she arrived at 124, she knew that her very identity depended upon her children's being absolutely hers.

There are strong reasons to accept Sethe's infanticide as a desperate act of self-definition: By claiming her child absolutely, she claimed her identity as a mother, not a breeder. But in grounding her defense of her identity as a mother in the murder of her own child, she opened new possibilities of being viewed as an animal. The responses of Denver and Paul D, like the absence of Howard and Buglar, remind us that Sethe's self-definition was also the "crawling already?" baby's murder. Was it a thing outside or a thing inside that made Sethe do what she did? Was slavery an external force or an internal presence? By giving Beloved a consciousness, however briefly and elliptically, Morrison seems to suggest that we cannot entirely cast the murder of a baby as an act of heroic, if tormented, resistance. By peopling Beloved's consciousness with memories that evoke the slave ships of the middle passage, she seems to suggest that we cannot entirely divorce the murder of this baby from the slavery that shaped its murdering mother's life.

In her own way, Harriet Jacobs insisted that slavery corrupted everyone it touched. But, in sternly repressing her most painful personal angers, she left the impression that it affected behavior more than identity. Linda Brent's personal war with slavery, as embodied in her master, left her identity as mother largely intact, blemished only by a few understandable lapses. Significantly, her daughter seems almost bemused that her mother feels obliged to ask her forgiveness. Morrison, in contrast, shows slavery as cutting to the quick of Sethe's innermost being—jeopardizing any possibility of even beginning to sort out rights and wrongs. And the anger that Jacobs cloaks with a veneer of respectable discourse, emerges in *Beloved* as the unquietable rage of the murdered "crawling already?" baby girl, whose ghost also embodies the boundary-obliterating love that joins mother and child.

The parallels between the two narratives bridge the chilling and the reassuring, leaving us only with the certainty that each embodies a different way of telling an impossible story. Slavery's contempt for the humanity of motherhood corrupted everyone it touched—black and white, slave and free, female and male. Jacobs could only begin to hint at the elements of the story, steadfastly distancing her protagonist from personal experience of the most searing pain and humiliation. Morrison has bravely attempted to capture the subjective perspective—to tell the story that was not fit for passing on and to explain the story of the forgetting. But to do so, even she had to create a ghost since memory alone demonstrably would not serve.

Throughout American slave societies, mothers have enjoyed a special place in humanizing a too-frequently dehumanizing social system, in standing as the last bastion against the full horror of social death. Many have chosen to see the predominance of mothers in different African-American communities as a sign of pathology or social breakdown. From another perspective, mothers constituted the last bastion against the evil that slavery could wreak. And the power to define and defend motherhood emerged as the battleground over the irreducible minimum of the slaves' social identities. In that struggle, it understandably appeared threatening to expose the worst horrors for fear that they confirm the worst consequences of enslavement. In this perspective, slavery's power to define motherhood becomes the power to define the slaves' humanity and the slaves' power to defy the definition becomes the cornerstone of collective resistance. What, then, to do with the ghosts—the "unspeakable thing unspoken"? For Harriet Jacobs, the risks of speaking were too high. But in the hands of Toni Morrison the speaking of unspeakable thoughts has emerged as the necessary recovery of a buried history—the cornerstone of a new resistance.

Thus Morrison, in the frontispiece to *Beloved,* quotes Romans 9:25: "I will call them my people, which were not my people; and her beloved, which was not beloved." Beloved, the ghost, acquired her name at the moment of her burial when Sethe had to provide a name for the tombstone of the "crawling already?" baby girl who had had no name in life. Her choice resulted from her having loved the words of the minister at the funeral service, "Dearly beloved, we are gathered together. . . . " Had that baby been killed in the name of the too-thick love that sought to put her beyond the claims of slavery, or had she been sacrificed to her mother's fierce determination to define her own identity as a mother? In the end, the choice is no choice at all, for the baby died, her ghost born as a result of the intertwining of both.

Sethe had grown up with the knowledge that a mother's love and behavior did not always observe the conventions that enshrined it. Had she not insisted that her own mother could not have been killed when she was running away, for no little girl's mother would run away and leave her? And does not the reader, like some part of Sethe herself, know that running away was precisely what her mother was doing? If slavery did make it almost impossible for women to be mothers, then, in the measure that they could not, the children and frequently the children's children suffered the consequences. The horror of slavery, Morrison seems to be saying, lies in the intractability of two opposing truths: Mothers might murder their own babies out of love and in an act of resistance, but that expression of love and of resistance nonetheless resulted in the extinction of a baby they had suckled and loved. There is no easy way to construct a vision of humanity out of the murder of children—especially one's own children. Only by telling the real story—by refusing the superficially ennobling conventions and relinquishing the pretension that the inequities of slavery as a social system left the hearts and minds of the enslaved untouched—would it be possible to reclaim an impossible past as the foundation for a possible future. Only by exposing their scars, could African-Americans as a people expose the full costs of the oppression they had suffered.

Notes

1. Toni Morrison, *Beloved* (New York, 1987).

2. Eric Foner, *Free Soil, Free Labor, Free Men: The Ideology of the Republican Party before the Civil War* (New York, 1970); Frederick Douglass, *Life and Times of Frederick Douglass: Written by Himself* (1892; repr. New York, 1962); Frederick Douglass, *My Bondage and My Freedom* (New York, 1866); Frederick Douglass, *Narrative of the Life of Frederick Douglass, an American Slave, Written by Himself* (1845; repr. New York, 1968); Robert W. Fogel, *Without Consent or Contract: The Rise and Fall of American Slavery* (New York, 1988).

3. Eugene D. Genovese, *Roll, Jordan, Roll: The World the Slaves Made* (New York, 1975); Herbert G. Gutman, *The Black Family in Slavery and Freedom, 1750–1925* (New York, 1976); Lawrence Levine, *Black Culture and Black Consciousness: Afro-American Folk Thought from Slavery to Freedom* (New York, 1977); John W. Blassingame, *The Slave Community: Plantation Life in the Antebellum South,* rev. and enl. ed. (New York, 1979); George P. Rawick, *From Sundown to Sunup: The Making of the Black Community* (Westport, Conn., 1972).

4. Robert W. Fogel and Stanley L. Engerman, *Time on the Cross: The Economics of American Negro Slavery,* 2 vols. (Boston, Mass., 1974).

5. Deborah G. White, *Ar'n't I a Woman? Female Slaves in the Plantation South* (New York, 1985).

6. Lucille Mathurin, *The Rebel Woman in the British West Indies during Slavery* (Kingston, Jamaica, 1975); Hilary McD. Beckles, *Natural Rebels: A Social History of Enslaved Black Women in Barbados* (New Brunswick, N.J., 1989); Barbara Bush, *Slave Women in Caribbean Society, 1650–1838* (Kingston, Jamaica and Bloomington, Ind., 1990); Marietta Morrissey, *Slave Women in the New World: Gender Stratification in the Caribbean* (Lawrence, Kan., 1989).

7. Elizabeth Fox-Genovese, *Within the Plantation Household: Black and White Women of the Old South* (Chapel Hill, N.C., 1988), esp. ch.3.

8. On the repudiation of passion, see Nancy Cott, "Passionlessness: An Interpretation of Victorian Sexual Ideology, 1790–1850," *Signs* 4, no. 2 (Winter 1978): 219–36. For recent evaluations of the extensive discussions of separate spheres, see Linda Kerber, "Separate Spheres, Female Worlds, Women's Place: The Rhetoric of Women's History," *Journal of American History* 75, no. 1 (June 1988): 9–39 and Elizabeth Fox-Genovese, *Within the Plantation Household,* ch. 1, and *Feminism Without Illusions: A Critique of Individualism* (Chapel Hill, N.C., 1991), passim. It has long seemed to me (again on the

basis of psychoanalytic theory) that the ideology's repudiation of women's anger was at least as important as its repression of women's sexuality. Close attention to the experience of slave women helps to illuminate the point.

9. The most celebrated example is obviously Harriet Beecher Stowe, *Uncle Tom's Cabin, Or, Life Among the Lowly,* ed. Ann Douglass (1852; repr. New York, 1981).

10. Barbara McCaskill, "'Eternity for Telling': Topological Traditions in Afro-American Women's Literature," Ph.D. diss., Emory University, 1988; George Rawick, ed., *The American Slave: A Composite Autobiography,* 19 vols. (Westport, Conn., 1972); and George Rawick, ed., *The American Slave: A Composite Autobiography. Supplement,* 12 vols. (Westport, Conn., 1977).

11. Women's narratives of infanticide do exist. See, esp., Deborah Symonds, "The Transformation of Women's Work and Culture in Scotland, 1760–1820," Ph.D. diss., SUNY Binghamton, 1984; George Eliot, *Adam Bede* (1859; repr., New York and London, 1908).

12. For examples of inadequate mothers, see, e.g., *Uncle Tom's Cabin*; Caroline Lee Hentz *The Planter's Northern Bride* (1854; repr., Chapel Hill, N.C., 1970); and for an orphan, Augusta Jane Evans, *Beulah,* ed. Elizabeth Fox-Genovese (1859; repr., Baton Rouge, La., 1992).

13. Harriet Jacobs, *Incidents in the Life of a Slave Girl: Written by Herself,* ed. Jean Fagan Yellin (Cambridge, Mass., 1987). Page references to *Incidents* are in parentheses in the text.

14. See Yellin's introduction to Jacobs, *Incidents.*

15. Fox-Genovese, *Within the Plantation Household,* epilogue. See also, William L. Andrews, *To Tell a Free Story: The First Century of Afro-American Autobiography, 1760–1865* (Urbana, Ill., 1988), p. 252.

16. See, e.g., Susan Warner, *The Wide, Wide World* (1850: repr. New York, 1987); Maria Susanna Cummins, *The Lamplighter* (1854; repr. New York, 1968).

17. Why, she wonders, has her lot been so different from that of her mother? "She had been married, and had such legal rights as slavery allows to a slave" (p. 78). More important, "She was never in the power of any master, and thus she escaped one class of the evils that generally fall upon slaves" (p. 78).

18. For an elaboration and specific examples, see Fox-Genovese, *Within the Plantation Household,* esp. chs. 3 and 6.

19. Lou Smith in *The American Slave: A Composite Autobiography,* edited by George P. Rawick, Vol. 7, *Oklahoma Narratives,* pt. 1, p. 302. See also Fox-Genovese, *Within the Plantation Household,* pp. 323–24.

20. Orlando Patterson, *Slavery and Social Death: A Comparative Study* (Cambridge, Mass., 1982).

21. For a general analysis, see Eugene D. Genovese, *The World the Slaveholders Made: Two Essays in Interpretation* (New York, 1969) and his *From Rebellion to Revolution: Afro-American Slave Revolts in the Making of the Modern World* (Baton Rouge, La., 1979). See also, e.g., Fox-Genovese, *Within the Plantation Household,* ch. 6; Elizabeth Fox-Genovese, "Strategies and Forms of Resistance: Focus on Slave Women in the United States," in *In Resistance: Studies in African, Caribbean, and Afro-American History,* ed. Gary Y. Okihiro (Amherst, Mass., 1986), pp. 143–65 [article reprinted in this volume, pp. 3–26]; Barbara Bush, "'The Family Tree Is Not Cut': Women and Cultural Resistance

in Slave Family Life in the British Caribbean," in Okihiro, ed., *In Resistance,* pp. 117–32; Mathurin, *Rebel Woman.*

22. See Lucie Fultz, "Toni Morrison's Narrative Method," Ph.D. diss., Emory University, 1990.

23. All references to page are indicated in parentheses in the text.

Eleven

Introduction to *Beulah*

"Thou shalt not more be termed Forsaken; neither shall thy land any more be termed Desolate: but thou shalt be called Hephzibah and thy land Beulah: for the Lord delighteth in thee, and thy land shall be married." Early in Augusta Jane Evans' novel *Beulah,* the thirteen-year-old orphaned protagonist, Beulah Benton, responds to the bemused query about her name from Dr. Guy Hartwell, whom she has just met over the sickbed of an infant she is tending: "You need not tell me it is unsuitable; I know it; I feel it. Beulah! Beulah! Oh my father! I have neither sunshine nor flowers, nor hear the singing of birds, nor the voice of the turtle. You ought to have called me MARAH."[1] Hartwell responds, searching her face, "You have read the 'Pilgrim's Progress' then?" (35). Since Beulah does not answer him, we never know for sure, although we do know that Evans had read it. But there can be no doubt that Beulah has read her Bible and knows not merely the reference to Beulah in Isaiah but also the references to Marah. In Exodus 15, she would have read of how the children of Israel, under the leadership of Moses, celebrated their successful crossing of the Red Sea, singing of their Lord's strength, of how he "*is* a man of war" and how he "hath dashed in pieces the enemy." But then the Israelites went into the wilderness, where for three days they found no water. "And when they came to Marah, they could not drink of the waters of Marah, for they *were* bitter: therefore the name of it was called Marah." Beulah would also have known the passage in Ruth in which Naomi tells the people of Bethlehem, "Call me not Naomi, call me Mara: for the Almighty hath dealt very bitterly with me."[2]

Beulah's name governs the action and meaning of a novel that chronicles the anxious and conflicted coming-of-age of a young Southern woman in the late 1850s. The external action remains as circumscribed as a typical Southern woman's life, primarily moving through various domestic interiors in a single Southern city. But the internal action concerns all of the great theological, moral, and intellectual questions of the mid-nineteenth century. And to the conventional woman's drama of the appropriate claims of duty and ambition, independence and submission, it joins the framing drama of science and faith. Evans thus boldly and unapologetically locates the principal moral and intellectual struggles of her day in the mind of a woman. *Beulah* is a classic *Bildungsroman*—the narrative of a young woman's education and successful search for identity and a place in the world. But it should also be read as an allegory of Evans' own reflections on the role of women and the future of the South.

The publication of *Beulah* in 1859 fell at the end of the tumultuous decade of political disintegration that followed the Compromise of 1850. That mounting national confrontation over slavery and states' rights coincided with a coming-of-age of American women's fiction that itself manifested increasingly strong sectional and ideological allegiances.[3] In particular, Southern women writers took the publication of *Uncle Tom's Cabin* as a personal affront. While fathers and brothers struggled over Kansas and Nebraska, women turned their pens to the defense of Southern culture and the women who represented it.[4] Caroline Gilman, Mary Eastman, Marion Harland, Caroline Lee Hentz, Louisa S. McCord, and Mrs. Henry R. Schoolcraft rose enthusiastically to what they perceived as Harriet Beecher Stowe's wanton assault on everything they respected and held dear.[5] Notwithstanding considerable variation in specifics of plot and character, all focused on demonstrating that slavery as a social system represented a form of social organization superior to the system of free labor. Thus Marion Harland, in *Alone,* insisted that the "slave lies down at night, every want supplied, his family as well cared for as himself; not a thought of to-morrow! He is secure of a home and maintenance, without disturbing himself as to the manner in which it is to be obtained. Can the same be said of the menial classes in any other country under the sun?"[6] A distinct tradition of Southern women's domestic fiction was developing apace with rising sectional tensions.

Augusta Jane Evans belonged to that tradition and, arguably, took second place to none as a Southern polemicist. Yet, with the notable exception of *Macaria; or, Altars of Sacrifice,* her novels barely mention slavery, and even *Macaria* does not so much focus on slavery as on Southern political values.[7] The few slaves who figure in *Beulah* play minor roles at best, appearing as necessary but unremarkable features of Southern society. For Evans, the defense of Southern values transcended a narrow defense of slavery, the beneficent effects of which even she occasionally doubted.[8]

In *Beulah,* Evans infuses the Southern domestic tradition with a new concern with the inner lives of female characters, apparently reflecting the influence of Charlotte Brontë as well as her own Methodism. *Beulah* became a near best seller, with 22,000 copies printed in the first nine months, and won widespread critical acclaim. It probably owed much of its success to the growing taste for the "psychological" or "subjective" novel. In June of 1855, a reviewer in the *Southern Literary Messenger* had noted that "the most successful novels of the present day have been those in which the trials and sorrows, the love and despondency, the reverses and triumphs of this life, as they are experienced by women, are thrown in an autobiographical form before a sympathizing world." According to this reviewer, Charlotte Brontë had initiated the form but had since had many successors.[9]

Evans had probably read the review in the *Southern Literary Messenger.* She had certainly read Charlotte Brontë. Indeed, one of her few openly hostile reviewers in 1859 dismissed *Beulah* as a "'very humble and feeble and intellectually unremunerative' imitation of *Jane Eyre.*" The male reviewer for the Baltimore *Daily Exchange* had a special reason to be annoyed, for according to John Derby, *Beulah*'s publisher and Evans' friend, he had read the novel in manuscript and advised Appleton's against publication.[10] Other reviewers responded more favorably, and overall, the response was remarkably appreciative, especially in view of the long pages devoted to difficult philosophical speculation.

In a brief notice, the reviewer for *De Bow's Review,* a journal devoted more to political economy than belles lettres, warmly praised both novelist and novel. Evans, identified as a charming young lady of Mobile, was commended for "sprightliness," "depth of intellect," "a wide and varied range of information," and "much boldness in the discussion of social and philosophical subjects." *Beulah,* he wrote, "may be considered one of the best American novels." It details the interesting history "of a very gifted and ambitious woman . . . who earnestly strove to discharge the duties of her position, and consecrated her talents to the service of the Good, the True, and the beautiful." In another brief review, the *Methodist Quarterly Review* compared *Beulah* favorably to George Eliot's *Adam Bede,* which Evans herself disliked, and praised it for exposing "the baseless and unsatisfying character of rationalism—the exaggerated subjective religion of some of our 'great thinkers'—as a substitute for the truth as it is in Jesus."[11]

The *Southern Literary Messenger* devoted seven pages to *Beulah* and praised it highly, especially for its contribution to a distinct Southern literature. The literature of the North, the reviewer contemptuously noted, reveals in "its threadbare character" the "region of its birth," which "speaks rather from the head than from the heart." The South, in contrast, was beginning to produce a literature that within a few years was "destined to startle the world." Calling *Beulah* "brilliant," this reviewer commended it for its characters, "elegant diction, refined sentiment, and lofty philosophy." But he also criticized it for being too much a "modern novel" and especially for "its want of geographical location." Admittedly, it is set "in the Southern portion of our country, and those knowing the history of the writer have but little difficulty in determining the State and the city, but these nowhere appear in the book." Less ambiguously, Marion Harland pronounced *Beulah* "the best work of fiction ever published by a Southern writer," indeed the best by any American woman writer. And James Spaulding, who reviewed *Beulah* enthusiastically for the New York *Courier and Enquirer,* was so taken with it that he called upon the author. He told Derby that Evans obviously "knew what she was writing about."[12] Evans and Spaulding soon became engaged, although after Lincoln's election they broke off the engagement because of irreconcilable political views.

Evans' willingness to sacrifice personal happiness to her political commitments testifies to the depths of her allegiance to the South. In 1860, following Spaulding's visit to Mobile and the end of their engagement, she wrote with a "*very sad heart*" and considerable outrage to her aunt, Mary Howard Jones, in Milledgeville, Georgia, protesting the rumors that were circulating (presumably as a result of her aunt's indiscretion) about her purported engagement to Mr. Spaulding, a "Black Republican." She had told her aunt in strictest confidence of a tentative engagement and could not bear to have it publicly known in Milledgeville that she might marry "such a creature." And by early 1861, with her political passions at white heat, she wrote to Mrs. L. Virginia French angrily refusing to have her name appended to the antisecessionist memorial that Mrs. French was circulating among Southern women for presentation to the Georgia legislature. Unlike Mrs. French, who had "espoused the *Union* cause," Evans wrote, "I am an earnest and most uncompromising Secessionist" who believed "prompt and separate state action . . . to be the *only* door of escape from the worse than Egyptian bondage of Black Republicanism."[13]

Evans' interest in politics had apparently developed early. Her first novel, *Inez, a Tale of the Alamo,* published when she was twenty but mostly written, according to family lore, when she was fifteen, focused on the confrontation between Texans and Mexicans on the eve of annexation. Even then Evans covertly engaged in a defense of Southern values, improbably likening the aggression of the Mexicans against the Texans to that of the North against the South. Her gothic portrayal of a villainous Jesuit priest's sinister campaign to gain control of the souls and fortunes of unsuspecting Protestants was intended obliquely to represent the intentions of fanatical abolitionists upon Southern values. Even the most sympathetic critics have dismissed *Inez* as at the best an interesting youthful effort, but amidst its melodramatic excesses lay the themes that would preoccupy Evans throughout her career: women's identities and roles, Southern values, and religion.

Between the publication of *Inez* in 1855 and that of *Beulah* in 1859, Evans found the focus and voice that would, in one way or another, characterize all of her subsequent novels.[14] During those decisive years, she experienced a searing crisis of faith from which, with the help of a young minister, William Harriss, she emerged the devout Methodist that she remained throughout her life.[15] A youthful confrontation with Catholicism did much to provoke the crisis, but so, doubtless, did her extensive reading in literature and philosophy. *Beulah* provides a fictional account of her experience from the safe remove of her own dearly won religious conviction.

Beulah's central plot follows the familiar conventions of domestic fiction, which Alexander Cowie has teasingly, although not unsympathetically, summarized: "First, take a young and not-too-pretty child about ten years old. Boys are possible, but girls are to be preferred, for the author and the increasing majority of women readers will be more at home in the detail. Make sure that the child is, or shortly will be, an orphan." If by chance the child's mother is living, she must be gently put to death. Her father will, of course, already have perished, and if not must now be married to a shallow, fashionable woman. The heroine, accordingly, falls to the untender mercies of a stepmother or a cruel housekeeper but benefits from the tempering influence of some other worthy woman, who "is destined to die about two-thirds of the way through the book of badly-diagnosed tuberculosis." The story can end after the mentor's edifying death but is better carried on "in order that the heroine may be menaced and morosely loved by a proud, handsome, moody, Rochester-like man aged about thirty who has traveled and sinned (very vaguely) in the Orient." Shocked by the heroine's refusal of his hand in marriage, the tempestuous hero again departs for foreign parts, preferably the Orient, whence he returns chastened, wealthy, and maybe even a minister. Meanwhile, the heroine has shed "her fantastic notions of female independence" and come to recognize that "a woman's greatest glory is in wifely submission."[16]

In conformity with this model, *Beulah* traces the formative decade in the life of a young woman, opening with Beulah Benton's entrance into adolescence at not quite fourteen and concluding with her marriage at twenty-four. At the outset, Beulah is indeed living in an orphanage, from which she is rapidly sent forth to take up uncongenial duties as a nursemaid. In quick succession fate deprives her of her last remaining relative, her beloved younger sister, Lilly, and provides her with the occasion to meet the wealthy, morose, and unmarried Guy Hartwell, who takes her into his home as a protégée. But as she matures, Beulah embarks on the path of skepticism and determines to establish her independence from Hartwell by becoming a self-supporting teacher and writer. Only after years of lonely wrestling with doubt does she finally regain her faith, discover that she loves Hartwell, and decide that, if he returns safely from the Orient, to which he had fled following her repeated rejections of his attentions and gifts, she will marry him. He does, and the novel concludes with her resolution to convert him to her faith.

The formal similarities to *Jane Eyre* are striking: Beulah, like Jane, begins as an orphan who is taken into the home of the older man she will ultimately marry; Hartwell bears a strong resemblance to Edward Rochester; Beulah, like Jane, addresses her suitor as "sir," and he addresses her as "child"; Beulah, like Jane, is courted by an apparently suitable man, whom she rejects even though she has already rejected Hartwell. Both orphaned heroines struggle to earn their living, cope with the arrogant dismissals of fashionable society, and experience a difficult coming-of-age, including a search for personal independence. Evans also followed Charlotte Brontë in exploring the dynamics of female strength and independence without overtly challenging the social structures that hedged women in. But Evans was much less conflicted than Brontë seems to have been about the value of those structures and the dangers of individualism.

Most likely, Evans took *Jane Eyre* as a model, not least because, for both financial and personal reasons, she sought to appeal to a broad female readership. But she departed from *Jane Eyre* in primarily focusing on her protagonist's spiritual crisis. The success of *Beulah* is all the more remarkable because of the stringent intellectual demands that it makes upon its readers. Long passages in the novel more closely resemble an intellectual tract than a domestic fiction, and Evans' quasi-exhibitionist displays of erudition led some uncharitable critics to complain that she simply collected facts from an encyclopedia. Even Mary Forrest, who admired Evans' work, admitted that "Beulah Benton and Guy Hartwell are much more familiar with Carlyle's 'Herr Teufelsdrockh' than with Ovid's 'Art of Love.' They make a grim pair of lovers enough, and throw into spasms of impatience all who are wading through 'ontology,' 'psychology,' 'eclecticism,' etc . . . but they . . . are in keeping with the austere, determinate character of the book." That austerity, Forrest insisted, derived from the most worthy of purposes, namely Evans' determination to wage war against skepticism, "the Upas tree of the age."[17]

Throughout the novel, Beulah's story intertwines with the stories of an array of other characters to illuminate her own struggles and temptations.

But the central dynamic remains Beulah's personal journey through doubt into faith—through the thickets of nineteenth-century science and skepticism finally to end upon the rock of Methodist conviction. Since Beulah's ultimate victory over doubt results in her apparent acceptance of subordination within marriage, some modern feminist critics read the novel as a narrative of thwarted female independence. Thus Anne Goodwyn Jones, one of the most thoughtful critics of Southern women's writing, concludes that in *Beulah* "the prescription (for individual female growth) does turn to protest and finally, depressingly, to capitulation."[18] For Jones, Evans' commitment to the Southern social order and to woman's allotted role within it should be understood as a mask. In this perspective, the true life of the novel lies in Beulah's assertion of her independence, and her renunciation of it must be seen as a betrayal.

Evans' contemporaries read it differently. Many readers responded with as much enthusiasm as Fannie Page Hume, who noted in her diary, "I devoured 'Beulah' this morning till it was time to dress for Mr. Smith's."[19] Countless other women, who, like Hume, were struggling to understand their specific vocation as women, found Beulah's struggle inspiring. Few, if any, of Evans' late-adolescent, nineteenth-century women readers, especially those in the South, would have found anything objectionable either in her interest in personal conversion or in her choice of marriage as a woman's appropriate calling. It nonetheless remains difficult to determine how many even of her most devoted women readers enjoyed—or even followed—the erudition and philosophical speculation that lie at the center of the novel. But the better educated surely did.

There is every reason to believe that many aspects of *Beulah* conform closely to Evans' personal experience, notably the crisis of faith. Obviously the experience of being an orphan does not; nor, significantly, does the marriage. Evans herself never taught, as Beulah does. But in other important respects *Beulah* embodies concerns that lay close to Evans' own experience and, probably, to those of many of her readers. Since much of Evans' correspondence for the years between the publication of *Inez* and that of *Beulah* has disappeared, the evidence necessarily remains indirect, but some of it bears directly on the novel.

During the years that immediately preceded the publication of *Beulah*, Evans was living in Mobile with her parents and siblings in straitened financial circumstances. As a young woman in her early twenties, she would normally have expected to be preparing for marriage. We will probably never know whether her failure to become engaged during those years resulted from her singular intellectual accomplishments and desire for independence or from her father's economic reversals. Both of Evans' parents came from well-to-do slaveholding families, her mother from the socially and politically prominent Howard family of Virginia, South Carolina, and Georgia. But if her father's economic difficulties prevented her from engaging in the social life of the slaveholding elite, her background would doubtless have led her to recoil from anything less prestigious.

Notwithstanding the carping of the *Messenger*'s reviewer that Evans did not explicitly identify the city in which *Beulah* was set, her descriptions of it in the novel hewed very close to reality. During the late 1850s Evans was living with her family in a rented house on Government Street in Mobile. She had become a member of the board of the Protestant Orphanage, which she and her mother had been instrumental in rebuilding. As recently as the 1930s, many older residents of Mobile remembered the pine grove behind the brick orphanage building that figures prominently in *Beulah*'s opening chapter. Evans, who had lived through the worst yellow fever epidemic in Mobile's history, graphically describes it in *Beulah*. Although Mobile had no public library, it did have two rental libraries and a Franklin Society. The accounts of Beulah's trotting around town borrowing and returning books probably depict Evans' own experience. Even the names of her characters come directly from the Mobile of the 1850s: Hammonds, Hartwells, Graysons, Martins, and Asburys may all be found in the city directory for 1858–59. And many of the homes in which they are said to have lived can be identified.[20] Even to the description of views from houses of the waves breaking in the Mobile River, *Beulah* is as faithful to Evans' immediate environment as any travelogue.

William Fidler, the literary historian and critic who read Evans' letters to the Reverend Mr. Harriss, confirms that Beulah's crisis of faith has much in common with Evans' own. Evans' letters to her friends, notably Rachel Lyons, during the year following *Beulah*'s publication further suggest how deeply she had been thinking about the issues of the novel. At the end of July, 1860, Evans wrote Lyons to encourage her to take up writing as a way out of the depression from which she was apparently suffering. She especially advises Lyons, a Jew, to write a Jewish tale "and make it a substratum on which to embroider your views of life, men, women, Art, Literature." She acknowledges that women writers suffer greater trials than the world imagines, but nonetheless insists that they also enjoy special pleasures. "I speak now not of mere *gratified ambition*; I point you to the nobler aim of doing *God's work*." Evans herself had thought much on these topics and concluded that "while literary women as a class, are *not as* happy . . . as women who have Husbands and Children to engage their attention and monopolize their affections; yet in the faithful employment of their talents, they experience a deep peace and satisfaction, and are crowned with a glory such as marriage never gave." Yes, she does mean that literature and marriage are antagonistic. "No loving wife and mother can sit down and serve two masters, Fame and Love—. It is almost impossible—." If Lyons were married, as she apparently wished, Evans would say, "God bless." But so long as she was not, "I wish you would *write*."[21]

In August and November, Evans wrote again, underscoring her conviction that work and more work provided the best antidote to depression and, presumably, to being unmarried. The letters also contain advice on how to write a novel, suggesting that Evans had thought carefully about her own writing. Lyons should not be obsessed with "the mere accumulation of information; for after all, it is an author's own deep, original thoughts, which are remembered, and prized; and not the rehashing of classical or medieval sentiments." She should start with the plot, which must be clearly traced to the very end before a line is written. Then she would find no difficulty in embroidering and polishing. She must also be sure to "*select* the *very highest types* of character for the standard has sadly deteriorated of late in works of fiction." Many novelists had fallen into a "too-close imitation of <u>Nature</u>" and, worse, into "the error of patronizing coarseness, vulgarity, and ignorance." Evans remarks that in *Adam Bede* George Eliot especially errs in this regard. "The world needs *elevating,* and it is the peculiar province of the Novelist to present the very highest *noble types* of human nature."[22]

In these letters, Evans arrestingly combines her theories of novel writing with her thoughts about the situation of women like Lyons and herself. The intermixture confirms the profound importance of women's narratives to women's identities. Novels—good novels—do offer models of being and thinking; they are taxonomies of the soul and road maps for the difficult journey toward becoming a self. For Evans, this aspect of women's fictions could not be separated from the development of literature in general. In the fall of 1859, she wrote a series of articles for the Mobile *Daily Advertiser* in which she vigorously defended a distinct Southern literature. Northern publishers, she argued, are subjugating Southern writers and repressing the development of their genius in an attempt to ensure that the South remain inferior to the North in the worlds of national and international letters.[23] In Evans' view this gambit was of a piece with the Northern attempt to undermine Southern institutions, notably slavery. In Northern literature, "the low sensual African is dragged up from his normal position and violently thrust into an importance which the Creator has denied him by indications as strong as physical inferiority and mental incapacity could make them." If literature failed to respect the differences between whites and blacks, she insisted, the nation would begin to ignore them as well—thereby jeopardizing "national harmony."[24]

In these articles Evans forcefully condemns the tendency to "render all classes of society dissatisfied with their normal condition." Such literature was drawing the North into chaos. In contrast, the South enjoyed the stability promoted by its own institutions. "Next to the British aristocrat, we know of no position in the world more desirable than that of the Southern planter," who belongs to the "most enlightened" class of any country. The entire nation should look to the "sons of our planters" for the "talents, learning and statesmanship" so sorely lacking in contemporary politics. In combating this persecution, Southern writers should aspire to rise above special pleading and write for the most enlightened and discriminating readers throughout the English-speaking world. Evans expresses the desire that Southern writers be read "wherever the English language is spoken and read" and that their works "be written in language whose style will fall under the most severe rules of literary taste."[25]

The *Daily Advertiser* articles unmistakably corroborate Evans' passionate identification with proslavery Southern politics, but also help to explain why she did not follow other Southern women novelists in endowing her novel with an overtly proslavery cast. She aspired to follow the advice she had given Lyons—to write about what she knew, but to present it in a language that would meet the most discriminating tastes throughout the English-speaking world. She ought to produce a Southern literature that, although firmly grounded in the life and values of her region, would engage the human condition. The resemblances between *Beulah* and *Jane Eyre* may be taken as evidence of Evans' determination to model her work on that of the most prestigious and influential British novelist, but they do not fully account for the specific content of *Beulah,* notably its preoccupation with the struggle between skepticism and faith. On this matter, Evans was more deeply influenced by Samuel Taylor Coleridge, Thomas Carlyle, and William Hamilton than by even the most accomplished women writers.[26]

If *Beulah* follows *Jane Eyre* in plot and aspects of its rhetoric, it less obviously, but no less closely, follows "The Rime of the Ancient Mariner." At one point, Evans has Beulah herself make the correspondence explicit. Reginald Lindsey, who wishes to marry Beulah and has just loaned her his copy of Sir William Hamilton's *Philosophy of the Conditioned* to help her through her spiritual crisis, reminds her that those with a solid Christian faith know that on earth "'we see through a glass darkly.' Better this than the starless night in which you grope, without a promise of the dawn of eternity, where all mystery shall be explained. Are you not weary of fruitless, mocking speculation?" (367). She replies, "Ah, yes; weary as the lonely mariner, tempest-tossed on some pathless ocean, without chart or compass. In my sky, even the star of hope is shrouded. Weary? Yes, in body and mind" (367).

In many respects the similarities between the plot and the philosophy of *Beulah* and those of "The Ancient Mariner" are striking. Beulah, like the Mariner, has a story that must be told and retold, as a cautionary tale for listeners and as a sign of salvation for the teller. For Beulah, too, that story progresses from a dangerous voyage to the appearance of an Albatross to the killing of the Albatross to the utter abandonment of solitude upon the "rotting sea" to the recovered ability to pray, and from thence to return to the world of the living. Coleridge's lines perfectly capture the frozen state of Beulah's heart after the death of her sister Lilly:

> Nor shapes of men nor beasts we ken—
> The ice was all between.
> The ice was here, the ice was there,
> The ice was all around.[27]

The appearance of Guy Hartwell may be likened to the appearance of the Albatross, and Beulah's rejection of his love to the Mariner's slaying of the Albatross. After Hartwell's departure, Beulah feels, like the Mariner, "Alone, alone, all, all alone, / Alone on a wide wide sea!" (ll. 232–33). Also like the Mariner, she

> looked to heaven, and tried to pray;
> But or ever a prayer had gusht,
> A wicked whisper came, and made
> My heart as dry as dust.
>   (ll. 244–47)

And for both only when "A spring of love gushed from my heart" did prayer finally become possible and, with prayer, release from the carcass of the Albatross (l. 284). Thus could Beulah second the Mariner's final sentiments:

> He prayeth well, who loveth well
> Both man and bird and beast.
> He prayeth best, who loveth best
> All things both great and small.
>   (ll. 612–15)

But unlike the Mariner, Beulah gets a second chance to love the love that she had sought to kill.

The similarities between *Beulah* and "The Rime of the Ancient Mariner" confirm that for Evans the central problem concerned a loss and repossession of faith. In October, 1859, she attempted to explain Beulah's struggle with doubt to Rachel Lyons, who felt that "Beulah's speculative doubts were not satisfactorily answered." The truth of the matter, Evans replied, "lies in

a nut shell[:] Our religious states are determined by *Faith, not Reason.*"
Beulah, Evans insisted, erred in constituting "her Reason the sole criterion
of truth." But she kept encountering "insolvable mysteries—found that unaided by that Revelation which her reason had ignored, that she was utterly
incapable of ever arriving at any belief." Evans explained that "the object of
the book was to prove the fallacy of all human, philosophical systems, the
limited nature of human faculties, the total insufficiency of our reason to
grapple with the vital questions which are propounded by every earnest
mind." So long as Beulah "trusted to Rationalism, she was wretched and
sceptical; but when she put *faith* in the word of the Living God, she *found
'the ways of pleasantness and the paths of peace.'*"[28]

Whatever Evans' intentions, she represented the progress of Beulah's
loss of faith as something more than an infatuation with the power of
human reason. On Evans' own showing, Beulah's doubts sink their roots in
the losses of her childhood and adolescence: How can she continue to pray
to a God who manifestly disregards her prayers? Who strips her successively
of mother, father, and sister? Almost from the outset, cheerfulness comes
hard to Beulah, who has lost everything that she held dear. Significantly, her
mother's death, which occurred very early in her life, receives almost no
attention, either as an event or as a cause of Beulah's doubts. Even her
father's death, which resulted in her removal to the orphanage, had not initially shaken her trust in God, to whom she had continued to look "for
relief and reward. But the reward came not in the expected way. Hope died;
faith fainted; and bitterness and despair reigned in that once loving and gentle soul. Her father had not been spared in answer to her frantic prayers.
Lilly had been taken" (59). She had put her trust in the Lord, "and He has
forgotten me" (60).

But if Beulah's doubts have their source in personal despair, their development is fed by extensive reading in philosophy and literature, especially
nineteenth-century skeptical thought. Even when she is still in the orphanage, her paleness is attributed to her reading too much (9). Given free access
to her guardian's library, she begins a determined course of intellectual
exploration. Edgar Allan Poe, in particular, "was the portal through which
she entered the vast Pantheon of Speculation" (121). Hartwell had warned
her against Poe, "but the book was often in his own hand, and yielding to
the matchless ease and rapidity of his diction, she found herself wandering
in a wilderness of baffling suggestions" (121).

From Poe, Beulah moves to Thomas De Quincey's "Analects from
Richter" and on to Jean Paul. When Hartwell questions her about the solidity of her faith, she replies. "Of course, of course! What could shake a faith
which years should strengthen?" (129). Watching her, Hartwell recognizes

the progress of doubt: "Do you want to be like me? If not, keep your hands off of my books" (129). But her obsession with books steadily grows. "The Ancient Mariner" is to her "the most thrilling poem in the English language" (158). Books, she tells her friend Clara, "are to me what family, and friends, and society, are to other people" (161). She reads Carlyle's works for hours without fatigue, but when midnight forces her to lay the book aside, "the myriad conjectures and inquiries which I am conscious of, as arising from those same pages, weary me beyond all degrees of endurance" (199). As she ever more frenetically reads, she becomes visibly thinner and more drawn; her normally white skin becomes whiter, her eyes strained, her hands almost transparent. Her speculations, Clara sadly reproaches her, have brought her to doubt the Bible. Her speculations, Evans firmly reminds us, are inexorably leading her to a skepticism that sees creation and creator as one. "Unluckily for her, there was no one to direct or assist her" (209).

In the absence of guidance, Beulah is no longer studying for the sake of learning alone. The riddles with which she is grappling "involved all that she prized in Time and Eternity, and she grasped books of every description with the eagerness of a famishing nature" (209). From German speculation she plunges into ethnology and then geology. "Finally, she learned that she was the crowning intelligence in the vast progression; that she would ultimately become part of the Deity" (210). And in the dark of night she fumbles along, following "that most anomalous of all guides, 'Herr Teufels-drockh'" (210). Kneeling in despair, she tries to pray but no longer knows to whom she should pray: to nature? to heroes? "She could not pray . . . 'Sartor' had effectually blindfolded her, and she threw herself down to sleep with a shivering dread, as of a young child separated from its mother, and wailing in some starless desert" (211).

Evans especially explores the consequences of Beulah's reading through long interchanges between Beulah and her friends Clara and Cornelia. The haughty Cornelia engages Beulah in a searching discussion of Emerson, in which Beulah remonstrates with her that surely Cornelia is not an Emersonian. To Beulah, his writings are "like heaps of broken glass, beautiful in the individual crystal, sparkling, and often dazzling, but gather them up, and try to fit them into a whole, and the jagged edges refuse to unite" (229). She had long sought a creed in Emerson but had come to recognize him as the very prince of Pyrrhonists. She can accept his law of compensation "as regards mere social position; wealth, penury, even the endowments of genius. But further than this, I do not accept it" (230). Beulah cannot relinquish the idea of an immortal soul and continues to "desire something more than an immutability, or continued existence hereafter, in the form of an abstract idea of truth, justice, love or humility" (230). Cornelia, who is dying and hopes only for an unbroken and eternal sleep, feels like "that miserable, doomed prisoner of Poe's 'Pit and Pendulum,' who saw the pendulum, slowly but surely, sweeping down upon him" (231).

Cornelia's death is extraordinary, if not unique, in mid-nineteenth-century women's fiction. Evans' willingness to explore the possibility that a good woman—and even evil women were normally represented as converting on their deathbeds—might die without a shred of religious feeling demonstrates her refusal to limit the capacities of women's minds. Kneeling beside the bed of her friend who has died bereft of faith, Beulah agonizes about the meaning of that death, wonders what philosophy has to say about such grim hours of struggle and separation: "Was she to see her sister no more? Was a moldering mass of dust all that remained of the darling dead— the beautiful angel, Lilly, whom she had so idolized? Oh! was life, then, a great mockery, and the soul, with its noble aims and impulses, but a delicate machine of matter? Her brain was in a wild, maddening whirl; she could not weep; her eyes were dry and burning" (319).

She asks herself, was that death? "Oh, my God, save me from such a death!" (321). At Cornelia's funeral, she writhes in the nadir of despair. "What availed all her inquiries, and longings, and defiant cries? She died, no nearer the truth than when she began. She died without hope and without knowledge" (321). But could a loving God refuse to save her? And how different was Beulah's own situation? How different would her death be? Even the terrifying lesson of Cornelia's death does not immediately save Beulah from her ceaseless questioning, although later that year, exhausted by her struggles, she reembraces faith.

The turning point comes when Beulah recognizes that her suitor, Reginald Lindsey, believes she has rejected his proposal because of her love for Guy Hartwell: "Then, for the first time, his meaning flashed upon her mind. He believed she loved her guardian" (368). As the thought seeps into Beulah's consciousness, her normally pale face is suffused with a burning flush. "Oh! how unworthy I am of such love as his? how utterly undeserving!" (368). Evans does not clarify the referent of *his.* Logically, it should be Lindsey; psychologically, it must be Hartwell; metaphorically, it is God. Later that evening, Beulah reads the book that Lindsey had brought her, Hamilton's *Philosophy of the Conditioned,* and reviews the progress of her own skepticism, her proud and fruitless search for truth: "A Godless world; a Godless woman" (370). She recognizes that "philosophy! thou hast mocked my hungry soul; thy gilded fruits have crumbled to ashes in my grasp" (371). At that moment, Evans informs us, Beulah's "proud intellect was humbled, and falling on her knees, for the first time in many months, a sobbing prayer went up to the throne of the living God" (371).

Time and again, Evans insists that Beulah's struggle with Christianity derives primarily from the evils of individualism and the temptation to believe that the human mind can encompass all knowledge. She assumed that her readers would be familiar with Hamilton's argument, which was widely discussed in religious circles in the late 1850s. In fact, in July of 1859, about the time that *Beulah* appeared, the *Southern Literary Messenger* ran an article on *Philosophy of the Conditioned*. Hamilton was best known for his dictum, "The first act of philosophy is to doubt our knowledge, and the last act of it is to be certain of our ignorance." Directly engaging the problems of faith and reason that bedeviled Beulah, Hamilton argued that the purpose of philosophy "is to establish the theory of human ignorance and to determine the boundaries of human thought." The proliferating concern with the power of reason, he believed, had led to the proliferation of infidelity—the contempt for sacred truths and the undermining of morals. Under such conditions, the task of philosophy is to "show the insufficiency of logic as the invariable standard of truth; to demonstrate the limits of human understanding." To this end, Hamilton divided knowledge between the conditioned and the unconditioned, identifying the former as finite ideas, which we can know positively, and the latter as infinite ideas, which we can know only negatively. "The Infinite, the absolute, the one, the identical, the abstract, the substantial, the noumenal, the pure, the necessary, are unconditioned." Knowledge of the conditioned leaves a broad field for human reason, but beyond it we cannot positively go.[29]

Evans doubtless appreciated Hamilton's position as possible grounds from which to salvage religious faith from the greatest presumptions of secular knowledge. No human being can aspire to be God; the attempt to grasp the ultimate mysteries of life, death, and eternity is doomed to failure—and, worse, is presumptuous. In considering the great nineteenth-century struggles between faith and reason, Evans drew upon Hamilton to argue that faith and reason are of different orders. But in accepting faith as a knowledge of the heart rather than of the head, she did not repudiate the pleasures and challenges of intellectual inquiry. She simply insisted that they unfold within their allotted sphere and serve, rather than challenge, divine truth. In this respect, *Beulah* closely follows Carlyle's *Sartor Resartus* in simultaneously exploring the myriad intellectual temptations of the age and elaborating a pattern of conversion.[30]

The power of *Beulah* largely derives from Evans' ability to ground demanding intellectual debates in the psyche of a young woman. Beulah's main drama, her struggle for faith, lies at the core of her identity. Evans' depiction of Beulah emphasizes the ways in which emotional and intellectual development intertwine. And for Beulah, as for Evans herself, the problems of female identity have much to do with the acceptance or rejection of woman's ascribed sphere and role. Significantly, during her period of gravest doubts, Beulah becomes an author, first anonymously, then under her own name. Hartwell attributes her rejection of his proposal of marriage directly to her quest for literary fame. Evans herself associates Beulah's literary career with an interest in woman's independence. Beulah's valedictory address upon graduation had been devoted to "Female Heroism"; her writings had touched upon the possible benefits of a woman's remaining single as well as upon questions of philosophy and faith. But Evans does not condemn Beulah for writing or for publishing: She condemns her for her pursuit of unlimited individualism and for the infidelity to which it must lead. And she does, to the disgust of subsequent feminist critics, insist that infidelity is even worse in a woman than in a man.

Beulah manifests a relentless determination to establish and defend her independence—to impose her will and to realize her self-appointed duty, notably by earning her own living. It humbles her to hear a "woman bemoaning the weakness of her sex, instead of showing that she has a soul and mind of her own, inferior to none" (116). Haughtily, she reproaches Clara for preferring to be cared for: "You are less a woman than I thought you, if you would be willing to live on the bounty of others when a little activity would enable you to support yourself" (115). Clara counters that the issue is not merely "the bread you eat or the clothes that you wear; it is sympathy and kindness, love and watchfulness" (115). Those, truly, are the things a woman needs. Can "grammars and geographies, and copy books" fill a woman's heart? (115). Can the conviction that "you are independent and doing your duty" satisfy all other longings? (115–16). Beulah will have none of it. "What was my will given to me for, if to remain passive and suffer others to minister to its needs? Don't talk to me about woman's clinging, dependent nature. You are opening your lips to repeat that senseless simile of oaks and vines; I don't want to hear it; there are no creeping tendencies about me" (116).

Hartwell yet more impatiently condemns Beulah's quest for independence. Attributing her refusal of his offers of support and his gifts to her literary ambition, he reproves her, "Ambition such as yours, which aims at literary fame, is the deadliest foe to happiness" (328–29). To a woman's heart, ambition is a tempting fiend, the siren call of fame but an illusion (329). And he chastises Beulah: "You are a proud, ambitious woman, solicitous only to secure eminence as an authoress. I asked your heart; you have now none to give" (330). Beulah does not yield but, heartsick, returns to her desk to complete an article "designed to prove that woman's happiness was not necessarily dependent on marriage. That a single life might be more useful, more tranquil, more unselfish" (331).

Throughout the novel, Beulah insists that in the behavior that others, notably Hartwell, view as willful she is merely following her duty. Thus when Hartwell tells her that her "rash obstinacy" has tortured him beyond expression, she retorts, "I have but done my duty" (167). Similarly, when Pauline, Hartwell's niece and Beulah's friend, asks what possessed her to forsake comfort in order to teach "little ragged, dirty children their A, B, Cs," Beulah responds, "duty" (249). And when Mrs. Williams, the matron of the Asylum whom Beulah deeply loves, reproaches her with having abandoned her faith, Beulah tells her, "I am trying to do my duty just as conscientiously as though I went to church" (314). But, Mrs. Williams counters, "If you cease to pray and read your Bible how are you to know what your duty is?" Mrs. Williams' question cuts to the heart of the problem. It is all very well for Beulah to claim that she is following the path of duty, but perhaps she is merely confusing duty with her own recalcitrant pride. How is she to know?

Evans leaves little doubt that Beulah risks self-delusion. She represents Beulah, during an especially dark period after Cornelia's death, as sitting by a window of a Sunday morning, thinking of her childhood practice of going to church. Now, Evans tells us, "she felt doubly orphaned. In her intellectual pride, she frequently asserted that she was 'the star of her own destiny'"; but this morning she cannot shake the memories of her own previous faith (253). In her unhappiness, Beulah picks up her Bible, which falls open to the thirty-eighth chapter of Job. There the Lord speaks to Job out of a whirlwind, asking him, "Who is this that darkens counsel by words without knowledge?" After reading the chapter with its unrelenting condemnation of the perils of intellectual arrogance, Beulah departs for church to hear Ernest Mortimer's sermon on the text of two verses from the first and last chapters of Ecclesiastes: "For in much wisdom is much grief; and he that increaseth knowledge, increaseth sorrow," and "Of making many books there is no end, and much study is a weariness of the flesh."[31] Mortimer insists that the only certainty lies in fearing God and keeping his commandments, "for this is the whole duty of man" (254).

Beulah spends many lonely months thereafter wrestling with her angel, insisting upon her independent ability to find the truth. Never does she forsake her quest for an absolute, never does she succumb to total skepticism, which she views with fear and loathing. Throughout her journey, she insists upon the words of the Christian tradition—especially "duty"—but she persists in that most horrendous of sins, pride. In a moment of despair, she poignantly tells Hartwell: "There is a truth for the earnest seeker somewhere—somewhere! If I live a thousand years, I will toil after it till I find it" (264). What else, she implores, is life for? Merely to sleep and eat? That she refuses to accept. "No, no. My name bids me press on; there is a land of

Beulah somewhere for my troubled spirit" (264). And she promises to persist in her studies "unguided, unassisted even as I have begun" (264).

Evans' correspondence with Rachel Lyons demonstrates that she, like her heroine, had thought about the respective rewards of a literary and a married life. By the time that she had completed *Beulah,* she was able to write with calm assurance on the matter to her friend. By then, she was also enjoying the considerable financial rewards of her work, which permitted her to buy a house for her parents and to think of traveling to Europe. But we know less about her feelings before and while she wrote the novel. No doubt the ability to earn her living appealed to the young woman whose family was experiencing financial difficulties. No doubt the idea of literary success appealed to the young woman who may have harbored doubts about whether she would ever have the opportunity to marry according to her station. Evans had, in short, her own good reasons to understand the appeal of female independence.

Yet many have read *Beulah* as a blanket condemnation of female independence. That interpretation results from Evans' merciless exposure of the ways in which Beulah's struggle to establish her independence derives from a stubborn, willful pride and from her confusion of the fulfillment of her duty with the mere assertion of her will. In the novel, Evans chooses not to depict the attractions of "single blessedness," although she does have Beulah enjoy a brief period of single tranquility. By that time, however, she has recovered her faith and recognized that she loves Hartwell. Throughout most of the novel, Evans portrays Beulah's determination to establish her independence as frenetic. She invites the reader to see Beulah's interest in economic independence as primarily motivated by—indeed inseparable from—the arrogance that assumes that she can, by reason alone, comprehend the mysteries of the universe.

If Evans does not approve Beulah's presumption, she does treat it with great compassion, implicitly inviting identification with Beulah's struggles. The mainspring of that identification, even for readers who do not share Beulah's intellectual passion, lies in the subtext of Beulah's emotional and psychological development. As Beulah herself insists to Hartwell, her restless search sinks its roots in her childhood, for, she tells him, the questions that trouble her "are older than my acquaintance with so-called philosophic works. They have troubled me from my childhood" (261). But even Beulah does not entirely recognize their deep personal roots. As an orphan, Beulah lacked the formative love of parents and, at the onset of adolescence, saw those she held most dear snatched from her. Tellingly, throughout most of the novel she insists that she has no home—that Hartwell may offer her a house, but never a home. Yet more tellingly, she rarely mentions her childhood and almost never her mother. When Clara asks her why, she replies that it was "all dark and barren as a rainy sea" (213). And when Clara presses for particulars, Beulah responds that she loves her father's memory. "Ah! it is enshrined in my heart's holiest sanctuary. He was a noble, loving man, and my affection for him bordered on idolatry" (213). But of her mother, she says only that she "knew little of her. She died before I was old enough to remember much about her" (213).

Evans describes Beulah's face after this interchange as "full of bitter recollections" and her eyes as if "wandering through some storehouse of sorrows" (213). *Beulah* figures as a protracted account of melancholia, of pathological and self-destructive mourning. Shortly after Lilly's death, when Eugene, the companion of her childhood in the Asylum and the object of her devotion, is about to depart, she tells him, "When you are gone, everything will be dark—dark!" (42). The image of darkness recurs throughout the novel, invariably signaling Beulah's progressive emotional detachment from the world. At the nadir, the bleak Christmas of her extended conversations with Clara and Cornelia, Beulah is depicted as "a young child separated from its mother, and wailing in some starless desert" (211). Only after Beulah has recovered the unconscious and denied roots of her loss—the loss of the mother she claims not even to remember—can she finally begin to accept the love of those who wish her well, and then a husband. Evans thus links Beulah's loss of faith to the psychological depression that derives from the loss of all of those she loved. She also links Beulah's recovery of faith to her feelings for Hartwell. The depths of her unconscious struggles emerge from her refusal to be indebted to him for material goods, her refusal to call his house her home, her refusal, above all, to recognize that he loves her. In the end, Evans, by linking Beulah's recognition that Hartwell loves her to her recognition that she can love God, invites some confusion. Does she intend, as Anne Goodwyn Jones has argued, to suggest that Beulah ultimately loves God in Hartwell?[32]

The evidence that Evans intends no such thing is strong, notwithstanding contrary intimations that she might. Jones's argument depends upon the assumption that in consigning Beulah to the role of devoted wife, Evans is consigning her to defeat. Jones thus assumes that Beulah's struggles to realize her own individualism and independence were positive. Evans gives scant reason to think that she would concur. For Evans, conversion and faith represented the highest human accomplishment, the surest foundation for identity and peace. She valued women's strength and independence but mistrusted unbridled individualism for women or men. In her view, Beulah's struggles for independence could not be divorced from that intellectual presumption that destroys faith—the true threat of individualism as a systematic creed. In *Beulah,* Evans is celebrating not Beulah's defeat but her triumph. She does, to be sure, accept and celebrate the ordained differences between men and women, but in having Beulah willingly accept her highest destiny as a woman she is not celebrating Beulah's subordination to Guy Hartwell: She is celebrating Beulah's subordination to God. And in the novel's concluding lines she entrusts Hartwell's salvation to Beulah.

Beulah's tragedy lies in her frozen heart—her inability to recognize and accept love. Her heart, Evans insists, is a woman's heart. But Evans never endorses the view that Beulah had scornfully rejected woman's nature as dependent and clinging. She simply insists that woman's nature, like man's, requires divine assistance in order to recognize the path of duty. To determine duty for the self is to assume the place of God, to accept the pernicious Emersonian view that creation and creator are one. In this respect, Evans was articulating the distinct Southern view of identity as grounded in particular stations—a view that women must accept their natures and their proper social roles. But she was not endorsing the view that women depend on men for their salvation. Women, like men, must accept their guidance direct from God. Women, like men, are capable of rejecting true duty and forfeiting salvation.

Evans clearly intends Beulah's name to figure as a primary sign in the novel. In the third chapter, a brash girl, daughter of the parvenu woman whom Beulah is serving as nurse, snidely comments, "Beulah—it's about as pretty as her face" (26). By this time the reader knows that Beulah is not beautiful, that she can even be seen as downright ugly, and that her lack of conventional female prettiness has caused her to be sent to work as a servant. But only after the occurrence of these material misfortunes, succeeded by the tragedy of losing her beautiful younger sister and idol to adoption by a fashionable couple, does her name become an issue. The name thus presides over the main plot of the novel: Beulah's progress from the predictable woes of unfortunate humanity through the seemingly inescapable slough of despond to renewed faith and ultimately marriage.

Critics have frequently emphasized the meaning of Beulah's name as "married woman" but have generally paid less attention to its meaning as "(married) land," thus ignoring the possibility that Evans intended her novel to double as an allegory of the South as a whole. Beulah's struggle with religion, Evans carefully demonstrates, is also tied to her disgust with "fashionable" religion. The novel abounds with examples of women who attend the correctly fashionable church while disregarding the true claims of religion: the lady managers of the orphanage, May Chilton, the Graysons. Materialism has invaded the very fabric of belief, reducing it to nothing more than a complacent, self-serving practice for the wealthy. That shallow observance of the forms of faith, with no regard for its substance, is as threatening to the fabric of Southern society as the skepticism that bedevils Beulah. But Evans also demonstrates, in the persons of Clara, Mrs. Williams, and Mrs. Asbury, that true faith, like true charity, remains possible. Materialism and hypocrisy may rightfully disgust the serious believer but cannot alone account for loss of faith, although they can testify to a radical deterioration in society as a whole.

In this respect, the novel may be read as an allegory of the crisis of Southern society in the 1850s, with Beulah's struggles taken as signs of the struggles of the Southern people. Certainly, as early as the 1850s, the great Southern divines were beginning to launch those appeals for self-reformation that would reach a crescendo during the dark years of the Civil War. The virtues that they were urging upon their fellow Southerners strongly resembled those that Evans urges upon her heroine, notably the virtue of a deep, trusting faith that puts aside the graven images of materialism and, especially, unbridled individualism. The good of the self can only be found in the good of the whole, in hewing to the lines that God has laid down.

For generations after its publication, *Beulah* spoke to countless women—and no few men. For these readers, it embodied a great human drama, which it resolved in the appropriate manner with a return to a reinvigorated faith. In so doing, it insisted that the struggles of a young orphan girl mattered, not simply as an object of charity but as a mirror and enactment of social values in general. *Beulah* conveys a forceful sense of the power and significance of women's intellectual and spiritual lives.

Beulah's undoubted appeal is all the more remarkable because of the learning, even pedantry, with which it abounds. Evans' endorsement of a distinct woman's role should not be confused with an endorsement of women as frail, clinging creatures, much less as a rejection of women's intellectual capacity. Whatever *Beulah*'s weaknesses, it testifies to Evans' possession of a powerful and wide-ranging intellect. Since Evans enjoyed exercising and displaying that intellect, *Beulah* contains innumerable explicit and implicit allusions, ranging from the Bible to classical myths to German philosophers. Many of these references will seem obscure to modern readers, as they did to many of Evans' contemporaries. Some probably reflect a mild exhibitionism, for Evans delighted in what she knew. Most are integral to the main narrative—a running commentary on the referents of Beulah's consciousness and identity.

The final chapter presents the marriage of Beulah Benton and Guy Hartwell. Marriage, Evans reminds her readers, is not the end of a life, but the beginning of a new course of duties through which she cannot follow Beulah. Evans does allow Beulah one final reflection on her past, which, she tells

Hartwell, "can never die" (418). She frequently ponders the past, and the recollection of her struggles and her search for a "true philosophy" keeps her humble. "I was so proud of my intellect; put so much faith in my own powers; it was no wonder I was so benighted" (418). And in the final pages, Beulah explains her mature views on science and religion to her husband. Science, she insists, can accomplish wonders, and its powers and scope will continue to advance with the progress of human knowledge. Faith remains a matter of divine mystery: "Truly, 'a God comprehended is no God at all!'" (419). Christian rules of life and duty are clear as crystal.[33] Whatever else, the ending confirms the paramount importance Evans attached to her heroine's thought—to her grasp of and interest in the greatest problems of her age. And she represents Hartwell as respectfully and deferentially attending to Beulah's views.

Notes

1. Isa. 62:4; Augusta J. Evans, *Beulah: A Novel,* 35 herein. All references are to the current edition, which is based on the 1900 edition published by the Federal Book Company in New York. See note 33.

2. Exod. 15:23; Ruth 1:20.

3. See Mary Kelly, *Private Woman, Public Stage: Literary Domesticity in Nineteenth-Century America* (New York, 1984); Jane Tompkins, *Sensational Designs: The Cultural Work of American Fiction, 1790–1860* (New York, 1985). See also Helen Waite Papashvily, *All the Happy Endings: A Study of the Domestic Novel in America, the Women Who Wrote It, the Women Who Read It, in the Nineteenth Century* (New York, 1956); Ann Douglas, *The Feminization of American Culture* (New York, 1977); Nina Baym, *Woman's Fiction: A Guide to Novels by and about Women in America, 1820–1870* (Ithaca, N.Y., 1978); Joyce W. Warren, *The American Narcissus: Individualism and Women in Nineteenth-Century American Fiction* (New Brunswick, N.J., 1989); Fred Lewis Pattee, *The Feminine Fifties* (New York, 1940); Alexander Cowie, *The Rise of the American Novel* (New York, 1948); Herbert Ross Brown, *The Sentimental Novel in America, 1789–1860* (Durham, 1940); E. Douglas Branch, *The Sentimental Years, 1836–1860* (New York, 1934).

4. See especially L.S.M. [Louisa S. McCord], "Uncle Tom's Cabin," *Southern Quarterly Review,* XXIII (January, 1853), 81–120. On Louisa McCord and on Southern women's response to *Uncle Tom's Cabin* in general, see my *Within the Plantation Household: Black and White Women of the Old South* (Chapel Hill, 1988). On the various women writers of the South, see, among many, Kelly, *Private Woman, Public Stage;* Robert LeRoy Hilldrup, "Cold War Against the Yankees in the Antebellum Literature of Southern Women," *North Carolina Historical Review,* XXXI (July, 1954), 370–84; Jeannette Reid Tandy, "Pro-Slavery Propaganda in American Fiction of the Fifties," *South Atlantic Quarterly,* XXI (January, 1922), 41–50, (April, 1922), 170–78; Elizabeth Moss, *Domestic Novelists in the Old South: Defenders of Southern Culture* (Baton Rouge, 1992); Amy Thompson McCandless, "Concepts of Patriarchy in the Popular Novels of Antebellum Southern Women," *Studies in Popular Culture,* II, No. 2 (1987), 1–15. Anne Goodwyn Jones, in *Tomorrow Is Another Day: The Woman Writer in the South, 1859–1936* (Baton Rouge, 1981), discusses Augusta Jane Evans but not the antebellum tradition as a whole.

5. See, among many, Caroline Gilman, *Recollections of a Southern Matron* (New York, 1858), 107; Mrs. Mary H. Eastman, *Aunt Phillis's Cabin; or, Southern Life as It Is* (1852; rpr. New York, 1968), 93; Marion Harland, *Alone* (Richmond, 1854) and *Mossside* (New York, 1857); Caroline Lee Hentz, *The Planter's Northern Bride* (1854; rpr. Chapel Hill, 1970); Mrs. Henry R. Schoolcraft, *The Black Gauntlet: A Tale of Plantation Life in South Carolina*, in *Plantation Life: The Narratives of Mrs. Henry Rowe Schoolcraft* (1852–60; rpr. New York, 1969).

6. Harland, *Alone*, 116.

7. See Drew Gilpin Faust's introduction to the new edition of *Macaria; or, Altars of Sacrifice* (Baton Rouge, 1992).

8. See, for example, Augusta J. Evans to Hon. J. L. M. Curry, July 13, 1863, in J. L. M. Curry Papers, Library of Congress. Evans entertained the idea that slavery might have a deleterious effect on the character of Southern women because the constant attendance of servants deprived them of exercise.

9. Nina Baym, *Novels, Readers, and Reviewers: Responses to Fiction in Antebellum America* (Ithaca, 1984), 94; William Fidler, *Augusta Evans Wilson: A Biography* (University, Ala., 1951), 79; Jones, *Tomorrow Is Another Day*, 61; *Southern Literary Messenger* review, quoted in Baym, *Novels, Readers, and Reviewers*, 94–95.

10. Baltimore *Daily Exchange* review, quoted in Fidler, *Augusta Evans Wilson*, 79; J. C. Derby, *Fifty Years Among Authors, Books, and Publishers* (New York, 1884), 390.

11. "Editorial Miscellany," *De Bow's Review*, XVII (October, 1859), 491; "*Beulah*," *Methodist Quarterly Review*, XX (January, 1860), 112.

12. "*Beulah*," *Southern Literary Messenger*, XXXI (October, 1860), 241, 242–43, 243–44; Marion Harland, publisher's advertisement of *Beulah* in New York *World*, June 14, 1860, quoted in Fidler, *Augusta Evans Wilson*, 80; James Spaulding, New York *Courier and Enquirer* review, quoted in Derby, *Fifty Years*, 392. It seems likely that Evans subsequently used an adapted account of her meeting with Spaulding in *St. Elmo.*

13. Augusta Jane Evans to Mary Howard Jones, November 26, December 4, 1860, in Benning/Jones Collection, Chattahoochee Valley Local & Oral History Archives, Columbus College Library, Columbus, Georgia; Augusta Jane Evans to Mrs. V. French, January 13, 1861, ibid.

14. *Macaria; or, Altars of Sacrifice* (1864), *St. Elmo* (1866), *Vashti* (1869), *Infelice* (1875), *At the Mercy of Tiberius* (1887), *A Speckled Bird* (1902), and *Devota* (1907), which was a brief novella but published as an independent book at her publisher's insistence.

15. We have little specific information about her life and thoughts during these years. The main evidence of her crisis of faith is presented by her biographer, William Fidler, who read the letters between Evans and the Reverend Mr. Harriss. Those letters have since disappeared from circulation, and I was unable to consult them.

16. Cowie, *Rise of the American Novel*, 413, 414.

17. Derby, *Fifty Years*, 396–97; Mary Forrest, *Women of the South Distinguished in Literature* (New York, 1861), 331–32.

18. Jones, *Tomorrow Is Another Day*, 91.

19. Fannie Page Hume Diary, March 1, 1860 (MS in Southern Historical Collection, University of North Carolina, Chapel Hill).

20. Sidney C. Phillips, "The Life and Works of Augusta Evans Wilson" (Ph.D. dissertation, Alabama Polytechnic Institute, 1937), 27–31. My warmest thanks to Leah Atkins for calling this dissertation to my attention.

21. Augusta Jane Evans to Rachel Lyons, July 30, 1860, in possession of William Fidler, Tuscaloosa, Alabama. I wish to express my deep thanks to Mr. Fidler for sharing this letter and others of Augusta Jane Evans with me.

22. Augusta Jane Evans to Rachel Lyons, August 28, November 13, 1860, in possession of William Fidler.

23. Mobile *Daily Advertiser,* November 6, 1859. The articles were unsigned, but William Fidler has identified their writer as Evans. See his "Augusta Evans Wilson as Confederate Propagandist," *Alabama Review,* II (1949), 32–44. See also the thoughtful discussion of these articles in Moss, *Domestic Novelists in the Old South,* Chap. 5.

24. Mobile *Daily Advertiser,* October 10, 1859.

25. Ibid., October 30, November 6, 1859. For my own views on the complex role of proslavery thought in antebellum Southern literature, see my article "The Fettered Mind: Time, Place, and the Literary Imagination of the Old South," *Georgia Historical Quarterly,* LXXVI (Winter, 1990), 622–50.

26. On the general problem of faith and unbelief in nineteenth-century American culture, see James Turner, *Without God, Without Creed: The Origins of Unbelief in America* (Baltimore, 1985).

27. Samuel Taylor Coleridge, "The Rime of the Ancient Mariner," Ernest Hartley Coleridge, ed., in *Coleridge Poetical Works* (New York, 1988), ll. 57–60. Subsequent line references will appear in the text. I am indebted to James Turner for thoughtful discussions about the relation between *Beulah* and "The Rime of the Ancient Mariner."

28. Augusta Jane Evans to Rachel Lyons, October 17, 1859, in possession of William Fidler.

29. "Sir William Hamilton's Philosophy," *Southern Literary Messenger,* XXIX (July, 1859), 3, 6.

30. On this aspect of Carlyle, see Walter L. Reed, "The Pattern of Conversion in *Sartor Resartus,*" *English Literary History,* XXXVIII (September, 1971), 411–31.

31. Job 38:1; Eccles, 1:18, 12:12.

32. Jones, *Tomorrow Is Another Day,* e.g., 76, 84, 88.

33. There are a few slight alterations in this final chapter in the 1887 edition, published by Martin & Hoyt Co. in Atlanta. The significance of the changes does not seem great, although they include the dropping of Evans' paean to those who toil in laboratories and chart the frontiers of scientific discovery. Since the 1900 edition (reproduced here) is identical with the original, New York edition of 1859, it is possible that the changes simply resulted from an inadvertent omission. It is also possible that they reflected deference to what were assumed to be post-Reconstruction Southern sensibilities.

Twelve

Texas Women and the Writing of Women's History

Looking at the richness and variety of Texas women's experience, it is tempting to say that all the world is Texas. Yet, notwithstanding the extraordinary flowering of women's history during the past three decades, the history of Texas women remains comparatively unexplored. Happily, some important recent dissertations, like the papers in this volume, are beginning to fill the gaps. And as new work begins to appear, it is becoming clearer than ever that any attempt to write Texas women's history necessarily intersects with the most pressing issues of theory and method in women's history in general.

As a growing body of work in women's history has taken shape, the attention of scholars has increasingly moved from the accumulation of (previously neglected) information to the consideration of theory. It has become a cheerful commonplace that we have transcended our own recent naive projects to recover women worthies and to restore women to the existing (male) models of history, primarily understood as the history of political power. Women's history, many proudly proclaim, has its own logic and dynamic, its own "dialectic," which challenges the most entrenched assumptions about how history should be written and interpreted. Thus, for growing numbers of scholars, women's history has become feminist history, although differences about the meaning of "feminist" persist.

This extraordinary transformation has occurred as women's historians, in step with a variety of other critics of Western culture and its fundamental presuppositions, have discovered pluralism, diversity, and multiculturalism. Having begun with the assumption that the recovery of women's experience required the restoration of woman to man's self-serving accounts, women's historians are now acknowledging that any simple model of woman itself denies the complexity of the experience of women in all their diversity. Gender, race, and class have, in the process, emerged as the signposts of any women's history that claims to attend to the differences among women.

The discovery of diversity has, in some respects, moved women's history in healthy new directions. No longer is it safe to assume that the experience and values of white, middle-class, normally Northeastern women are an acceptable proxy for the experience and values of women of different classes, races, and ethnicities throughout the country, much less the world. It is no longer even safe to assume that the ideology of separate spheres, which had long been taken to articulate the experience and values of white, middle-class women, faithfully captured the reality of any women's lives. Many, perhaps most, American women never enjoyed the luxury of remaining at home to raise their children amidst sparkling cleanliness and an ample store of provisions. With a few privileged exceptions, American women have known not leisure, but long hours, days, and lives of strenuous labor. As slaves, sharecroppers, migrant farm laborers, factory workers, domestic servants, laundresses, and even teachers, librarians, nurses, and clerical workers, most American women have combined their domestic responsibilities with labor outside the home. And many of those who have been able to remain within their homes have combined domestic labor with labor for others than their own families, taking in laundry, piecework, or boarders.

As with experience, so with values. It is now widely recognized that not all women internalized the values of the cult of domesticity with its implicit white, middle-class biases. Working-class women frequently defied even the most benevolent and well-intentioned efforts to remake them closer to the middle-class norm of propriety. African American women, in slavery times and since, have learned to practice a form of dissemblance that masks their innermost thoughts and feelings, protecting them from potentially demeaning or destructive white incursions on their privacy. Women of all ethnic groups have frequently cherished and preserved the values and traditions of their own people. Today, attention to the differences among women by race and class is rivaling attention to the similarities that unite women as members of a sex.

However welcome, this new attention to the diversity of women's experience and values harbors some potential dangers. For in essential respects, attention to diversity has simply discredited the universal claims of previous theories without reconstructing them. Confusion has resulted. Many of those who most enthusiastically champion the claims of diversity have, in effect, openly repudiated the ideal of a general theory, or even a general narrative, of women's history. At least for the moment, it is said, we can at best hope to know only "partial truths."[1] Since our primary responsibility remains to recapture the voices of discrete women and groups of women with as much immediacy as possible, we should do better to avoid generalizations entirely. Yet others, who are no less interested in the differences among women, cling to some notion of a women's culture—to the sense that women are, in important and historically significant respects, different from men. The problems with both positions are legion, but do usefully highlight the most pressing challenges in women's history.

Significantly, those who focus most explicitly on the irreducible diversity of women's experience are also focusing on women's subjective assessment of their own experience. Such scholars, especially when explicitly influenced by postmodernist literary theory, are quick to dismiss any attempt to generalize beyond women's immediate experience as an illegitimate exercise of power. For, they reason, the generalizations that our culture has produced have invariably promoted binary oppositions, such as black and white, male and female, self and other, that have legitimated women's oppression. Freedom for women, in this view, must begin with an attack on these most crippling and deeply entrenched forms of oppression. Women, above all, should understand that the time-honored opposition between male and female has regularly resulted in women's being cast as "the other," and in the denial of women's independent claims to subjective authority.[2] And if the problem is acute for women in general, how much more acute must it be for women of disadvantaged class, ethnic, and racial groups? Would it not be ultimately presumptuous for white women to impose their own categories upon the experience of African American women, who have suffered unique forms of oppression from which white women have frequently benefitted? If African American women's experience and values have demonstrably not conformed to white, middle-class paradigms, must we not reject those paradigms and, more ominously, reject any paradigms that do not emerge directly from African American women's own lives?[3] The same questions, obviously, arise for Native American, Hispanic American, and other women.

This position, at the extreme, holds that the only possible legitimate knowledge must arise from unmediated consideration of the specific features of specific women's lives. In this respect, the position privileges the social and cultural history of everyday life, which alone can hope to capture ordinary women's experience—their actual behavior and, to the extent we can determine, their actual thoughts. Pursuit of these goals has resulted in newly rich and evocative pictures of the lives of people whom historians had too frequently dismissed as lost to historical knowledge. But such history, notwithstanding its considerable appeal and value, does make generalization, not to mention narrative or a sense of historical development, notoriously difficult.

Postmodernists would counter that their purpose is precisely to complicate, deconstruct, and even sabotage the possibility of a comprehensive narrative. Arguing that power resides in language, they insist upon the necessity for each to reclaim her own voice and, above all, to refuse being encoded in the dehumanizing language of others. The very idea of difference, notably the difference between male and female, they proclaim, must be recognized as an artifact of language, as a manifestation of illegitimate power.[4] Men, who have monopolized cultural as well as social, political, and economic power, have cast women as different in order to subordinate them. So long as difference persists, so will hierarchy.

Difference in this sense apparently means binary difference, or the notion of difference in the abstract. For those who most enthusiastically repudiate difference as an organizational paradigm no less enthusiastically celebrate the multiplicity of differences that distinguish all human beings from one another. It takes little imagination to grasp that the concept of difference, specifically sexual difference, has served to disadvantage women. But that very difference which has so effectively helped to limit women to subordinate roles and ambitions also affords the primary justification for women's history as a subject. How, in other words, does the abolition of difference as an overarching category not result in the abolition of women as an historical subject? The emphasis on diversity at the expense of difference would seem to open the possibility that more divides women among themselves than divides women as a group from men. Under these conditions, the common experience and values of those individuals who are able to bear and suckle children evaporates under the weight of the various aspects of their condition that divide them.

To be sure, some of those who emphasize the social, economic, and political divisions among women nonetheless remain loyal to the notion of a women's culture. As the psychologist Carol Tavris has argued, the notion of a distinct, much less uniform women's culture raises other problems.[5] Any notion of a women's culture must rest on some assumptions about experiences or values that women share independent of class, race, ethnicity, nationality, or historical epoch. Intuitively most of us accept that women, or most women, do in fact tend to behave more like each other than like men. But most of our intuitions derive from our own experience. The women we know tend to behave more like each other than like the men we know: women are more likely to prefer shopping to a boxing match; or, in the more popular example, women are more likely to cherish children and hate war.

Cross-cultural comparisons have, nonetheless, taught us to be suspicious of easy generalizations on these matters. There are cultures in which men delight in shopping. The association of women with the nurture of children and men with warfare is more pervasive across cultural boundaries, but even that association may be modified in particular cases. Should we therefore conclude that all differences between women and men result from culture and are, accordingly, subject to modification or even abolition? If not, should we assume that physiological characteristics, which women do share across cultural boundaries, determine women's culture? And, if so, does history not offer grim lessons? How, in short, do women's historians propose to separate women's culture from women's subordination?

The dilemma starkly exposes the greatest challenges that confront women's history as a coherent discipline. In effect, as theories, both the postmodernist and the women's culture positions inadvertently end in a denial of history. In practice, however, both can be understood to underscore the centrality of history to any serious interpretation of women's experience and values. As Ramon Saldivar has argued for the Chicano narrative, "*history* is the subtext we must recover because history itself is the subject of its discourse."[6] In the case of women, to cast history simply as the background or context of experience and values is to radically divorce women from history rather than understand that, divorced from history, women become either biological beings or abstractions. History constitutes the essence of women's experience and values, the very structure of their lives and their minds. This insistence upon the historical contingency of all human experience should not be taken as a repudiation of physiological differences between women and men or even of abiding values; it does, however, focus attention upon the social consequences that different peoples in different eras attribute to those differences, and to the salient political, social, economic, and cultural relations within which they are elaborated.

There is no easy way of writing a satisfying women's history and no ready-made grand theory to encompass the entire corpus of women's experience. Any adequate theory of women's history must simultaneously attend to similarity and difference, always asking similar to and different from whom, and in which ways. The task is all the more complicated since all of us, willy-nilly, write from within the Western tradition in general and the American tradition in particular. However much we may protest the injustices, oppressions, and exclusions of that tradition, our deepest assumptions, beginning with our attitudes towards women, derive from it. Thus even if we successfully expose the operation of the ideology of separate spheres as misleading and oppressive, every time we speak of women as a group—or as individuals—we betray our complicity with it.

The complicity is not, in my judgment, especially dangerous, provided we retain our critical vigilance. For the very tradition that so successfully propounded the universal ideology of spheres also propounded the universal ideology of individual freedom and individual rights that has proven our strongest basis for criticizing it. It is, in short, our history, the fabric of our identity. No determination to repudiate difference as inherently hierarchical can eradicate a past in which most women experienced their difference from men as central to their sense of self and to the rhythm of their lives. No enthusiasm for women's culture can transform a past in which most women found their difference from women of other groups as important as their difference from the men of their own group.

In this perspective, the most important task that women's historians confront remains a vast increase in information about women. Perhaps the most daunting feature of women's history lies in the interrelated tasks of distinguishing among and appropriately grouping together women. For most of human history and, more to the point, most of American history (however defined), most women have spent most, if not all, of their lives as daughters, sisters, wives, and mothers within rural households. From the perspective of the women themselves those lives have been as varied as the human species. The food women have eaten, the shelters in which they have lived, the languages in which they have spoken, the ways in which they have worshipped, the clothing they have worn, the goods they have been able to barter or to trade, the ways in which they have raised their children, and their relations with their kin and neighbors. Like snowflakes, no two women are alike. But then neither are any two men.

From the perspective of generalization or analysis, however, the similarities are no less decisive. Throughout rural societies, women's lives have followed the patterns of the seasons and their own life-cycles just as they have fallen into predictable patterns of work. Throughout rural societies, women have traditionally assumed responsibility for the preservation and preparation of food, the rearing of children, the making and repairing of clothing, the care of the sick and the elderly, the carrying of water, and frequently the smoothing and sustaining of relations among generations and kin. It would be possible, with no gross violations of accuracy, to use the same words to describe the lives of rural women in early modern Europe, precolonial West Africa, the antebellum South, and late-nineteenth-century Texas. With no greater violation of accuracy it is also possible to use the same words to describe the lives of African slave women, Hispanic women, Anglo women,

Italian peasant women, Serbian Jewish women, and Swedish women in Minnesota.

Somewhere between the diversity and the similarity lies the substance of women's history. To make sense of that history we need, in the first instance, enough information to generalize. For example, we learn little, if anything, from repeated pronouncements about the oppression of African American and Hispanic women in Texas. We learn a great deal from Julia Kirk Blackwelder's discussion of the employment experience of different groups of women in San Antonio during the Depression.[7] Suddenly, oppression acquires a specific content: as the economy worsened, women of socially advantaged ethnic groups displaced those less advantaged. Anglo women took jobs previously held by Hispanic women who, in turn, took jobs previously held by African American women, who were pushed back into domestic service and laundry work, if they could secure employment at all. To talk seriously of the experience of different groups of women, we need innumerable other studies of this kind. Otherwise we will only be able to persist in our tiresome groaning about oppression or to relate detailed personal stories of individual women, which may or may not be typical of anything.

We also need enough knowledge to assign women to the appropriate groups. We now have ample evidence that, in general, Hispanic women fared less well in Texas than Anglo women. But that generalization obscures significant variations. As Jane Dysart has demonstrated, during the early American period some Hispanic women in San Antonio married well-placed Anglo men.[8] As a rule, those who did tended to be of light skin and of politically powerful, wealthy families. These women brought their husbands important political connections and frequently substantial economic assets as well, largely because Mexican law prescribed equal inheritance for daughters and sons. As married women, moreover, they continued to participate in many aspects of their own culture. Even when their husbands were Protestant, they raised their children as Catholics, maintained strong ties to their own kin, and gave their children Hispanic *compadres,* or godparents. In the end, however, they paid what many might view as a stiff price for their membership in the political and social elite, for most of their children came to identify with their fathers' culture. And, tellingly, Anglo and Hispanic culture, notwithstanding pronounced differences in customs and manners, shared a strong emphasis on male authority and values. It is surely significant that during the same period San Antonio witnessed almost no marriages between Anglo women and Hispanic men.

Studies such as this one provide the essential building blocks for any comprehensive theory of women's history. The experience of these women encapsulates in microcosm some of the many complexities that bedevil women's history. Not unlike the free women of color of the Gulf Coast during the antebellum period, they rank as an anomalous minority. Yet their anomalous status illuminates much about women's roles in mediating between racial and ethnic groups, just as it illuminates the dangers in arbitrarily codifying women by their gender, race, or ethnicity with no attention to class. It is hard to imagine that these women did not employ Hispanic servants, and hard to imagine that they did not regard those servants as socially inferior to themselves. To be sure, they may have employed Irish or German servants, or even owned African American slaves. Whatever the case, as upper-class women they surely did have servants and surely did, in part, define themselves in relation to them.

How they defined themselves in relation to their husbands and redefined themselves through their husbands in relation to the ethnic community into which they were born constitutes a separate and no less interesting problem. From an anthropological perspective, they can easily be recognized as objects of exchange, pawns in the consolidation of a new elite. Whether they saw themselves in that way remains unknown. There is no evidence to suggest that the free women of color of the Gulf Coast identified with slave women, and abundant evidence to suggest that they fiercely defended their free status. However deep these Hispanic women's religious, cultural, and personal ties to their communities of origin, their marriages represented a limited kind of upward mobility and perhaps the realization of personal ambition. Since we know that men may experience the conflicting claims of ambition and cultural roots, on what grounds can we assume that women may not?

My plea for a massive increase in what we know about women should not be confused with a commitment to Rankean empiricism. To the contrary, information about women's lives and values is always more difficult to come by than comparable information for men. Thus even the questions and hypotheses that lead us to seek certain kinds of information represent preliminary contributions to any serious theory. More important, however, only substantial and comparable data about the specific features of women's lives could permit us to ascertain how to appreciate women's historical roles. We have, for example, become reasonably sophisticated in our understanding that, at least from the early decades of the nineteenth century in the United States, women have tended to become church members in larger numbers than men. Elizabeth Turner, drawing upon the work of Ann Boylan, has even argued convincingly that the kinds of churches to which women belonged tended to play a role in their attitudes towards benevolence and reform. But, to take only the case of Texas, we know a good deal less about the social attitudes and activities of practicing Catholic women than their Protestant counterparts.

The issues are not trivial. There is good reason to believe that church membership, and beyond it faith, simultaneously empowered and restricted women. Church activities introduced women to new roles and responsibilities outside their immediate families, frequently encouraged them in a sense of social responsibility, and frequently encouraged them to work with other women. Faith frequently endowed women with a sense of righteousness and of serving a cause with which man had no right to interfere. But the ministers, priests, and texts of faith normally reminded women of their own secondary status and not infrequently imbued them with the conviction of their own sinfulness. If faith, in other words, offered many women a purpose and even a structure for their self-representations, it also constantly reminded them that they were women in a world dominated by men.[9] But in communities rent by social inequality and ethnic difference, the observance of faith in specific denominations probably did not lead all women into the belief that they shared a culture with all other women. Indeed, to the extent that women have experienced religion as central to their culture, many may have drawn upon it to define and differentiate other groups of women.[10]

That class position, like ethnicity and race, divided women no longer comes as a surprise to scholars in women's history. And many have taken the recognition of these divisions as evidence that the general ideologies of womanhood do not apply to the experiences of all women. The concept of separate spheres, as most of us now acknowledge, was a myth. We have further learned that innumerable women rejected the myth as an adequate description of their own lives and, especially, their ambitions. But as Megan Seaholm has demonstrated, elite women devised ways of turning the myth to their advantage. Seaholm's elegant dissertation on club women in Texas argues, among other things, that Texas club women drew upon the myth of separate spheres to claim aspects of the public sphere as peculiarly and appropriately their own.[11] In so doing, they were simultaneously strengthening their own roles as women within the white elite and drawing attention to the needs of other women who were divided from them by class, ethnicity, and race. We do not need, naively and inaccurately, to assume that such women felt bound in sisterhood to women less fortunate than they in order to accept that they did believe that women's position in society required active defense and even improvement. Nor do we need, just as naively and inaccurately, to believe that less fortunate women were deluded by the invocation of women's sphere into believing that privileged women fully understood or defended their needs. But we might begin by acknowledging that women of very different conditions could, for their own reasons, draw upon an ideology of separate spheres to pursue specific, and frequently divergent, goals.

In this perspective we can, again, recognize Texas as all the world. For the extraordinary complexity of Texas, with its multiple nationalities, its slave-holding, farming, ranching, and urbanizing sectors, its religious and cultural diversity, and its indomitable sense of its own destiny and power, offers a microcosm of the complexity of the United States as a whole. If we can begin to understand the place of women in the Texas which has recently given us Ann Richards, Sarah Weddington, Barbara Jordan, and Sissy Farent-hold, we might begin to piece together a theory adequate to understanding the history of women in the United States and the world.

In the end, any theory of women's history depends upon our ability to accumulate information that permits us to identify the similarities and differences in women's lives. In this quest, no presuppositions will serve. Women have always shared much as women; women have always been divided by much as historical, which is to say social and political, beings. The history of men, as written by men, cannot be dismissed as alien to women's experience and values, for women have always participated in it. But until we can write with confidence of the experience of different groups of women, we will not be able to reason intelligently about women's participation. Until we can write with confidence of the experience of different groups of women, we will not even know how the groups should be defined. Somewhere between the multiplicity of individual women and the culture of all women lies the history of how women have historically related to each other, to men, and to the American past.

Notes

1. Jacqueline Dowd Hall, "Partial Truths: Writing Southern Women's History," in *Southern Women: Histories and Identities,* eds. Virginia Bernhard, Betty Brandon, Elizabeth Fox-Genovese, and Theda Purdue (Columbia: University of Missouri Press, 1992).

2. The best-known formulation of the problem of women as other to male consciousness is Simone de Beauvoir, *The Second Sex,* trans. H. M. Parshley (New York: Knopf, 1952). For a thoughtful recent discussion of the problem, see Nancy K. Miller, *Subject to Change: Reading Feminist Writing* (New York: Columbia University Press, 1988).

3. See, for example, Patricia Hill Collins, *Black Feminist Thought: Knowledge, Consciousness, and the Politics of Empowerment* (London: Harper Collins Academic, 1990).

4. See, for example, Joan Wallach Scott, *Gender and the Politics of History* (New York: Columbia University Press, 1988).

5. Carol Tavris, *The Mismeasure of Woman* (New York: Simon and Schuster, 1992).

6. Ramon Saldivar, *Chicano Narrative: The Dialectics of Difference* (Madison: University of Wisconsin Press, 1990), 5.

7. Julia Kirk Blackwelder, *Women of the Depression: Caste and Culture in San Antonio, 1929–1939* (College Station: Texas A&M University Press, 1984).

8. Jane Dysart, "Mexican Women in San Antonio, 1830–1860: The Assimilation Process," *Western Historical Quarterly,* XVII (Oct., 1986), 365–376.

9. See Elizabeth Fox-Genovese, "Religion in the Lives of the Slaveholding Women of the Antebellum South," in *That Gentle Strength: Historical Perspectives on Women in Christianity,* eds. Lynda L. Coon, Katherine J. Haldane, and Elisabeth W. Sommer (Charlottesville: University Press of Virginia, 1990), and Jean E. Friedman, *The Enclosed Garden: Women and Community in the Evangelical South, 1830–1900* (Chapel Hill: University of North Carolina Press, 1985).

10. Elizabeth Fox-Genovese, *Within the Plantation Household: Black and White Women of the Old South* (Chapel Hill: University of North Carolina Press, 1988).

11. Megan Seaholm, "Earnest Women: The White Women's Club Movement in Progressive Era Texas, 1880–1920" (Ph.D. diss., Rice University, 1988).

Thirteen

Stewards of Their Culture

Southern Women Novelists as Social Critics

The temptation to view Southern women as committed, if frequently secret, social critics has been strong but may rest on a misunderstanding. For the view of women—any women—as social critics too frequently rests on the assumption that women will, first and foremost, criticize their own social subordination. There is, in other words, a strong tendency to associate women as social critics with the emergence of feminism. This tendency especially derives from the pioneering work in women's history that linked the rise of feminism to women's associations for the moral reform of society, particularly to the rise of antislavery, which, it is argued, provided women with a powerful analogy for their own subordination.[1] It rests on the further and palpably false assumption that women, as social critics, inevitably favor an expanded democratization of society and politics.

One premise of this argument, at least, is compelling. Feminism as a social movement has, as its most vociferous critics have always insisted, tended to promote the leveling of hierarchies, beginning with that most resilient of all, the hierarchy of gender relations within the family. But the argument also rests upon a serious fallacy, namely the assumption that all women equate social criticism with feminism. It ignores, in other words, the evidence that many women, like many men, criticize society from a conservative position; it assumes that women's social criticism necessarily presupposes a commitment to women's equality—either with men or among themselves.

"Stewards of Their Culture: Southern Women Novelists as Social Critics." In *Stepping Out of the Shadows: Alabama Women, 1819–1990,* edited by Mary Martha Thomas, 11–27. Tuscaloosa: University of Alabama Press, 1995. Copyright 1995 by the University of Alabama Press. All rights reserved. Used by permission of the publisher.

Today we are beginning to understand that women may criticize aspects of their society and may even support elements of feminism without embracing the sisterhood of all women across class and racial lines. But even those who recognize this much may balk at the recognition that some women actively oppose even the basic equality between women and men implied by mainstream bourgeois feminism, if they perceive it as threatening other social values that they cherish. We are loathe to see women actively championing what we now view as repressive regimes and, perhaps, are even more loathe to see them as complicit in their own subordination.[2]

The work of feminist scholars on women's culture, especially the tradition of sentimental or literary domesticity, has taught us to recognize the ways in which women manipulated the discourses available to them to criticize a variety of social relations and practices. Mary Kelly and Jane Tompkins have especially insisted upon the conflicts about authority and role that wracked women writers, and upon the ways in which they manipulated conventions of proper male and female roles to subvert prevailing discourses and relations of power.[3] Today domestic sentimental novels are no longer dismissed as a "sub-literary" genre unworthy of serious critical attention and are widely, if not universally, recognized as "powerful and important in their own right."[4] According to Tompkins, sentimental fiction may rank as "the most influential expression of the beliefs that animated" the widespread religious revival movement of the antebellum period. For, like the evangelical reformers themselves, "the sentimental novelists wrote to educate their readers in Christian perfection and to move the nation as a whole closer to the City of God."[5] The leading exponents of the sentimental tradition set themselves nothing less than a millennial mission to relocate the very center of power, from the government, the courts of law, the factories, and the marketplace, to the kitchen.[6] Thus, even when overtly embracing their culturally prescribed roles as angels of the hearth, they sought to draw from their subordination a transformative social vision.

Antebellum Southern women writers, whom many have viewed as participating in the sentimental domestic tradition, would have agreed with Tompkins's assessment of what their Northern counterparts were about. But they did not approve. Roundly castigating Northern literary domestics, above all Harriet Beecher Stowe, for their poorly disguised, revolutionary, and socially disruptive intentions, they berated them for precisely those subversive tendencies for which modern critics praise them. Under the protective mantle of self-proclaimed womanly virtue, Northern women were foisting a radical, leveling social vision upon an unsuspecting public. Claiming to realize the deepest evangelical implications of woman's domestic mission, they were, in fact, undermining it and everything else that respectable folks held dear.

Throughout the antebellum period, Southern women novelists diverged from their Northern counterparts, primarily by developing their own interpretation of domesticity, which always included an acceptance of slavery as an appropriate foundation for a worthy society. During what has been called the "feminine fifties," the tensions between Northern and Southern domesticity erupted in an outright literary war. In this war, Southern women novelists united in their defense of their region, specifically its values and social system. But as the war unfolded, they also began to develop variations upon their common theme. And increasingly, in the common effort, Caroline Lee Hentz and Augusta Jane Evans, both of whom were living in Alabama, took the lead, thereby supplanting the traditionally genteel voice of Virginia women with the more modern and, if anything, more unambiguously proslavery voice of the Cotton Kingdom of the Old Southwest.

The political turmoil of the decade that opened with the Compromise of 1850 and closed with the election of Lincoln found its sharpest literary expression in the realm of domestic fiction. The appearance of *Uncle Tom's Cabin* in 1852, which crystallized Southern women writers' opposition to the subversive tendencies of Northeastern literary domesticity, provoked them to a succession of direct and indirect responses and, above all, prompted them to undertake a searching examination of their own social vision. Caroline Lee Hentz and Mary Eastman attacked directly, seconding in their fiction the anger and the social values that Louisa McCord had displayed in her polemical review. Caroline Gilman, Maria McIntosh, Mary Virginia Terhune, and Augusta Jane Evans avoided a frontal attack on Stowe but took her challenge no less seriously.[7] And Hentz and Evans especially defended the experience and attitudes of the Deep South.

Uncle Tom's Cabin rent the veil of genteel domesticity that had shrouded the growing divergence of Northern and Southern domestic fiction. Its very success precluded polite dissembling by associating the dominant female literary voice with the cause of antislavery.[8] Doubt was no longer possible. At issue was not merely a struggle over competitive social systems, but a struggle over the very definition of womanhood. Domestic fiction, apparently the privileged locus of consensus and harmony, became a distinctly female battleground, although unlike Louisa McCord, the Southern literary domestics did not plunge into unfeminine polemics. Ever mindful of their manners, ever respectful of the characteristic domestic idiom, they persisted in wrapping their message in the conventional package of woman's duty, religious uplift, and domestic values. But decorum and literary convention notwithstanding, they increasingly insisted that the North, led by its women, was proceeding rapidly to perdition—down the road of revolution.

If *Uncle Tom's Cabin* brought the issues into focus, it did not inaugurate them. By 1852, as Elizabeth Moss argues, Southern literary domesticity, which she sees as extending from Caroline Lee Hentz's *Lovell's Folly* of 1833 to Mary Virginia Terhune's *Sunnybank* of 1866, had a respectable pedigree.[9] Caroline Gilman's pair of novels, *Recollections of a New England Housekeeper* (1834) and *Recollections of a Southern Matron* (1838), laid the true foundations of the genre, which owed as much to the emerging genre of plantation fiction as to Northern literary domesticity.[10] From the start, the Southern literary domestics, like their Northern counterparts, believed themselves the embodiments of a mission. And, again like their Northern counterparts, they believed that that mission above all concerned women's special role in the defense of fundamental religious and familial values.[11] But the similarities ended where they began, at the general levels of passion and rhetoric. For the Southern women knew from the start that the values that they were defending depended upon the persistence of slavery as a social system. And well before the tide of Northern antislavery began to crest, they perceived that the North was embarked on a course that threatened everything they cherished.

During the 1830s and the 1840s, Southern literary domestics, like South ern writers in general, primarily came from the elite of the more settled states, notably Virginia and South Carolina. They tended to represent Southern values as the aristocratic values of the entire country, claiming that the South embodied the true legacy of the American Revolution. Thus they associated what they viewed as the more radical of Northern values with the disruptions of accelerating capitalist development. Borrowing from late eighteenth- and early nineteenth-century classical republican rhetoric, notably its suspicions of commerce and celebration of rural virtue, Gilman sharply criticized the fashionable corruption of urban life, to which she attributed the dissolution of woman's virtuous character and sturdy independence. Superficially, that critique had much in common with many Northern women writers' distrust of the corrosive and debilitating effects of fashion, but Gilman endowed the general trope with specific social referents. "What a blessed thing to childhood," she writes in *Recollections of a Southern Matron*, "is the fresh air and light of heaven! No manufactories, with their over-tasked inmates, to whom all but Sabbath sunshine is a stranger, arose on our plantation." Slaves enjoyed an infinitely superior fate to that of Northern workers. "Long before the manufacturer's task in other regions is closed, our labourers were lolling on sunny banks, or trimming their gardens, or fondling their little ones, or busy in their houses, scarcely more liable to intrusion than the royal retirement of a Guelph or a Capet."[12]

There is no mistaking Gilman's intent. Slaves, who lead a healthier life than urban workers, enjoy the benefits of leisure, gardens, children, and private homes—explicitly identified as their castles. Membership in a plantation household, moreover, ensures their full exposure to the highest benefits of civilization. The influence of the plantation mistress's manners "was evident on the plantation, producing an air of courtesy even among the slaves," who held her in the deepest reverence and who were themselves capable of the most unswerving loyalty.[13] A planter's daughter, Gilman notes in passing, "fears none but white men."[14] She assuredly credits the beneficent influence of country life upon the character and bearing of women, whom cities can transform from healthy lasses into polished belles, who spend their time "calculating all night and dressing all day."[15] The country she celebrates is not rural life in general; it is the Southern household within the confines of which slavery exercises a mutually beneficial influence on owners and owned. Enslavement affords slaves the benefits of religion, decent living conditions, and frequently an appreciation for refined taste unknown to Northern workers. Most Southern plantations, Gilman insists, "were regulated with almost military precision. No punishment was ever inflicted but by an authorized person, and if he overstepped the boundaries of mercy in his justice, he was expelled from his authority. From my infancy, I had never seen a gentleman forget the deportment of a gentleman to our slaves."[16]

Even as the responsibilities of slaveholding encourage the development of the highest gentlemanly conduct, so do they encourage the development of responsible womanhood. The plantation mistress does not preside over a limited household, but over a number of dependents who "would constitute a village." Obliged to listen to grievances, to nurse the sick, and to distribute "the half-yearly clothing," a planter's lady lives with the "arduous" responsibility of keeping "so many menials in order . . . and the *keys* of her establishment are a care of which a Northern housekeeper knows nothing, and include a very extensive class of duties."[17] To meet these responsibilities, "many fair, and even aristocratic girls, if we may use this phrase in our republican country," must develop the ability to measure supplies "with the accuracy and conscientiousness of a shopman," and matrons "who would ring a bell for their pocket-handkerchief to be brought to them, will act the part of a surgeon or physician with a promptitude and skill which would excite astonishment in a stranger."[18]

Thus Gilman, at the dawn of the Southern domestic tradition, establishes slavery as the necessary foundation for the general discourse of virtuous womanhood upon which both Northern and Southern writers drew. Systematically appropriating the values of religion, duty, charity, and social responsibility for the particular condition of the slaveholding woman, she conjoins to them the more masculine values of a shopman's accuracy and a physician's skill. In training to assume the position of Southern matron, her protagonist, tellingly named Cornelia, shares equally with her brothers the instruction of a tutor. Initially, her father worries that "the full cultivation of [her] mind in the branches studied by [her] brothers" would "lead her to consider herself more learned than her father." And why, the deeply religious tutor counters, "should she not . . . if humility be so wrought in her as to make her feel her own inferiority to the true standard of mind?" The father has no grounds to fear. "Intellectual women are the most modest inquirers after truth, and accomplished women often the most scrupulous observers of social duty."[19]

Slavery and sincere religion, which constitute the twin poles of an orderly society, provide a structure within which women should be free to cultivate their intelligence.[20] Gilman, like many of her successors, notably Augusta Evans Wilson, refused to deny women the full cultivation of their minds, provided that they cultivate them in the service of higher values. To be sure, she deplored women's self-aggrandizement, but, for her, fashion, not intellect or learning, constituted its premier sign. Fashion, which she associated with urban mobility and corruption, resembled free labor in corroding society and religion. Female intellect and learning, in contrast, could serve them and, pursued in the proper spirit, offered no challenge to established hierarchies, notably gender hierarchy. In Gilman's view, a primary commitment to slavery and religion permitted women the freedom of a responsible self-cultivation by ensuring that their accomplishments would enhance their contributions to their households and society rather than lead them into wanton individualism.

Gilman's contemporaries Caroline Lee Hentz and Maria McIntosh embroidered the same themes in their fiction of the 1830s and 1840s. Never complacent in their defense of Southern society and values, they, like she, remained alert to the internal dangers that might threaten it. In *Recollections of a Southern Matron,* Gilman herself introduces what would emerge as one of Southern literary domestics' favorite targets, the dissolute elite Southern man. Lewis Barnwell, heir to the plantation adjacent to that of Cornelia Wilton's father, possesses all of the advantages of class and breeding but is marred by a deep-seated strand of self-indulgence. The reader first learns of this charmer's weakness when Cornelia discovers a young male slave whom he has inappropriately beaten. Slaves, Gilman insists, require "a strict superintending hand . . . to maintain that discipline, without which not even the social hearth can be preserved from strife." But "Lewis's was not the hand to chastise" the slave. And Cornelia, observing the young slave, "could not check the mental inquiry if one who could yield to his passions with an inferior, would not be an imperious companion with an equal."[21]

Events confirm Cornelia's fears. Lewis's unchecked passions lead him from the abuse of slaves into the tentacles of fashionable life—drinking and gambling—from which he lacks the character to extricate himself. The tragic death of the young woman who loves him unmistakably signals the infectious danger of his proclivities. Gilman, like other Southern literary domestics, warns her readers that men's passions threaten the very fabric of the households and society that men should protect and order. The attack on men's capacity for irresponsibility echoes an older strand in women's fiction but acquires new meaning in the Southern context.[22] For Southern women writers, like their British predecessors and Northern counterparts, a man's dissolution frequently testifies to his parents', normally his mother's, failures or absences and thus testifies to the importance of maternal guidance to the development of male character. And in this view, the women were overwhelmingly seconded by the articulate men of the South, especially the ministers and educators.

Southern literary domestics also normally attribute special importance to distinct attributes of manhood, notably the ability to command others responsibly, which is the necessary sign of the ability to command oneself. Frequently loathe to criticize an older generation of plantation masters, whom they are wont to associate directly with the legacy of the Revolution, they may fall back on the notion of an inherited strand of weakness to explain the failure of men to rise to the exigencies of household governance. For, however essential a mother's influence, male character requires appropriate male guidance.[23]

The dissolute young man, who recurs throughout Southern domestic fiction, acquires special resonance as the distorted reflection of male strength. His vices invariably represent the pernicious excesses of necessary male virtues. In his characteristic incarnation, he succumbs to the lure of drink, gambling, fast horses, and unbridled temper. He thus offers a terrifying caricature of the qualities of command and daring that are essential to the man who must master other men. The unflinching will of the good master surfaces in the dissolute rake as the unbridled willfulness of the unsocialized child. Southern literary domestics' abiding preoccupation with male strength and its perversions reflects their abiding commitment to a distinct, socially grounded ideal of maleness, which they deem necessary to the survival of their most cherished institutions. The dissolute young man appears early in the Southern domestic tradition and persists to the end as the sign of a continuing attempt to sustain a viable model of masculinity. From Lewis Barnwell in *Recollections of a Southern Matron* to Eugene (Rutland) Graham in *Beulah,* he manifests the same flaws and falls prey to the same temptations, but as the debate over slavery intensifies, his virtuous alter ego gradually changes. Increasingly, Southern women writers focus their primary effort on the presentation of a compelling model of male strength.

Throughout the antebellum period, the dissolute young man figures as a primary object of Southern women writers' social criticism. In so using him, they are superficially following a path similar to that followed by the Northern literary domestics, but beneath the surface, they are elaborating a very different agenda. Whereas the Northerners increasingly sought to make men more like women, to subject them to domestic standards, Southerners sought to make them adhere more closely to traditional standards of manhood. In their hands, the weakness of the dissolute young man disconcertingly evokes effeminacy, merging with their image of undisciplined women. Their determined insistence upon the significance of sharp distinctions between male and female excellence testifies to their commitment to differentiating the values of slave society from what they perceive as the corruption of capitalist society. In this spirit, they invariably link male dissolution to the contagion of fashion as embodied in urban life. The line that Northern women writers figuratively draw between the home and the world, Southern women writers draw between the North and the South, although by the late 1850s, many are reluctantly acknowledging that Northern corruption is extending its tentacles into Southern cities.

Even when Southern domestic writers most sharply castigate the failures of their own society, they link those failures to Northern values and forms of behavior and even to direct Northern influences. Where Harriet Beecher Stowe attributes Southern vices to slavery, Southern domestic writers attribute them to the erosion of slavery as a social system—or to Northern intrusion into Southern life. In the 1830s, Caroline Gilman could present slaveholding households under the governance of strong masters as the natural embodiment of the principles of the Revolution. Her novels thus echo an indigenous Southern representation of slavery as a positive good. By the 1850s, Southern domestic writers, like Southern proslavery writers in general, are inescapably slipping into a more polemical, defensive tone in their attempts to answer the rising criticism of their values and institutions. The predilection to present themselves as the true heirs of the Revolution persists, but increasingly it is enlisted to combat a newly aggressive Northern definition of freedom as the natural right of each individual and as the absolute antithesis of slavery.

Under the Northern onslaught, Southern literary domestics intensify their defense of their region and their concomitant outright attack on the North, but as the issues become more complex, they branch out into a variety of arguments. Caroline Lee Hentz, in *The Planter's Northern Bride,* takes on Stowe most directly. Reversing every one of Stowe's premises, Hentz depicts the North as the graveyard of young women. She opens with a heart-rending portrayal of a young worker whose wages afford her aged mother's only support but who, suffering from tuberculosis, is being turned out into the snow by her heartless employer. To drive the point home, she has her heroine, Eulalia, come close to death because of her fatuous abolitionist father's refusal to allow her to marry the gallant Southern planter whom she loves. The threat of her death chastens her father, who permits the marriage but does not forswear his destructive principles. Safely removed to the South, Eulalia thrives, learning more each day of the goodness and strength of her husband. But renewed threats to the felicity and stability of their lives surface, first, in the form of his first wife, a willful and undisciplined, if lusciously beautiful, orphan daughter of traveling musicians. They surface a second time when an abolitionist preacher, who insinuates himself into the confidence of the master in order to foment a revolt of his slaves, in effect offers the master his finest moment. The discovery of the plot to revolt leads Moreland, who customarily adopts a demeanor of loving compassion, to reveal the unflinching strength and iron will that undergird and inform his customary gentleness. Facing down his slaves, who cower under his gaze, he embodies the very essence of the right to command and incarnates the substance of righteous justice. He plays out, in short, the Southern man's favorite role of the chivalric knight, at once personally gentle and yet ever ready to mete out stern justice in the name of social duty.

For Hentz, the core of the response to Stowe lay in the concept of slavery as a beneficent social system—as the best way of ordering a society in which some are necessarily unequal to others. Good women, she demonstrates, benefit from men's protective strength, while flawed women deservedly provoke their repudiation and wrath. Slaves, too, benefit from the protective structure of slavery. Never homogenizing her black characters into a single type, she nonetheless assumes that only fools could view them as the equals of whites. Allowing for considerable variation in personality, she assumes that slavery provides the best possible structure for them. Like Mary Eastman, who in *Aunt Phillis's Cabin* also engaged the confrontation with Stowe, she offers a searing picture of the desperate plight of free blacks. Both Hentz and Eastman include discussions of slaves who succumb to the lure of abolitionists and attempt to trade their comfortable situations for the chimera of freedom. In both instances, the misguided slaves find themselves abandoned or even preyed upon by their purported saviors and rapidly come to regret the security they have so thoughtlessly jeopardized.

Unlike Hentz, who would tolerate no chink in the proslavery armor and no defensiveness in the proslavery tone, Eastman is even willing to acknowledge that slavery may have disadvantages, but she does so in a way that prompts her to greater racism without softening her attacks on Northerners in general and abolitionists in particular. Northerners, she insists, maintained slavery so long as it suited their economic interests. And their slavery was altogether more draconian than anything known in the South, as one of her Southern gentlemen pointedly reminds a Northern acquaintance. Northerners too had slave laws, he insists, and pretty tight ones at that. "'A woman could be picked up and whipped, at the report of any body, on the naked body.'" Not so in the South. "'Why, sir, if we had such laws here, it would be whipping all the time, (provided so infamous a law could be carried into execution).'" Northerners made the most of slavery while it suited their convenience, and now that it does not, they attempt to foist their "principles" on others. But do they consider the best interests of the slave? No. Their principles reduce to their pockets. If the abolitionists mean what they say, why do they not give the profits from their books "to purchase some of these poor wretches who are whipped to death, and starved to death, and given to the flies to eat up, and burned alive"?[24]

Southerners, who have been "left with the curse of slavery upon us (for it is in some respects a curse on the negro and the white man)," know enough to leave the ending of slavery to God.[25] They also know that it is impossible for slaves to enjoy freedom within the United States. Virginia's laws prohibit freed people from remaining in the state of their birth. Northern states exploit all free laborers, white or black, Irish or African, with a draconian cruelty unimaginable in the South. Eastman's Southern gentleman, Mr. Chapman, has seen enough in England to last him a lifetime. "I saw some of your redeemed, regenerated, disenthralled people—I saw features on women's faces that haunted me afterward in my dreams. I saw children with shrivelled, attenuated limbs, and countenances that were old in misery and vice."[26] If the abolitionists had a shred of conscience, they would cease their irresponsible meddling, spend some of their wealth to purchase slaves, and send them to Liberia. But it is too much to expect them to behave according to reason. *Aunt Phillis's Cabin*, Eastman states in her preface, is not intended as a history of slavery or abolition. "Slavery, authorized by God, permitted by Jesus Christ, sanctioned by the apostles, maintained by good men of all ages," she explains, in a rehearsal of familiar Southern arguments, "is still existing in a portion of our country." And only "the

Almighty Ruler of the universe" can determine "how long it will continue, or whether it will ever cease." Abolition, "born in fanaticism, nurtured in violence and disorder," also exists. "Turning aside the institutions and commands of God, treading under foot the love of country, despising the laws of nature and nation, it is dead to every feeling of patriotism and brotherly kindness; full of strife and pride, strewing the path of the slave with thorns and of the master with difficulties, accomplishing nothing good, forever creating disturbance."[27]

The abolitionists, in their fanaticism, are turning their backs on scripture and history. "Knowing that the people of the South still have the views of their revolutionary forefathers, we see plainly that many of the North have rejected the principles of theirs." The constitution, like scripture, recognized slaves as property. "Our country was then like one family—their souls had been tried and made pure by a united struggle—they loved as brothers who had suffered together. Would it were so at the present day."[28] Eastman's view of slavery as an unavoidable evil concedes the possibility of its historical disappearance but rejects the abolitionist claim that it must be acknowledged a sin. To follow that view would be to have the father no longer control the child, the master no longer control the apprentice. "Thus the foundations of society would be shaken, nay destroyed." Christ, she enjoins her readers, "would have us deal with others, not as they desire, but as the law of God demands: in the condition of life in which we have been placed, we must do what we conscientiously believe to be our duty to our fellow men." And Christ, she adds, "alludes to slavery, but does not forbid it."[29]

Eastman's position suggests that she, like her sister Virginian Mary Virginia Terhune, basically identifies with the Southern Whig tradition. Proposing a qualified acceptance of historical development and cautiously endorsing some benefits of modernity, she entertains the possibility of slavery's eventual disappearance and thereby edges away from the extreme proslavery position of her South Carolinian contemporary Mrs. Henry Schoolcraft. In "The Black Gauntlet," Schoolcraft, explicitly arguing the proslavery case from the perspective of both masters and slaves, insists that the scriptural and historical cases for slavery are as one. History demonstrates that slavery "has been the efficient cause of civilization and refinement among nations."[30] For South Carolinians in particular, the "exemption from *manual* labor" afforded by slaves "is at the foundation of a class of elevation and refinement, which could not, under any other system, have been created," and which provides for the slaves with a care and instruction that far exceeded anything provided to Northern workers.[31] Let the abolitionists look to "perfecting the morals of those poor, degraded pale-faces, that surround the doors of their own State," who suffer an oppression so intense "that negro slavery is far preferable."[32]

Writing in the midst of mounting sectional crisis, Schoolcraft, like East-man and Hentz, is in part responding to the abolitionists, but more than the others, she is challenging frontally, not merely the abolitionists' actions, but also their worldview. South Carolinians, she approvingly avows, are "'old fogies'" who, unlike the abolitionists, do not believe "that *God* is a progres-sive being; but that throughout eternity *He* has been the same; perfect in wisdom, perfect in justice, perfect in love to all his creatures." From this per-spective, she finds it impossible to credit "the new-light doctrine, 'That slav-ery is a sin.'"[33] Mrs. Stowe's vision of a world in which "all are born equal" is nothing but a millennial fantasy. Even Thomas Jefferson's celebrated words in the Declaration of Independence defy six thousand years of historical ex-perience, not to mention scripture, and have caused nothing but mischief.[34]

For each of these writers, differences notwithstanding, women may appro-priately take up their pens as social critics when the stakes are high. As social critics, they understand their primary responsibility to lie in the defense of their own people, institutions, and region, which, they staunchly insist, em-body the highest social principles. And they all take as objects of their criti-cism, not the failings of slave society, but the failings of the North. Above all, they berate Northerners, including Northern women, for abandoning scripture, the foundation of true religion, and for espousing the destructive doctrines of individualism and equality, including abolition and women's rights. She who cares to see the consequences of such pernicious doctrines has only to look at the Northern laboring poor and ponder the dissolution of family and social ties inherent in their condition. Among the ranks of those poor, she will find abundant examples of faithless men and women; drunken, violent, and improvident husbands; downtrodden, overworked, and fatally ill women; broken marriages; neglected children; and impover-ished, despairing elderly people. Although few Southern literary domestics explicitly label their project, they are, in effect, holding up the dregs of North-ern poverty as a harbinger of what the free market threatens to impose on the South and the world. A people that heedlessly repudiates the divine and natural order of hierarchical conditions is asking for what it will get. What can women expect of a world in which each is free to labor and think as she pleases? Household drudgery, brutal and faithless husbands, and wanton children—in sum, the destruction of precisely those domestic values that Northern women writers believe they are extending into the public sphere.

In the measure that the Southern domestics admit that the vices of free society are beginning to infect their own region, they tend to attribute them to Northern intervention: the actual intervention of abolitionist agitators and the metaphorical intervention of Northern ideas. During the fifties, those who accept the explicit struggle over slavery as the principal arena of combat are especially likely to focus their novels on the slavery question and thereby allow their opponents to define the terrain. Their social criticism, accordingly, more often than not focuses on slavery narrowly defined as the condition of workers, and they risk falling into the trap of juxtaposing material well-being against legal condition. In this context, freedom can appear as a mere ideological dream that counts for little against the assurance of adequate food and housing, reasonable working hours, and support in old age.

Augusta Jane Evans of Mobile, arguably the most passionate and assuredly the most learned of these female defenders of Southern values, avoids the trap.[35] Her two antebellum novels, *Inez* of 1855 and *Beulah* of 1859, barely mention slavery and do not so much as acknowledge Stowe's existence. Yet in *Inez*, she turns the tables on Stowe by equating Northern aggression with expansionist Catholicism and by casting her two young Southern women protagonists as the defenders of true Protestant values.[36] In *Beulah*, Evans further adapts the classic domestic novel to her own purposes, attacking her Northern counterparts on the high ground of woman's identity and purpose.[37]

Beulah contains none of the familiar pictures of degraded Northern laborers or of happy, well-fed slaves. It does contain a healthy dose of social criticism, most of it directed against Southerners whose misguided lives testify to the disarray into which their society is plunging. Eugene Graham dramatically evokes the pitfalls of Southern manhood gone astray. His proclivities toward self-indulgence and material comfort lead him to marry his beautiful, wealthy, and irredeemably selfish cousin, and the disastrous marriage accelerates his own collapse into dissipation. Excessive drinking and gambling destroy the last vestiges of his youthful promise; uncontrollable horses almost destroy his life. His stepsister, Cornelia Graham, embodies the tragic decline of the ideal of republican motherhood that her name evokes. Pampered from childhood by irresponsible parents, she suffers from an incurable heart ailment. But the physical weakness of her heart pales beside the consuming cynicism of her spirit. Bereft of faith and all but bereft of meaningful human attachments, Cornelia dies in a spiritual desert, an index of the barren prospects of a people that has lost its spiritual moorings.

Both Eugene and Cornelia, amply seconded by an array of fashionable, materialist, and faithless characters, represent the pernicious penetration of Northern values into the very heart of Southern society. Evans spares nothing in her castigation of their failings. Materialism, empty fashionable religion, and narrow selfishness all provoke her to a devastating critique of a society gone awry. Beulah herself, however, embodies the greatest trial of Southern society, for she falls prey to the siren call of learning and female independence. Most of the novel is taken up with extensive discussions of the reading and ambition that fuel her progress to the very brink of agnosticism.

Bypassing the specific question of women's rights, Evans plunges into the maelstrom of faith and skepticism. Shifting from the manifestations of corruption to its source, she scathingly attacks the temptations of Northern and European philosophy, denouncing the intellectual pretensions of the abolitionists as nothing less than the ambition to substitute the human mind for God. That she locates the struggle of faith against philosophy in the mind of a woman testifies above all to her conviction that to grant men the license of freethinking while holding women responsible for religion is sheer self-deception. Where man's mind roams, there will the intelligent woman's mind follow. Nothing is safe against the Northern onslaught— nothing, that is, save the will of the Southern people to save themselves.

Beulah's tragedy lies in her frozen heart, her inability to recognize and accept love. Her heart, Evans insists, is a woman's heart. But Evans never endorses the view that she has Beulah scornfully reject woman's nature as dependent and clinging. She simply insists that woman's nature, like man's, requires divine assistance in order to recognize the path of duty. To determine duty for the self alone is to assume the place of God Himself, to accept the pernicious Emersonian view that creature and creator are one. In this respect, Evans articulates a distinct Southern view of identity as grounded in particular stations, a view that women must accept their natures and their proper social roles. But she is not endorsing the view that women depend on men for their salvation. Women, like men, must accept their guidance direct from God. Women, like men, are capable of rejecting true duty and forfeiting salvation.

Beulah has most commonly been read as a female *Bildungsroman* laced with a heavy measure of social criticism. But it may also be something more. Those who have emphasized the meaning of Beulah's name as "married woman" have slighted its meaning as a (married) land. They have thus ignored the possibility that Evans intended her novel to double as an allegory for the South as a whole. In my judgment, the novel is best read as such an allegory, with Beulah's struggles taken as sign of the struggles of the Southern people. Certainly, well before the 1850s, the great Southern divines were launching those appeals for self-reformation that would reach a crescendo during the dark years of the war. The virtues that they were urging upon their fellow Southerners strongly resembled those that Evans urges upon her heroine, notably those of a deep and trusting faith that puts aside the graven images of materialism and, especially, unbridled individualism. The good of the self can only be found in the good of the whole, in hewing to the lines that God has laid down.

In many respects, the voices of the Southern sentimentalists merge in a distinct regional voice, for each, in her own way, strove to defend what she took to be the superior values of her region. Thus regional loyalty to what many Southerners were increasingly prepared to view as a separate society, if not a separate nation, tended to submerge differences by state in letters, just as it was coming to in politics. Yet within that regional convergence, Hentz and Evans, the two Southern women writers who arguably ranked first among their peers during the decisive 1850s and who both came from Alabama, seem to have been developing a voice and vision that reflected the distinct experience of the Old Southwest. For both of their works, especially that of Evans, embody a commitment to the South that has been hewed out of the frontier and still bears some of its traces. In their novels, the reader finds no lingering deference to Virginia as the cradle of the Revolution but rather finds a forthright celebration of the new world of a modern slave society that Southerners have wrought. No less significantly, they who most firmly insist upon the worth of the South's distinct social order also are most ready to generalize about social order and, above all, most ready—as their contemporary Henry Hughes of Mississippi was doing during the same decade—to defend Southern slave society not as a legacy of the past, but as a model for the future.[38]

The war and emancipation destroyed the foundations of this view.[39] In the aftermath, disillusioned Southern women writers did not abandon their commitments to the distinct values of their region, but they did confront the necessity to ground them in new institutions. Sadly, some, including Evans herself, increasingly turned to racism and sexism to justify what seem increasingly arbitrary restrictions. Others gradually groped toward a new critique of both. But that is another story.

Feminist scholarship, understandably concerned with recovering its legacy, has primarily focused on the ways in which women have struggled against the social relations and narrative traditions that have hedged them in. In this context, the Northeastern women novelists of the nineteenth century offered an especially attractive perspective. Protesting the twin and related injustices of chattel slavery and the subordination (even "enslavement") of women, they fashioned a narrative to which women can now comfortably turn. Women such as Harriet Beecher Stowe and Susan Warner also criticized aspects of emerging industrialization and may thus be said to have harbored their own ambiguously articulated reservations about capitalism. But even in criticizing what they viewed as capitalism's excesses, the Northeastern women critics remained generally committed to the core of the ideology of bourgeois individualism.[40]

The arguments for antislavery and woman's rights both rested squarely on individualist principles; both unquestionably assumed that the social relations of the capitalist North were essentially superior to those of the

slaveholding South. To the extent that Northeastern women criticized capitalist social relations—and they did—they sought to extend the sway of
women's values and, in some instances, to retard capitalist development.
Their Southern counterparts were more likely to see the vices of capitalism
as endemic to the system and, accordingly, to dismiss the possibilities for its
reform. For Southern women, the social relations of slavery, which, they
admitted, themselves required reform, offered a superior model. Above all,
the Southern domestic novelists assumed that women found their highest
calling as vigilant members of the communities into which they were born.

Notes

1. Blanche Glassman Hersh, *The Slavery of Sex: Feminist-Abolitionists in America*
(Urbana: University of Illinois Press, 1978); Carroll Smith-Rosenberg, *Religion and the
Rise of the American City: The New York City Mission Movement, 1812–1870* (Ithaca, N.Y.:
Cornell University Press, 1970); Jean Fagan Yellen, *Women and Sisters: Antislavery Fem-
inists in American Culture* (New Haven, Conn.: Yale University Press, 1990).

2. For a preliminary discussion of the conservatism of antebellum Southern women,
see Elizabeth Fox-Genovese, "Social Order and the Female Self: The Conservatism of
Southern Women in Comparative Perspective"; Barbara Jeanne Fields, "Commentary,"
both in *What Made the South Different?*, ed. Kees Gispen (Jackson: University of Mississippi Press, 1990), 49–70.

3. Mary Kelly, *Private Woman, Public Stage: Literary Domesticity in Nineteenth-
Century America* (New York: Oxford University Press, 1984); Jane P. Tompkins, *Sensational Designs: The Cultural Work of American Fiction 1790–1860* (New York: Oxford
University Press, 1989). See also Joyce W. Warren, *The American Narcissus: Individualism and Women in Nineteenth-Century American Fiction* (New Brunswick, N.J.: Rutgers
University Press, 1989), on the ways in which nineteenth-century American fiction made
no place for women as individuals.

4. Alexander Cowie, *American Novel* (New York: American Book Company, 1948),
413; Jane P. Tompkins, "The Other American Renaissance," in *The American Renaissance Reconsidered*, ed. Walter Benn Michaels and Donald E. Pease (Baltimore: Johns
Hopkins University Press, 1985), 35.

5. Tompkins, "Other American Renaissance," 35.

6. Tompkins, *Sensational Designs*, 185, 145.

7. Louisa S. McCord [L.S.M.], "Uncle Tom's Cabin," *Southern Quarterly Review*
23 (January 1853): 81–120. On Louisa McCord and on Southern women's response
to *Uncle Tom's Cabin* in general, see Elizabeth Fox-Genovese, *Within the Plantation
Household: Black and White Women of the Old South* (Chapel Hill: University of North
Carolina Press, 1988); Fred Lewis Pattee, *The Feminine Fifties* (New York: D. Appleton-
Century, 1940); Cowie, *Rise of the American Novel*, 413; E. Douglas Branch, *The Senti-
mental Years 1836–1860* (New York: D. Appleton-Century, 1934). On the various women
writers, see, among many, Kelly, *Private Woman, Public Stage*; Elizabeth Moss, *Domestic
Novelists in the Old South: Defenders of Southern Culture* (Baton Rouge: Louisiana State
University Press, 1992). Anne Goodwyn Jones, in *Tomorrow Is Another Day: The Woman
Writer in the South, 1859–1936* (Baton Rouge: Louisiana State University Press, 1981), discusses Augusta Evans Wilson, but not the antebellum tradition as a whole. Ann Douglas,

The Feminization of American Culture (New York: Alfred Knopf, 1977), focuses on the North.

8. For a general discussion of the reception of the novel, see Thomas F. Gossett, *Uncle Tom's Cabin and American Culture* (Dallas, Tex.: Southern Methodist University Press, 1976). See also Gillian Brown, "Getting in the Kitchen with Dinah: Domestic Politics in *Uncle Tom's Cabin*," *American Quarterly* 36, no. 4 (Fall 1984): 503–23; Tompkins, *Sensational Designs*.

9. Moss, *Domestic Novelists*, 31.

10. Francis Pendleton Gaines, *The Southern Plantation: A Study in the Development and Accuracy of a Tradition* (New York: Columbia University Press, 1924; reprint, 1962).

11. On the religious views of slaveholding women, see Elizabeth Fox-Genovese, "Religion in the Lives of Slaveholding Women of the Antebellum South," in *That Gentle Strength: Historical Perspectives on Women in Christianity*, ed. Lynda L. Coon, Katherine J. Haldane, and Elisabeth W. Sommer (Charlottesville: University of Virginia Press, 1990), 207–29. See also Jean E. Friedman, *The Enclosed Garden: Women and Community in the Evangelical South, 1830–1900* (Chapel Hill: University of North Carolina Press, 1985).

12. Caroline Gilman, *Recollections of a Southern Matron* (New York: Harper and Brothers, 1858), 107.

13. Ibid., 27.

14. Ibid., 70.

15. Ibid., 132.

16. Ibid., 71.

17. Ibid., 47.

18. Ibid., 47–48.

19. Ibid., 56.

20. Fox-Genovese, "Religion in the Lives of Slaveholding Women."

21. Gilman, *Recollections*, 71.

22. The Gothic tradition retained considerable resonance in nineteenth-century women's fiction. On the general phenomenon, see Judith Wilt, *Ghosts of the Gothic: Austen, Eliot, and Lawrence* (Princeton: Princeton University Press, 1980). For a specific example, see Charlotte Smith, *Emmeline: The Orphan of the Castle*, ed. Anne Henry Ehrenpreis (London: Oxford University Press, 1971).

23. The need for a father's participation in the education of sons frequently surfaces in the correspondence of slaveholding women whose husbands were too often absent on business or politics. See, for example, the letters of Anna Matilda King to Thomas Butler King, Thomas Butler King Papers, Southern Historical Collection, University of North Carolina, Chapel Hill. On gender conventions in general, see Fox-Genovese, *Within the Plantation Household*, 192–241, and Steven M. Stowe, *Intimacy and Power in the Old South: Ritual in the Lives of the Planters* (Baltimore: Johns Hopkins University Press, 1987).

24. Mrs. Mary H. Eastman, *Aunt Phillis's Cabin; Or, Southern Life as It Is* (Philadelphia: Lippincott, Grambo & Co., 1852; reprint, New York: Negro Universities Press, 1968), 93.

25. Ibid., 71.

26. Ibid., 95.

27. Ibid., 24.

28. Ibid., 21.

29. Ibid., 19.

30. Mrs. Henry R. Schoolcraft, "The Black Gauntlet: A Tale of Plantation Life in South Carolina," in *Plantation Life: The Narratives of Mrs. Henry Rowe Schoolcraft* (1852–60; reprint, New York: Negro Universities Press, 1969), 93.

31. Ibid., 227.

32. Ibid., 306–07.

33. Ibid., iv.

34. Ibid., v.

35. For the fullest account of Evans's life, see William Perry Fidler, *Augusta Evans Wilson, 1835–1900: A Biography* (University: University of Alabama Press, 1951).

36. See Moss, *Domestic Novelists,* for an arresting reading of the pro-Southern implications of *Inez.*

37. For a fuller development of my views on *Beulah,* see my "Introduction" to *Beulah,* ed. Elizabeth Fox-Genovese (Baton Rouge: Louisiana State University Press, 1992) [reprinted in this volume, pp. 194–217].

38. Henry Hughes, *Treatise on Sociology, Theoretical and Practical* (1854; reprint, New York, 1968). On Hughes, see Douglas Ambrose's excellent dissertation, "'The Man for Times Coming': The Life and Times of Henry Hughes" (SUNY Binghamton, 1991), subsequently published as *Henry Hughes and Proslavery Thought in the Old South* (Baton Rouge: Louisiana State University Press, 1996).

39. For a strong argument about Southern women's alienation during the war, see Drew Gilpin Faust, "Altars of Sacrifice: Confederate Women and the Narratives of War," *Journal of American History* 76, no. 4 (March 1990): 1200–1228, and her "Introduction" to *Macaria,* ed. Drew Gilpin Faust (Baton Rouge: Louisiana State University Press, 1992).

40. For a fuller development of this argument, see Elizabeth Fox-Genovese, *Feminism without Illusions: A Critique of Individualism* (Chapel Hill: University of North Carolina Press, 1990). See also the excellent discussion in Jeanne Boydston, Mary Kelley, and Anne Margolis, *The Limits of Sisterhood: The Beecher Sisters on Women's Rights and Woman's Sphere* (Chapel Hill: University of North Carolina Press, 1988).

Fourteen

Slavery, Race, and the Figure of the Tragic Mulatta, or, The Ghost of Southern History in the Writing of African-American Women

"I am afraid that I am destined to die at my post. I have no special friends in the North, and no home but this in the South. I am homeless and alone."[1]

Frances Ellen Watkins Harper, Iola Leroy,
Or Shadows Uplifted *(1892).*

I loved history as a child, until some clear-eyed young Negro pointed out, quite rightly, that there was no place in the American past I could go and be free.[2]

Sherley Anne Williams, Dessa Rose *(1986).*

Sadness was overtaking Lena's feeling of fear. She wanted to tell Rachel, "I'm just a little girl. I don't want to hear all of this. I don't want to know all of this. Please don't tell me any more." But Rachel just looked at the child's big brown eyes welling up with tears and slipped inside her head and thoughts again.

"Child," she said softly. "Do you know how long I been waiting for somebody like you to come along so I can tell them all of this, so

"Slavery, Race, and the Figure of the Tragic Mulatta, or, The Ghost of Southern History in the Writing of African-American Women." *Mississippi Quarterly* 49, no. 4 (1996): 791–817. Copyright 1996 by *Mississippi Quarterly*. All rights reserved. Used by permission of the publisher.

I can share some of this? You t'in I'm not gonna tell you now I got you here on my beach?"[3]

Tina McElroy Ansa, Baby of the Family *(1989).*

Everybody knew what she was called, but nobody anywhere knew her name. Disremembered and unaccounted for, she cannot be lost because no one is looking for her, and even if they were, how can they call her if they don't know her name? Although she has claim, she is not claimed. . . .

It was not a story to pass on. . . .

So they forgot her. Like an unpleasant dream during a troubling sleep. . . .

This was not a story to pass on.[4]

Toni Morrison, Beloved *(1987).*

The writings of African-American women writers abound with the ghosts and memories of a Southern history that anchors their own and their people's experience even as it challenges their ability to represent their own and their foremothers' sense of self. Like the Russian peasants' proverbial rat, Southern history has stuck in the throat of African-American women writers, who can neither swallow it nor spit it out. Toni Morrison's novel *Beloved* poignantly reminds us of the difficulty. How—in what voice—may a woman tell of women's experience of slavery? How may she represent the worst toll that slavery exacted from enslaved mothers and their children? Morrison represents those difficulties through the figure of a ghost, Beloved, that embodies the residue of what cannot be told. As the ghost of the murdered, "crawling already?" baby, Beloved dances though the pages of the text, yet ultimately remains disremembered and unaccounted for. No one is even looking for her. Murdered by her own mother, she cannot rest and must, like all disremembered slave children, devote herself to (as Baby Suggs puts it) "worrying someone's house into evil" (p. 5). Baby Suggs knows that there is "not a house in the country ain't packed to its rafters with some dead Negro's grief," and she tells Sethe to consider herself lucky that "this ghost is a baby," not an adult man (p. 5).

Like Baby Suggs, Sethe knows that memories—rememories—persist, even if you do not remember them yourself. What she does remember "is a picture floating around out there outside my head," and even if "I don't think it, even if I die, the picture of what I did, or knew, or saw is still out there. Right in the place where it happened" (p. 36). Those thought pictures, she tells her daughter, Denver, lie in wait, and one day you bump into one of them. You may think that the thought that enters your mind belongs to you, but it is really "a rememory that belongs to somebody else" (p. 36). Thus, even a picture of events that are "all over—over and done with"— will, if you go and stand in the place where the events occurred, "always be there for you, waiting for you" (p. 36). Even if Sethe does not think the thought picture, even if she dies, it will remain out there, waiting for someone to bump into it. Worse, as *Beloved* suggests, the most painful thought pictures do not remain bound to the place in which the events occurred, but migrate, permeating the entire country so that there is no place where one can escape them.

Even in Ohio, a free state, Sethe might suddenly find herself "remembering something she had forgotten she knew. Something privately shameful that seeped into a slit in her mind right behind the slap on her face and the circled cross" (p. 61). Beloved's fingers, massaging her neck, remind her of Baby Suggs's fingers, which had eased the pain when "her spirits fell down under the weight of the things she remembered and those she did not" (p. 98). However bad the things Sethe remembers, she knows the things she does not remember are worse. Fleetingly, the touch of Beloved's fingers seems exactly like that of the baby's ghost, but she shoves the "tiny disturbance" of that thought aside in the conviction that what now matters is to have Paul D in her life—that their shared trust and rememory will heal the wounds. "Her story was bearable because it was his as well—to tell, to refine and tell again. The things neither knew about the other—the things neither had word-shapes for—well, it would come in time: where they led him off to sucking iron; the perfect death of her crawling already? baby" (p. 99).

Throughout *Beloved*, Morrison reminds us that the sharing of rememories and the healing of wounds does not unfold as smoothly as Sethe hopes. The stories are not easy to tell, refine, and retell. Even when, haltingly, imperfectly, they have been told and a fragment of trust established, the powerful temptation to forget abides. Beloved, the ghost, is not claimed, for hers was not a story to pass on. And ultimately, the significance of the forgetting of that story supersedes the importance of the original event, so that the forgetting itself becomes a story that cannot be passed on. The easy part of Beloved's story, which is also inescapably Sethe's story, indicted the horrible cost of slavery for African-American slaves; the difficult part, as Morrison does not flinch from acknowledging, implicated the slaves themselves.[5] For the transformation of slaves from passive victims—mere objects—into active resisters of their own dehumanization necessarily invoked their accountability for their actions, however desperate, however constrained. The true price of their humanity lay in the scarring acknowledgement of their responsibility— that is, in their willingness to claim the story of slavery as their own subjective experience, to claim Southern history as their own.

The pain of that history has decisively complicated the challenge of claiming it as one's own, insidiously tempting its survivors into a manicheean vision of good and evil in which innocent victims confront evil oppressors. The manicheean vision has, since the nineteenth century, been fueled by the abolitionist fervor that condemned slavery as an unmitigated evil. But recognition of the injustice and the crimes of slavery as a social system does not tell us much about the character and humanity of those who participated in it. Even when we allow for the propensity of a social system to shape its participants, we are left with the knowledge that the experience of oppression does not inevitably transform fallible men and women into saints, any more than the exercise of domination inevitably transforms decent men and women into monsters.

These complexities and ambiguities have weighed heavily on black and white authors alike, but they have especially weighed upon the imaginations of black women writers, who have been most likely to attempt to capture the personal experience of slave women and their female descendants. Both blacks and whites have recognized the experience of slave women as, in some essential way, emblematic of the system as a whole. Sexually vulnerable as women, slave women were if anything more vulnerable to tragedy as mothers whose children might, at any time, be wrestled from them. Indeed, from the perspective of the black community, the greatest crime of slavery seems indeed to have been the separation of families, especially the separation of mothers and children. Slaveholders' sexual access to slave women ranked a close and closely related second, but was never taken fully to equal the separation of mother and child, at least in part because African cultures did not place the same weight as middle-class Anglo-Americans on women's premarital chastity. In the too frequent cases in which the separation was forcefully perpetrated by sale, the results were devastating but could at least be attributed to the malevolence of an external force. But what if it were perpetrated by the mother herself through running away, suicide, or infanticide?

If a slave woman's separation from her child might raise troubling questions, how much more so might her sexual relations with a white man? Instances of rape assuredly abounded, but so do instances of mutual consent and even love, as well as everything in between. Should writers represent slave women only as victims of rape, they would underscore the brutality of slavery, but would, by the same token, implicitly deny the special attractiveness of the individual woman: They would reduce her to a random object of the man's quest for power or his lust. We should not find it difficult to understand that black women writers might seek to endow their heroines with the charms and complexities of conventional white heroines and might even enjoy representing men who preferred a black woman to her white rivals, all the more since this choice, as the word rival implies, establishes the black woman as the white woman's equal. Many black women writers have resolved the tension between these two options by turning to the trope of the tragic mulatta—the beautiful woman who appears to be white, who manifests all of the personal graces fostered by freedom and privilege, but who, through the accident of a few drops of "black blood," is legally a slave.

The notion that a few drops of blood, of which the tragic mulatta manifested no external sign, could determine a woman's fate understandably chilled readers, as indeed it was intended to. Taking the drop of blood to represent the essence of a woman's identity captured the irrationality of racism and even uncomfortably evoked the concept of original sin—literally the sin of the parents bequeathed to the innocent child. Doubtless the certainty that readers would instinctively recoil from the injustice of an inherited destiny helps to explain the popularity of the trope among writers who sought above all to shock readers out of complacency. It is, nonetheless, worth noting that before emancipation the drop of black blood did not condemn a mulatta to slavery. Should a mulatta have had a slave father and a free mother, she would legally have been free—whether the mother was white or black. Under slavery, women—or men—were slaves because they inherited the condition from slave mothers, not because of the composition of their blood. And, as everyone knew, the probabilities were that a mulatta would have a slave mother and a free father. But then, the possibility that a mulatta might result from the intimacy of a slave father and a free mother was not one that antebellum whites liked to acknowledge, and black writers have not been quick to challenge their reticence.

Since Harriet Jacobs, black women writers have consistently preferred to emphasize blood rather than slavery, even when writing about the antebellum period. They have not been alone in evoking the trope of the tragic mulatta, but they have informed it with a complexity that no black man or white woman has easily appreciated. Knowing from experience the anguish of writing the story of the slave woman from a subjective stance, they have seized upon the trope of the tragic mulatta as a way simultaneously to gain sympathy for their heroines and to remain silent about the most disturbing aspects of black women's experience. The trope has permitted them to endow their heroines with the sensibilities and personal dignity that have conventionally been attributed to white women even as it has permitted them to drive home the horrendous injustice of slavery. By inviting the identification of white readers with the tragic mulatta, black women writers have lured them into the emotional recognition that skin color counts for nothing. In effect, they are saying "this tragic heroine, dear reader, could just as well be you." But the invitation to identification has come at the price of candor about the deepest wounds of slave women's experience. Thus the trope of the tragic mulatta has covered over the stories that, until recently, none have felt free to pass on, but that have, as in the case of Beloved, a disquieting ability to return as ghosts.

In *Dessa Rose*, Sherley Anne Williams evokes Dessa's reluctance to expose the scars around her loins where no hair would grow again and which, according to Rufel, "looked like a mutilated cat face" (p. 154). There, hidden beneath her clothes, her history had been graven on her flesh. Considering those hidden scars, Nehemiah wonders how many others "carried a similar history writ about their privates" (p. 21).[6] Rufel sees the scars when she inadvertently catches a glimpse of Dessa's nudity in a mirror. But Dessa refuses to discuss the part of her past to which they testify. "Even when the others spoke around the campfire, during the days of their freedom, about their trials under slavery, Dessa was silent. Their telling awoke no echoes in her mind. That part of the past lay sealed in the scars between her thighs" (pp. 59–60). Listening to Nathan's account of the travail that Dessa herself could not tell, Rufel wonders, "How did they bare such pain?" (p. 138).

Deborah McDowell calls attention to the visual implication of "bare" in contradistinction to the internal endurance of the "bear" the reader might have expected (p. 154). McDowell sees the scars of Dessa's history as "a script written in the slave master's hand and bound up in his enslaving psychosexual myths and fantasies" and her refusal to display them as "a radical act of ownership over her own body/text in a system that successfully stripped slaves' control over this, their most intimate property" (p. 154). In McDowell's reading, the refusal becomes "both an act of resistance (she is the repository of her own story) and a means of containing the pain by forgetting the past" (p. 155).

Writing, like Morrison, in the 1980s, when the willingness to acknowledge both the brutality of slavery and the vitality of African-American culture ran high, Sherley Anne Williams has no qualms about representing a slave woman as physically scarred or speaking in dialect. But she holds to the notion that containment of the pain requires "forgetting the past." The recovery of African-American history, which Carter G. Woodson and W. E. B. DuBois, among other black scholars, inaugurated early in the twentieth century and which flowered in the 1960s and 1970s, brought the horrors of slavery and the extraordinary cultural resilience of slave communities to national attention.[7] Within this context, Williams, like other black women novelists, could forsake the concern for respectability that had weighed upon earlier generations of African-American women writers and draw upon the cadences and traditions of folk culture. Yet more important, Williams, like Morrison, could attribute the most painful scars to her female protagonist. Even so, Williams does not have Dessa tell her own story, which the reader learns through the accounts of other characters. As a result, the reader learns only those parts of the story that others have learned, and the subjective story remains buried in Dessa's determined forgetting of the past. Thus does Williams suggest that continued resistance to the wounds of oppression requires resistance to history itself.

Williams's resistance to the most painful memories contrasts sharply with Morrison's determination to expose them and, thereby, to cauterize the wounds. The deteriorating social and economic condition of many black Americans during the 1980s may have tempted Williams, as it tempted others, to see an encompassing continuity between slavery and the present. This understandable discouragement had two important consequences. First, and most obviously, it prompted a rejection of confidence in the possibility of historical change on the assumption either that nothing ever changes or that the more things change the more they stay the same. Second, it discouraged searching and candid explorations of the history of slavery on the grounds that to bare the scars of the past would be to bare those of the present. Thus even as Williams, like other black women writers, admitted that slavery had happened to women like her, she remained reticent about the highest and most personal costs. This determined preservation of privacy, however admirable, has risked opening the door to insistent ghosts, for the repressed does have a way of returning.

Williams reflects briefly upon history in her "Author's Note" to *Dessa Rose,* which she claims to have based upon two specific historical incidents: the experience of a pregnant black woman who helped to lead a slave uprising, was caught, convicted, and sentenced to death, but not hung until after the birth of her baby, and the account of a white North Carolina woman who reportedly provided sanctuary to runaway slaves. In addition, she admits to having also written an outraged response to William Styron's *Nat Turner,* which, in her view, confirms that "Afro-Americans, having survived by word of mouth—and made of that process a high art—remain at the mercy of literature and writing; often these have betrayed us" (p. 5). Williams leaves no doubt that the betrayal of literature and writing rests upon the betrayal of history itself, for "there was no place in the American past where I could go and be free." Slavery, she has learned, "eliminated neither heroism nor love; it provided occasions for their expression" (p. 6). Yet her representation of slavery strips the demonstrable expressions of heroism and love of the less admirable responses that bound them to a multi-dimensional and credible humanity.

II.

As impassable as a rain-swollen river, Southern history runs like a deep dangerous current between the black American present and past. Those who would turn their eyes to an African legacy must somehow get across it; those who prefer to focus upon the recent contributions of free black communities must explain how its encompassing waters have nourished subsequent harvests. The hold of Southern history has weighed as heavily upon Northern as Southern black women writers, for all concur that it embodies the crimes that have been perpetrated upon their people. And although they know that the North also practiced slavery and then discriminated brutally against blacks, and that the trans-Atlantic slave traders were generally Northern, they reserve a special indignation for the full-blown slave society of the South.[8]

Rarely have the historical imaginations of African-American woman novelists reached back beyond 1820. The reasons why most turn to the 1850s for the seedbed of the stories they wish to tell are numerous, but high among them ranks a reluctance to focus upon a life that ended as it began under slavery. A woman protagonist who had come of age much before the 1850s would not plausibly have experienced the full fruits of post-Civil War freedom or have been young enough when she did to engage readers' imaginations. But if the personal situation of a heroine has largely dictated novelists' concern with the 1850s, other considerations have also had their say. For the 1850s could plausibly be represented as the flowering of slavery as a social system—as a designed and crafted society that self-consciously defended the bondage of the African-American people. In addition, the 1850s brought to a crescendo an abolitionist discourse that proclaimed a non-negotiable moral line between North and South.

Antislavery and uncompromising abolitionist discourses were hardly new in the 1850s, but the Compromise of 1850, especially its Fugitive Slave Law, lent them an urgency they had previously lacked. And the outpouring of writings, fictional as well as theoretical, theological, and political, on both sides of the divide crystallized what we may call a dominant pattern of discourse. The character of the debate is familiar enough. While Northern abolitionists preached the inviolability of freedom ("free soil, free labor, free men") and immorality of bondage, proslavery Southerners preached the necessity of social hierarchy and the wanton cruelty of free labor. Intermingling with and enriching the abstract arguments about first principles and social systems, novelists on both sides wove a tapestry of human examples designed to show the direct consequences of the two systems for specific people.[9] This climate encouraged the publication of first-hand accounts of slavery by black writers, most of whom viewed their literary efforts as an important contribution to the abolitionist struggle. Yet the racism of many Northern readers, as well as their own discretion, also encouraged blacks to create protagonists who met white expectations of respectability. The trope of the tragic mulatta perfectly served their purposes.

The pioneering African-American writers of the 1850s, especially the women, were late-comers to the raging discussion about their condition. William Wells Brown, who led the way with his novel, *Clotel, or the President's Daughter,* set a precedent that many would follow by taking as his heroine a mulatta (the quintessential "high yaller") woman, who, betrayed and abandoned by the white planter who claimed to love her, ultimately dies.[10] Brown's role in establishing the beautiful mulatta as the exemplary black heroine has cast a long shadow and received much attention from subsequent critics. What has received less attention is his adaptation of a distinct Southern pastoral mode to his own purposes.[11] To drive his point home, Brown set his novel in Virginia and attributed Clotel's parentage to none other than Thomas Jefferson, thus linking high professed political principle to the despoiling of slave women. None of Brown's female successors would follow his lead in this regard, not even in consigning their heroines to an untimely death. But then Brown depicted Clotel as a cast-aside wife (although legally she was never married) rather than as a young girl exposed to all the horrors of random sexual exploitation. Not until the Northern black woman writer Pauline Hopkins picked up Brown's story in *Hagar's Daughter* (1901) would the figure of the slave woman as forsaken wife reappear, this time with a dramatically different ending.[12]

Brown, an abolitionist who wrote primarily for Northern and, especially, British readers, wrote the story of the slave woman into the fabric of Southern life and discourse, not least by offering Southern readers a disquieting mirror of their own professed principles. Brown firmly opposed slavery as a social system, but however broad and generous his sympathies with the great mass of slaves, he focused upon the ways in which the system most cruelly betrayed those whom it might have embraced—literally its own offspring as embodied in a beautiful, virtually white, articulate woman. He primarily evoked Clotel's delicacy, refinement, and nobility of sentiments, together with her creamy skin, to signal the hypocrisy of a society that professed to love freedom and equality. He made much of the betrayal of Clotel's womanly qualities, but always from an objective perspective. Thus, although he represented her as the novel's heroine, arguably, he did not take her as its subject.

Rather than subject, Clotel may best be understood as a figure—a distillation of discourses—that designates the condition of the tragic mulatta which itself represents the inherent contradictions of Southern society.[13] For unlike most of those who came after, Brown locates the conception of freedom (Jefferson) and the possibility of social tranquility (the garden) within the South itself. Paradoxically, by not making Clotel the center of subjectivity, he permits her a coherence of character, a freedom from soul-wrenching conflict that black women writers' protagonists frequently lack. As author and narrator, Brown offers an unapologetic and unconflicted interpretation of Southern history. And since his narrative focuses directly upon his principal protagonists, whom he carefully inscribes in literate culture, the history he explores and criticizes belongs essentially to the realm of public discourse rather than to that of the memories of oral culture and the ghosts of scarred imaginations.

Brown's contemporary, Harriet Jacobs, followed his lead in directly engaging the public debate over slavery, although unlike him, Jacobs located the subjectivity of her protagonist, Linda Brent, at the center of her narrative, *Incidents in the Life of a Slave Girl*.[14] Drawing heavily upon abolitionist discourses, Jacobs followed Harriet Beecher Stowe and other antislavery women writers in emphasizing the ways in which slavery as a social system negated all social order, corrupting the integrity of domestic relations, white and black. Calling slavery an "obscene cage of birds," Linda Brent insists she can testify from "my own experience and observation, that slavery is a curse to the whites as well as to the blacks. It makes the white fathers cruel and sensual; the sons violent and licentious; it contaminates the daughters, and makes the wives wretched" (p. 52). "As for the colored race," she continues, "it needs an abler pen than mine to describe the extremity of their sufferings, the depths of their degradation" (p. 52). But Jacobs's use of pronouns, which juxtaposes "my" pen to "their" sufferings, dramatically, if inadvertently, betrays the conflicts that plague her attempt to bare a woman's subjective experience of slavery.

The split between "my" pen and "their" sufferings pervades Jacobs's attempt to conjoin Linda Brent's experience with the history of slavery in the South, and, in the end, she does not succeed. Casting Brent as a real woman rather than a literary figure, she cannot draw directly upon the complexities of the figure of the mulatta, although more than occasionally she appears to evoke them. Her representation of Linda Brent as a slave formally acknowledges the legal condition that governs Linda's destiny, yet her distancing of Linda from the other slaves and, indeed, from the darker blacks very much resembles other writers' representation of free mulattas who are punished for their possession of a few invisible drops of black blood. If the history of Southern slavery is as bleak as Jacobs must paint it as being in order to justify Linda Brent's actions—including her taking of a white lover and her abandonment of her children—then it cannot be allowed to shape Linda Brent's character. For if Linda Brent had indeed been marked by slavery's evil, how could she have developed the instinctive nobility and love of freedom that inspire her to risk everything, including life and "virtue," to elude its grasp? Ironically, the very abolitionist beliefs that permit Jacobs to write at all make it virtually impossible for her to ground Linda's history in the history of the South as the abolitionists present it. Here and there, hints of Southern black history flicker in the pages of the text, notably when she links Linda Brent's experience in the swamp with the folklore of black oral culture. But in general, and especially in narrative voice, she claims as much distance as possible between Linda and the history that produced her.

Incidents in the Life of a Slave Girl contains virtually no references to history or even to the variations in Southern society. Proceeding from the consciousness of Linda Brent, the narrative encompasses only those incidents which her mind has encountered, whether family traditions, cases of brutality, or random comments on proslavery religion. Jacobs's South seems cut almost entirely from manicheean abolitionist cloth and meshes comfortably with Orlando Patterson's conception of slavery as social death.[15] In the measure that Jacobs pays any attention to history, she restricts it to family history, primarily to establish a pedigree of fair skin, literacy, respectability, and quasi-freedom for herself. And in the end, her falling off from the standards of her forebears matters considerably less than her having been reared with them in the first place. Indeed, Jacobs seems to be suggesting that her very lapses from the norms of middle-class respectability confirm her personification of the fundamental ideals they embody. For, even as Linda Brent enjoins her readers to "pity" and "pardon" her lapses from the highest standards of womanly virtue, she reminds them that they "never knew what it is to be a slave; to be entirely unprotected by law or custom; to have the laws reduce you to the condition of a chattel, entirely subject to the will of another" (p. 55).

Such conditions make a mockery of conventional morality. Thus a slave woman who retains "any pride or sentiment" may well taste "something akin to freedom" in taking a lover who is not her master, even if he cannot be her lawful husband. Such moral principles, Linda Brent allows, may seem like sophistry, "but the condition of a slave confuses all principles of morality, and, in fact, renders the practice of them impossible" (p. 55). She knows that her mother and grandmother cleaved to moral principles, but they were spared the unmediated power of a master and, by implication, did not really experience the full weight of slavery's most destructive power.

To guarantee Linda Brent's immunity to the demoralizing power of slavery, Jacobs effectively endows her with a Northern history and emphasizes her grandmother and parents' possession of the skills and independence of artisans and the domestic values that flow therefrom. Slaves they may have been, but they lived largely as if they had been free. Similarly, Jacobs introduces the worst specific abuses of slavery as reports rather than as subjective experiences. Had she not, she would have had to represent Linda Brent— and by implication herself—as the victim of indiscriminate lust, and she would thereby have reduced Linda to that status of object to which the logic of chattel slavery pointed. To underscore the moral and cultural distance between Linda and her family from the mass of slaves, she represents them as speaking the purest English and the other slaves as speaking in dialect.

Harriet Jacobs's difficulty in coming to terms with Southern history, above all slavery, derives from her fierce rejection of its possible consequences for slave women—for Linda Brent and, by implication, for Jacobs herself. This was not a story she could tell, much less a story to pass on. Yet the problems with her denial of its bearing permeate her narrative. If slavery does "confuse" moral principles and make their practice "impossible," then how may she, a former slave, claim basic moral decency? Tactically, Jacobs attempts to place the blame upon the slaveholders who, as a class, corrupt everything and everyone they touch. Yet this history of abuse never seems to ground Linda Brent's identity, and Jacobs consistently presents Linda Brent's lapses from Northern standards of female virtue as external rather than internal to her character.

With the benefit of hindsight, we may recognize Jacobs's narrative as haunted by ghosts that never appear in the text. Avoiding bitter engagement with the specter of racism and the significance of African traditions, Jacobs, to the extent possible, adopts the perspective of her presumed abolitionist readers and refrains from offending their sensibilities. This respect for Northern sensibilities leads her to minimize Linda Brent's ties to the community of black slaves, whose sufferings have etched the costs of slavery upon their persons and character. Taking Northern, middle-class domesticity as a universal norm and especially reproving slavery for depriving the majority of slaves of its benefits, she represents Linda Brent as a woman with whom her Northern readers may readily identify. Jacobs takes special pains to present Linda's desertion of her children as a violation of the tradition in which her family reared her. On the eve of Linda's flight, her grandmother begs her to endure a while longer if the children must be left behind. "Nobody," she reminds Linda, "respects a mother who forsakes her children; and if you leave them, you will never have a happy moment" (p. 91).

Pleas and admonitions notwithstanding, Linda persists in her plans. Throughout the years of her hiding and after her final escape to the North, she remains concerned about her children's fate, but refuses to accept that her first obligation is to remain with them at any cost to herself. Jacobs never says that slavery makes it impossible for anyone to be a good mother, but her endorsement of Linda's actions strongly suggests that she believes it. In effect, she claims that Linda's flight, even though it entails temporary separation from her children, is the only way she can defend her right to be a good mother. For as Sethe tries to explain to Paul D in *Beloved*, under slavery you could not really love anyone at all. Pushed to the limit, Sethe kills her "crawling already?" baby girl rather than lose the right to be a loving mother that freedom had provided her. But just as Paul D and the other members of the black community shudder at Sethe's radical interpretation of the dictates of true motherhood, so does Linda's grandmother question Linda's claim that only freedom will permit her to mother properly. Thus, beneath the claim that Linda is seeking her own freedom the better to care for her children lurks the haunting possibility that she is seeking it because slavery has so weakened family ties as to cut her innermost identity loose from them. And beyond that possibility lurk the ghosts of all the children who are "worrying someone's house into evil" because, as Morrison suggests, they may have had their own views of good mothering and may have preferred to have their mother's presence even at the cost of her self-respect.

Successful flight to the North no more solves Linda's problems than it does Sethe's. Once there, she still feels that "I could never go out to breathe God's free air without trepidation at my heart," which hardly seems "a right state of things in any civilized country" (p. 195). Even at the North, she can only secure her freedom through purchase. That purchase assures that she and her children are "as free of the power of slaveholders as are the white people of the North; and though that, according to my ideas, is not saying a great deal it is a vast improvement in *my* condition" (p. 201). But even freedom does not realize her dream of a home of her own, much less liberate her from the pervasive shadow of racism.

Jacobs exercises great caution in expressing her reservations about Northern society, which we know abounded with racism. The main complaint she makes openly concerns the extent to which Southern slavery compromised Northern institutions—the familiar abolitionist complaint about the long arm of the Fugitive Slave law. But in closing the narrative with Linda Brent's still working as a servant and still lacking a home of her own, she guardedly points the way toward subsequent criticisms of the devastating economic consequences of Northern racism for black people. And by ending with the consoling memory of her grandmother, she suggests that the roots of her personal history lie in the South.

III.

Jacobs does not openly embrace the figure of the beautiful mulatta, but in essential respects she might just as well have. She represents Linda Brent as having more in common with educated white women than with the illiterate and abused women of the slave community. In her pages, Linda never suffers a whipping or a rape, and even when she is consigned to wear modest clothing, her natural beauty does not diminish. The difficulties of the escape leave scratches on Linda's hands and face (significantly, the rest of her body remains covered), but her everyday life leaves no marks. Unlike Dessa Rose, she has no physical scars to conceal or bare.

Since slave status was transmitted through the mother and since the absence of legal marriage among slaves left fathers peculiarly exposed, the transmission of history through women assumed special importance for the African-American community. Even after emancipation and the emergence of solid marriages and families, women remained privileged custodians of the history of their people under slavery. To say as much is to slight neither the sufferings of African-American men under slavery nor their centrality to African-American communities. It is simply to suggest that slavery oppressed women and men less as couples or members of coherent families than as isolated individuals who might or might not be able to establish human ties strong enough to withstand slavery's deadly tendency toward atomization.

As a people, African-American slaves did withstand the worst of the atomization, notably through their creation of communities that transcended family units and that could always absorb and support those whose immediate families had been torn from them. These communities proved reliable custodians of collective memories, including those of African practices and beliefs. To these traditions they added the Anglo-American Christianity and messages of political freedom that predominated in the South, interweaving all into a sustaining culture of their own design. The message of abolition contributed a new attention to individualism. For while the slaves had never needed anyone to tell them they wanted to be free, abolition's emphasis on individualism ran counter to older collective traditions. The tension between the individual and the community informed every attempt to come to terms with the Southern slave experience of African-Americans. For some, like Jacobs and Williams, the balance shifted in favor of the individual who had suffered unspeakable wrongs and frequently led to the refusal to "bare" the wellsprings that might expose the barer to unbearable pain.

Frances Ellen Watkins Harper and Pauline Hopkins, writing after Reconstruction, were both supremely conscious of women's responsibility to tell the history of slavery and to assess its implications for a free present and future. Both were no less conscious, during an era of vicious and institutionalized racism, of the pressing need to shift the balance toward the history of the African-American community rather than the isolate individual. Tellingly, both returned to Brown's figure of the tragic mulatta to carry the burden of that history, although, unlike Brown, both allowed their mulatta heroines to triumph, pointing the way in their persons, their works, their marriages, and their offspring to a promising future for their people.

Harper and Hopkins both attended carefully to the broad historical context of their protagonists' dramas, grounding the events that followed emancipation in the slavery that came before. Hopkins, a proud New Englander to her core, had no patience with the South, notwithstanding her clear-sighted recognition of the centrality of slavery to African-American history. Harper, coming from Baltimore, shared Hopkins's harsh judgment of slavery but showed more understanding of the South as the region in which the majority of African-Americans had their roots and felt at home.

Harper's *Iola Leroy,* which opens in the middle of the Civil War, plunges the reader directly into the community of slaves with a conversation between Robert Johnson and Thomas Anderson, both slaves, who, under the cover of reports on freshness of butter and fish, trade notes about the progress of the Union forces. In a few brief chapters, Harper evokes the main features of slavery and the diverse personalities of Robert, Thomas, and the other slave men she introduces. From the start the reader learns that some masters and mistresses are better than others, although even Robert's indulgent mistress regards him as a "pet"; that, notwithstanding prohibitions, the slaves have a complex network of prayer meetings; that some have learned to read although most have not; that some plan to leave and join the Union forces, whereas others feel bound by loyalties to blacks and whites to remain where they are. Deftly, Harper brings to life a small-slaveholding region of North Carolina and the textured relations and personalities of the slaves who inhabit it.[16]

With great skill, Harper simultaneously convinces the reader that her subjects, who have not been flattened by the weight of slavery, have built a rich human community and that slavery is morally and politically wrong. The differences between her and Jacobs's depiction of North Carolina slavery are subtle but arresting, primarily because of Harper's sympathy for the variety of personalities and cultural vitality among the slaves. Judging the slaveholders harshly, she nonetheless insists that slavery did not deaden the humanity of the slaves, and she unflinchingly attributes the ultimate responsibility for slavery to the country as a whole. Slavery, she avers, "had cast such a glamour over the Nation, and so warped the consciences of men, that they failed to read aright the legible transcript of Divine retribution which was written on the shuddering earth, where the blood of God's poor children had been as water freely spilled" (p. 14).

Significantly, the reader first glimpses Iola Leroy through the eyes of Tom, one of the local slaves, who describes her to Robert as "a mighty putty young gal," whom her owners have been selling all over the country, because "she's a reg'lar spitfire; dey can't lead nor dribe her" (p. 38). Adoring Iola and fearing for her safety in the grip of her "reckless and selfish master, who had tried in vain to drag her down to his own level of sin and shame," Tom moves Robert to persuade the Union Commander of the local fort to secure her release and to take her as a nurse in the field hospital. The General, to whom she is taken, is astonished by her beauty and refinement. "Could it be possible that this young and beautiful girl had been a chattel, with no power to protect herself from the highest insults that lawless brutality could inflict upon innocent and defenseless womanhood?" (p. 39). How could he take pride in his American citizenship "when any white man, no matter how coarse, cruel, or brutal, could buy or sell her for the basest purposes?" (p. 39).

Only sixty pages into the novel does the reader learn how one as fair and unmarked by toil as Iola Leroy could indeed be a slave. Daughter of a fair-skinned slave woman and the wealthy Louisiana planter who loved, educated, and married her, Iola grew up with no knowledge of her mixed racial heritage. As a student at a New England boarding school, she treats her anti-slavery classmates to a spirited defense of slavery, cheerfully insisting that slavery could not be wrong, "for my father is a slave-holder and my mother is as good to our servants as she can be" (p. 97). And when challenged that even the most luxurious treatment cannot outweigh the priceless good of freedom itself, she innocently counters, "Our slaves do not want their freedom. They would not take it if we gave it to them" (pp. 97–98). Only upon her father's untimely death does she come to the understanding of the true meaning of enslavement and the subjective value of freedom. Following that death, a vicious, greedy cousin, to whom Iola's father has naively confided the secret of his wife's birth, persuades a judge to overturn the father's will and remand the mother and their children into slavery. The youngest girl mercifully dies of brain fever, the son is kept safely in school at the North, but Iola and her mother are turned over to slave-traders.

With minor variations, Iola's story became the prototype for the gothic horror of the inherent evil of slavery. One may plausibly assume that Harper herself did not necessarily view the plight of the fair-skinned woman who had been raised in the lap of luxury as slavery's worst evil. But she assuredly knew her readers and doubtless believed that to whites like the General the idea that a single drop of black blood could throw a young woman like their own daughters onto the vilest of sexual marketplaces would be infinitely more moving than the plight of a dark-skinned, illiterate laborer, male or female. Thus when Iola's father, Eugene, tells his cousin of his plan to marry a beautiful fair-skinned mulatta woman, Marie, the cousin responds, "Don't you know that if she is as fair as a lily, beautiful as a houri, and chaste as ice, that still she is a negro? . . . One drop of negro blood in her veins curses all the rest" (p. 67). Yet under slavery, it was the condition of enslavement, passed through the mother, that counted, whereas after emancipation, when the condition no longer existed, the drop of black blood replaced it and could be transmitted by either parent. Writing after emancipation and the beginning of Jim Crow, Harper conflates slavery and race to strengthen the impact on her audience, which had but recently been horrified by tales of the white slave trade.

Harper relied upon the moving appeal of the figure of the beautiful mulatta to bind the open racism of her day to the condition of slavery that the Civil War had purportedly destroyed—to carry the message that she feared even antislavery readers would find difficult to accept. The novel leaves no doubt that Harper's main quarrel was with the racism of the 1890s. In locating the origins of her story in slavery, she doubtless hoped to tap the wellsprings of that Northern sense of moral superiority which triumphed with victory in the war. The conflation of slavery and racism permitted her, in effect, to displace some of her outrage at bourgeois racism and say to her Northern readers: This injustice, which you are so proud of yourselves for having fought against, you surely will not now tolerate it in your midst.

In addition, Harper, who had a genuine feel for the strengths and vulnerabilities of the community of ordinary slaves, seems purposefully to have located the dramatic abuses of slavery in Louisiana with its special aura of mystery and corruption, thus underscoring the gothic dimension of Iola's personal story. In contrast, she represents the slaves of North Carolina who befriend Iola as varied and engaging human beings who have suffered the debilitation of slavery, but have assuredly not been crippled by it.

Pauline Hopkins, notably in *Contending Forces* and *Hagar's Daughter,* also embraces the figure of the tragic mulatta as a vehicle for expressing her passionate indictment of racism, but even more than Harper, she locates the story in a broad historical canvas. *Contending Forces* opens with the arrival in Bermuda of the news of the impending British abolition of slavery.[17] Upon learning the news, Charles Montfort, a wealthy planter, determines to move his family and slaves to the more "congenial" climate of North Carolina, notwithstanding his determination eventually to free his own slaves. Hopkins takes his arrival in New Bern as the occasion to depict what she considers the most loathsome members of Southern society: corrupt and greedy planters, overseers, and ordinary white riff-raff—stock characters who manifest the crudest possible racial and sexual attitudes.

The forces of evil swiftly wreak their jealous vengeance on Charles Montfort and his family, driving his wife, Grace, whom they have charged with being a mulatta, to her death, and forcing his younger son into slavery. The older son escapes the worst only because a visiting English gentleman succeeds in buying him. Hopkins's historical object lesson apparently bears little relation to the rest of the novel, which takes place in Boston around the turn of the century, although at the end we discover that the members of the Smith family, principal participants in the main story, descend from the younger Montfort son, who had eventually made his escape.

The historical prologue nonetheless permits Hopkins to ground the novel in what she views as the distinctly sinful history of the antebellum South and, thereby, to link the racism of the 1890s directly to the sins of slaveholding. It also permits her to link Boston to Britain's legacy of freedom and, above all, to show that even marriage to the wealthiest of men cannot protect the woman suspected of being a mulatta. The story of Grace Montfort thus prefigures that of Sappho Clark, the beautiful mulatta who plays a central role in the novel's main plot, who, at the age of fourteen, had been forced into slavery and raped and who is now in Boston, supporting herself and the child who resulted from the rape. Like Harper before her, Hopkins locates the scene of her beautiful mulatta's tragedy in Louisiana, underscoring the dangerously exotic—almost un-American and certainly un-British—aspect of slavery.

The acutely intelligent and impressively learned Hopkins understands full well that racism pervades the "free" capitalist North. Her articulate, genteel, light-skinned black characters all encounter difficulties in education or employment. Worse, as she underscores, their problems are being exacerbated by politicians who, while congratulating themselves on their opposition to slavery, regard racism as acceptable and even necessary to a rapidly industrializing society. At a meeting of the American Colored League to protest a recent lynching in the South, the Honorable Herbert Clapp, a Northern Democrat with pro-Southern sympathies, insists that the "problem is national, not sectional. The sin of slavery was the sin of the nation. . . ." Clapp tries to convince his black audience that their brothers in the South are doing well, but the North has other problems: "Here at the North the pressure is so great from the white laborer that we are forced, to some extent, to bar against the colored brother" (p. 248).

Hopkins, who understands perfectly the nature of Clapp's arguments, will have none of them. The next speaker, Luke Sawyer, the son of a free black from Louisiana—who in telling his personal history reveals Sappho's history as well without naming her—passionately argues that "conservatism, lack of brotherly affiliation, lack of energy for the right and the power of the almighty dollar . . . are the forces which are ruining the Negro in this country" (p. 256). Finally, Will Smith, Hopkins's hero, who strikingly resembles the young W. E. B. DuBois, speaks, presumably articulating her views.

Opening with a broadside against the South, Will avers that "to the defense of slavery in the past and the inhuman treatment of the Negro in the present, the South has consecrated her best energies. Literature, politics, theology, history have been ransacked and perverted to prove the hopeless inferiority of the Negro and the design of God that he should serve by right of color and physique" (p. 266). But, he continues, the South has convinced none but herself and is still smarting under the "bitterer than double-distilled gall" of the Federal victory (p. 266). Now the South aims at nothing less than the disfranchisement of blacks. There are those who would deprive blacks of education on the grounds that they are incapable of absorbing and profiting from it. Yet education provides black Americans with their best hope of escaping the legacy of slavery—that is, the essential way of ridding "the Negro" of "any tendency toward vice that he may be thought to possess, and *which has been largely increased by what he has imbibed from the example and the close,* immoral association *which often existed between the master and the slave*" (pp. 268–269).

Historically, the responsibility for the plight and condition of the mass of black people demonstrably lies with the South. Yet the South, Will continues, "declares that she is no worse than the North, and that the North would do the same under like provocation. Perhaps so, if the offender were a Negro" (p. 271). Human nature, after all, is everywhere the same, and "the characteristic traits of the master will be found in his dog" (p. 272). The problem defies easy solutions and above all requires the formation of public opinion. Like the antislavery apostles of a previous generation, blacks must go out to "appeal for the justice of our cause to every civilized nation under the heavens," lifting "ourselves upward and forward . . . until 'Ethiopia shall indeed stretch forth her hand and the princes shall come out of Egypt'" (p. 272).

In the manner of DuBois, Hopkins weaves a complex historical and political argument especially designed to meet the needs and aspirations of elite, Northern blacks.[18] In the end, the tragic mulatta remains virtually incidental to her main purposes, serving primarily to add an element of mystery and suspense to the plot. In *Hagar's Daughter,* however, the story of the beautiful mulatta returns to center stage, this time featuring the vicissitudes of a mother and daughter.[19] As in *Contending Forces,* Hopkins begins with a historical prologue, here the secession convention in Charleston. The main action of the novel, however, unfolds in Washington during Reconstruction and focuses on the domestic consequences of slavery, especially its infinitely complex interracial sexual bonds.

The mulatta Hagar, who is not recognized for who she is throughout much of the novel, lives out the end of Clotel's story. Forsaken, like Clotel, by her white slaveholding husband, Hagar, like Clotel, throws herself into the Potomac. But, as we ultimately learn, unlike Clotel, she survives the jump, as does her baby daughter, Jewel, and the two (unbeknownst to Hagar) are soon reunited as mother and stepdaughter when Hagar, known throughout most of the novel as Mrs. Bowen, marries the wealthy Westerner, Zenas Bowen, who has already adopted the purportedly orphan Jewel. Bowen's election to the Senate brings the family to Washington, where much of the action of the endlessly intricate plot unfolds. The plot unites the corrupt minutiae of politics with the disastrous and interlocking influences of slavery upon domestic life. At the end, Hopkins's narrative voice summarizes the lesson: "The holy institution of marriage ignored the life of the slave, breed [sic] indifference in the masters to the enormity of illicit connections, with the result that the sacred family relation is weakened and finally ignored in many cases" (p. 284). In *Hagar's Daughter,* the price of this neglect is the untimely death of Jewel, which simultaneously punishes her slaveholding father for his abandonment of his wife and child and her New England betrothed, Cuthbert Sumner, who could not face marriage to a woman with even a drop of black blood.

Sumner, much like Dr. Gresham of *Iola Leroy,* represents the flower of white New England youth and its commitment to the antislavery cause.[20] Gresham eventually overcomes his instinctive prejudice of race, although he does not win Iola, but Sumner cannot. As he tells a friend, who has been arguing that the amalgamation of the races is inevitable, "The mere thought of the grinning, toothless black hag that was her foreparent would forever rise between us" (p. 271). He is willing "to allow the Negroes education, to see them acquire business, money, and social status within a certain environment. I am not averse even to their attaining political power" (p. 271). More than that he cannot countenance. So, his friend counters, "this is the sum total of what Puritan New England philanthropy will allow—every privilege but the vital one of deciding a question of the commonest personal liberty which is the fundamental principle of the holy family tie" (p. 271).

Sumner cannot be moved. Given the "ignorance, poverty and recent degradation" of black people, how can Anglo-Saxons not attempt to keep their own race as pure as possible? Sadly, his friend reminds him that there is a higher law than those of earth and predicts that Sumner may one day find that his own nature has more nobility than he suspected. By the time he does, Jewel is dead. And Hopkins has made her point that for personal liberty to flourish it must be grounded in the family.

Throughout *Hagar's Daughter,* Hopkins demonstrates that the mixture of the races had proceeded further than anyone suspects and its greatest casualty is the mulatta woman. Speaking of Aurelia Mason, another beautiful mulatta who, lacking Hagar and Jewel's advantages of family and character, has led the life of a courtesan, Sumner's secretary, Elsie Bradford, muses that although the loveliness of such women is often marvelous, their condition is too frequently deplorable.

> Beautiful almost beyond description, many of them educated and refined, with the best white blood of the South in their veins, they refuse to mate themselves with the ignorant of their own race. Socially, they are not recognized by the whites; they are often without money enough to bu[y] the barest essentials of life; honorably, they cannot procure sufficient means to gratify their luxurious tastes; their mothers were like themselves; their fathers they never knew; debauched white men are ever ready to take advantage of their destitution, and after living a short life of shame, they sink into early graves. Living, they were despised by whites and blacks alike; dead, they are mourned by none. (p. 159)

Elsie Bradford, having had an illicit liaison that resulted in the birth of her son, has reason to understand something of Aurelia Mason's situation although Elsie is white, not mulatta. In using Elsie to offer the one guardedly negative, if empathetic, assessment of the beautiful mulatta, Hopkins shows the full danger and loneliness of the mulatta's situation. Yet in so doing, she shifts the emphasis in the beautiful mulatta's tragedy from the drop of black blood to the liminality of her sexual situation, thereby inviting white women to respond with "there but for the grace of God go I." Elsie's words thus subtly recast the figure of the beautiful mulatta as none before Hopkins had dared. Doubtless Hopkins was emboldened by her growing commitment to full integration, including inter-racial marriage, as the best way to raise the mass of blacks from the swamp into which slavery had plunged them.

For all her boldness, even Hopkins does not assign Elsie's convention-defying words to the compromised Aurelia Mason herself, much less to Hagar or Jewel. Neither she nor Harper was willing to risk a subjective expression of the greatest dangers of the beautiful mulatta's situation. Iola, Sappho, Hagar, and Jewel all remain essentially innocent, however much the forces of evil may threaten and even harm them. Even their most debasing experiences apparently leave no scar upon the purity of their souls.

IV.

Notwithstanding Harper's and Hopkins's narrative deployment of the plight of the beautiful mulatta to engage the imaginations of their readers, they were ultimately more concerned with the fate of their people than with the personal stories of individuals. Their politics were more national than personal: Both placed their greatest faith in the responsible and creative leadership of a respectable, family-based black elite, although Hopkins in her last novel also turned her attention to Africa.[21] The figure they use to dramatize their message remains effectively, indeed strikingly, silent about her own worst experiences. Like Linda Brent, Harper's and Hopkins's mulatta women do not personally tell of the worst injuries of the history they so passionately protest against, although, unlike Linda Brent, they unambiguously identify with the other members of the black community.

The figure of Aurelia Mason confirms how much they would have had to lose by breaking that silence. For Aurelia, notwithstanding some claims upon the reader's compassion, descends from and remains associated with the worst villains of the conventional antislavery melodrama—the uncouth and unfeeling slave-trader. If Hopkins is correct, as we know she is, about the ubiquity of interracial sex in the antebellum South, we may assume that for every Iola Leroy or Sappho Clark there were at least two Aurelia Masons and, beyond them, countless numbers of ordinary slave women, like Margaret Walker's Vyry Dutton,[22] whose fathers happened to be their masters. Not all mulatta women were beautiful; most probably did not speak flawless English. Most, in other words, were slave women like others, except perhaps for lighter skin or straighter hair. In this respect, we should do well to ponder Hopkins's explicit evocation of the biblical Hagar, slave of Abraham and mother of his son Ishmael. In invoking the biblical precedent, Hopkins transforms it, suggesting that in her time the line that descended from Hagar was not male but female and thereby reminding her readers that women alone transmitted the condition of enslavement to their daughters.

To engage their reader's sympathy, Harper and Hopkins represented their mulatta heroines as essentially white—as elite young women who by the trick of a cruel fate were doomed by a few drops of black blood to slavery. Their texts carried the thinly veiled message that their unmerited destiny could threaten countless other unsuspecting young women. Iola Leroy and Sappho Clark ultimately choose to be black, willingly casting their fate with the African-American community. But their role within Harper's and Hopkins's texts precludes their telling the subjective story of the former slave women whose interest they represent. As figures, they embody and represent a history that their mouths may never speak.[23]

The real problem is not that Iola and Sappho could not speak, but that, even through the mediation of a narrative figure, Harper and Hopkins, neither of whom had been raised a slave, could not. The wounds were too painful, the scars too raw, and, possibly, the shame too great for public exposure. So the figures of Iola, Sappho, Hagar, and Jewel were shadowed by the ghosts of Aurelia Mason and countless others who had no voice of their own. With the passage of time, especially from the 1960s, those ghosts began to press more insistently against the consciousness of their heirs. Stories that no one had wanted to remember and could pass on only privately, if at all, began, hesitantly, indirectly, to be told. A tenacious bunch, the ghosts would not down. As Tina Ansa has Rachel say to Lena, "Do you know how long I been waiting for somebody like you to come along so I can tell them all of this, so I can share some of this? You t'in I'm not gonna tell you now I got you here on my beach?" But then, only Ansa's Lena, who was born with a caul and who grows up in a tight-knit black family enmeshed in a Southern black community, can begin to hear the ghosts and to absorb what Toni Morrison calls the "rememories" of the stories that could not be passed on.

Notes

1. *Iola Leroy, Or Shadows Uplifted* ([Philadelphia:] Garrigues Brothers, 1892), p. 60.

2. *Dessa Rose* ([New York:] William Morrow & Co., 1986), pp. 5–6.

3. *Baby of the Family* (New York: Harcourt Brace, 1989), pp. 163–164.

4. *Beloved* (New York: Alfred A. Knopf, 1987), pp. 274–275.

5. For a fuller discussion of my reading of *Beloved*, see Elizabeth Fox-Genovese, "Unspeakable Things Unspoken': Ghosts and Memories in African-American Women's Narratives of Slavery," Elsa Goveia Lecture, published as a pamphlet (Kingston, Jamaica: n. p., 1993) [reprinted in this volume, pp. 174–93].

6. For a discussion of *Dessa Rose*, see Deborah E. McDowell, "Negotiating Between Tenses: Witnessing Slavery After Freedom—*Dessa Rose*," in *Slavery and the Literary Imagination*, ed. Deborah E. McDowell and Arnold Rampersad (Baltimore: Johns Hopkins University Press, 1989), pp. 144–163.

7. Jacqueline Goggin, *Carter G. Woodson: A Life in Black History* (Baton Rouge: Louisiana State University Press, 1993); David Levering Lewis, *W. E. B. DuBois: Biography of a Race, 1868–1919* (New York: Henry Holt and Co., 1993). For the recent history of slavery, see especially, Eugene D. Genovese, *Roll, Jordan, Roll: The World the Slaves Made* (New York: Pantheon, 1975); Lawrence Levine, *Black Culture and Black Consciousness: Afro-American Folk Thought From Slavery to Freedom* (New York: Oxford University Press, 1977); Peter Kolchin, *Unfree Labor: American Slavery and Russian Serfdom* (Cambridge, Massachusetts: Harvard University Press, 1987); Elizabeth Fox-Genovese, *Within the Plantation Household: Black and White Women of the Old South* [(Chapel Hill: University of North Carolina Press, 1988)].

8. For a very different discussion than my own of the relation between African-American women novelists and history, see Missy Dehn Kubitschek, *Claiming the Heritage: African-American Women Novelists and Slavery* (Jackson: University Press of Mississippi, 1991).

9. Eric Foner, *Free Soil, Free Labor, Free Men: The Ideology of the Republican Party before the Civil War* (New York: Oxford University Press, 1970); Elizabeth Fox-Genovese, "Stewards of Their Culture: Southern Women Novelists as Social Critics," in *Stepping Out of the Shadows: Alabama Women, 1819–1990,* ed. Mary Martha Thomas (Tuscaloosa: University of Alabama Press, 1995), pp. 11–27 [reprinted in this volume, pp. 229–46]; Elizabeth Fox-Genovese, "To Be Worthy of God's Favor: Southern Women's Defense and Critique of Slavery," Fortenbaugh Lecture, Gettysburg College (1993), published as a pamphlet; Elizabeth Fox-Genovese, "Contested Meanings: Women and the Problem of Freedom in the Mid-Nineteenth-Century United States," in *Historical Change and Human Rights: The Oxford Amnesty Lectures 1994,* ed. Olwen Hufton (New York: Basic Books, 1995), pp. 179–216; Elizabeth Fox-Genovese and Eugene D. Genovese, "The Divine Sanction of Social Order: Religious Foundations of the Southern Slaveholders' World View," *Journal of the American Academy of Religion,* 55 (Summer 1987), 211–233; Jamie Stanesa, "Dialogues of Difference: Personal Identity, Social Ideology, and Regional Difference in American Women Writers, 1850–1860," Diss., Emory University, 1993.

10. William Wells Brown, *Clotel; or, the President's Daughter* (New York: Collier Books, 1975, 1970; orig. ed., London, 1853).

11. On the pastoral in Southern literature, see, especially, Lewis P. Simpson, *The Dispossessed Garden: Pastoral and History in Southern Literature* (Athens: University of Georgia Press, 1975). See also, Louis D. Rubin, Jr., *The Edge of the Swamp: A Study in the Literature and Society of the Old South* (Baton Rouge: Louisiana State University Press, 1989); Jan Bakker, *The Pastoral in Antebellum Southern Literature* (Baton Rouge: Louisiana State University Press, 1989); Elizabeth Fox-Genovese, "The Fettered Mind: Time, Place, and the Literary Imagination of the Old South," *Georgia Historical Quarterly,* 76 (Winter 1990), 622–650.

12. Pauline E. Hopkins, *Hagar's Daughter: A Story of Southern Caste Prejudice,* in *The Magazine Novels of Pauline Hopkins,* ed. Hazel V. Carby (New York: Oxford University Press, 1988), pp. 3–284. *Hagar's Daughter* was originally published in serial form in the *Colored American Magazine,* 2 (March and April 1901); 3 (May–October 1901); and 4 (November and December 1901, January and March 1902).

13. Michael Kreyling, *Figures of the Hero in Southern Narrative* (Baton Rouge: Louisiana State University Press, 1987).

14. Harriet A. Jacobs, *Incidents in the Life of a Slave Girl Written by Herself,* ed. Jean Fagan Yellin (Cambridge, Massachusetts: Harvard University Press, 1987; orig. ed., 1861).

15. Orlando Patterson, *Slavery and Social Death: A Comparative Study* (Cambridge, Massachusetts: Harvard University Press, 1982).

16. John Hope Franklin has explored the distinct world of free blacks in antebellum North Carolina in his *The Free Negro in North Carolina, 1790–1860* (Chapel Hill: University of North Carolina Press, 1943).

17. Pauline E. Hopkins, *Contending Forces: A Romance Illustrative of Negro Life North and South* (New York: Oxford University Press, 1988; orig. ed., 1900).

18. On domesticity in Hopkins, see Claudia Tate, *Domestic Allegories of Political Desire: The Black Heroine's Text at the Turn of the Century* (New York: Oxford University Press, 1992), e.g., p. 149. On the young DuBois, see Lewis, *W. E. B. DuBois.*

19. Hopkins, *Hagar's Daughter,* in Carby, ed., *The Magazine Novels of Pauline Hopkins,* pp. 3–284.

20. Cuthbert Sumner bears a strong enough resemblance to Dr. Gresham, who proposes to and is rejected by Iola Leroy, to suggest that Hopkins may have been consciously glossing Harper's text. But whatever Hopkins's intention in this regard, it seems clear that the New England man who prided himself on his antislavery liberalism while harboring an intractable racism was emerging as a trope of African-American women's fiction.

21. Pauline E. Hopkins, *Of One Blood Or, the Hidden Self* in Carby, ed., *The Magazine Novels of Pauline Hopkins. Of One Blood* was originally published in the *Colored American Magazine,* 1902–1903. See Tate, *Domestic Allegories,* on the importance of family.

22. Margaret Walker, *Jubilee* (Boston: Houghton Mifflin, 1966).

23. For a related discussion of Iola's virtual voicelessness, see Elizabeth Ammons, *Conflicting Stories: American Women Writers at the Turn into the Twentieth Century* (New York: Oxford University Press, 1992), p. 31.

Fifteen

"To Weave It into the Literature of the Country"

Epic and the Fictions of African American Women

Toward the end of Frances Ellen Watkins Harper's novel, *Iola Leroy,* Dr. Frank Latimer asks Iola Leroy (to whom he will shortly propose marriage), who is seeking to do "something of lasting service" for her people, why she does not write a "good, strong book that would be helpful to them?" More than willing, she reminds him that the writing of a successful book requires leisure and money and, even more, "needs patience, perseverance, courage, and the hand of an artist to weave it into the literature of the country."[1]

By the time that Harper published *Iola Leroy; or, Shadows Uplifted* in 1892, she had been a successful and admired writer for almost forty years, as well as an indefatigable worker for the advancement of her people, but she had never previously published a novel. With empathetic hindsight, it should be possible to understand why she had not. Leisure and money had their say for her and, even more, for other African American women writers, but may not alone have accounted for the apparent difficulty of telling the story of African American women or even for the difficulty of African American women's telling the story of their people.

Consider the special qualities that Harper thought such a telling required: "patience, perseverance, courage, and the hand of an artist." She believed that those qualities were necessitated by what must be the object of such a telling: "to weave it into the literature of the country." Today, it has become a commonplace among many critics, especially those interested in the writing of women and African Americans, that the literature of the country was not noticeably receptive to dissident points of view. Many, indeed, would hold that those to whom the dominant culture has been less than receptive have no call to respect its sensibilities and, yes, prejudices. How, such critics ask, can you be expected to write yourself into a culture that trivializes or stereotypes, when it does not blatantly ignore, your experience?

The prospect appears all the more daunting when we acknowledge that African American women knew that their experience turned the expectations and assumptions of the dominant culture topsy-turvy. Harriet Wilson, the first African American woman (so far as we know) to try her hand at novel writing, saw her only effort, *Our Nig,* sink into oblivion.[2] On reflection, the fate of *Our Nig* should not occasion undue surprise. It was, if ever there was one, a countertext and an almost unbearably angry one at that. Harriet Wilson had no truck with the sentimental domestic pieties of mid-nineteenth-century American culture, and from its opening pages *Our Nig* reverses all of them.

Within two brief chapters, Wilson sketches the spiraling "degradation" of Mag Smith, white mother of her mulatto protagonist, Frado. Abandoned after having succumbed to the seduction of a man who considerably outranks her in social station, Mag bears an "unwelcomed" child, who almost immediately dies. Mag welcomes the death, which Wilson suggests her readers should acknowledge as a "blessed release." What, she ponders, could have been the fate of such a child? "How many pure, innocent children not only inherit a wicked heart of their own, claiming life-long scrutiny and restraint, but are heirs also of parental disgrace and calumny, from which only long years of patient endurance in paths of rectitude can disencumber them" (6–7). Wilson has thus identified her text with the seduction and abandonment of what, at this point in the novel, appears to be her main female character, the birth and death of her illegitimate child, and the passing assertion that many of those who are formulaically called "pure, innocent" children inherit wicked hearts of their own.

In defying the conventions of womanhood and the prescribed feelings of motherhood, Mag has embraced a fate from which she can no longer escape. When a move to another town fails to free her from her past or to improve her material circumstances, she returns to the scene of her disgrace, eking out a meager living from the few odd jobs that immigrant laborers disdain. The black man, Jim, who supplies her with wood, offers the only human fellowship she experiences, and when he asks her to marry him, she listlessly acquiesces. Viewing his white wife as a "treasure," Jim does his best to provide well for her. Together, they have two children, including the girl Frado. But after Jim dies of consumption, Mag spirals even lower, living, unmarried, with his black business partner, Seth Shipley.

Wilson explains that Mag, having lived for years as an outcast, had stifled the feelings of penitence and the agonies of conscience. "She had no longings for a purer heart, a better life. . . . She entered the darkness of perpetual infamy. She asked not the rite of civilization or Christianity. Her will made her the wife of Seth" (16). And, when circumstances again worsen, Seth persuades her to give the children away. The main story begins with Mag's leaving Frado at the house of the affluent, white Bellmont family. Throughout the first day, "Frado waited for the close of day, which was to bring back her mother. Alas! it never came. It was the last time she ever saw or heard of her mother" (23). Yet in comparison with Mrs. Bellmont, an acknowledged "she-devil," whose viciousness dominates Frado's experience throughout the remainder of the novel, Mag ranks as the good mother.

These opening chapters stand alone among the writings of nineteenth-century American women, perhaps alone among all nineteenth-century American literature. And they introduce what probably qualifies as the angriest and least compliant novel by a nineteenth-century woman writer. The willful noncompliance with cultural conventions and fierce determination to tell a story that few were eager to hear do much to account for the oblivion to which *Our Nig* was relegated. On the face of it, nothing could seem further from Harper's determination to write her story into the literature of the country. The simple lesson to be drawn from *Our Nig* is that the attempt to write the story of African American women into the literature of the country runs into what may well be insuperable obstacles. Wilson seems to suggest that if you tell the truth, no one will read you, which is tantamount to saying that you cannot both tell the truth and meet prevailing literary expectations. Conversely, if you do meet prevailing literary expectations, you will not be telling the truth, which may make it very difficult for you to write with power and conviction.

It would be easy, but not entirely accurate, to attribute the long disappearance of *Our Nig* to racial and sexual prejudice.[3] In publishing the novel, Wilson clearly understood the risk she ran of alienating even those most likely to be sympathetic. In the preface, she attempts to anticipate and disarm hostility. First, she mobilizes the conventions of her own lack of talent and the distressing circumstances that have nonetheless driven her to write. Even the most pressing misfortunes would not, however, lead her to "palliate slavery at the South, by disclosures of its appurtenances North" (3). Her mistress's principles were wholly "*Southern.*" And had she recounted every misery of her life, as she has not because of her reluctance to provoke shame in her antislavery friends, "the unprejudiced would declare [her treatment] unfavorable in comparison with treatment of legal bondmen" (3). Like other authors before and since, Wilson dares to hope that her candid confession will disarm the severest criticism. And finally, she appeals to all of her "colored brethren" for "patronage, hoping they will not condemn this attempt of their sister to be erudite" (3).

In essential respects, as Wilson may have known or at least suspected, *Our Nig* has more in common with antebellum Southern women's writing than with Northern women's. I know of no Southern woman writer who had the audacity to claim that the brutal neglect of white working women in the North drove them into the arms of free black men, but many claimed that it drove them to death. Wilson's portrait of Mrs. Bellmont's cruelty, bad faith, and lack of manners should have warmed the heart of Caroline Lee Hentz, Mary Eastman, or Louisa McCord.[4] *Our Nig* offers little or nothing to flatter the sensibilities of antislavery Northerners. To the contrary, it forcefully suggests that the curse of racism has so infected the United States as to make the choice between sections, and even the choice between slavery and freedom, virtually meaningless. To drive the point home, Wilson introduces into her own antislavery text a final ironic gloss by having her protagonist, Frado, marry a black man who was working for abolition and who falsely claimed to be a former slave. Thus Wilson, admittedly against the odds, was trying to make her readers understand that even the righteous work of antislavery may not be what it seems. This was not a story that many readers would have found useful to pass on.

If Wilson could lay any claim to having written her story into the literature of the country, it could only be by a series of reversals that bordered on insults none was willing to accept. Yet if one gets beyond what we might call the overt political "message" of her story, the ways in which she was trying to weave it into the literature of the country command attention. Unlike Harriet Jacobs, Wilson did not drop so much as a passing curtsy to prevailing views about the purity of women or the devotion of mothers. Whereas Jacobs goes to great lengths to establish the respectability of her mother and her own devotion to her, Wilson represents her mother as abandoning her as the logical and unemotional consequence of a degraded life. Where Jacobs represents her fair-skinned, literate black mother as having enjoyed a loving and respectable marriage to a man who had all the feelings of a free man, Wilson represents her white mother as having had a bastard before marrying a black man simply to put bread on the table.

Henry Louis Gates sees *Our Nig* as essentially autobiographical with Frado as Wilson's persona, and he calls attention to the ways in which Wilson slipped into the use of personal pronouns to refer to relations that properly adhere to Frado. Similarly, Jacobs used the persona of Linda Brent to disguise her own identity and, presumably, to conceal aspects of her experience. Jacobs' greatest disguise, however, lies in the language in which she wrote and represented Linda Brent as speaking and in the middle-class sensibilities that she represented Linda Brent as embodying. Notwithstanding Linda Brent's profuse apologies for having had her children by a man to whom she was not married, there is nothing about *Incidents in the Life of a Slave Girl* that would not have passed muster in any respectable Northern, middle-class home.

Our Nig is another matter entirely. Wilson made virtually no concessions to middle-class sensibilities. Not only did she represent white folks in a harsh light but she unambiguously represented the debilitating cost of their behavior for black folks. Being abandoned and abused does not transform Frado into a long-suffering saint. Wilson represents Frado as openly hating her mistress and as taking her revenge any way she can. Tellingly, Wilson forthrightly acknowledges that children may inherit a wicked heart that is all their own and that requires restraint. Throughout *Our Nig,* in other words, Wilson frontally attacks the comfortable pieties that might have made her novel palatable to white readers. Suffering, abuse, and discrimination, she insists throughout, do not necessarily—and perhaps do not ever—transform fallible human beings into saints.

Wilson's uncompromising insistence on disrobing the most cherished white, middle-class icons indirectly confirms that she knew that which she was attacking. Her request that her colored brethren not condemn their sister's attempt to be erudite was probably no casual figure of speech. A comparison of her and Jacobs' texts strongly suggests that she was, if anything, the more learned of the two. Like so many African American writers, Wilson manifests considerable knowledge of American and British elite culture. She borrowed many of the epigraphs at the head of each chapter from highly appreciated white poets, primarily of the first half of the nineteenth century: Shelley, Byron, Thomas Moore, Martin Tupper, Eliza Cook, and, for the final chapter, the book of Ecclesiastes.

Notwithstanding dramatic differences in tone and diction between the epigraphs and the chapters, the ways in which they complement and gloss each other are clear. Thus, the verse from Thomas Moore that introduces the first chapter about Mag Smith speaks of the grief beyond all others that

> First leaves the young heart lone and desolate
> In the wide world, without that only tie
> For which it loved to live or feared to die;

> Lorn as the hung-up lute, that ne'er hath spoken
> Since the sad day its master-chord was broken!

And, immediately following the verse, the chapter begins, "Lonely Mag Smith! See her as she walks with downcast eyes and heavy heart. It was not always thus. She *had* a loving, trusting heart" (5). But Mag, like her daughter after her, had lost her parents early and been left to develop into womanhood, "unprotected, uncherished, uncared for" (5). Wilson does not specify whether the loss that cripples Mag's ability to feel is her loss of her parents, especially her mother, or her loss of the well-born lover to whom she transferred that most basic love "for which she loved to live and feared to die."

The fourth chapter, "A Friend for Nig," in which James Bellmont first appears, is preceded by a verse from Byron on the blessings of friendship. The verse emphasizes the unique place of friendship in youth, "When every artless bosom throbs with truth, / Untaught by worldly wisdom how to feign." Youth, it concludes, is the time

> When all we feel our honest souls disclose—
> In love to friends, in open hate to foes;
> No varnished tales the lips of youth repeat,
> No dear-bought knowledge purchased by deceit.

The chapter that follows contains two references to Frado's loss of her mother. In the first, she tells the friendly Aunt Abby, "'I've got to stay out here and die. I ha'n't got no mother, no home. I wish I was dead'" (46). In the second, she responds to James's assurance that she will not be whipped because she ran away and his injunction that she must try to be a good girl. "'If I do, I get whipped. . . . They won't believe what I say. Oh, I wish I had my mother back; then I should not be kicked and whipped so. Who made me so?'" (51).

When James responds to her query that God made her so, just as He made James, and Aunt Abby, and her mother, she asks if the same God made her as made her mother. And when James assures her that He did, she responds that then she does not like that God, "'Because he made her white, and me black. Why didn't he make us *both* white?'" (51). James, at a loss to answer her "knotty questions," encourages her to go to sleep, promising that she will feel better in the morning. It took, Wilson informs us, "a number of days before James felt in a mood to visit and entertain old associates and friends" (51).

In these instances, as in innumerable others throughout the novel, Wilson demonstrates a remarkable literary skill that is all the more difficult to appreciate because it is so very much her own. Her striking mixture of voices combines the spare, almost modernist, narrative of the early chapters about Mag Smith; the direct and unvarnished conversations, including Frado's dialect; and occasional interventions of an omniscient narrator in a rather studied neoclassical voice. The various voices tend to be divided between the specific situations and general reflections. Thus the chapter that follows the passage from Byron and introduces James begins, "With what differing emotions have the denizens of earth awaited the approach of to-day" (40).

In some ways, the alternation between the specific and the general resembles the alternation between the use of the personal pronouns that identify Mag Smith as "my mother" and the use of Frado to identify the protagonist who, by the logic of Mag Smith as "my mother," should be I. The novel never pretends to resolve these apparent contradictions. It does not even explicitly acknowledge them. Throughout, the voice of Harriet Wilson remains somewhat confused and divided among Frado and the various narrative voices. Unlike Harriet Jacobs, she does not try to fit the voice of her protagonist into the rhetoric of domestic fiction. And unlike Harriet Jacobs, she does not restrict her judgments about human nature and the order of the universe to the formulas of domestic fiction. *Our Nig* never attains the unity of tone that characterizes *Incidents in the Life of a Slave Girl*. To put it differently, *Incidents* attempts to placate its readers; *Our Nig* does not.

Jacobs, it appears, believed that to write the story of African American women into the literature of the country, the story would, at least in some measure, have to be tailored to the expectations of its prospective readers. Wilson was no less interested in having readers appreciate and, especially, buy her book, which she claimed to have written out of a desperate need for money, but she proved less able or willing than Jacobs to force either her story or her language into the prevailing mode of domestic fiction.

Even the cautious Jacobs hinted that the conventions of domestic fiction did not perfectly capture her own experience, but she steadfastly persevered in shaping that experience to fit the conventions as closely as possible. She especially exploited the dictum of the leading domestic sentimentalists, notably Harriet Beecher Stowe, that slavery represented the absolute contradiction of domestic norms. Adherence to this dictum permitted her to present her own lapses from domestic virtue as the consequence of slavery, not of her character or breeding. To represent her mother as the model of domesticity, she emphasized the ways in which her mother's experience had resembled that of a free woman.

Freedom, in Jacobs' pages, emerges as the condition of and proxy for female virtue. This assumption perfectly mirrored the most cherished claims to moral superiority advanced by white Northeastern women writers. It further linked virtuous female behavior to the ideology of male individualism that was, increasingly, condemning slavery as the antithesis of freedom.[5] For the majority of the Northeastern domestic sentimentalists, the natural corollary to their belief in the complementarity of female domestic virtue and male individualism was human perfectibility. In their view, children, who were born innocent, confirmed the innate goodness of human nature which, with proper nurturing, could continue to perfect itself throughout life.

The assumptions and goals of the domestic sentimentalists left little place for tragedy. As a rule, occurrences that presumably contradicted their commitment to perfectionism—losses, reversals of fortune, deaths, evil deeds, the breaking up of families—resulted from specific character failings or corrupt social institutions or bad mothering. By attributing these failings to specific causes, rather than to the inherent tragedy of the human condition or the innate possibilities for evil in human nature, the domestic sentimentalists successfully presented evil as correctable and tragedy as avoidable. Thus they rarely distinguished between the evils inherent in slavery and those which must attend any social system. And they thereby dramatically narrowed the variety of human experience. Clinging firmly to the belief that their values embodied the highest aspirations of humanity, they blithely assumed that those values should be acknowledged as moral norms. In any event, nineteenth-century American politics increasingly confirmed their view of their values as normative. The triumph of bourgeois individualism in politics proceeded in tandem with and ensured its triumph in literature.

It is safe to assume that Harriet Wilson sensed what was coming and that *Our Nig* embodies her rejection of it. Northeastern, middle-class complacency did not, in her view, exhaust either the complexities of human nature or the possibilities of literature. After the Civil War, at an accelerating rate, others would come to criticize what they perceived as the self-satisfied narrowness of middle-class American culture. In general, their criticisms did not overturn the paradigmatic narratives of individualism. Many recent critics have called attention to the ways in which women writers began to wrestle with the inherently masculine assumptions of the master plots of American culture, but their primary mission has been to reclaim individualism for women.[6] The same, with appropriate qualifications, can be said for African American male writers, who from slavery days have focused on their own exclusion from individualism's promises of male authority and autonomy.

Thus following the Civil War, as before it, the political and literary premises of individualism dominated what Harper called "the literature of the country." These premises, which explicitly emphasized individual autonomy and responsibility as universal attributes, implicitly harbored sexual and racial assumptions that restricted access to an authoritative literary voice. Perhaps more important, they intertwined with a vision of the history of the country that continued to feature slavery as the antithesis of freedom. The persistence of slavery as the sign of national sin proved wonderfully compatible with the commitment to perfectionism. Northerners enthusiastically embraced anti-slavery as the sign of their own transcendence of sin. Southerners never accepted the equation of slavery with sin, but they also faced serious obstacles in writing their distinct views into the literature of the country. Before the war, their defense of slavery as the foundation of a more humane social order met with irate resistance from the antislavery North. After the war, defeat stripped Southerners of the will to defend slavery as an alternate vision of social order, and they settled upon a racism that had disfigured but by no means overwhelmed their antebellum worldview.

Harriet Wilson shared the Northern opposition to slavery but not white Northerners' righteous conviction that they had put slavery behind them. As she suggested in the preface to *Our Nig,* she believed that the most insidious forms of slavery did persist in the North. Her fictional illustration of this persistence resulted in a comprehensive and angry indictment of the many insidious forms that slavery can take. Obviously, Mrs. Bellmont's abuse of and disregard for the humanity of Frado top the list and constitute the primary focus of the novel. But the early chapters on Mag Smith add an important dimension that links Wilson's work to a distinct tradition of African American women's writing.

Wilson depicts the free white Mag Smith as eerily similar to unfortunate black slave mothers. Mag is drawn, by overwhelming circumstances, into bearing and abandoning mulatto children. As she tumbles toward the nadir of her misfortunes, she enters into a marriage sanctified only by her own will. On the face of it, the use of Mag to introduce Frado's story seems puzzling. Many domestic novelists chose to make their heroines orphans, but normally paid little attention to their mothers, who were invariably presented as having died. To the extent that white domestic novelists, notably Harriet Beecher Stowe, considered the circumstances of slave mothers, they wrote them directly into the conventions of maternal devotion and attributed their possible failures to fulfill those conventions to the brutality of slavery. In *Incidents,* Harriet Jacobs hewed closely to this model, with respect both to her own mother and to her attitudes toward her own children.

In *Our Nig,* Wilson implicitly asserts that prevailing domestic conventions cannot be stretched to fit the story she wants to tell. But, in so doing, she confronts the intractable problem of how it is possible to tell the story, especially the woman's story, of slavery. As a free white woman whose life resembles that of a black slave woman, Mag Smith represents a double inversion: the inversion of the conventional story of free white women by behaving like a slave; the inversion of the story of black slave women by being white. Her life confuses the neat boundaries favored by the narrative of individualism. It is no wonder that *Our Nig* did not attract a large readership. And because it fell into such a long neglect, it is difficult to argue that Wilson's concerns directly influenced subsequent African American women writers. Yet I am prepared to argue that the themes of *Our Nig* continued to engage the imaginations of African American women who struggled, with mixed success, to write their own story into the literature of the country. Above all, however, *Our Nig* suggests the magnitude of the obstacles African American women writers confronted.

Many African American writers tried to solve some of the problems by selecting mulatto heroines. Such heroines, of whom Clotel, Iola Leroy, Sappho Clark, and Hagar Ellis are but the better known, offered the perfect compromise between the virtues of freedom and the degradation of slavery. The compromise worked especially well with fair-skinned female protagonists who could plausibly be described as innately virtuous and innocent victims. (Victimization posed problems for the representation of men, as the figure of Uncle Tom confirms.) Such heroines could plausibly be represented as beautiful by white standards, as speaking in perfect English, and, frequently, as having been raised in the belief that they were white, which means having been raised to observe the conventions of bourgeois domesticity.

Such a sketch of the mulatto heroine should clarify the problems that confronted any African American woman writer who attempted to write of a woman's experience of slavery from the subjective perspective. The main requirement for the high yaller heroine was that she have internalized none of the abuses of slavery. She must be a victim, but only in her external circumstances. Her scars must never be those of character. The formula of the mulatto heroine contains a significant measure of racism, especially in its assumption that white standards of female beauty are normative. More important, however, the formula betrays the hold of the individualist narrative on the literary imagination. For the individualist narrative, in emphasizing women's difference from men, effectively cast all women as victims and claimed that they willingly embraced their victimization. White women had a point, albeit a more limited one than they admitted, in comparing the condition of women to the condition of slaves. But then, free white women and black slave women shared an unwillingness to speak openly of the most scarring pains of their situation.

Normally the critics who write about mulatto heroines do not include Frado. Yet Frado was a mulatto. She differed from her literary sisters in having a white mother and a black father, in her appearance, and, above all, in the anger with which she responded to the indignities of her situation. In essential respects, Frado represents the inversion of the "tragic" mulatto of convention. Where the tragic mulatto is patient and long-suffering, Frado is angry and rebellious. Unlike the conventional mulatto heroine, Frado exposes the internal scars that her experience has traced in her mind. In many ways, she more closely resembles a heroine in an ancient Greek tragedy than the heroine of a domestic novel. No comforting domestic pieties can encompass the experience of the child who has been born into an interracial union based on economic dependence and who has been abandoned, again for economic reasons, by the mother she loves but whom she also resents for not having made her white. Wilson's evocation of Frado carries an especially bitter and biting irony because enslavement did follow the condition of the mother.

Frado's conflicted feelings about her mother begin to hint at what may have been the conflicted feelings of slave girls toward their mothers. Such conflicts are, indeed, the stuff of tragedy. But the domestic tradition did not allow for tragedy in the sense of inherent and irreconcilable conflicts. The orphan heroines of domestic fiction do not admit to having hated the mothers who abandoned them, if only through a death that was no fault of their own, and whom they also loved. Harriet Jacobs firmly assures us that Linda Brent's daughter felt no resentment toward her mother. And as African American women began to write their story into the literature of the country, they were understandably tempted to sustain the silence.

It is safe to assume that the oral culture of slaves, most of whom were not literate, found a way of preserving some of the conflicts and tensions. The sources abound with examples of slave mothers who beat their own children out of the panicky determination to teach them that the world was a dangerous place. The same mothers frequently risked their own safety to provide their children with tokens of love. And, yes, occasionally a slave mother, who could take no more, ran off, abandoning her children. Now and then a slave mother even killed one of her children to put it out of the reach of conditions she finally judged intolerable. But these were not stories that could easily be woven into the literature of the country. In *Beloved,* Toni Morrison breaks the silence, but until recently this was truly, in her words, "not a story to pass on."[7]

Following emancipation, African American women were primarily concerned with establishing families and communities and beginning to enjoy the prerogatives of freedom. Even when their hopes were most sorely deceived, many remained committed to the ideal of comfortable respectability. And then, for those who could write of their experience, there was the problem of shame. The literature of the country did not invite women's public confessions of sexual abuse, much less confessions of extramarital sexual pleasure or conflicted feelings toward children. In the end, the real cost and horror of slavery did not lend themselves to the narratives of bourgeois individualism, if only because whoever told the story would have to admit that this was done to me. And admitting that this was done to me amounted to writing oneself out of the story entirely.

In trying to write themselves into the literature of the country, African American women were, if for understandable reasons, also tempted to write themselves out of the oral culture of their people and into the "proper-speaking" English that signaled middle-class respectability. More dangerous yet, they were tempted to deny or bury the truth about the real suffering of their mothers and grandmothers. The conventions of domestic fiction offered them no way to write of that experience, primarily because the conventions remained so closely tied to individualist premises. And, pretenses to universality notwithstanding, the individualism of American culture trailed innumerable assumptions about the specific ways in which women, slaves, and blacks related to the free white male embodiment of individualism. Individualism thus confronted African American women writers with a wall of denial. If they wrote as women, they had to write themselves white—and passive. If they wrote as blacks, they had to write themselves male. In retrospect, it appears that this overdetermined denial of African American women's experience may account for the extraordinary vitality of their writing in our own time.

To break the stranglehold of silence, African American women writers have had to find ways to tell stories that fundamentally challenged the most unyielding assumptions of the literature of the country. More than has commonly been recognized, Harriet Wilson pointed the way. However significant *Our Nig* remains for having been the first novel written by an African American woman, it deserves special attention for throwing down the gauntlet to received conventions, even as it proclaimed its author's conversance with high literary tradition.

Recall, if you will, that Wilson prefaced each of her chapters with a passage of verse. She apparently wrote some herself; others she borrowed from the most appreciated literature of her day. In general, her choices were excellent, especially because, on first reading, they serve to assimilate her story to the prevailing sensibilities of her epoch. The verses apparently confirm that Mag and Frado's emotional travails echo those that preoccupied established poets. The borrowed verses thus suggest that Mag and Frado's pain merges with a universal experience. But look again. When Wilson quotes Byron on the ways in which youth honestly discloses the soul and disdains deceit, does she really mean that school boys are honest with each other in a way that adults are not? Or is she subtly mocking the claim of honesty and casting her readers, by implication the American public, as the foes who deserve open hate? To choose one reading or another would miss the complexity of her intent. She wanted both.

Wilson, by her use of those verses, was proudly writing herself into the literature of the country. By the double entendre with which her text endowed them, she was also serving notice that to accommodate her story the literature would have to change. Her strategy unmistakably implied that the literature of the country would have to allow for conflicted readings and multiple perspectives. In this respect, Wilson bequeathed an important legacy to her most talented successors, who, even if they had never read her, drew something of her sensibility from the experience that they shared with her.

African American women's experience of slavery indelibly colored their relation to the literature of the country, because the pieties of that literature could not encompass their experience. Gradually and unevenly, African American women writers have created an alternative literature that features collective rather than individual subjects. The point is not, as some like to claim, that they repudiated the dominant (white male) literary tradition. They did not. From Wilson's evocation of Byron and Shelley to Hurston's love of Shakespeare and Milton to Morrison's admiration for the ancient Greek dramatists, their continuing engagement with the high Western literary tradition resonates throughout their work. But as they have increasingly felt freer to try to tell the hard, unvarnished truth of their mothers' and grandmothers' lives, they have been led to conjoin the oral tradition of their people with the literary tradition of their aspirations.

The most compelling work of African American women writers draws its peculiar vitality from its attempt to fuse disparate oral and literate traditions and from its determination to make the literary tradition apply. Like Harriet Wilson, they are implicitly posing the question, If this is beautiful and moving, then what is it about? And they are answering that if it is indeed about you, must it not also be about me? Their insistence is helping to move the literature of the country away from the narrow assumptions of individualism toward a properly epic vision. The story of African American slavery is, ultimately, an epic that implicates all of us. The abolitionists' attempt to cast it as a Manichaean struggle between the forces of good and evil rested on an individualist vision of the good that denied the slaves' experience. Today, the descendants of slaves are forcefully reminding us that their experience has been and may yet be ours. In this spirit, Harriet Wilson chose, for the last chapter of *Our Nig*, an epigraph that ironically invoked a biblical favorite of the slaveholders—as if, once again, to demonstrate the strange and conflicted close connection between the two variants of Southern culture. She chose the words of the biblical preacher, "Nothing new under the sun."

Notes

1. Frances Ellen Watkins Harper, *Iola Leroy; or, Shadows Uplifted* (New York, 1988), 262.

2. Harriet E. Wilson, *Our Nig; or, Sketches from the Life of a Free Black, in a Two-Story White House, North, Showing that Slavery's Shadows Fall Even There, by "Our Nig,"* ed. Henry Louis Gates, Jr. (1859; New York, 1983), hereinafter cited parenthetically by page number in the text. For the history of the novel and a discussion of its relation to the culture of the period, see Gates's Introduction.

3. See ibid., xxxi–xxxiv, on the paucity of references to it.

4. Caroline Lee Hentz, *The Planter's Northern Bride* (Chapel Hill, 1970); Mary Eastman, *Aunt Phillis's Cabin* (Philadelphia, 1852); Louisa S. McCord, Review of *Uncle Tom's Cabin, Southern Quarterly Review,* XXIII (n.s. VII) (January, 1853), 81–120.

5. See Elizabeth Fox-Genovese, *Feminism Without Illusions: A Critique of Individualism* (Chapel Hill, 1991), for a discussion of the ideology of bourgeois individualism and its implications for women.

6. See, among many, Jane Tompkins, *Sensational Designs: The Cultural Work of American Fiction, 1790–1860* (New York, 1985). Many feminist critics argue that women's literature embodied different values from those of men, but in my judgment even when the purported female values appear most harshly to criticize (male) competitive self-assertion, they remained tied to the fundamental premises and worldview of individualism, which was responsible for a specific vision of female nature and values. For a fuller development of the argument, see Fox-Genovese, *Feminism Without Illusions.*

7. Toni Morrison, *Beloved* (New York, 1987). For references to such events in the lives of slave women, see also Elizabeth Fox-Genovese, *Within the Plantation Household: Black and White Women of the Old South* (Chapel Hill, 1988).

Selected Bibliography of Works by Elizabeth Fox-Genovese

Compiled by Ehren K. Foley

This bibliography provides a listing of those works written by Elizabeth Fox-Genovese that deal substantially with the themes of this volume. It is divided into books, coauthored books, edited and coedited works, and articles, including contributed chapters and review essays. Items in each section are listed chronologically by date of original publication. Included are items in this volume, related items in other volumes of this series, and those items that were excluded from this volume by constraints on space or by editorial decision. While the bibliography does strive for comprehensive coverage, it doubtless falls short of that goal. Several conscious omissions are worth noting. The bibliography does not include the many short book reviews and articles that Fox-Genovese authored during her career. It also omits those items that deal with themes addressed in the other volumes of this series, though there is some overlap between volumes. A full sense of the breadth of Fox-Genovese's work therefore requires perusal of each of the first four volumes of the selected edition of Elizabeth Fox-Genovese's writings and its accompanying bibliography.

Books

1988

Within the Plantation Household: Black and White Women of the Old South. Chapel Hill: University of North Carolina Press, 1988.

1993

To Be Worthy of God's Favor: Southern Women's Defense and Critique of Slavery. 32nd Annual Robert Fortenbaugh Memorial Lecture. Gettysburg: Gettysburg College, 1993.

Unspeakable Things Unspoken: Ghosts and Memories in the Narratives of African-American Women. 1992 Elsa Goveia Memorial Lecture. Mona, Jamaica: Department of History, University of the West Indies, 1993.

Coauthored Books

2005

With Eugene D. Genovese. *The Mind of the Master Class: History and Faith in the Southern Slaveholders' Worldview.* New York: Cambridge University Press, 2005.

Edited and Coedited works

1992

With Virginia Bernhard et al. *Southern Women: Histories and Identities.* Columbia: University of Missouri Press, 1992.

1994

With Virginia Bernhard et al. *Hidden Histories of Women in the New South.* Columbia: University of Missouri Press, 1994.

Journal Articles and Sections of Books

1979

"Kate Chopin's Awakening." *Southern Studies* 18, no. 3 (1979): 261–90.

1981

"Scarlett O'Hara: The Southern Lady as New Woman." *American Quarterly* 33, no. 4 (1981): 153–79.

1983

"Antebellum Southern Households: A New Perspective on a Familiar Question." *Review* [Fernand Braudel Center] 7 (Fall 1983): 215–53.

1986

"Strategies and Forms of Resistance: Focus on Slave Women in the United States." In *In Resistance: Studies in African, Caribbean, and Afro-American History,* edited by Gary Y. Okihiro, 143–65. Amherst: University of Massachusetts Press, 1986.

1987

"To Write My Self: The Autobiographies of Afro-American Women." In *Feminist Issues in Literary Scholarship,* edited by Shari Benstock, 161–80. Bloomington: Indiana University Press, 1987.

1988

"*The Awakening* in the Context of the Experience, Culture, and Values of Southern Women." In *Approaches to Teaching Chopin's "The Awakening,"* edited by Bernard Koloski, 34–39. New York: Modern Language Association of America, 1988.
"My Statue, My Self: Autobiographical Writings of Afro-American Women." In *The Private Self: Theory and Practice of Women's Autobiographical Writings,* edited by Shari Benstock, 63–89. Chapel Hill: University of North Carolina Press, 1988.

1989

"To Write the Wrongs of Slavery." *Gettysburg Review* 2 (Winter 1989): 63–76.

1990

"Between Individualism and Community: Autobiographies of Southern Women." In *Located Lives: Place and Idea in Southern Autobiography,* edited by J. Bill Berry, 20–38. Athens: University of Georgia Press, 1990.
Foreword to *Fanny Kemble: Journal of a Young Actress,* edited by Monica Gough, ix–xx. New York: Columbia University Press, 1990.

"Myth and History: Discourse of Origins in Zora Neale Hurston and Maya Angelou." *Black American Literature Review* 24, no. 2 (1990): 221–35.

"Religion in the Lives of Slaveholding Women of the Antebellum South." In *That Gentle Strength: Historical Perspectives on Women in Christianity,* edited by Lynda L. Coon, Katherine J. Haldane, and Elisabeth W. Sommer, 207–29. Charlottesville: University Press of Virginia, 1990.

"Social Order and the Female Self: The Conservatism of Southern Women in Comparative Perspective." In *What Made the South Different? Essays and Comments,* edited by Kees Gispen, 49–62. Jackson: University Press of Mississippi, 1990.

1991

Introduction to *A Blockaded Family: Life in Southern Alabama during the Civil War,* by Parthenia Antoinette Hague, ix–xxviii. Lincoln: University of Nebraska Press, 1991.

"Family and Female Identity in the Antebellum South: Sarah Gayle and Her Family." In *In Joy and in Sorrow: Women, Family, and Marriage in the Victorian South, 1830–1900,* edited by Carol Bleser, 15–31. New York: Oxford University Press, 1991.

1992

Introduction to *Beulah,* by Augusta J. Evans, xi–xxxvi. Baton Rouge: Louisiana State University Press, 1992.

1993

Afterword to *Lamb in His Bosom,* by Caroline Miller, Modern Southern Classics Series, 346–55. Atlanta: Peachtree, 1993.

"Texas Women and the Writing of Women's History." In *Women and Texas History: Selected Essays,* edited by Fane Downs and Nancy Baker Jones, 3–14. Austin: Texas State Historical Association, 1993.

1994

Afterword to *Hidden Histories of Women in the New South,* edited by Virginia Bernhard et al., 224–38. Columbia: University of Missouri Press, 1994.

1995

"Stewards of Their Culture: Southern Women Novelists as Social Critics." In *Stepping Out of the Shadows: Alabama Women, 1819–1990,* edited by Mary Martha Thomas, 11–27. Tuscaloosa: University of Alabama Press, 1995.

1996

"Slavery, Race, and the Figure of the Tragic Mulatta, or, The Ghost of Southern History in the Writing of African-American Women." *Mississippi Quarterly* 49, no. 4 (1996): 791–817.

1997

"Education of Women in the United States South." *Journal of Women's History* 9, no. 1 (1997): 203–11.

"'To Weave It into the Literature of the Country': Epic and the Fictions of African American Women." In *Poetics of the Americas: Race, Founding, and Textuality,* edited by

Bainard Cowan and Jefferson Humphries, 31–45. Baton Rouge: Louisiana State University Press, 1997.

1999

Foreword to *Parlor Ladies and Ebony Drudges: African American Women, Class, and Work in a South Carolina Community,* edited by Kibibi Voloria C. Mack, xiii–xviii. Knoxville: University of Tennessee Press, 1999.

"Mothers and Daughters: The Tie That Binds." In *Southern Mothers: Fact and Fictions in Southern Women's Writing,* edited by Nagueyalti Warren and Sally Wolff, xv–xvii. Baton Rouge: Louisiana State University Press, 1999.

2002

"Southern History in the Imagination of African American Women Writers." In *The History of Southern Women's Literature,* edited by Carolyn Perry and Mary Louise Weeks, 156–63. Baton Rouge: Louisiana State University Press, 2002.

Index